166900

The Evolution of Economic Thought

The Evolution of Economic Thought

THE Evolution OF Economic Thought

JACOB OSER
Utica College

HARCOURT, BRACE & WORLD, INC.

New York · Burlingame

© 1963 BY HARCOURT, BRACE & WORLD, INC.

Library of Congress Catalog Card Number: 63-14622

PRINTED IN THE UNITED STATES OF AMERICA

TO
David Kenneth
WHO, DANGEROUSLY ENOUGH,
ARRIVED ON THE DAY THE BIOGRAPHY OF
JOHN STUART MILL
WAS BEING WRITTEN

Preface

SOME seventy-two major economists and their ideas are presented in
this book. Many more might have been included, and one could argue
persuasively that others should have been substituted for some who were
included. In covering more than four hundred years of economic thought,
many important figures necessarily had to be omitted. A vast multitude
of actors parading across the stage provided here might be confusing, and
most of the *dramatis personae* would necessarily have to be limited to
bit parts. A kind of Malthusian overpopulation of historic figures presented in a single moderately sized volume could exhibit the erudition of
the author but at the same time bewilder the reader. The stage has been
rather sparsely peopled here so that each character can be seen and heard.

The extensive quotations from original sources included in this book
are meant to serve two major purposes. First, they illustrate the ideas of
major economic thinkers; second, they will hopefully whet the reader's
appetite for more, so that he will turn to the original works to read further.

It is both customary and proper for an author to thank those who
assisted him and at the same time to absolve them of any censure. The
typical author claims competence to write his book, he persuades his
friends and relatives to read his untidy manuscripts, and he exercises veto
power over their advice and suggestions. Undoubtedly most books benefit, as this one has, from the suggestions of interested readers. It is not
the responsibility of readers, however, to produce a masterpiece.

My greatest debt of gratitude is owed to Professor John S. Gambs of
Hamilton College. He carefully read the entire manuscript and suggested
numerous improvements. More than a few felicitous phrases are due to
his mastery of the art of writing.

Mrs. Dorothy Judd Sickels of Hamilton, New York, edited the manuscript, read proof, and did much of the work required to prepare the index.

My wife, Kathleen Johnson Oser, has found time to read and criticize the entire manuscript in spite of all the household duties she assumed in order to relieve me of my share of them and in spite of her other interests and activities that were sometimes slighted to assist me in my work.

Finally, I owe heartfelt thanks to those custodians of the accumulated wisdom—and some nonsense—of the past, the librarians of Utica College, Hamilton College, Syracuse University, and the New York Public Library at Forty-second Street.

JACOB OSER

Clinton, New York
January 3, 1963

Contents

List of Tables and Figures

The Evolution of Economic Thought

The Evolution of Economic Thought

CHAPTER I

Introduction

O UR STORY of the evolution of economic thought will begin in the sixteenth century with mercantilism. Economic problems and economic thinking about them can, of course, be traced back to antiquity. However, to discuss the economic ideas of the middle ages, the ancient Greeks, Romans, Egyptians, and those to be found in the Bible, would make this book too long. Moreover, we can use 1500 A.D. as a dividing line between two epochs with vastly different economic characteristics. We can find a truly enormous range of different economic conditions from 1500 A.D. back to 3000 B.C., when man began to record his history in picture language. But the whole epoch generally had these common characteristics: there was little trade, and most goods were produced for consumption in the community that produced them without first being sent to market; money was therefore not widely used, although it existed in ancient times; strong national states and integrated national economies had not yet developed; systematic economic theorizing had not yet evolved to any considerable extent, nor had any schools of thought been formed.

During the period since 1500 we can also find the most divergent economic conditions in both time and space. Yet the general characteristics of this epoch differentiate it from the earlier period. Trade was expanding rapidly, with the great geographical explorations both resulting from this process and accelerating it; the money economy increasingly superseded the natural or self-sufficient economy; national states and unified national economies became a dominant force; economic schools arose, representing unified and systematic bodies of thought and policy formation.

We shall be concerned with economic thinking since 1500 and not before because it copes with problems that are nearest to us in time, it is most relevant to current ideas, and it is most systematic and therefore most interesting from the viewpoint of unified and coherent theory.

Economic thought is woven into the complex fabric of society. We should not wrench it loose and display it isolated from its social context. It must be analyzed and judged from the standards of the society out of which it grew. But this does not preclude our using the wisdom of hindsight to judge it in relation to its time.

In economics, social relationships and institutions probably are as important as individual efforts and accomplishments. That is why it is worthwhile to examine society as a whole when looking at a set of economic ideas. We can thereby better explain why certain theories were brought forth, why they achieved some measure of popularity or success, and why they declined and sometimes disappeared.

The Five Major Questions

AS EACH important school of economic thought is introduced, five major questions about it will be considered. This method will serve to provide perspective on the school and the social background that produced it. Such a concise summary at the outset will help clarify the main points as we study the ideas of the leading economists. The study of each economist will illustrate the characteristics of the school with which he has been linked. Extensive quotations will indicate the flavor and trend of his thinking.

First question: What was the social background of the school? Here we will look at the social background that produced a system of thought. The assumption is that economic theory developed in response to changes in the environment that in turn drew attention to new problems. Men's ideas grew out of current problems and issues. Some knowledge of the times is essential if we are to understand why men thought and acted the way they did. It is true, of course, that many systems of thought exist simultaneously in the heads of many individuals. People can spin out a wide multiplicity of ideas, ranging from the most sensible to the wildly fantastic, or so they seem to contemporaries. Ideas irrelevant to society at the time they are presented wither and die. Those that are useful and effective in answering at least some questions and in solving some problems are disseminated and popularized, thereby making their authors famous. An Adam Smith contributed much to economic thinking, but had he never lived, can anyone doubt that the same ideas would have been forthcoming? Perhaps they would have come somewhat later. Perhaps they would not have been expressed as well or as clearly. Then thinking men would have stumbled about a bit more before they found themselves on the path that he so clearly laid out. Smith made a great contribution because his ideas answered the requirements of his time.

The theory of comparative advantage in international trade, had it been discovered in the feudal epoch, would have been without any significance in a world of local self-sufficiency with a minimum of trade. The dispute over the corn laws in England in the early 1800's brought forth the theory of rent. Had Keynes published *The General Theory of Employment, Interest, and Money* in 1926 instead of in 1936, it probably would have attracted far less attention than it did. The social milieu in which ideas grow is important.

Second question: What was the essence of the school? Here we will make generalizations about the ideas of successive economic schools. The strength of such a procedure is that we can get at the heart of the matter very concisely. The weakness is that there will be exceptions that cannot be taken up in detail. A succinct summary presents patterns of uniformity in the ideas of an epoch. The exceptions may contain the seeds of ideas that may triumph in the future. Thus we will argue that mercantilists favored the accumulation of gold and silver; yet there were voices among them that took an antibullionist position. They were overwhelmed and scarcely heard at first, but ultimately their ideas were vindicated. Similarly, the classical school believed in free foreign trade; yet Malthus, a classical economist, was a protectionist.

Third question: What groups of people did the school serve or seek to serve? If economic theory seeks answers to questions, it is important to know what questions are asked, and who asks them. Questions that are dominant in the thoughts of one group may be insignificant to another. Theologians in the middle ages were very much concerned about the compatibility of charging interest for money lent out and the salvation of one's soul. With the passage of time this problem seemed less important. The merchant capitalist in his heyday asked, How can a country best accumulate gold and silver? The classical economist was more concerned with, How can we increase production? The socialist wanted to know, How can we best improve the condition of the working classes? A system of ideas must fit the needs of all of society, or it must suit a segment of society that will try to defend, develop, and popularize it.

Most economic theorists assume that self-interest of the individual is dominant and guides the economic process. Yet individual self-interest does not result in the chaotic condition of each person going his own way in opposition to the rest of society. Individuals are guided by market, social, political, and ethical forces to cooperate with their fellow men in organizing a reasonable working relationship with society. Moreover, they coalesce into groups because of social pressures, common interests and ideas, and man's gregariousness. Thus there are religious, political, aesthetic, social, economic, and other groups, each of which presents a unified outlook and program in its sphere of special interest. We are concerned here with groups of people who develop common economic ideas based partly on self-interest, and partly on other considerations that help shape the concept of how an economy should be organized and in what direction it should move. We shall try to identify the groups that supported each school of thought, and the groups to which each school appealed for support, successfully or unsuccessfully.

Fourth question: How was the school valid, useful, or correct in its time? We have to find our way between two opposing dangers. One is the erroneous idea that thinkers of the past were wrong, naïve, ignorant, or foolish; we, being much wiser, have discovered the final truth. Thus, J. B. Say, writing over 150 years ago, asked:

What useful purpose can be served by the study of absurd opinions and doctrines that have long ago been exploded and deserved to be? It is mere useless pedantry to attempt to revive them. The more perfect a science becomes the shorter becomes its history.

This view, popular as it has been since Say expressed it, is rejected here. It applies more to the physical than to the social sciences. Since the universe has not changed perceptibly during recent centuries, the physical laws under which it operates have not changed much either. Since our scientific knowledge has grown, we have approached ever closer to the truth. Nevertheless the history of physical science also is meaningful. But as society evolves, the ideas with which we seek to explain and improve it must change also. What was a plausible theory or policy in the 1600's would be questionable three hundred years later.

The other extreme is to find every dominant idea of the past right, just, and good in its time. While the possible validity of economic ideas must be related to their time and place, they may have been wrong or unreasonable even when first presented. This critical approach may well be applied to current thinking also. When John Maynard Keynes implied that pyramid-building in ancient Egypt was a counterdepression measure, he was wrong, for he confused two different societies; public works in Egypt did not arise for the same reasons as ours. The writer who recently stated that mercantilists followed a full employment policy suffered from a similar confusion; mercantilists were primarily concerned, not with unemployment, but rather with pushing more and more men, women, and children into the workshops. Concepts which are serviceable today may have been inapplicable in earlier times, and they may become inappropriate in the future;

widely accepted ideas of today may be erroneous or inappropriate, but they persist because of the difficulty of changing men's minds.

Fifth question: How did the school outlive its usefulness? Ideas that once were useful can outlive their usefulness as social conditions change. The evolutionary approach to economic thinking recognizes that society is changing continually. New problems arise, and new analyses become appropriate.

These five questions will be used as guides for presenting the historical background, the content, and the relevance of economic schools. The bibliography for this chapter at the end of the book includes some of the general works covering the history of economic thought.

CHAPTER 2

The Mercantilist School

THE TYPE of economic doctrine known as mercantilism falls between the middle ages and the period of the triumph of laissez faire. It can be dated roughly from 1500 to 1776, although the dates vary in different countries and regions.

Overview of Mercantilism

The social background of the school. The self-sufficiency of the feudal community slowly gave way to the new system of merchant capitalism. Cities, which had been growing gradually during the middle ages, became increasingly important. Trade flourished, both within each country and between countries, and the use of money expanded. The discovery of gold in the Western Hemisphere facilitated the growing volume of commerce and stimulated theorizing about the precious metals. Great geographical discoveries, based in part on the development of navigation, were extending the sphere of commerce. Production was small scale, but the merchant more and more stood between the producer and the consumer. The merchant capitalist, although he was a contemptible tradesman in the eyes of the landed aristocracy, became the key figure in the world of business.

National states were arising, and the most powerful of them were acquiring colonies and spheres of influence. Economic rivalries between nations were intensified. A body of doctrine was required to supersede feudal concepts, to promote nationalism, to give new dignity and importance to the merchant, and to justify a policy of economic and military expansion.

The essence of the mercantilist school. The main principles can be summarized as follows:

1. Mercantilists regarded gold and silver as the most desirable form of wealth. Some mercantilists seemed to believe that the precious metals were the only type of wealth worth pursuing. All of them valued bullion as the

means by which power and riches could be achieved. A surplus of exports from a country was therefore necessary if payments were to be received in hard money. Even if one's country were at war, goods would be exported to the enemy if they were paid for in gold.

Mercantilist writers in Austria, a silver-producing country, estimated that if mining silver exactly paid for its cost of production, the enterprise was as profitable to the state as a 100 per cent profit would be to a private person. If the silver sold for one-half its cost of production, the profit was 50 per cent, but in either case only the state could undertake the mining.

2. Mercantilists promoted nationalism. All countries could not, of course, simultaneously enjoy a surplus of exports. Therefore one's own country should promote it at the expense of its neighbors. Wealth could thereby be accumulated to the detriment of foreigners. Only a powerful nation could capture and hold colonies, dominate trade routes, win wars against rivals, and engage successfully in economic warfare. According to this static concept of economic life, there was a fixed quantity of economic resources in the world; one country could increase its resources only at the expense of another. The French essayist Michel de Montaigne wrote in 1580: "The profit of one man is the damage of another. . . . No man profiteth but by the loss of others."

Mercantilistic nationalism of course meant militarism. Strong navies and merchant fleets were an absolute requirement for their purposes. As fisheries were "nurseries for seamen," the mercantilists imposed "political Lent" on England in 1549. People were forbidden by law to eat meat on certain days of the week. This enactment was vigorously maintained for about a century, and it did not disappear from the statute book until the nineteenth century.

3. Mercantilists advocated the import of raw materials without tariffs if they could not be produced at home, protection for manufactured goods and raw materials which could be produced at home, and the restriction of the outward movement of raw materials. This emphasis on exports, this reluctance to import, has been called "the fear of goods." The interests of the merchant took precedence over those of the consumer. Prices would be kept high, and gold would accumulate. Antoine de Montchrétien, the French playwright and economist, in 1615 wrote the first book using the term "political economy"; in it he said: "He who wishes for good order in the arts and maintenance of their standing, must never decrease profits through abundance. The brightness of the lamp is dimmed if it be too plentifully filled with oil."

An act passed in 1565–66 during Queen Elizabeth's reign forbade the export of live sheep, the penalties being confiscation of property, a year in prison, and cutting off of the left hand. The death penalty was provided for a second offense. The export of raw wool was prohibited and the same penalties were applied in a law enacted during the reign of Charles II (1660–85).

4. The merchant capitalists believed in dominating and exploiting colonies, and in monopolizing colonial trade for their own benefit. They wanted to keep the colonies eternally dependent on and subservient to their nations. If any benefits from the home country's economic growth and military power spilled over to the gain of the colonies, this was an accidental by-product of the policy of exploitation.

The English Navigation Acts of 1651 and 1660 were good examples of this policy. Goods imported into Great Britain and the colonies had to move in English ships, which included colonial bottoms, or in ships of the country where the goods originated. Certain colonial products had to be sold only to England, and others had to be landed in England before being shipped to foreign countries. Foreign imports into the colonies were restricted or prohibited. Colonial manufacturing was curbed or in some cases outlawed, so that dependent territories would remain suppliers of raw materials and importers of English manufactured goods.

5. To promote their business interests, mercantilists believed in free trade within a country. That is, they were opposed to internal taxes, tolls, and other restrictions on the movement of goods. However, they did not favor free internal trade in the sense of allowing anybody to engage in whatever trade he wished. On the contrary, mercantilists preferred monopoly grants and exclusive trading privileges whenever they could acquire them.

Tolls and taxes could throttle business enterprise. On the Elbe River in 1685 a shipment of sixty planks from Saxony to Hamburg required the payment of fifty-four planks at toll stations, and only six arrived at the destination. But at least with payments in kind, the total tolls had to be less than 100 per cent. If cash had been paid, the charges could have added up to much more than the original value of the goods.

6. Mercantilism favored a strong central government to enforce the regulation of business. The government granted monopoly privileges to companies engaged in foreign trade. Free entry into business at home was restricted in order to limit competition. Agriculture, mining, and industry were promoted with subsidies as well as tariffs. Methods of production and quality of goods were closely regulated so that a country would not get a bad name for its products in foreign markets, which would hamper exports. In other words, mercantilists did not trust the judgment and honesty of the individual merchant, and their common interest required that poor workmanship and shoddy materials be prohibited by the government.

A strong central government was therefore required to insure uniform, national regulation. Strong national governments also were necessary to achieve the goals discussed above: nationalism, protectionism, colonialism, and internal trade unhampered by tolls and excessive taxes.

7. The mercantilists favored a large population that would work hard for low wages. Idleness and begging by able-bodied people were dealt with harshly, and thievery was impermissible. During the reign of Henry VIII in Great Britain (1509–47), 7,200 thieves were hanged. In 1536 it was decreed that "sturdy vagabonds" should have their ears cut off, and death was the penalty for the third offense. In 1547 anyone who refused to work was condemned to be the slave of whoever denounced him. A law passed in Queen Elizabeth's reign in 1572 decreed that unlicensed beggars of fourteen years or older were to be flogged and branded unless someone were willing to employ them; for a second offense they were to be executed unless someone would take them into service; for a third offense they were to be executed without mercy as felons.

Bernard de Mandeville (1670?–1733), the Dutch philosopher, satirist, and medical doctor who settled in London, wrote:

In a free Nation where Slaves are not allow'd of, the surest Wealth consists in a Multitude of laborious Poor. . . . As they ought to be kept from starving, so they should receive nothing worth saving. . . . It is the Interest of all rich Nations, that the greatest part of the Poor should almost never be idle, and yet continually spend what they get. . . . The Poor should be kept strictly to Work, and that it was Prudence to relieve their wants, but Folly to cure them. . . . To make the Society happy and People easy under the meanest Circumstances, it is requisite that great Numbers of them should be Ignorant as well as Poor.

The mercantilist doctrine was wealth for the nation, but wealth from which most people must be excluded. A large population would provide not only cheap laborers but also an abundance of soldiers and sailors who would be ready to fight for the glory of the nation and the enrichment of their masters.

What groups of people did the mercantilist school serve or seek to serve? Obviously this doctrine served the merchant capitalists, and also the kings and their immediate followers. But it especially served those interests that were most powerful and entrenched, and that had the most favored monopolies and privileges. In England, for example, the wool interests saw to it that importing printed calicoes was prohibited. In 1721 the use of printed calicoes was outlawed, but exports were allowed. Not until 1774 was the domestic consumption of such cloth permitted. In the late 1600's the law required the dead to be buried in woolen shrouds even though religious traditions required linens.

In France mercantilism had a stronger feudal flavor, and the entrenched monopolistic interests were even more successful in having the government intervene on their behalf. From 1686 to 1759 the production, import, and use of printed calicoes was prohibited. In armed conflicts and executions arising out of the enforcement of these measures, it is estimated that sixteen thousand people died. Many more were sent to the galley ships.

A host of government officials, inspectors, judges, and enforcement officers also gained from mercantilist regulations. The French government (but not the English) received significant revenue from fines, concessions, and monopoly privileges sold to businessmen. Officials kept a percentage of the fines levied against violators of the many government regulations.

How was the mercantilist school valid, useful, or correct in its time? The arguments for bullionism, although exaggerated, made some sense in a period of transition between the predominantly self-sufficient economy of the middle ages and the money and credit economy of modern times. The rapid growth of commerce required more money in circulation, and banking was insufficiently developed to produce it. Wars were fought on a pay-as-you-go basis, and bullion provided a reserve that could be used to hire soldiers and pay for their upkeep, build ships, buy allies, and bribe enemies.

Mercantilists were also aware that an influx of precious metals made tax collection easier. They knew that prices would rise, or at least not fall, if the quantity of money increased as trade expanded. Not only was the volume of output expanding, but the self-sufficient household was being drawn into the market economy. More money was therefore needed to maintain the same volume of output. Mercantilists were aware of the quantity theory of money, but they usually overlooked the significance of the velocity of circulation.

Mercantilists understood that an increased quantity of money would lower the rate of interest, thereby promoting business. They also made a lasting contribution by overcoming the medieval ethical and religious scruples about usury.

Mercantilism permanently influenced prevailing attitudes toward the businessman. Formerly the approach of the medieval aristocracy was that the man of business was a contemptible second-class citizen who was immersed in the muck of business and money. The mercantilists gave respectability and importance to the businessman who, they argued, enriched not only himself but also the kingdom and the king. The landed aristocrats eventually were allowed to participate in business ventures without losing their status and dignity. Ultimately they gave their children in marriage to the offspring of business families, thereby merging aristocratic lineages with great commercial fortunes.

Mercantilism had a lasting impact by promoting nationalism, a force that is very much alive today. Central government regulation was necessary when uniform weights, measures, coinage, and laws had to be imposed on local authorities; when production and trade had not yet developed enough to rely on competition to give the consumer a wide choice of goods; when the risks of trade were high, and monopoly privileges may have been necessary to induce more risk-taking than would otherwise have occurred.

The privileged chartered companies, ancestors of the modern corporation, were promoted under mercantilism. They helped transform the economic organization of Europe, bringing in new goods, providing outlets for manufactured goods, and furnishing incentives to the growth of capital investment. By colonizing abroad they expanded the market economy.

Mercantilism made a permanent contribution by expanding the internal market, promoting the free movement of goods unhampered by tolls, establishing uniform laws and taxes, and protecting people and goods in transit within each country and abroad.

How did mercantilism outlive its usefulness? The growth of banking overcame the need to rely so heavily on bullion and coin. The further expansion of the market economy revealed that real estate, factories, machinery, inventories of goods, and money in checking accounts were more important items of wealth than gold and silver. The industrial revolution replaced the merchant capitalist with the industrial entrepreneur as the key figure. Economic growth permitted society to rely on competitive forces and on laissez faire rather than on promoting and regulating monopolies. The phenomenal progress made in science, technology, and invention enabled people to see that a country could become richer not only by impoverishing its neighbors but also by mastering the forces of nature more efficiently, by investing more capital, by making labor more effective. All countries could enrich themselves simultaneously. When progress was slow, world resources, output, and wealth seemed fixed, and attempts were made to redistribute wealth, as the mercantilists did, in favor of themselves. But when progress was rapid, new hopes were aroused for a great increase of wealth without conflicting interests upsetting world peace.

Even if the regulations protecting the quality of goods were once necessary, they ultimately became a barrier to progress. The published rules in France from 1666 to 1730 on textiles alone were printed in seven huge volumes. The dyeing manual, alleged to be the best set of instructions on dyeing technique at the time, contained 317 articles. These regulations prevented inferior methods from being used. But they also seriously impeded experimentation and improvements.

Mercantilistic regulations to promote a large population, hard work, and low wages were no longer required by the late 1700's. After workers had been dispossessed from their tools and denied access to the land, laws to keep their wages down became unnecessary. During the industrial revolution, high birth rates and lower death rates increased the population without government intervention. Farmers, handicraftsmen, women, and children were driven into the factories by economic necessity.

Mun

THOMAS MUN (1571–1641), the son of a dealer in textile fabrics, acquired wealth and reputation while a merchant in the Italian and the Near Eastern trade. After he was elected a director of the East India Company, he became involved in a controversy over that company's policy and published a tract in its defense. Critics objected to the company's exporting gold. Mun in 1621 published *A Discourse of Trade from England unto the East Indies,* in which he argued that so long as total exports exceeded total imports, the drain of specie from a country in any one branch of trade did not matter.

Around 1630 Mun wrote his famous exposition of mercantilist doctrine in *England's Treasure by Forraign Trade,* published posthumously by his son in 1664. The title of Chapter 2 of this work posed a key problem: "The means to enrich the Kingdom, and to encrease our Treasure." And how was the kingdom enriched? Not by production, not by the accumulation of capital. The answer lay, according to Mun, in a surplus of exports. Of course one must produce in order to export, but production was subservient to the grand design, to accumulate gold. The first page of the two-page chapter reads as follows:

Although a Kingdom may be enriched by gifts received, or by purchase taken from some other Nations, yet these are things uncertain and of small consideration when they happen. The ordinary means therefore to encrease our wealth and treasure is by *Forraign Trade,* wherein wee must ever observe this rule; to sell more to strangers yearly than wee consume of theirs in value. For suppose that when this Kingdom is plentifully served with the Cloth, Lead, Tinn, Iron, Fish and other native commodities, we doe yearly export the overplus to forraign Countries to the value of twenty two hundred thousand pounds; by which means we are enabled beyond the Seas to buy and bring in forraign wares for our use and Consumptions, to the value of twenty hundred thousand pounds; By this order duly kept in our trading, we may rest assured that the Kingdom shall be enriched yearly two hundred thousand pounds, which must be brought to us in so much Treasure; because that part of our stock which is not returned to us in wares must necessarily be brought home in treasure.

Mun argued that although England was rich, she could be still richer if she used waste land to grow hemp, flax, cordage, tobacco, and other things "which now we fetch from strangers to our great impoverishing." Exports should be carried in English ships to gain insurance and freight charges.

In defending the East India Company's export of gold to pay for goods, Mun in the same book argued for multilateral rather than bilateral trade.

In some Countrys we sell our commodities and bring away their wares, or part in mony; in other Countreys we sell our goods and take their mony, because they have little or no wares that fits our turns: again in some places we have need of their commodities, but they have little use of ours: so they take our mony which we get in other Countreys: And thus by a course of traffick (which changeth according to the accurrents of time) the particular members do accommodate each other, and all accomplish the whole body of the trade.

Mun was looking at the over-all balance of trade rather than at the separate account with each foreign country. In addition, more imports would increase England's stock of precious metals if she exported the wares to some other country at a profit. Therefore the export of gold should be allowed to pay for the import of goods which would in turn increase the total volume of goods exported.

Why should we then doubt that our monys sent out in trade, must not necessarily come back again in treasure; together with the great gains which it may procure.... If we only behold the actions of the husbandman in the seed-time when he casteth away much good corn into the ground, we will rather accompt him a mad man than a husbandman: but when we consider his labours in the harvest which is the end of his endeavours, we find the worth and plentiful encrease of his actions.

But the emphasis was on purchase and sale at a profit rather than the processing of imported raw materials into manufactured goods, although the latter was mentioned in the case of textiles.

The emphasis on importing treasure led to the strange conclusion that trade at home could not enrich a country.

We may exchange either amongst our selves, or with strangers; if amongst our selves, the Commonwealth cannot be enriched thereby; for the gain of one subject is the loss of another. And if we exchange with strangers, then our profit is the gain of the Commonwealth.

Malynes

GERARD MALYNES (died 1641) was born in Antwerp of English extraction. He returned to England and became a merchant in foreign trade. Not being very successful in this occupation, he spent a short term in a debtor's prison. He also served as the English commissioner of trade in Belgium, a government advisor on trade matters, an assay master of the mint, and commissioner of mint affairs.

In *Lex Mercatoria: or, the Ancient Law-Merchant*, published in 1622 and reissued in a new edition in 1686, Malynes observed that trade was considered too low for the aristocracy, yet too important for incompetents. He cited a long list of savants "and divers other Doctors and learned of the civil Law" who concerned themselves with merchants.

And hereunto thay add a declaration of such as may trade; and by the contrary thereof, is to be understood who may not trade, *viz.* Clergy-men, Noblemen, Gentlemen, Souldiers, Counsellors at the Laws both Ecclesiasticall and Temporal, publick Officers and Magistrates, frantick persons and mad-men, Youths under years, Orphans, Lunaticks and Fools, all these are exempted to be Merchants.

But Malynes sprang to the defense of merchants:

For the maintenance of Traffick and Commerce is so pleasant, amiable and acceptable unto all Princes and Potentates, that Kings have been and at this day are of the Society of Merchants: And many times, notwithstanding their particular differences and quarrels, they do nevertheless agree in this course of Trade, because Riches is the bright Star, whose height Traffick takes to direct it self by, whereby Kingdoms and Common-weals do flourish; Merchants being the means and instruments to perform the same, to the Glory, Illustration, and benefit of their Monarchies and States. Questionless therefore the State of a Merchant is of great dignity, and to be cherished; for by them Countries are discovered, familiarity between Nations is procured, and politick experience is attained.

The regulation of goods to assure good quality was defended by Malynes in a section of *Lex Mercatoria* headed "Benefits which will arise by the true making of Clothes in England, according to the Statute made in the fourth year of His Majesties raign of Great Britain":

The Cloth being truly made, will be more vendible beyond the Seas, where many complaints are daily made of the false making thereof; ... hereby traffick

will increase for the general good of the Realm, and his Majesties Custom will be duly payed, according to the said Statute, and all will tend to the glory of God, and honour of the King, in all Equity and Justice to be observed in all well-Govrened Commonweals.

While most mercantilists wanted a large population that would work hard for low wages, Malynes had an almost Malthusian fear of overpopulation:

For unless the three Impostumes of the World, namely Wars, Famine, and Pestilence, do purge that great Body, all Kingdoms and Countreys become very populous, and Men can hardly live in quiet, or without danger. Merchants therefore seeking to discover new Countreys, are much to be commended and cherished.

The mercantilist idea that more money in a country would raise prices and thereby stimulate good business was developed by Malynes as follows:

Plenty of Mony maketh generally all things dear, and scarcity of Mony maketh generally things good cheap: Whereas particularly Commodities are also dear or good cheap, according to plenty or scarcity of the Commodities themselves, and the use of them. Mony then (as the blood in the body) containeth the Soul which infuseth life: for if Mony be wanting, Traffique doth decrease, although Commodities be abundant and good cheap: And on the contrary, If Monies be plentiful Commerce increaseth, although Commodities be scarce, and the price thereof is thereby more advanced.

Davenant

CHARLES DAVENANT (1656–1714), the son of Sir William Davenant, the poet and dramatist, spent much of his life in various government posts having to do with taxes, imports, and exports. He was also a member of Parliament.

Davenant has been called an enlightened mercantilist, an eclectic who tried to blend the old and the new, a man who foreshadowed more of the argument of laissez faire than any other influential mercantilist. So he was. But an examination of his writings indicates that in some respects he was a conventional, orthodox mercantilist.

He developed a bullionist argument in *An Essay on the East-India Trade* (1698):

I have often wonder'd upon what Grounds the Parliament proceeded in the Act for Burying in Woollen: It Occasions indeed a Consumption of Wooll, but such a Consumption, as produces no advantage to the Kingdom. For were it not plainly better, that this Wooll made into Cloth, were Exported, paid for, and worn by the Living abroad, than laid in the Earth here at home. And were it not better, That the Common People (who make up the Bulk and are the great Consumers) should be bury'd in an old Sheet, fit for nothing else, as formerly, than in so much new Wooll, which is thereby utterly lost. . . . For it is the Interest of all Trading Nations whatsoever, that their Home-Consumption should be little, of a Cheap and Foreign Growth, and that their own Manufactures should be sold at the highest Markets, and spent Abroad; since by what is Consum'd at Home, one loseth only what another gets, and the Nation in General is not at all the Richer; but all Foreign Consumption is a clear and certain Profit.

In *An Essay on the Probable Means of Making the People Gainers in the Balance of Trade* (1699) Davenant argued that the entire value of the exported product was gained to the kingdom, if made from domestic raw materials. If raw materials were imported and the product exported, the net profit was the difference between the two values.

In *Discourses on the Publick Revenues, and On the Trade of England* (1698), Davenant expressed a preference for wars fought within a country rather than abroad:

A Foreign War must needs drein a Kingdom of its Treasure. . . . *France*, from the time of *Charles* IX to the Reign of *Harry* IV, had a continual Civil War in its Bowels, and was often ravag'd by Armies from *Spain* and *Germany;* but this War exporting no Treasure, did not Impoverish the Kingdom.

In the same work Davenant called for government regulation of business because merchants were not to be trusted:

There is hardly a Society of Merchants, that would not have it thought the whole Prosperity of the Kingdom depends upon their single Traffick. So that at any time, when they come to be Consulted, their Answers are dark and partial; and when they deliberate themselves in Assemblies, 'tis generally with a byass, and a secret Eye to their own Advantage. . . . And 'tis now to be apprehended, That they who stand possess'd of the ready Cash, when they discover the Necessities of other People, will, in all likelihood, prompted by their Avarice, make a use of it very distructive to their Fellow-Subjects, and to the King's Affairs, if not prevented by the Care and Wisdom of the State.

Davenant was enlightened enough to say that the wealth of a country is what it produces, not gold or silver. Trade governs money rather than the other way around. Wealth invested in ships, buildings, manufactures, furniture, apparel, etc., constitutes riches as much as coins and bullion. He favored a surplus of exports because if the quantity of money increases, interest rates fall, land values rise, and taxes increase. But too much gold and silver can be detrimental, as with Spain, where Spanish affluence caused neglect of the arts, labor, and manufactures. Davenant defended both the Navigation Acts and multilateral trade. In other words, where possible, a nation should enforce bilateralism between itself and its colonies, excluding foreigners from trading there. But among equals, multilateral trade is desirable.

Colbert

JEAN BAPTISTE COLBERT (1619–83) represents the heart and soul of mercantilism, which in France is called Colbertism. He was the French Minister of Finance from 1661 to 1683 under Louis XIV. In spite of his modest origin (he came from a family of dry-goods merchants) he rose to a position of great power, often by unscrupulous means. Matching his unbounded ambition was a tremendous capacity for work and attention to the most minute details of his office.

Colbert was a bullionist. He felt that the strength of a state depended on its finances, its finances on its taxes, and the collection of taxes on an abundance of money. He favored expanded exports, reduced imports, and the retention of bullion within the country by law.

Colbert was an arch-nationalist and militarist. He held that there were four professions that were useful for great purposes: "Agriculture, trade, war on land, and that on sea." Colonies were desirable as markets for French goods and as sources of raw materials. A big navy and merchant marine were essential. He felt that one nation could become richer only at the expense of another, because the volume of trade, the number of ships engaged in commerce, and the production of manufactured goods were all relatively fixed. Commerce, therefore, was a continual and bitter war among nations for economic advantage.

Colbert did his best to facilitate internal trade. He tried to give France a uniform system of weights and measures, but was rebuffed by feudal localism and tradition, and the vested interests of the church and the nobility. He opposed, unsuccessfully, tolls on the movement of goods, internal customs barriers, and excessive local taxes. He subsidized the construction of the Canal of Languedoc, which joined the Atlantic and the Mediterranean. By enforcing the feudal system of compulsory labor of peasants on the roads, the *corvée*, he made himself thoroughly hated; but fifteen thousand miles of roads were surfaced.

Government regulation of business, which in France had a strong feudal flavor, was an important feature of Colbert's policies. He thought businessmen a shortsighted, selfish, grasping lot who sacrificed the national interests for their own profit. The quality of goods and methods of production were closely regulated to attain uniformity, protect the consumer, and earn a good name for French goods in foreign markets. Monopoly privileges and subsidies were offered for new industries, especially those that were difficult and expensive to establish. But the system could be abused, and some monopolies were granted to raise money for the state or to endow favorite courtiers.

The feudal contempt for men of business prevailed in Colbert's time. But he had laws passed that permitted aristocrats to participate in commerce without losing their status and privileges. An edict of 1669 declared: "We desire that a gentleman shall have the right to participate in a company and take a share in merchant vessels, so long as he does not sell at retail."

Colbert favored a large, hard-working, poorly paid population. No child, he thought, was too young to enter industry, and the power of the state should enforce child labor. He remarked in 1665 that "experience has always certainly shown that idleness in the first years of a child's life is the real source of all the disorders in later life." In a decree of 1668 he commanded that all the inhabitants of Auxerre should send their children into the lace industry at the age of six, or pay a penalty of thirty *sous* per child.

Colbert regarded monks, nuns, lawyers, and officials as unproductive idlers, and he tried to reduce their number. Attempts were made to curb religious feelings and limit religious institutions. He canceled seventeen holy days, leaving only twenty-four in addition to Sundays when work ceased.

In an edict of 1666 people were exempted from taxes for a number of years if they married early. Every father of ten living children was also exempted from taxes; interestingly enough, sons who died in the armed forces were counted as living, but priests, nuns, and monks were not counted. This law was revoked in 1683 because of widespread fraud.

It remained for the French Revolution of 1789 to abolish feudal rights, internal tolls and tariffs, special privileges, and local power. The practice of openly selling offices was discontinued. Taxes were equalized and weights and measures standardized on the basis of the metric system. These measures opened the way for further great advances in French commerce, industry, and agriculture.

Petty

SIR WILLIAM PETTY (1623–87) was a mercantilist who offered some new ideas that foreshadowed classical economics.

Before his sixteenth year he had mastered Latin, Greek, French, mathematics, astronomy, and navigation. The son of a poor clothier, he achieved

great wealth, fame, and honor. During his busy life he was a sailor, a physician, a professor of anatomy, an inventor, a surveyor, a member of Parliament, a promoter of iron and copper works, an experimental shipbuilder,
an author, a statistician, and a large landowner.

We shall first discuss his mercantilist views, and then his ideas that broke
new paths toward the economics of Adam Smith.

Petty's mercantilist views. In *A Treatise of Taxes and Contributions*
(1662) Petty was concerned with "this supernumerary 100" unemployed
out of a thousand people for whom there is food enough in the nation; he
complained that they starve, beg or steal. For the latter the penalty might
be hanging or exile. But he was opposed to these remedies. "I think 'tis
plain, they ought neither to be starved, nor hanged, nor given away." Indigent people should be employed on roads, making rivers navigable, planting trees, building bridges, mining and manufacturing. But true mercantilist
that he was, Petty added:

Now as to the work of these supernumeraries, let it be without expence of
Foreign Commodities, and then 'tis no matter if it be employed to build a use-
less Pyramid upon *Salisbury Plain*, bring the Stones at *Stonehenge* to *Tower-
Hill*, or the like.

He was a harbinger of Keynes's theory that in both ancient and modern
times building pyramids was an antidote to unemployment!

How would these public works be paid for? By taxes. As people were
concerned with their relative incomes as compared with their neighbors',
a proportional tax would not matter, as long as the money was spent within
the country.

Let the Tax be never so great, if it be proportionable unto all, then no man
suffers the loss of any Riches by it. For men (as we said but now) if the Estates
of them all were either halfed or doubled, would in both cases remain equally
rich. For they would each man have his former state, dignity and degree; and
moreover, the Money leavied not going out of the Nation, the same also would
remain as rich in comparison of any other Nation.

Petty favored a large population because he recognized increasing returns to governing, but failed to see decreasing returns to farming:

Fewness of people, is real poverty; and a Nation wherein are Eight millions of
people, are more then twice as rich as the same scope of Land wherein are but

Four; For the same Governours which are the great charge, may serve near as well, for the greater, as the lesser number.

In the work cited above, Petty expressed his enthusiasm for the mercantilist version of "full employment." The argument in favor of a poll tax was: "It seems to be a spur unto all men, to set their Children to some profitable employment upon their very first capacity, out of the proceed whereof, to pay each childe his own Poll-money."

He also was against hanging thieves, but hardly from humanitarian motives:

Why should not insolvent Thieves be rather punished with slavery then death? so as being slaves they may be forced to as much labour, and as cheap fare, as nature will endure, and thereby become as two men added to the Commonwealth, and not as one taken away from it; for if *England* be under-peopled (suppose by half) I say that next to the bringing in of as many more as now are, is the making these that are, to do double the work which now they do; that is, to make some slaves.

In his analysis of foreign trade Petty expressed views ahead of his time. He favored freer foreign trade, partly to circumvent smuggling. But he wanted imported consumer goods taxed so that they "may be made somewhat dearer then the same things grown or made at home, if the same be feasible." Imports of raw materials and tools ought to be "gently dealt with." He opposed laws prohibiting the export of money. But in *Political Arithmetick* he deplored the money paid to foreigners for shipping, to Hollanders for their fishing trade "practised upon our Seas," and the money spent on imported commodities that could be manufactured in England.

Petty as a forerunner of classical economics. Petty was a pioneer statistician. In the preface of *Political Arithmetick*, written from 1672 to 1676 and first published in 1690, he stated: "Instead of using only comparative and superlative Words, and intellectual Arguments, I have taken the course . . . to express my self in Terms of *Number, Weight,* or *Measure*." He made some rash calculations. For example, he wanted to know the number of people in Ireland in 1641, before the rebellion against Cromwell's England had been crushed. As one-third more oxen, sheep, butter, and beef were exported in 1664 than in 1641, he concluded that there were one-third more people in 1641 than in 1664! But this lapse does not detract from the fact that he was a founder of the science of statistics.

In the same work he pointed out the economies of the division of labor. He also noted that, "There is much more to be gained by Manufacture than

Husbandry, and by Merchandize than Manufacture." This is mercantilist thinking, but he placed more emphasis on manufacturing than most of his contemporaries.

In *Verbum Sapienti*, probably written in 1667 and first published in 1691, Petty de-emphasized the importance of the quantity of money. He recognized that the velocity of circulation, as well as the quantity, was important. If payments were made weekly rather than quarterly, less money would do the same work. He even suggested that there might be too much money as well as too little. "For Money is but the Fat of the Body-politick, whereof too much doth as often hinder its agility as too little makes it sick." He recommended the sale of surplus gold abroad to prevent harm at home.

In *A Treatise of Taxes and Contributions* Petty arrived at a primitive theory of rent:

Suppose a man could with his own hands plant a certain scope of Land with Corn, that is, could Digg, or Plough, Harrow, Weed, Reap, Carry home, Thresh, and Winnow so much as the Husbandry of this Land requires; and had withal Seed wherewith to sowe the same. I say, that when this man hath subducted his seed out of the proceed of his Harvest, and also, what himself hath both eaten and given to others in exchange for Clothes, and other Natural necessaries; that the remainder of Corn is the natural and true Rent of the Land for that year.

This analysis of rent as the surplus from land was a real advance in economic thinking. But he did not separate the return to capital from the return to land—an error easy to commit in the 1600's, when capital investments in tools and fertilizer were insignificant. Nor did he show rent to be a differential return arising at the extensive and intensive margins of cultivation. But he did realize that land near a market produced a higher rent because the cost of transporting the produce was lower.

Petty probed the role of capital in terms similar to Eugen von Böhm-Bawerk's theory of roundabout production presented more than two hundred years later. In *The Political Anatomy of Ireland*, written in 1672 and first published in 1691, he wrote:

We must make a Par and Equation between Art and Simple Labour; for if by such Simple Labour I could dig and prepare for Seed a hundred Acres in a thousand days; suppose then, I spend a hundred days in studying a more compendious way, and in contriving Tools for the same purpose; but in all that hundred days dig nothing, but in the remaining nine hundred days I dig two hundred Acres of Ground; then I say, that the said Art which cost but one hundred days Invention is worth one Mans labour for ever; because the new Art, and one Man, perform'd as much as two Men could have done without it.

Very unmercantilist is his emphasis on production rather than on exchange.

Petty developed a labor theory of value, saying that labor is the father and land the mother of wealth. In *A Treatise of Taxes and Contributions* (1662) he said that the value of a bushel of corn will be equal to that of an ounce of silver if the labor necessary to produce each is the same.

Petty's groping for a theory of value that determines price initiated a new line of reasoning. His ideas were to be extended and improved by others who came later.

CHAPTER 3

The Physiocratic School

THE PHYSIOCRATS appeared in France toward the end of the mercantilist epoch. The beginning of this school can be dated at 1756, when
Quesnay published his first article on economics in the *Grande Encyclo-
pédie*. The school may be said to have ended with the downfall of Turgot
from his high office and the publication of Smith's *Wealth of Nations*, both
events occurring in 1776. But the significance and influence of the physiocrats lasted beyond the two decades during which they led the world in
fresh economic thinking.

Overview of the Physiocrats

The social background of the school. Physiocracy was a reaction to mercantilism and to the feudal characteristics of the old regime in France. Yet
it could not completely escape the medieval concepts that pervaded French
society.

The minute government regulation of production, even specifying the
required threads per inch of cloth, may once have promoted good order
and high quality. It certainly imprisoned production in a strait jacket that
did not allow for experimentation, improved methods of production, or
changing consumer tastes. A corrupt and extravagant government made
equitable enforcement of the rules impossible. The growth of business enterprise and increasing competition made such rules unnecessary.

French industry was retarded in its development by the local authorities
who imposed internal tolls, taxes, and tariffs, thereby impeding the movement of goods. French agriculture was burdened by the conditions enforced by the landowning nobility. Peasants were subject to taxes on land
and on the profits of farming, while the nobility and the clergy were exempt. Taxes varied from year to year, depending on the whim of the col-
lector and the wealth of the peasants. Incentives to accumulate wealth and

expand investments were thereby seriously impaired. Peasants had to pay dues to the lord when they inherited a holding or when they transferred it through sale. They had to do business with and pay heavy charges to the lord's millers, bakers, and wine-pressers. The nobles had the right to hunt game across the cultivated fields of their peasants, and game laws prohibited weeding and hoeing if young partridges would be disturbed. The hated feudal *corvée*, revived by Colbert and perpetuated after him, forced the peasants and their draft animals to work without pay on the public roads, largely for the benefit of others.

For centuries the French government and the authorities in the towns had subjected the grain trade to a bewildering mass of regulation. The little freedom allowed to other kinds of trade was denied to that in grain. The export of grain from France was prohibited—a typically feudal law that was more concerned with adequate supplies than with good business and high prices. But exceptions were granted in years of plenty. Special permits to individuals might be issued indicating the quantity and kind of grain to be exported, and frequently its destination. Within the kingdom, grain and flour could not be moved from one province to another without permission. To receive a license to sell grain between provinces, all details of the enterprise had to be submitted to an inspector; after the grain had been transported, a certificate had to be produced showing that the consignment had actually reached the prescribed destination. Within each province grain was subject to further restriction. Laws specified where grain was to be sold and what the price should be. In times of shortage, marketing was compulsory to prevent hoarding. Tolls as well as regulations impeded the grain trade, so that in one area surpluses might glut the warehouses while a few miles away people starved.

The guilds, which arose during the medieval period, persisted longer in France than in England. Their character changed as national authorization and regulation of guilds replaced the authority of towns or feudal lords. But down to 1789 guilds impeded the free entry of labor into certain occupations, restricted and regulated output, fixed prices, and fought against competition between towns and from abroad. Guild jurisdictional quarrels and litigation dragged on for generations and centuries at great cost in time and money. The annual cost of legal battles to the Paris guilds during the middle 1700's was eight hundred thousand to one million livres. Goose-roasters and poulterers quarreled for half a century until the latter were finally restricted to the sale of uncooked game. The successful roasters then turned on the cooks who had won a triumph over the sauce-makers. A three-hundred-year litigation between the secondhand-clothes-dealers and the tailors in Paris had not been resolved by 1789, when the Revolution swept the guilds aside and destroyed them.

It was through this corrupt and decayed society that physiocratic ideas swept like a fresh breeze.

The essence of the physiocratic school. The concepts of this school may be summarized as follows:

1. The physiocrats developed the idea of natural order. According to this belief human societies were subject to laws of nature such as govern the physical world. It was necessary, therefore, that all human activities be brought into harmony with these laws of nature. The object of all scientific study was to discover the laws to which all the phenomena of the universe were subject. In the economic sphere the chief natural right of man was to enjoy the fruits of his own labor, provided that such enjoyment be consistent with the rights of others. Governments, it followed, should never extend their interference in economic affairs beyond the minimum absolutely essential to protect life and property and to maintain freedom of contract.

2. The physiocrats were opposed to almost all feudal, mercantilist, and government restrictions. Vincent de Gournay (1712–59), an inspector of the quality of products as guaranteed by trade marks, is credited with uttering the famous phrase "laissez faire, laissez passer." This may be freely translated as freedom of business enterprise at home and free trade abroad. Gournay was not the only high functionary of the mercantilist system who became an adherent of laissez faire as a result of his experiences.

3. They thought that industry, trade, and the professions were useful but sterile, simply reproducing the value consumed in the form of raw materials and subsistence for the workers. Only agriculture (and possibly mining) was productive. It produced a surplus, a net product, above costs of production.

4. They thought that as only agriculture produced a surplus and this went to the landowner, only the landowner could or should be taxed. All taxes imposed on others would be passed on to him anyway. A direct tax was preferable to indirect taxes, which increased as they were passed along to others.

5. They opposed the consumption of luxury goods as being a barrier to the accumulation of capital.

6. They looked at the economy as a whole and analyzed the circular flow of wealth.

What groups of people did the physiocratic school serve or seek to serve? The peasants stood to gain from these ideas if all the heavy and onerous obligations to the landowners could be shaken off; but if the physiocrats had had their way, the peasants would have become wage laborers on large farms. Businessmen would be better off if all restrictions on production and the movement of goods were removed. The physiocrats, by advocating the doctrine of laissez faire, were promoting industry, even though this was not their intention. With their emphasis on agriculture, they were interested in encouraging freer internal grain trade and in stimulating the export of farm products and the import of manufactured goods.

The physiocrats especially favored capitalistic farmers using wage labor and advanced techniques. These progressive farms could be found mostly in northern France. The big producers with surpluses for sale would be favorable to the emphasis on agricultural development and free internal trade in grain. The tax on the surplus produced in agriculture would have lowered land values and hurt the landowning nobility instead of the current or prospective farm entrepreneurs who paid rent. A multiplicity of taxes that burdened the commoner landowners exempted the nobility and clergy. A single tax applicable to all land in production would have helped the non-titled owners.

The physiocrats tried to placate the nobility by genuinely defending their right to own land and receive rent. Unlike Henry George (see Chapter 16), who later wanted to abolish private landownership by taxing away all economic rent, the physiocrats thought that a tax taking one-third of the economic surplus would be sufficient. This, they believed, would not redistribute wealth from the rich to the poor, because the landowners paid all taxes in any case; they argued that converting the taxes from an indirect to a direct basis would lower the over-all burden. In their view the nobility would be aided if their program were enacted; but this was erroneous, based on their faulty analysis which held that all taxable surpluses could come only from the land.

How was the physiocratic school valid, useful, or correct in its time? Before the industrial revolution, industry was, in a sense, sterile because of the extremely low productivity of a handicraft economy. This was especially true of France during the last decades of the *ancien régime*. Farming, however, sometimes produced bountiful harvests in spite of the primitive methods of cultivation. Agriculture often provided the surpluses that could be saved and reinvested to initiate a rising rate of economic growth.

In promoting laissez faire, the physiocrats were opposing obstacles to capitalistic economic development. They unwittingly promoted the French Revolution, which swept away the numerous obstacles to progress. By emphasizing the productivity of agriculture, they were getting away from the older concept that only commerce produces wealth and adds to it; the physiocrats emphasized production rather than exchange as a source of wealth. In their analysis of taxes they favored direct rather than the in-direct taxes that pervaded and corroded French society of their time. They favored capital accumulation through reduced consumption by the wealthy. By looking at society as a whole and analyzing the laws that governed the circulation of wealth and goods, they were the founders of economics as a science.

How did physiocratic doctrine outlive its usefulness? This school was always wrong to consider industry and trade as sterile. The more industry and trade developed in France, the more conspicuously incorrect their analysis became. This fault led to another error, that only landowners should be taxed because only land could yield a surplus. The wealthy in-dustrialist could smile as he endorsed the doctrine that he should not be made to pay the tax because he added nothing to wealth. This anomaly in-spired Voltaire to write a lively satire, *The Man with Forty Crowns;* in it the wealthy financier who escapes taxation taunts the poor farmer who pays taxes for both, although his income is only forty crowns.

The physiocrats would promote the capitalistic farmer as the key figure in French economic development, but they were wrong on two counts. First, the industrialist became the important man in the economic growth of the country, while the relative importance of agriculture declined. Sec-ond, the small peasant farmer rather than the large farm entrepreneur be-came typical in France. Had the land remained in the hands of the nobility, a tax on land ownership would have curbed wasteful luxury consumption. But when the small peasants got the land after the Revolution, they would have borne the bulk of the tax burden.

Quesnay

FRANÇOIS QUESNAY (1694–1774) was the founder and leader of the physiocratic school. He was the court physician of Louis XV and Mad-ame de Pompadour. To him society was analogous to the physical or-ganism. The circulation of wealth and goods in the economy was like the circulation of blood in the body. The name physiocracy was derived from the Greek, meaning the rule of nature. Man-made laws should be in har-mony with natural laws.

The dauphin of France once bemoaned to Quesnay the difficulties of the office of king, which he was not destined to live to assume. "I do not see," said Quesnay, "that it is so troublesome." "What then," asked the dauphin, "would you do if you were king?" "Nothing." Asked who would govern, he said cryptically, "The Law." He meant natural law.

His famous *Tableau Économique*, constructed for the king of France in

1758 and revised in 1766, depicted the circular flow of goods and money in an ideal freely competitive economy. This was the first systematic analysis of the flow of wealth on what later came to be called a macroeconomic basis. Economists such as Smith, Marx, and Keynes, who favored the description of economic activities in terms of large aggregates, paid tribute to Quesnay for originating this approach. Neoclassical economists, who prefer the microeconomic approach of describing activities in terms of individuals, have tended to belittle him.

The *Economic Table* foreshadowed national-income analysis and led toward statistical work to describe an economy. Quesnay himself tried to estimate the values of annual output and other aggregates. The table also explicitly conveyed the concept of equilibrium of the whole economy, for if one of the interdependent variables changed, others would also change.

Quesnay assumed that only farmers, who make up the productive class, create a surplus, which is paid to the landowners in the form of rent. In his scheme, this payment is used to finance the consumption of farm products by landowners and the sterile class—the people engaged in non-agricultural work. Farmers produce goods worth five billion francs. Of this, two billions do not circulate, because one billion is used for the farmers' own subsistence, and one billion replaces the capital used up in the form of feed for livestock and seed. The remaining three billion francs worth of goods constitutes the net product or surplus. The farmers sell this and pay two billions in rent to the landowners. The landlords pay one billion to the farmers for agricultural products, and one billion to the sterile class for manufactured goods. The farmers use their remaining billion of income to buy manufactured goods from the sterile class. That class now has two billions to spend on raw materials and food supplied by farmers. The cycle of payments is now complete and can be repeated.

It was odd that Quesnay called non-agricultural production sterile, yet he did not question the right of the proprietors of the soil to receive rent. It is nature that produces the surplus, he said, and not the worker. The landowner therefore has a right to the surplus product, which goes with the title to the land. His class makes the original capital investment in land to make it productive, and he is entitled to the surplus product. But Quesnay's proposal (later taken up by Henry George) to tax only landowners was an attack on their interests.

Quesnay argued that "an excess of luxury in the way of decoration may quickly ruin with magnificence an opulent Nation." He preferred spending on raw materials. This was the language of economic growth at a time when the aristocracy was wasteful in its consumption, and industry was far less important than agriculture and mining as a source for accumulating wealth for further investment.

The medieval flavor of Quesnay's thinking was apparent in his glorification of agriculture, and in his belief that the government should fix the rate of interest, although Turgot and Du Pont opposed usury laws. He also favored the "just price." But he relied on a free market rather than on regulation by authority to achieve it.

Turgot

ANNE ROBERT JACQUES TURGOT (1727–81) was born of a noble family of Normandy that for several generations had furnished the state with able administrative officials. As a younger son, he was educated for the church. But after receiving his theological degree, he decided instead to enter the judicial and administrative service. He rose in the ranks of government service until, in 1774, he became the finance minister of France; this had been Colbert's office a hundred years earlier. In less than two years in office, he introduced antifeudal and antimercantilist measures in keeping with physiocratic ideas. Freedom of internal grain trade was ordered, and the hated *corvée* was replaced by a tax which all landowners had to pay. He decreed the abolition of guilds and privileged trading corporations. Plans were presented to tax the nobility and to establish the principle that every man had a right to work at any occupation without restriction. Turgot's edicts and plans aroused the most determined opposition from the nobility, the financiers, the clergy, the rich and entrenched bourgeoisie of Paris, and others interested in maintaining existing conditions. He was dismissed by Louis XVI because of the protests of the court and Marie Antoinette. Turgot's reforms were at once canceled, not to be introduced again until the French Revolution.

Turgot, like other physiocrats, believed in an enlightened absolutism and he looked to the king to carry through all reforms. He opposed the interference of parliaments in legislation. A plan that he submitted to the king would allow only landed proprietors to form the electorate, and the elected body would have no legislative powers. It would administer taxation, education, and poor relief. Obviously Turgot and the other physiocrats had their roots in the old feudalistic regime of France, and they were reformers rather than revolutionaries. But the reactionary French regime could not stomach their reforms.

In *Reflections on the Formation and the Distribution of Riches*, written in 1766, Turgot developed a theory of wages. Competition among workmen lowers the wage to the minimum of subsistence, an early statement of what was later called "the iron law of wages." Only farmers produce a surplus, which is used to feed and provide raw materials for all of society.

He [the husbandman] is, therefore, the sole source of the riches, which, by their circulation, animate all the labors of the society; because he is the only one whose labor produces over and above the wages of the labor. . . . It is the earth which is always the first and only source of all wealth; it is that which as the result of cultivation produces all the revenue.

Turgot, using the term *Entrepreneur*,* said that the capitalist tenant farmer is most capable of efficient farming. Being rich, he has the capital to invest in the soil. He receives profits and the return of his investment with interest. Entrepreneurs reinvest most of their profits and savings, but not so the landlords:

It is even generally true that, although the proprietors have a greater superfluity, they save less because as they have more leisure, they have more desires and more passions; they regard themselves as more assured of their fortunes; they think more about enjoying it agreeably than about increasing it: luxury is their inheritance.

Turgot, in a letter to David Hume written in 1767, stated that taxes imposed on other groups were passed on to the landowner. A tax on wage earners would not be passed on only if wages were above the minimum of subsistence, but this was a temporary deviation. Wages at the minimum of subsistence could not be lowered by taxes because workers had to earn enough to survive. A direct tax on the landowner was therefore preferable to indirect taxes, which were passed on to him. This inevitable incidence of taxes was also the best for economic development, as implied above, because the landlord wasted his share of the revenue.

Turgot was a persistent advocate of economy in government. In a letter to Hume in 1766 he wrote:

You also know as well as I do what is the great end of all governments on earth: submission and money. The object is, as they say, to pluck the bird without making it squeal; now it is the proprietors who are squealing, and one has always preferred to attack them indirectly, because then they notice the harm only when the thing has become an accepted fact.

Turgot's greatest contribution in the realm of economic theory was in correctly presenting the law of diminishing returns. This appeared in his *Observations sur un Mémoire de M. de Saint-Péravy*, written about 1767. It can never be imagined, he said, that a doubling of expenditure in agriculture would double the product.

* Before him, Quesnay used the term in his encyclopedia article on "Grain," 1757. Richard Cantillon wrote about the entrepreneur before 1734.

The earth's fertility resembles a spring that is being pressed downwards by the addition of successive weights. If the weight is small and the spring not very flexible, the first attempts will leave no results. But when the weight is enough to overcome the first resistance then it will give to the pressure. After yielding a certain amount it will again begin to resist the extra force put upon it, and weights that formerly would have caused a depression of an inch or more will now scarcely move it by a hair's breadth. And so the effect of additional weights will gradually diminish.

It is curious that Adam Smith, who knew Turgot and his work, did not apply the law of diminishing returns to agriculture. The doctrine was later used in the analysis of rent by Ricardo, Malthus, and Edward West; but none of them recognized, as Turgot did, the possibility of increasing returns in the early stages of adding successive units of variable factors of production to a fixed factor, land.

Du Pont de Nemours

PIERRE SAMUEL DU PONT DE NEMOURS (1739–1817) became an intimate disciple of Quesnay, Turgot, and others of the physiocratic school. He advocated their doctrine of free trade in his *Exportation et importation des grains* (1764). The name for this school was taken from his book, *La physiocratie* (1767). Du Pont served as editor, journalist, secretary, biographer, and friend of the school and its leaders. He was a government official, an advisor to foreign princes, and in 1790 he was elected president of the revolutionary constituent assembly. But in 1792, after taking the side of the king, he was driven into hiding. When he was arrested and imprisoned, only the death of Robespierre saved him from the guillotine.

In 1797 Du Pont's house was sacked by a mob, and two years later he emigrated to the United States. Jefferson asked him to design a system of national education, which was published in 1800. He returned to France, where he lived and held high offices from 1802 to 1815. Then he went to the United States once again. He died near Wilmington, Delaware, where his son, Eleuthère Irénée du Pont de Nemours had founded a small gunpowder mill in 1802.

CHAPTER 4

The Classical School:

FORERUNNERS

THE BEGINNING of the classical school can be dated at 1776, when Adam Smith's great book was published. It ended in 1871, when both W. Stanley Jevons and Carl Menger published works expounding what was later called neoclassical theory. There were, of course, advanced thinkers before Smith, including the physiocrats, who influenced his thinking. This in no way detracts from the tremendous contribution he made.

Overview of the Classical School

The social background of the school. In the seventeenth century England was behind Holland in commerce and behind France in manufacturing production. By the middle of the eighteenth century England was supreme in commerce and industry. Both classical political economy and the industrial revolution developed first in England. Smith and his contemporaries, living during the early stages of the industrial revolution, could not adequately identify the significance of this phenomenon and the direction its development would take; such wisdom is usually displayed through hindsight. But they were aware of the substantial growth of manufacturing, trade, inventions, and the division of labor. The growth of industry led to increased emphasis on this aspect of economic life in current thinking.

By 1776 England, being the most efficient and powerful country in the world, could afford free trade without fear of foreign competition. With entrepreneurs becoming strong enough to stand on their own feet, they no longer had to rely on subsidies, monopoly privileges, and tariff protection. With entrepreneurs becoming numerous enough to make monopoly agreements difficult to achieve and enforce, competition could be depended upon to establish moderate prices and products of good quality. Many mercantilist practices were breaking down under the upsurge of business activity, which spread in every direction.

The world of business and industry required a free, mobile, poorly paid, hard-working labor force. Before the final triumph of classical political economy, national and local governments regulated labor and working conditions. Sometimes labor was protected, but more frequently employers were favored. Wages in England had been regulated by local justices of the peace for centuries, with wage ceilings usually being imposed. This practice died out by 1762, however, for wages could be kept low through the workings of a free-market economy. Enclosures drove tenant farmers and even many small owners off the land; wage earners lost their right of access to the village pastures and woodlands where they once could graze a cow or a pig and gather fuel. Handicraftsmen lost their independence as the putting-out system of the merchant, and later the factory system, turned them into wage laborers. A high birth rate and a falling death rate increased the population, and child laborers and bankrupted Irish peasants who went to England also augmented the labor force. Government steps to keep wages down were therefore no longer necessary, and laissez faire became the gospel of the businessman. Then it was the workers who tried, unsuccessfully, to invoke government regulation to establish minimum wages.

In eighteenth-century England one could still find vestiges of feudal-agrarian paternalism that showed some concern for the welfare of the poor. But it was giving way to the harsh, impersonal relations of early industrialism. Taxes on the landowners provided funds for poor relief, paid through local government. Parishes tried to unload their poor on other parishes from which the indigent had come. Even preventive expulsion—removal of the poor to their home parishes if they might some day need relief—was practiced. Dying people or women in labor were rushed to their places of birth by officials who wished the present or future financial burdens to fall elsewhere. Preventive expulsion, which impeded the mobility of the population, was abolished in 1795; after that only people actually on relief could be sent back to their original parish. And the poor laws were made so harsh in 1834 that many people preferred to starve quietly at home rather than undergo the indignities of poor relief and workhouses.

The Speenhamland Law of 1795 provided that the poor should have a minimum income irrespective of their earnings. The family income was linked to the price of bread, and if earnings were below the prescribed level, allowances from taxes would make up the difference. This system prevailed in most of the rural areas and in some manufacturing districts. Workers were pauperized and demoralized when their welfare was no longer so directly dependent on their wage rates or productivity. When the Speenhamland system was ended in 1834, a competitive labor market was fully established in England.

The essence of the classical school. Classical doctrine is frequently called economic liberalism. Its bases are personal liberty, private property, and individual initiative and control of enterprise. These rest on the laissez faire doctrine. The term "liberalism" should be considered in its historical context. Classical ideas were liberal in contrast to feudal and mercantilist restrictions on choice of occupation, land transfers, trade, etc. But today we would hardly call a person liberal if he advocated an unmodified laissez faire program.

The major features of this body of thought may be summarized briefly as follows:

1. The first principle of the classical school was laissez faire. That government is best which governs least. The forces of the free, competitive market guide production, exchange, and distribution. The economy was held to be self-adjusting and tending toward full employment without any government intervention.

2. The existence of a harmony of interests was emphasized, with Ricardo being an important exception. Each individual, seeking his own interests, serves the best interests of society.

3. The classicists emphasized the importance of all economic activities, especially industry. The mercantilists had said that wealth is derived from commerce; the physiocrats had seen in agriculture the source of all wealth; the classical school added industry to the other two, and regarded all three as productive.

4. The classical school made tremendous contributions by providing a method of analyzing the economy and the economic laws that operate within it.

5. Classical economists sought to promote maximum economic growth and development.

6. They looked at the economy as a whole—the macroeconomic approach.

What groups of people did the classical school serve or seek to serve? In the first instance, it served businessmen. It gave them respectability in a world that offered the greatest honors to the landowning nobility and the gentry. Businessmen, especially industrialists, achieved a new status and dignity as the promoters of a nation's wealth. Entrepreneurs were assured that by seeking profit they were serving society. These doctrines also led to more material benefits, for they helped create the political, social, and economic climate that promoted industry, trade, and profit.

In the long run classical economics served all of society because the application of its theories promoted capital accumulation and economic growth. Historically speaking, we can apply the harmony-of-interests doctrine to classical theories. Somebody had to pay the heavy costs of industrialization. In Great Britain it was the wage earners who bore the heaviest share of the costs through long hours of hard work at low pay. But ultimately economic progress enabled them to improve their own position. In this sense classical economics served them too. Although their slice of the total pie was relatively small, the growth of the pie benefited succeeding generations of workers along with all other groups.

How was the classical school valid, useful, or correct in its time? The new doctrine was a rationalization of practices engaged in by enterprising men because they were profitable. It justified the overthrow of mercantilist restrictions, which had outlived their usefulness. Competition was a rising phenomenon, and reliance upon it as the great regulator of the economy could be defended. Governments were notoriously wasteful and corrupt, and under the circumstances, the less government intervention the better. By helping to remove the remnants of the feudal system, classical economics promoted business enterprise. For example, when feudal land laws were abolished and land could serve as security for credit, large sums could be raised by landowners for investment in agriculture or industry.

When industrialization was beginning, society's greatest need was to concentrate resources on the maximum possible expansion of production. The elevation of the private sector over the public sector served this end admirably. With consumers generally poor and investment opportunities seemingly unlimited, capitalists had every incentive to reinvest most of their profits. The outcome was a rapid expansion of output. Any growth of the public sector would have required increased taxation, thereby diverting resources from private capital formation.

Classical economics and the businessmen who endorsed it enlarged the market, not only by achieving freer international trade, but also by promoting an urban labor force. A subsistence farmer might consume much that he produced himself while he bought little in the market; an urban laborer of the late 1700's might consume less but buy much more from others. The food supply was absorbed into the monetary sector of the economy, and the merchant and processor came between the farmer and the consumer.

The classical economists gave the best analysis of the economic world up to their time, far surpassing the analyses of the mercantilists and the physiocrats. They laid the foundation of modern economics as a science, and the generations that followed built upon their insights and achievements. Their emphasis on the division of labor, the gains from international trade, and economic development are still basically compatible with the goals that modern societies have set for themselves.

How did the classical school outlive its usefulness? The doctrine of laissez faire succumbed as business fluctuations shook capitalistic society to its core, and as competition gave way to changing market structures characterized by quasi-monopoly, oligopoly, regulated industries, etc. The harmony of interests could no longer be defended when the concentration of wealth produced great disparity in bargaining power among individuals. Classical economists were frequently opposed to humane poor laws, and to factory acts, especially those that regulated the conditions of adult labor. The government was increasingly relied upon to ameliorate social conditions and to regulate and curb conflicting interests. Even where competition survived, it was not always deemed to be an efficient enough regulator of economic activities. Health laws, for instance, became more necessary with the growth of cities. In 1800 a small farmer's infected milk supply might sicken a few neighbors; a century later contaminated milk could produce a massive epidemic. Competition in the milk industry does not preclude strict government regulation.

Laissez faire was carried to absurd extremes by the advocates of classical economics. To cite but one example, the London *Economist* of July 13, 1850, criticized the "sanitary movement," which urged that the government require a pure water supply and proper sewage disposal. Even after sewage lines were built, owners of houses were not required at first to hook up to them. The *Economist* declared that poor housing and high urban death rates

spring from two causes, both of which will be aggravated by these new laws. The first is the poverty of the masses, which, if possible, will be increased by the taxation inflicted by the new laws. The second is that the people have never been allowed to take care of themselves. They have always been treated as serfs or children, and they have to a great extent become in respect to those objects which the government has undertaken to perform for them, imbecile.... There is a worse evil than typhus or cholera or impure water, and that is mental imbecility.

Classical economists committed the error of thinking that what applied to contemporary England was valid everywhere for all time. When they predicted, for example, that rents would rise and the rate of profit would fall, they were belittling future technological change. Their enthusiastic endorsement of free trade was good for England, but it could harm underdeveloped countries then and now. They viewed economic laws as immutable, not to be tampered with or thwarted. They and their followers could not understand that economic laws, which are generalizations about tendencies, can be curbed, overcome, or redirected. Man can control economic life. Economic laws that are valid under laissez faire may become inoperative in a regulated economy; the classical school did not admit this was possible or desirable. Theirs was a static analysis.

Classical economics was especially deficient in the analysis of demand, interest, and the role of money in a private enterprise system.

Finally, classical economics with its labor theory of value led to socialist doctrines; it was therefore condemned as pernicious theory by the defenders of private enterprise.

North

SIR DUDLEY NORTH (1641–91), living during the height of the mercantilist period, struck hard at the heart of mercantilist doctrine. He was a wealthy merchant in the Turkish trade. Later he became commissioner of customs and then a treasury official. He has been called the world's first prominent free-trader.

His brief tract, *Discourses upon Trade*, was his only published work. It appeared anonymously in 1691. Such caution was understandable in a merchant and high government official of a prominent family who did not conform to prevailing ideas. Decades later his brother hinted that the publication was deliberately suppressed. When Ricardo read a reprinted edition, he wrote: "I had no idea that any one entertained such correct opinions, as are expressed in this publication, at so early a period."

North emphasized that trade is not a one-sided benefit to whichever country realizes a surplus of exports. Rather, it is of mutual advantage. Its object is not to accumulate specie but to exchange surpluses. A division of labor and international trade would promote wealth even if there were no gold and silver in existence.

Trade is nothing else but a Commutation of Superfluities; for instance: I give of mine, what I can spare, for somewhat of yours, which I want, and you can spare.... He who is most diligent, and raiseth most Fruits, or maketh most of Manufactory, will abound most in what others make, or raise; and consequently be free from Want, and enjoy most Conveniences, which is truly to be Rich, altho' there were no such thing as Gold, Silver, or the like amongst them.

North repudiated the concept that wealth should be measured by the precious metals one has. His emphasis was on business enterprise and accumulation. Here he struck at the theory rather than the practice of the mercantilists. But, understandably for his time, he did not include manufacturing production in his list of productive activities. Even taking its original meaning of "making by hand," manufacturing was relatively unimportant in the seventeenth century.

No Man is richer for having his Estate all in Money, Plate, etc. lying by him, but on the contrary, he is for that reason the poorer. That man is richest, whose Estate is in a growing condition, either in Land at Farm, Money at Interest, or Goods in Trade: If any man, out of an humour, should turn all his Estate into Money, and keep it dead, he would soon be sensible of Poverty growing upon him, whilst he is eating out of the quick stock.

But to examine the matter closer, what do these People want, who cry out for Money? I will begin with the Beggar; he wants, and importunes for Money: What would he do with it if he had it? buy Bread, etc. Then in truth it is not Money, but Bread, and other Necessaries for Life that he wants. Well then, the Farmer complains, for the want of Money; surely it is not for the Beggar's Reason, to sustain Life, or pay Debts; but he thinks that were more Money in the Country, he should have a Price for his Goods. Then it seems Money is not his want, but a Price for his Corn, and Cattel, which he would sell, but cannot.

The profound truth of the last paragraph has not yet been mastered by most people even today. We want all the money we can get (if the effort is not too great) if money is considered as a measure of value. But with money as a means of payment, we want it only to part with it, except for working balances.

North observed that commerce among nations distributes the money supply according to the needs of trade:

For it hath been observed, that where no Mints were, Trade hath not wanted a full supply of Money; because if it be wanted, the Coyn of other Princes will become currant, as in *Ireland,* and the *Plantations.* . . . Then let not the care of Specifick Money torment us so much; for a People that are rich cannot want it, and if they make none, they will be supplied with the Coyn of other Nations.

North argued for laissez faire and a harmony of interest in trading, both within a country and internationally. This was bold theorizing in an age of rampant nationalism.

Now it may appear strange to hear it said, That the whole World as to Trade is but as one Nation or People, and therein Nations are as Persons. That the loss of a Trade with one Nation, is not that only, separately considered, but so much of the Trade of the World rescinded and lost, for all is combined together. That there can be no Trade unprofitable to the Publick; for if any prove so, men leave it off; and whereever the Traders thrive, the Publick, of which they are a part, thrives also. That to force Men to deal in any prescrib'd manner, may profit such as happen to serve them; but the Publick gains not, because it is taking from one Subject, to give to another. . . . That Money is a Merchandize, whereof there may be a glut as well as a scarcity, and that even to an Inconvenience. That a People cannot want Money to serve the ordinary dealing, and more than enough they will not have. . . . In short, That all favour to one Trade or Interest against another, is an Abuse, and cuts so much of Profit from the Publick.

Although North believed that free trade would help both the traders and the country, he did not profess a crude harmony-of-interest doctrine. He saw many special interests that were profiting at the expense of the public. This they accomplished by using the power of government for privileges on their own behalf. The authorities therefore should not support narrow private interests, which was quite contrary to mercantilist doctrine.

Whenever Men consult for the Publick Good, as for the advancement of Trade, wherein all are concerned, they usually esteem the immediate Interest of their own to be the common Measure of Good and Evil. And there are many, who to gain a little in their own Trades, care not how much others suffer; and each Man strives, that all others may be forc'd, in their dealings, to act subserviently for his Profit, but under the covert of the Publick.

So Clothiers would have men be forc'd to buy their Manufacture; and I may mention such as sell Wool, they would have men forc'd to buy of them at an high Price, though the Clothier loseth. . . . And in general all those who are lazy, and do not, or are not active enough, and cannot look out, to vent the Product of their Estates, or to Trade with it themselves, would have all Traders forc'd by Laws, to bring home to them sufficient Prizes, whether they gain or lose by it.

North disagreed with the mercantilist concept that war and conquest enrich a country. "Money Exported in Trade is an increase to the Wealth of the Nation; but spent in War, and Payments abroad, is so much Impoverishment." By payments abroad he probably meant payments without receiving an equivalent in return, as in the case of military subsidies to allies. If this promotes exports, of what virtue is that if an equivalent of imports does not follow? These are antimercantilist views of the strongest kind, which many would not endorse wholeheartedly even today.

Cantillon

RICHARD CANTILLON (1680?–1734) was born in Ireland. He spent many years in Paris, becoming a wealthy banker and successful speculator in stocks and foreign currencies. In 1734 he was murdered, robbed, and had his house set afire, probably by a cook he dismissed ten days earlier. His only book, *Essai sur la Nature du Commerce en Général*, written between 1730 and 1734, was published in French in 1755. It may have been translated by Cantillon himself from his English manuscript, which was never found.

Cantillon developed a theory of value and price. His emphasis on the role of land and labor, on supply and demand, and on the fluctuations of price around intrinsic value place him squarely as a forerunner of classical economics.

The Villagers come to Town on Market-Days to sell their produce and to buy the things they need. Prices are fixed by the proportion between the produce exposed for sale and the money offered for it. . . . When the price has been settled between a few the others follow without difficulty and so the Market-price of the day is determined. . . .

The Price or intrinsic value of a thing is the measure of the quantity of Land and of Labour entering into its production, having regard to the fertility or produce of the Land and to the quality of the Labour.

But it often happens that many things which have actually this intrinsic value are not sold in the Market according to that value: that will depend on the Humours and Fancies of men and on their consumption. . . .

If the Farmers in a State sow more corn than usual, much more than is needed for the year's consumption, the real and intrinsic value of the corn will correspond to the Land and Labour which enter into its production; but as there is too great an abundance of it and there are more sellers than buyers the Market Price of the Corn will necessarily fall below the intrinsic price or Value. If on the contrary the Farmers sow less corn than is needed for consumption there will be more buyers than sellers and the Market Price of corn will rise above its intrinsic value.

There is never a variation in intrinsic values, but the impossibility of proportioning the production of merchandise and produce in a State to their consumption causes a daily variation, and a perpetual ebb and flow in Market Prices.

The importance of the velocity of circulation of money was recognized by him, with a faster circulation requiring a smaller quantity.

But it usually happens in States where money is scarcer that there is more Barter than in those where Money is plentiful, and circulation is more prompt and less sluggish than in those where Money is not so scarce. Thus it is always necessary in estimating the amount of money in circulation to take into account the rapidity of its circulation.

Cantillon used the term "entrepreneur" and emphasized his role in economic life. Businessmen commit themselves to definite payments in expectation of uncertain receipts; this risk-taking is remunerated by profit that competition tends to reduce to the normal value of their services. He analyzed interest as a reward for the risk in lending; it is based on profits that the entrepreneurs can make out of borrowing and investing. Bankers, he pointed out, create credit, for if a hundred thousand ounces of gold are deposited with them, as much as ninety thousand can be lent out; such loans will not, of course, diminish the original demand deposit.

With one foot in the mercantilist camp, Cantillon preferred a surplus of exports; this is good for business. But gold and silver mined at home would not serve the same purpose. The emphasis was on the production of goods and their sale abroad, so that business would flourish. But he believed that an export surplus could not be maintained indefinitely; a self-balancing mechanism would wipe it out. His emphasis on the sale of goods rather than on the accumulation of gold, no matter how, and the equilibrium of forces that prevent a perpetual export surplus, came close to classical thinking.

The discovery and exploitation of rich mines of gold and silver, he said, would raise prices, rents, and wages. This would promote imports to the detriment of domestic workers and manufacturers. Money would flow out of the country. "The great circulation of Money, which was general at the beginning, ceases: poverty and misery follow and the labour of the Mines appears to be only to the advantage of those employed upon them and the Foreigners who profit thereby." That was what happened to Spain, he said.

But if the increase of money comes from a surplus of exports of goods, it enriches merchants and entrepreneurs and gives employment to workmen. However, as money flows into the country and business prospers, consumption and prices rise, spending on foreign luxury grows, and the export surplus dwindles. The state begins to lose some branches of its profitable trade, and workmen leave the country.

This will gradually impoverish the State and cause it to pass from great power into great weakness. When a State has arrived at the highest point of wealth (I assume always that the comparative wealth of States consists principally in the respective quantities of money which they possess) it will inevitably fall into poverty by the ordinary course of things. The too great abundance of money, which so long as it lasts forms the power of States, throws them back imperceptibly but naturally into poverty. Thus it would seem that when a State expands by trade and the abundance of money raises the price of Land and Labour, the Prince or the Legislator ought to withdraw money from circulation.

No reliance on laissez faire here!

Cantillon was mercantilistic—and probably realistic—in his emphasis on the uses of money in warfare:

If of two Princes who war upon each other for the Sovereignty or Conquest of a State one have much money and the other little money but many estates which may be worth twice as much as all the money of his enemy, the first will be better able to attach to himself Generals and Officers by gifts of money than the second will be by giving twice the value in lands and estates. Grants of Land are subject to challenge and revocation and cannot be relied upon so well as the money which is received. With money munitions of war and food are bought even from the enemies of the State. Money can be given without witnesses for secret service. Lands, Produce, Merchandise would not serve for these purposes, not even jewels or diamonds, because they are easily recognised.

This hard-headed businessman regretted that both nobles and monks lived in luxury and idleness. But noblemen are a great ornament to the country, and during wartime they will at least use their retinues and horses for victory, "while the Monks are, as people say, neither useful nor ornamental in peace or war on this side of heaven." Furthermore, he said, there are too many holy days in Catholic countries "which diminish the labour of the People by about an eighth part of the year."

Cantillon anticipated Malthus on population by saying that "Men multiply like Mice in a barn if they have unlimited Means of Subsistence."

A thread of physiocratic thought can be detected. Writing a generation before Quesnay constructed his Economic Table, Cantillon stated:

Cash is therefore necessary, not only for the Rent of the Landlord, . . . but also for the City merchandise consumed in the Country. . . . The circulation of this money takes place when the Landlords spend in detail in the City the rents which the Farmers have paid them in lump sums, and when the Entrepreneurs of the Cities, Butchers, Bakers, Brewers, etc. collect little by little this same money to buy from the Farmers in lump sums Cattle, Wheat, Barley, etc.

Hume

DAVID HUME (1711–76) was born in Scotland twelve years before his fellow countryman and friend, Adam Smith. He entered the University of Edinburgh at twelve years of age and left at fourteen or fifteen without taking a degree. Later, eminent as a philosopher, he was twice refused a chair in philosophy at Edinburgh because of his skeptical spirit and unorthodox thinking. In fact Adam Smith was once nearly expelled from Oxford University because a copy of Hume's *A Treatise of Human Nature* was found in his rooms.

Hume spent his life as a tutor to a marquis and as a minor government official. In retirement he returned to his inherited estate where he wrote prolifically. His fame as a historian derived from his multi-volume *History of England,* which went through numerous editions. His reputation as an economist was established by his economic essays in *Political Discourses,* published in 1752. Of all the forerunners of classical economics, Hume came closest to the ideas of Smith. Had he written a complete and systematic treatise on economics, he would have ranked near the top as one of the founders of the science.

Hume's greatest contribution was in presenting what has later been called the price specie-flow mechanism. The mercantilists wanted to promote a surplus of exports to accumulate specie. In the somber view of Cantillon, this was self-defeating because more money would raise prices and promote imports, while money would be shipped abroad, leaving poverty and bankruptcy behind; therefore the government should prevent an excess of money. The physiocrats were basically unconcerned with foreign trade, except that they wished to permit the free flow of grain abroad. But Hume, accepting the quantity theory of money as did Cantillon, analyzed the mechanism of international equilibrium that would occur without government intervention. Laissez faire could prevail with happy results. In his essay "Of the Balance of Trade" (1752), Hume wrote:

Suppose four-fifths of all the money in GREAT BRITAIN to be annihilated in one night, and the nation reduced to the same condition, with regard to specie, as in the reigns of the HARRYS and EDWARDS, what would be the consequence? Must not the price of all labour and commodities sink in proportion, and everything be sold as cheap as they were in those ages? What nation could then dispute with us in any foreign market, or pretend to navigate or to sell manufactures at the same price, which to us would afford sufficient profit? In how little time, therefore, must this bring back the money which we had lost, and raise us to the level of all the neighbouring nations? Where, after we have arrived, we immediately lose the advantage of the cheapness of labour and commodities; and the farther flowing in of money is stopped by our fulness and repletion.

Again, suppose, that all the money of GREAT BRITAIN were multiplied fivefold in a night, must not the contrary effect follow? Must not all labour and commodities rise to such an exorbitant height, that no neighbouring nations could afford to buy from us; while their commodities, on the other hand, became comparatively so cheap, that, in spite of all the laws which could be formed, they would be run in upon us, and our money flow out; till we fall to a level with foreigners, and lose that great superiority of riches, which had laid us under such disadvantages?

Hume was aware of another factor that precedes price changes and gold movements in promoting equilibrium in international trade. When exchange rates fluctuate between the gold points, an imbalance of trade tends to correct itself. In a footnote to the same essay, Hume wrote:

There is another cause, though more limited in its operation, which checks the wrong balance of trade, to every particular nation to which the kingdom trades. When we import more goods than we export, the exchange turns against us, and this becomes a new encouragement to export; as much as the charge of carriage and insurance of the money which becomes due would amount to. For the exchange can never rise but a little higher than that sum.

An increase of imports, Hume emphasized, would stimulate exports. He was aware of the concept of elasticity of demand, saying that if duties on wine are lowered, the government will collect more revenue. He did not realize that with an inelastic demand for a country's products abroad, a surplus of imports that would cause a price drop at home would not stimulate exports enough to produce equilibrium.

In "Of the Jealousy of Trade" (1758) Hume disputed the mercantilist concept that trading states are rivals, with one gaining at the expense of the other.

In opposition to this narrow and malignant opinion, I will venture to assert, that the encrease of riches and commerce in any one nation, instead of hurting, commonly promotes the riches and commerce of all its neighbours; and that a state can scarcely carry its trade and industry very far, where all the surrounding states are buried in ignorance, sloth, and barbarism.

He perhaps exaggerated the international harmony of interest, but this was a healthy antidote to the suspicion and the economic warfare of the eighteenth century.

Hume was egalitarian, recognizing the diminishing marginal utility of added units of wealth. In his essay "Of Commerce" he wrote:

A too great disproportion [of income] among the citizens weakens any state. Every person, if possible, ought to enjoy the fruits of his labour, in a full possession of all the necessaries, and many of the conveniencies of life. No one can doubt, but such an equality is most suitable to human nature, and diminishes much less from the *happiness* of the rich than it adds to that of the poor.

In "Of the Refinement in the Arts" Hume repudiated the idea of defending luxury for making work, as Malthus later proposed, although he was not opposed to luxury spending based on individual preferences. "The same care and toil that raise a dish of peas at Christmas, would give bread to a whole family during six months."

He also anticipated Malthus in "Of the Populousness of Ancient Nations": "Almost every man who thinks he can maintain a family will have one; and the human species, at this rate of propagation, would more than double every generation."

In a letter to Lord Kames in 1758, Hume displayed an optimism about underdeveloped countries that in the main has not been justified during the more than two hundred years since then. He pointed to the advantages that rich nations enjoy: extensive commerce, great capital, developed industry, skilled labor, etc. Will these advantages persist and increase? No, they must check themselves, he said. Provisions and labor become dearer. The poorer countries can then compete successfully in the coarser manufactures, and later in those that are more elaborate. Then laissez faire and the international harmony of interest will reign supreme in the best of all possible worlds.

Hume, in a letter to Turgot in 1766, opposed the physiocratic idea that all taxes must fall on the landowner. If laborers got more than the minimum of subsistence, they might pay the taxes instead of passing them along to someone else. Labor, he pointed out, is dearer in Switzerland, where there are no taxes, than in France, where there are many. There are almost no taxes in the English colonies, yet labor is three times dearer than in any country of Europe. Wages of labor depend, he said, on the supply of and demand for labor and not on taxes. Where a tax is laid on consumption, the immediate consequence is that people consume less or work more. The tax is not simply passed on to the landowner.

Hume displayed insight into rent theory in a letter to his good friend Adam Smith. On April 1, 1776, after having read Smith's *Wealth of Nations*, he wrote:

I am much pleas'd with your Performance. . . . If you were here at my Fireside, I should dispute some of your Principles. I cannot think, that the Rent of Farms makes any part of the Price of the Produce, but that the Price is determined altogether by the Quantity and the Demand. . . . But these and a hundred other Points are fit only to be discussed in Conversation; which, till you tell me the contrary, I shall still flatter myself with soon. I hope it will be soon: For I am in a very bad state of Health and cannot afford a long Delay.

Less than five months later Hume was dead, but Smith had visited him during the last days of his illness.

CHAPTER 5

The Classical School:

ADAM SMITH

ADAM SMITH (1723–90), the kindly, brilliant founder of the classical school, was born in the seaport and manufacturing town of Kirkaldy, Scotland. His father, comptroller of the customs in the town, died before his son was born. Margaret Douglas Smith provided a home for her son until her death in 1784 in her ninetieth year.

Young Smith attended Glasgow College at fourteen years of age, and later he studied moral and political science and languages at Balliol College, Oxford. He then returned to his mother's home to continue independent studies for two years. After that he moved to Edinburgh, where he gave lectures on rhetoric and literature. He was elected professor of logic at Glasgow College in 1751, and in the following year he was given the chair of moral philosophy, which he held for nearly twelve years. In 1759 he published his *Theory of Moral Sentiments*, after which his lectures concentrated less on ethical doctrines and more on jurisprudence and political economy.

Smith resigned his professorship to become the tutor of the stepson of Charles Townshend, chancellor of the exchequer, who later came to prominence in America on the issue of the colonial tea tax. Smith spent more than two years with his charge in France, where he established close personal friendships with the physiocrats, including Quesnay and Turgot. After returning home he retired on the three-hundred-pounds-per-year pension that his tutorship paid him for the rest of his life.

In 1776 Smith published his monumental work, which he had begun in France: *An Inquiry into the Nature and Causes of the Wealth of Nations*. Its fame was immediate and Smith's reputation was established forever. During his lifetime the book went through five editions.

The two years after the publication of his book were spent in London, where Smith mingled with the leading intellectuals of his day. Then, on being appointed commissioner of customs in Scotland, he went to live in Edinburgh with his mother. Much of his income is believed to have been spent secretly on charities. He was always happy to receive his friends at dinner, even without the formality of an invitation, and his Sunday suppers were long celebrated in Edinburgh. Among the honors bestowed on him was election as lord rector of Glasgow College. Shortly before he died in 1790, most of his manuscripts were destroyed according to his wish and without explanation.

Laissez Faire and the Harmony of Interests

SMITH was the great advocate of laissez faire, nonintervention by government in business. Governments were wasteful, corrupt, inefficient, and the grantors of special privileges to the detriment of society as a whole. Individuals, if left to pursue their own interests, would serve society even though this was not their intention. He applied the free-enterprise doctrine to both domestic and international affairs. *Wealth of Nations* contained a devastating attack on mercantilism, with 230 of 900 pages devoted to a critical analysis of that system.

Smith's defense of laissez faire, the harmony of interests, and free foreign trade can best be summarized in his own colorful language. "It is not from the benevolence of the butcher, the brewer, or the baker, that we expect our dinner, but from their regard to their own interest." [Bk. I, Ch. 2]

Every individual necessarily labours to render the annual revenue of the society as great as he can. He generally, indeed, neither intends to promote the public interest, nor knows how much he is promoting it. By preferring the support of domestic to that of foreign industry, he intends only his own security; and by directing that industry in such a manner as its produce may be of the greatest value, he intends only his own gain, and he is in this, as in many other cases, led by an invisible hand to promote an end which was no part of his intention. Nor is it always the worse for the society that it was no part of it. By pursuing his own interest he frequently promotes that of the society more effectually than when he really intends to promote it. I have never known much good done by those who affected to trade for the public good. It is an affectation, indeed, not very common among merchants, and very few words need be employed in dissuading them from it.

What is the species of domestic industry which his capital can employ, and of which the produce is likely to be of the greatest value, every individual, it is evident, can, in his local situation, judge much better than any statesman or lawgiver can do for him. The statesman, who should attempt to direct private people in what manner they ought to employ their capitals, would not only load himself with a most unnecessary attention, but assume an authority which could safely be trusted, not only to no single person, but to no council or senate whatever, and which would nowhere be so dangerous as in the hands of a man who had folly and presumption enough to fancy himself fit to exercise it.

To give the monopoly of the home-market to the produce of domestic industry, in any particular art or manufacture, is in some measure to direct private people in what manner they ought to employ their capitals, and must, in almost all cases, be either a useless or a hurtful regulation. If the produce of domestic can be brought there as cheap as that of foreign industry, the regulation is evidently useless. If it cannot, it must generally be hurtful. It is the maxim of every prudent master of a family, never to attempt to make at home what it will cost him more to make than to buy. The taylor does not attempt to make his own shoes, but buys them of the shoemaker. The shoemaker does not attempt to make his own clothes, but employs a taylor. The farmer attempts to make neither the one nor the other, but employs those different artificers. All of them find it for their interest to employ their whole industry in a way in which they have some advantage over their neighbours, and to purchase with a part of its produce, or what is the same thing, with the price of a part of it, whatever else they have occasion for.

What is prudence in the conduct of every private family, can scarce be folly in that of a great kingdom. If a foreign country can supply us with a commodity cheaper than we ourselves can make it, better buy it of them with some part of the produce of our own industry, employed in a way in which we have some advantage. [Bk. IV, Ch. 2]

Elsewhere he also spoke about foreign trade overcoming the narrowness of the home market and thereby promoting a better division of labor. Exports also remove surplus products for which there is no demand at home and bring back something else for which there is a demand.

Smith's distrust even of England's government was unequivocal. Yet we should remember that the regime he was criticizing probably was one of the more honest and efficient ones that could then be found anywhere in the world.

But though the profusion of government must, undoubtedly, have retarded the natural progress of England towards wealth and improvement, it has not been able to stop it. The annual produce of its land and labour is, undoubtedly, much greater at present than it was either at the restoration or at the revolution. The capital, therefore, annually employed in cultivating this land, and in maintaining this labour, must likewise be much greater. In the midst of all the exactions of government, this capital has been silently and gradually accumulated by the private frugality and good conduct of individuals, by their universal, continual, and uninterrupted effort to better their own condition. It is this effort, protected by law and allowed by liberty to exert itself in the manner that is most advantageous, which has maintained the progress of England towards opulence and improvement in almost all former times, and which, it is to be hoped, will do so in all future times. England, however, as it has never been blessed with a very parsimonious government, so parsimony has at no time been the characteristic virtue of its inhabitants. It is the highest impertinence and presumption, therefore, in kings and ministers, to pretend to watch over the œconomy of private people, and to restrain their expence, either by sumptuary laws, or by prohibiting the importation of foreign luxuries. They are themselves always, and without any exception, the greatest spendthrifts in the society. Let them look well after their own expence, and they may safely trust private people with theirs. If their own extravagance does not ruin the state, that of their subjects never will. [Bk. II, Ch. 3]

Contrary to the mercantilist belief that each nation enriches itself at the expense of its neighbors, Smith believed in the international harmony of interest.

The wealth of a neighbouring nation, however, though dangerous in war and politics, is certainly advantageous in trade. In a state of hostility it may enable our enemies to maintain fleets and armies superior to our own; but in a state of peace and commerce it must likewise enable them to exchange with us to a greater value, and to afford a better market, either for the immediate produce of our own industry, or for whatever is purchased with that produce. As a rich man is likely to be a better customer to the industrious people in his neighbourhood, than a poor, so is likewise a rich nation. [Bk. IV, Ch. 3]

Smith was suspicious of businessmen, who were ready and willing to sacrifice everybody else's interests to promote their own. How, then, could they be trusted to foster the general welfare? Competition was the answer. They could not unscrupulously enrich themselves at the expense of the rest of society, even though they usually tried; extraordinary profits would attract others who would compete and wipe out such excessive gains. "People of the same trade seldom meet together, even for merriment and diversion, but the conversation ends in a conspiracy against the public, or in some contrivance to raise prices." [Bk. I, Ch. 10]

The prejudices of some political writers against shopkeepers and tradesmen, are altogether without foundation. So far is it from being necessary, either to tax them, or to restrict their numbers, that they can never be multiplied so as to hurt the publick, though they may so as to hurt one another. The quantity of grocery goods, for example, which can be sold in a particular town, is limited by the demand of that town and its neighbourhood. The capital, therefore, which can be employed in the grocery trade cannot exceed what is sufficient to purchase that quantity. If this capital is divided between two different grocers, their competition will tend to make both of them sell cheaper, than if it were in the hands of one only; and if it were divided among twenty, their competition would be just so much the greater, and the chance of their combining together, in order to raise the price, just so much the less. Their competition might perhaps ruin some of themselves; but to take care of this is the business of the parties concerned, and it may safely be trusted to their discretion. It can never hurt either the consumer, or the producer; on the contrary, it must tend to make the retailers both sell cheaper and buy dearer, than if the whole trade was monopolized by one or two persons. [Bk. II, Ch. 5]

Smith always attacked government intervention on behalf of the special, narrow interests of businessmen. In condemning bounties on exports he defended consumers in opposition to businessmen in language that might be applied to United States farm and export policies:

Whatever extension of the foreign market can be occasioned by the bounty, must, in every particular year, be altogether at the expence of the home market; as every bushel of corn which is exported by means of the bounty, and which would not have been exported without the bounty, would have remained in the home market to increase the consumption, and to lower the price of that commodity. The corn bounty, it is to be observed, as well as every other bounty upon exportation, imposes two different taxes upon the people; first, the tax which they are obliged to contribute, in order to pay the bounty; and secondly, the tax which arises from the advanced price of the commodity in the home market, and which, as the whole body of the people are purchasers of corn, must, in this particular commodity, be paid by the whole body of the people. In this particular commodity, therefore, this second tax is by much the heaviest of the two. [Bk. IV, Ch. 5]

If Smith relied on laissez faire to promote competition and the general welfare, what should be the role of the state? He saw three major functions of government: First, to protect society from foreign attack. Second, to establish the administration of justice within the country. Third, to erect and maintain those public works and institutions that private entrepreneurs cannot undertake profitably. But scattered throughout his book, Smith favored a variety of state interventions that can be fitted into the above three categories, or that enlarge the scope of acceptable government action. He thought the law should enforce the performance of contracts. Control over the issue of paper money by bankers is necessary even though it might be considered as a violation of natural liberty. Legal control over interest rates is acceptable; but the rate should be somewhat but not much above the lowest market rate to promote sound projects rather than frivolous, wasteful, and speculative ones, which high interest rates might permit. Laws insuring the security of the agricultural tenant are good because they promote improvements and investments in the land. He approved of patents and copyrights of limited duration. Smith even favored tariffs under two conditions: First, if some domestic industry is necessary for the defense of the country. Second, if a domestic industry is taxed, a tariff should be imposed on imports to equalize the burden. Otherwise free trade is in order; but if it is to be introduced after a long period of protectionism, it should be done gradually in order not suddenly to throw many people out of work and entrepreneurs into bankruptcy. Among the public works that a government should support are those which promote commerce and education, including bridges, canals, roads, harbors, post offices, coinage, schools, and churches.

To finance these government activities he recommended taxation. His four famous maxims for good taxes were: (1) Taxes should be equal, that is, in proportion to revenue enjoyed under the protection of the state. This was a drastic departure from the regressive taxes prevalent at the time. (2) Taxes should be certain and not arbitrary as to the time of payment, the manner of payment, and the amount to be paid. (3) Taxes should be levied at the time and in the manner most convenient to the contributor. (4) Taxes should be collected economically, at minimum cost.

The Economic Laws of a Free-Enterprise Society

Value. According to Smith, there are two kinds of value.

The word VALUE, it is to be observed, has two different meanings, and sometimes expresses the utility of some particular object, and sometimes the power of purchasing other goods which the possession of that object conveys. The one may be called "value in use;" the other, "value in exchange." The things which have the greatest value in use have frequently little or no value in exchange; and on the contrary, those which have the greatest value in exchange have frequently little or no value in use. Nothing is more useful than water: but it will purchase scarce any thing; scarce any thing can be had in exchange for it. A diamond, on the contrary, has scarce any value in use; but a very great quantity of other goods may frequently be had in exchange for it. [Bk. I, Ch. 4]

There would be no point, then, in comparing the magnitudes of different use values. But exchange value, the power which the possession of a commodity gives to purchase other goods, has been one of the central problems of economics since the market economy developed.

What determines exchange value, or just "value," of a commodity? What it really costs. Not simply the money, but "the toil and trouble of acquiring it." And how is this to be measured? Labor is the real measure of the value of all commodities. But labor is not typically used to estimate value. There are different qualities of labor, and allowance has to be made for the skill, the difficulty, and the ingenuity with which the labor is applied. The "higgling and bargaining of the market" adjusts these differences.

The labor theory of value immediately presents a contradiction. Imagine two commodities made from labor of equal difficulty and skill. Suppose we add up all the time required to make each commodity, including the labor necessary to produce the raw materials and the capital goods used up in its production. Let us assume that each commodity takes two hours to produce. But commodity A requires virtually no capital to produce—say, growing potatoes with a hoe where good land is abundant. Commodity B —cotton yarn—is produced only with intricate and expensive machinery. If a pound of cotton yarn and ten pounds of potatoes, each containing two hours of labor, could be exchanged for each other in the market, which would people produce? Potatoes, of course, because they could avoid investing large amounts of capital, and they would get the same return for their labor. This dilemma, of which Smith was aware, will come up later when Ricardo's and Marx's labor theories of value are discussed.

Smith realized that the growth of capital would vitiate a simple labor theory of value. He therefore believed that only "in that early and rude state of society which precedes both the accumulation of stock and the appropriation of land" do commodities exchange in proportion to the quantities of labor required to produce them. If among a nation of hunters, he said, it usually costs twice the labor to kill a beaver as a deer, one beaver will exchange for two deer.

In a society where capital investments become important, said Smith, goods will normally be exchanged for other goods, for money, or for labor at a figure high enough to cover both wages and profits of the entrepreneur. Moreover, profits will depend on the whole value of the capital advanced by the employer. After the land of a country becomes private property, rent also must be paid for. Prices of commodities therefore cover wages, profit, and rent. The real value of commodities can no longer be measured by the labor contained in them. They can, however, be measured by "the quantity of labour which they can, each of them, purchase or command." The quantity of labor which a commodity can buy exceeds the quantity of labor embodied in its production by the total profits and rents.

If, following Smith, we set up a relationship of equality between a commodity and the labor it will buy, we can reverse the equation and say that the value of labor is measured by the commodities it will buy. In a sense, Smith's definition of value is used in international comparisons of the well-being of people. If a worker in the United States can buy a pair of shoes with five hours of labor, while in the Soviet Union it takes twenty hours of labor, this becomes a meaningful comparison.

Demand, according to Smith, does not influence the value of commodities; only the cost of production, made up of wages, profit, and rent, determines value in the long run. This is a reasonable proposition if we base it on Smith's implicit assumption that production will expand or shrink at constant cost per unit of output. If we assume, however, either increasing or decreasing costs, Smith's principle becomes untenable. If the demand for products rises, and if as the industry expands it will produce the goods at higher costs, then the increased demand will cause a long-run rise in price. If rising output results in falling costs per unit, then an increased demand will be followed by a falling long-run price.

Market price. There are ordinary or average rates of wages, profit, and rent in every society or neighborhood. These Smith called the natural rates of wages, profit, and rent. When a commodity is sold for its natural price, there will be exactly enough revenue to pay the natural rates of wages, profit, and rent. The natural price is a long-run price, which is the lowest price at which the entrepreneur would *continue* to sell his goods. In a desperate situation he would sell goods cheaper, but this would not continue. He could always go out of business or enter another line of production.

The actual price at which any commodity is sold is called its market price. It may be above, below, or exactly the same as its natural price. Market price depends on the aberrations of short-run supply and demand, and it will tend to fluctuate around the natural price. If it is above, more goods will come to market, depressing the price. If market price is below natural price, some productive factors will be withdrawn, the quantity supplied will fall, and market price will rise toward the natural price. That is, short-run supply and demand are not fundamental determinants of price, but they cause market-price fluctuations around the natural price or value of commodities.

Wages. Smith saw a conflict of interest between workmen and their masters as each side tried to combine to influence wages.

It is not, however, difficult to foresee which of the two parties must, upon all ordinary occasions, have the advantage in the dispute, and force the other into a compliance with their terms. The masters, being fewer in number, can combine much more easily; and the law, besides, authorises, or at least does not prohibit their combinations, while it prohibits those of the workmen. We have no acts of parliament against combining to lower the price of work; but many against combining to raise it. In all such disputes the masters can hold out much longer. A landlord, a farmer, a master manufacturer, or merchant, though they did not employ a single workman, could generally live a year or two upon the stocks which they have already acquired. Many workmen could not subsist a week, few could subsist a month, and scarce any a year without employment. In the long-run the workman may be as necessary to his master as his master is to him, but the necessity is not so immediate. [Bk. I, Ch. 8]

The minimum rate of wages must be that which will enable a workman and his family to survive and perpetuate the labor supply. But when the demand for labor is high, wages will rise above this minimum. The rate of increase of national wealth determines the demand for labor and the wage. Therefore we have the emphasis on capital accumulation and economic growth. This produces the best conditions for the majority of people. If the wealth of a country were great but stationary, population would multiply beyond the employment opportunities, and wages would be at the minimum of subsistence. But where rapid expansion occurs, wages rise. Smith applauded this development, thereby opposing the low-wage doctrine of mercantilism.

Is this improvement in the circumstances of the lower ranks of the people to be regarded as an advantage or as an inconveniency to the society? The answer seems at first sight abundantly plain. Servants, labourers and workmen of different kinds, make up the far greater part of every great political society. But what improves the circumstances of the greater part can never be regarded as an inconveniency to the whole. No society can surely be flourishing and happy, of which the far greater part of the members are poor and miserable. It is but equity, besides, that they who feed, cloath and lodge the whole body of the people, should have such a share of the produce of their own labour as to be themselves tolerably well fed, cloathed and lodged. [Bk. I, Ch. 8]

When more workers are employed, wages rise, marriages are encouraged, and more children survive. The increased demand for labor thereby generates an increased supply. But when there is an oversupply of labor, wages will fall and the marriage rate and the survival rate of children will decline. High wages, however, increase the health and strength of the worker, animating him to do his best work because of the hope for an improved life.

Profit. Every investment, said Smith, is exposed to the risk of loss. The lowest rate of profit must be high enough to compensate for such losses and to leave a surplus for the entrepreneur. The gross profit includes compensation for loss and the surplus. Net or clear profit is the surplus only, the net revenue of the businessman.

Where countries are advancing rapidly in wealth, competition among businessmen lowers profit. The forces that raise wages thereby lower profit. The low rate of profit may compensate for high wage rates in the sale of commodities; therefore thriving countries may sell goods as cheaply as their less fortunate neighbors among whom wage rates may be lower.

Classical economists generally did not handle interest as a separate distributive share; it simply was a deduction from profit. The lowest rate of interest must be a little higher than the losses that sometimes occur through lending. The interest that the borrower can afford to pay is in proportion to the net or clear profit only, and the rate must generally be lower than the rate of profit in order to induce borrowing. As profits rise, more money will be sought by borrowers, and interest rates will rise; and conversely.

Rent. "As soon as the land of any country has all become private property, the landlords, like all other men, love to reap where they never sowed." [Bk. I, Ch. 6] Smith was not criticizing or condemning landlords; he merely was reporting the truth as he saw it.

Rent is the price paid for the use of land. It is the highest the tenant can afford to pay, after deducting wages, the wear and tear of capital, average profits, and other expenses of production. The rent of land "is naturally a monopoly price." In this Smith was of course in error. With the many owners of land, and even more actual or potential users, land is not ordinarily rented under monopoly conditions.

Rent is a surplus that varies with the fertility and the location of the land. High prices yield high rents, and low prices low rents. Yet earlier Smith had said that the rent of land enters into the price of the product. It was this statement that David Hume had criticized (see p. 47 above). Yet the two statements are not necessarily inconsistent. When Smith said that high rents were the effect rather than the cause of high prices, he was looking at changes in rents and prices, at causes and effects. But in the statement that Hume criticized, Smith was discussing the components of the price of commodities in general. When commodities are sold, the revenue received must cover wages, profit, and rent. Where else could rent come from? It is correct to say that rent is a component of prices in general, that prices break down into distributive shares that include rent. It is also correct to say that rental payments do not influence the level of prices; instead, the level of prices influences rents. It is only the marginal part of the supply of farm produce that contains no rent in its price. This Smith failed to see. These matters were developed more fully about forty years later by Ricardo.

If rent is a surplus above the return necessary for the worker and the entrepreneur, Smith said, the more productive the land, the greater the surplus and therefore the greater the rent. If we discovered a plant that was much more productive than wheat, production of foodstuffs would rise and rents on land producing it would rise. In this, of course, Smith was in error if population and demand are assumed to be constant. He failed to measure the surplus from the marginal land in use. He was also wrong in believing that the price of minerals is regulated by the richest mines.

Smith anticipated Henry George by advocating a tax on rent. It would not raise the rent of houses, nor would it discourage any sort of industry. It would fall altogether on the landowners, who, he said, always act as monopolists and charge the highest possible rents.

An adequate theory of rent came to be based on the law of diminishing returns, but Smith had only a rudimentary understanding of this law. He did apply it to fishing, but not to agriculture.

The theories that analyze how wages, profit, and rent are determined constitute a theory of income distribution. Smith's was a systematic and comprehensive theory of distribution, based in part on the theory of the physiocrats, but far superior to theirs.

The role of money and debt. Smith established the classical tradition of de-emphasizing the importance of money. Money was vital, to be sure, as a means of payment; without it business would be shackled with a barter system. But money itself does not add to the revenue of society. It facilitates the circulation of goods, but it is the latter's production that makes up the revenue. The gold and silver coins that circulate are a valuable part of the capital of the country but are dead stock, producing nothing.

Here Smith developed the idea that was the opposite of mercantilist doctrine. Paper money in place of gold and silver would do equally well and cost a lot less effort to produce. Gold and silver are like a highway that enables goods to be brought to market without being itself productive. Banking, he said, by providing paper money, would save the labor of producing gold, just as a highway through the air would save land that could be used for other things. As long as paper money would be redeemable in gold, a small reserve of metal would do.

The mercantilists argued that consumable commodities are soon destroyed, but gold and silver are of a more durable nature. Would we therefore reckon, asked Smith, that the exchange of English hardware for French wines is disadvantageous? We could augment our supply of pots and pans to an incredible degree, but we need only a certain limited supply of utensils. So it is with coin. We require only a certain amount to circulate goods, and an excess is unnecessary and will be exported rather than left idle at home. Smith's refutation of the mercantilistic overemphasis on gold ignored the special qualities of gold. By being a universally acceptable medium of exchange, it can, unlike pots and pans, be spent in any direction.

Smith deplored the growth of public debt and the taxes it required. The view among some Keynesians that internally held debt does not matter because we owe it to ourselves was voiced in Smith's time, and answered by him:

In the payment of the interest of the public debt, it has been said, it is the right hand which pays the left. The money does not go out of the country. It is only a part of the revenue of one set of the inhabitants which is transferred to another; and the nation is not a farthing the poorer. This apology is founded altogether in the sophistry of the mercantile system. [Bk. V, Ch. 3]

Smith was afraid that heavy taxes would induce merchants and manufacturers to invest their capital abroad to the detriment of the home country. Writing before the development of recurring business cycles, he was not concerned with government spending to counteract a depression. Assuming full employment, government debt and interest charges represented resources that might have been used productively by private individuals if government had not diverted them to its own purposes. With militaristic, corrupt, and wasteful governments far removed from the people and partial to the special interests, such a diversion of resources would not serve society.

Smith gloomily forecast that growing debts would in the long run probably ruin all the great nations of Europe. The British debt that troubled him so was £129 million in 1775.

Economic Development

SMITH looked at the economy as a whole, and he emphasized growth and development. Labor is the source of all value, and machinery and the division of labor increase the production of wealth. He began his volume with a chapter on the division of labor, a phrase not familiar in his time. The division of labor increases productivity, and the emphasis lies there rather than on trade and accumulating treasure. Labor specialization is limited by the extent of the market. Widening markets therefore increase productivity. Smith was concerned, however, with the personally stultifying effects of the division of labor. This could be counteracted, he said, by government promotion of education for "the labouring poor."

Smith discovered the great truth that the division of labor makes possible the introduction of machinery to increase man's productivity. When a man made a complete pair of shoes himself, there could be no single machine to do his work, for it was too complicated. But when shoemaking was broken down to a succession of simple operations, tools and machines could be invented that would replace hand labor. But writing as he did before the factory system became dominant, Smith failed to emphasize sufficiently the changes in technology that would improve the productivity of labor so tremendously. His emphasis was more on the improved dexterity that resulted from a division of labor, rather than on mechanization both as a result of the division of labor and as its cause.

Those who live by wages would benefit most, not from *great* national wealth, but rather from *increasing* wealth.

It deserves to be remarked, perhaps, that it is in the progressive state, while the society is advancing to the further acquisition, rather than when it has acquired its full complement of riches, that the condition of the labouring poor, of the great body of the people, seems to be the happiest and the most comfortable. It is hard in the stationary, and miserable in the declining state. The progressive state is in reality the cheerful and the hearty state to all the different orders of the society. The stationary is dull; the declining melancholy. [Bk. I, Ch. 8]

As capital accumulates more rapidly than population increases, competition among the capitalists will tend to lower profits. Economists after Smith returned to this idea of a falling rate of profit, but with different analyses to explain the theory.

As society progresses, the real rents of land rise for two reasons. First, with every improvement in cultivation, the surplus rises, and the surplus goes to the landlords. Second, as improvements in industry occur, the real price of manufactured goods falls. The landlords will then be able to exchange their share of the farm products for an increasing quantity of manufactured goods.

Therefore, concluded Smith, the interests of landlords and workers coincide with the general interest of society. These two groups progress together as society progresses. But the interests of businessmen who live by profit are opposed to those of society as a whole. They thrive when competition is limited and profits are high; the rest of society gains from increased competition and reduced profits.

Smith distinguished between productive labor, which adds value to a product, and unproductive labor, which does not. Productive employment stores up labor in a salable commodity. Unproductive labor has to do with the output of services. The unproductive laborers include kings, soldiers, churchmen, lawyers, doctors, men of letters, players, buffoons, musicians, opera singers, dancers, etc. Among the productive workers are "artificers, manufacturers and merchants."

To us it seems odd that Smith would say that the person who gives a public piano recital is unproductive, but the man who prints the tickets is productive. To Smith it would have seemed strange that we, in our national income accounting, say that payments to servants, military personnel, advertisers, and public officials are additions to national income. He would have considered such expenditures as deductions. But to understand Smith, we should look at the problem through his approach to capital accumulation and economic growth. In fact, he called Chapter 3 of Book II "Of the Accumulation of Capital, or of Productive and Unproductive Labour." Material goods can be accumulated and are therefore a potential means of increasing wealth. Even consumer goods produced today can be used to support workers in the future, thereby enabling them to work and produce more goods. But services are of the moment only; they vanish in the simultaneous act of production and consumption, and they cannot be accumulated. From this point of view they are unproductive, although in many cases useful.

In refuting the physiocratic concept of productive and sterile labor, Smith seemed to have caught a toe in the physiocratic trap. In opposing their doctrine he argued that merchants, artificers, and manufacturers are not sterile or barren, even if they only reproduce annually the value of their own consumption. "We should not call a marriage barren or unproductive, though it produced only a son and a daughter, to replace the father and mother." But a marriage that results in three children is more productive than one that produces two. "So the labour of farmers and country labourers is certainly more productive than that of merchants, artificers and manufacturers." The reason is that in agriculture, livestock and nature labor beside man to add to value. Ricardo objected, pointing out that even in manufacturing the assistance of nature is considerable. The powers of wind and water, the pressure of the atmosphere and the elasticity of steam, the heating of metals, dyeing and fermentation, all rely on the gratuitous assistance of nature.

Smith, writing at a time when investment and production were burgeoning, pinned his hopes on widening markets, increasing accumulation of capital, and continuous progress. Business cycles, overproduction, unemployed men, and redundant capital still lay in the future. The harmony of interests prevailed, with a free and competitive market forcing each individual to serve society while he served himself. No wonder Smith is called an optimist.

CHAPTER 6

The Classical School:

DAVID RICARDO

WHILE Smith was the founder of the classical school, David Ricardo (1772–1823) carried it to the highest peak of development. Around Ricardo rallied an ardent band of disciples who enthusiastically disseminated his doctrines. After him his followers changed and amended his theories, moving toward neoclassical positions.

David, the third of seventeen children, was born of Dutch Jews who had migrated to England. He was trained for his father's business of stockbroker, which he entered at fourteen years of age. At twenty-one he married a Quaker girl and left the Jewish faith to become a Unitarian. His father disowned him, but in later life there was a reconciliation. Young Ricardo entered the stock market on his own. Bankers who knew and trusted him advanced the funds. In a few years he was richer than his father, and at forty-three he began retiring from business with a considerable accumulation of wealth. At his death from an ear infection at fifty-one he left about £725,000, two-thirds of it in landed estates and mortgages.

Perhaps Ricardo's principles for making money on the stock exchange may be at least as interesting to many as his abstract economic theorizing. He was quoted as saying that he had made all his money by observing that people generally exaggerated the importance of events. If there was reason for a small advance in stocks, he bought because of the certainty that an unreasonable advance would be profitable to him. When stocks were falling, he sold in the conviction that alarm and panic would produce a decline not warranted by circumstances.

As a man of firm convictions and high principles, Ricardo frequently advocated policies that conflicted with his own personal interests. He argued against the excessive gains of the Bank of England when he was a stockholder of that institution. He defended the cause of investors in British government bonds when he had ceased to be one himself. Even after he had become a large landowner, he put forward theories that, according to his critics, would ruin the landlords. Parliamentary reform, which he supported with enthusiasm, would have deprived him of the seat he had bought representing an Irish constituency he had never lived in or even visited. He advocated a levy on capital to liquidate the national debt although he was one of the richest men in England.

Ricardo, without any formal schooling beyond the age of fourteen, turned to the systematic study of political economy rather late in life. In his spare time in his youth, he worked rather systematically at physical science and mathematics. Then, at twenty-seven years of age, he accidentally came across Smith's *Wealth of Nations*. This happy accident fixed his attention on economics. His first published work was a letter to a newspaper on currency problems in 1809 when he was thirty-seven years old. Within another decade he had completed his major contributions. To him writing was difficult and painful in spite of his keen, analytical mind. "Oh that I were capable of writing a book!" he wrote to his friend James Mill. And Mill urged him on: "For as you are already the best *thinker* on political economy, I am resolved you shall also be the best writer." Mill read and criticized Ricardo's writing, always driving him to produce when the latter felt that writing was impossible for him.

Ricardo was an outstanding example of a deductive thinker. He made sweeping generalizations, frequently based on premises which he failed to state, or which he changed without notice. These generalizations he called economic laws, and he considered the operation of laws as valid in economics as in physics. For example, there were laws that regulated the distribution of precious metals throughout the world, laws that governed the international exchange of goods, laws that regulated the distribution of income, and so on. Although Ricardo, through his personal experience, was very well acquainted with the facts of business and economic life, he did not use the inductive method; he did not reason from the part to the whole, from particulars to the general, from facts to theories. Instead, he enunciated sweeping laws and then sometimes drew upon facts to illustrate their operation. Yet the theoretical questions that interested Ricardo had a significant bearing on the practical problems of his time, and of later times.

Ricardo changed the emphasis of economic analysis from production to distribution. Adam Smith inquired into the nature and causes of the wealth of nations; in the very first page of his book, Smith stated that the well-being of a nation depends on the total production and the number of people who must share it. In contrast, the opening paragraph of Ricardo's *On the Principles of Political Economy and Taxation* raised as the key problem the division of the produce of the earth among the three classes: land-owners, capitalists, and laborers. Ricardo emphasized the division of income rather than the growth of income because of his pessimism; to him Smith's optimism about a constantly improving world was erroneous. Population pressure, thought Ricardo, would force men to till poorer soil and to work the better soil more intensively. Improved technology would not completely counteract this tendency. Therefore average output per worker or per pound sterling invested in agriculture would tend to fall, and this would impoverish mankind in the long run. The question of how and why a certain pattern of distribution of limited output developed among ever growing numbers of people seemed the central problem to Ricardo.

The Bullion Controversy

IN 1797, in the midst of more than two decades of warfare between England and France, a panic and a run on gold dangerously depleted the Bank of England reserves. The government suspended cash payments, and England found herself on an irredeemable paper standard. The price of gold gradually rose from its mint parity of £3.17s.10½d. per ounce to a market price of £5.10s. in 1813. A general price inflation was the result. Instead of gold being brought to the mint, it was sold privately in the domestic or foreign markets. The worrisome questions were, Why was the market price of gold rising? and, How could it be stopped?

Ricardo had immense transactions with the Bank of England, and he began to reflect and write on these problems. He charged that the Bank was overissuing currency because it was no longer checked by the requirement to pay in gold on demand. Printing and lending bank notes was a profitable operation, but hardly conducive to stable prices for gold or commodities. It was analogous to clipping coins.

The remedy Ricardo called for was to return to the gold standard. Then, if the price of gold in the market rose, currency would be exchanged for gold at the Bank at the mint price. Every overissue of bank notes would be canceled automatically by the flow of paper back to the Bank. The restoration of the gold standard would curb inflation.

The directors of the Bank of England and their friends argued that the market price of gold rose because of its scarcity; gold, not paper, changed its value. If the gold standard were restored, every gold guinea would leave the country.

Ricardo replied that there was evidence that paper, not gold, changed its value. An ounce of gold would buy as many commodities as it had previously. But the paper which gold represented at the mint price would buy far less. And as for gold fleeing the country, it was already doing so except for that held in the coffers of the Bank. The gold standard could be restored safely if the Bank first reduced its note circulation. To eliminate the cost of coinage, and to economize on gold that would otherwise circulate as coins, Ricardo proposed a gold bullion standard. The Bank should buy and sell gold bullion rather than coin on demand, with at least twenty ounces being the minimum transaction.

Ricardo's plan was adopted by Parliament in 1819, when the Bank was ordered to resume gold payments in ingots of sixty ounces. In 1821, a law was passed requiring payment in coin. The gold standard worked for over a century thereafter, except during major wars and financial crises.

Value and Price

RICARDO was concerned with relative values, not with absolute value. That is, he wanted to discover the basis for ratios of exchange between commodities. Utility, he said, is not the measure of exchangeable value, although it is absolutely essential to it. Possessing utility, commodities derive their exchangeable value from two sources: from their scarcity, and from the quantity of labor required to obtain them. The commodities whose value is determined by their scarcity alone are nonreproducible, such as rare works of art, scarce books, and coins. But most commodities are reproducible, and Ricardo assumed that they are produced under conditions of competition without restraint.

Ricardo was unconditionally committed to a labor theory of value. Unlike Smith, who applied the labor theory to primitive societies, Ricardo linked it to capitalistic society as well. The exchange value of a commodity depends on the labor time necessary to produce it. The labor time includes not only the work done in making the commodity itself, but also the work embodied in the raw materials and capital goods used up in the process of production.

This simple form of the labor theory of value would be logical (although not necessarily correct) under two conditions: if all industries had the same ratios of capital to labor, and if the capital investments in all industries had the same durability. As these conditions do not exist, if all commodities sold at their value as measured by labor time, the consequences would be unequal rates of return in different industries. Both Smith and Ricardo were aware of this dilemma, and we can best illustrate the problem by using Ricardo's example given in the third edition of his book, *On the Principles of Political Economy and Taxation*, 1821 (first edition 1817). [Vol. I, pp. 33–34]*

* All references in this chapter are to Piero Sraffa, ed., *The Works and Correspondence of David Ricardo*, 10 vols. (Cambridge, 1951–55).

Suppose a farmer employs a hundred men for a year to grow grain, and a cotton manufacturer employs a hundred men for a year to make a machine to produce yarn. The machine will have the same value as the grain. Now assume that during the second year the farmer again employs a hundred men, and the cotton manufacturer uses a hundred men to work the machine to produce the yarn. Disregarding wear and tear of the machine, the hundred men growing grain during the second year will produce commodities of less value than the hundred men spinning yarn, because the latter use capital and the former do not. If wage rates were £50 per year per worker and profits were 10 per cent, the value of the grain produced each year, and the value of the machine, would be £5,500. The yarn produced during the second year would be worth £6,050, because 10 per cent would have to be earned on the investment in the machine. Otherwise such capital investments would not pay. Here then are two capitalists employing the same quantity of labor on the production of their commodities, and yet the goods they produce differ in value because of the different quantities of fixed capital used by each.

Two additional difficulties bring into question the validity of the labor theory of value. First, how are profits explained if all value is derived from labor time? Second, how are rents explained?

Rent will be discussed in the next section. Here we can point out that according to Ricardian theory, rent payments do not influence the prices of goods. On the contrary, the prices of goods are one of the elements that determine rent. No rent is paid on marginal land, and the rate of profit on marginal land governs the rate of profit in the whole economy. Rent results from the extra productivity on the better than marginal land, and it does not influence prices.

If all goods sell at their value as measured by labor time, the explanation of profit would be a thorny problem only if we were concerned with *absolute* value. Marx was concerned with this problem. Ricardo, however, dealt only with *relative* values, as we said at the beginning of this section. Regardless of whether profits rose or fell, they would not influence the relative values of goods. If a pair of shoes embodying five hours of labor exchanges for a dress also made with five hours, a rise of wages and a fall of profits or vice versa will not affect the one-to-one ratio of exchange. Labor does not have to get the whole product simply because labor time is the measure of value. There is no hint of exploitation in Ricardo's analysis; in fact, he defended the institution of private property. It was Marx who later drew revolutionary implications from Ricardo's labor theory of value.

We remain, then, with the problem of different industries using fixed capital and labor in different ratios. Ricardo simply stated that this cause of variation in the value of commodities was slight in its effect. Much more important in determining the value of a commodity was the labor time required to produce it. Commodities would sell at somewhat more or less than their labor-time value if more or less capital than the average was tied up in their production.

Labor, in Ricardo's view, was the foundation of the value of commodities, but market prices would deviate from value or natural price, due to accidental or temporary fluctuations of supply and demand. If the market price rose above the natural price, profits would rise, and more capital would be used to produce the commodity. If the market price fell, capital would flow out of the industry. The actions of individuals, seeking maximum advantage, would tend to equalize the rates of profit and to keep market prices proportional to values. The short-run price depends on supply and demand, but long-run values depend on the cost of production, and the relative costs of production of two commodities are nearly proportional to the quantity of labor bestowed upon them from first to last.

However abundant the demand it can never permanently raise the price of a commodity above the expence of its production, including in that expence the profits of the producers. It seems natural therefore to seek for the cause of the variation of permanent price in the expences of production. Diminish these and the commodity must finally fall, increase them and it must as certainly rise. What has this to do with demand? [Vol. VII, pp. 250–51]

This is an interesting contrast to demand theory which was later introduced by neoclassical economics.

Ricardo agreed with Smith that riches or wealth represents "The necessaries, conveniences, and amusements of human life." Value differs from riches in that it depends, not on abundance, but on the difficulty or facility of production. If a certain number of men increase their production of stockings from a thousand pair to two thousand, riches increase but the value produced remains the same. If water became scarce and one man monopolized it, his riches would increase, for the increased value of water would enable him to buy a larger quantity of goods. But the rest of society would lose what he gained, and total wealth would not increase.

Because it has been said, that abundance may be prejudicial to the interests of the producers, it has been objected that the new doctrine on this subject is, that the bounty of Providence may become a curse to a country; but this is essentially changing the proposition. No one has said that abundance is injurious to a country, but that it frequently is so to the producers of the abundant commodity. [Vol. IV, p. 221]

Wages and Profits

LABOR, said Ricardo, like all other things which are bought and sold, has its natural and its market price. The natural price of labor is that price which enables workers to subsist and to perpetuate themselves without either increase or diminution of their numbers. The natural price of labor depends on the price of the necessities of life required by the laborer and his family. If the cost of necessities rises, money wages will rise so that the worker can continue to buy just enough to survive and perpetuate the labor force. If the cost of living falls, wages will fall. The market price of labor depends on supply and demand. But as with commodities, the market price tends to fluctuate around the natural price.

Both the natural price of labor and money wages have a tendency to rise, said Ricardo, because of the increased difficulty and cost of producing food for growing numbers of people. A counteracting force is exerted by improvements in agriculture and imports of food, which tend to lower the cost of living. Of the two sets of forces, Ricardo thought the first was predominant. Therefore money wages would have to rise to pay the higher cost of agricultural produce.

Ricardo's idea that in the long run the worker always gets the minimum of subsistence came to be known as "the iron law of wages." When the market price of labor rises above the natural price, a worker can rear a large and healthy family. As population increases, wages fall to their natural price and even below. When the market price of labor is below the natural price, misery reduces the working population and wage rates rise. The long-run tendency is therefore for workers to receive the minimum of subsistence.

There is a tendency, said Ricardo, for the rates of profit in different fields of enterprise within a country to become equalized. Entrepreneurs seek the maximum rate of profit, after allowing for the advantages or disadvantages that one occupation offers compared with another. Price movements influence rates of profit which in turn direct the flow of capital. The monied class in particular can quickly shift funds to the most profitable businesses. The free, competitive market and the actions of individuals tend to produce rates of profit in all types of businesses which are equal or equally advantageous, all things considered.

Ricardo, concentrating on the division of national income rather than on its growth, emphasized that profits and wages vary inversely. One increases at the expense of the other. Why, we may ask, must higher wages come out of profits instead of being passed on in higher prices? The answer lies in the equation of exchange and the international balance of payments. If prices are to rise, more money will be required to sell a given quantity of goods. Where would the money come from? Instead of gold flowing in from abroad, gold would leave the country because prices abroad would be lower than at home. With a shrinking money supply, prices cannot rise. Therefore employers themselves must bear the higher money costs of production, and wage increases come out of profits. Conversely, if wages were to fall, prices would not fall. If they did, gold would flow into the country, and prices would rise again. Therefore a fall in wages will result in a rise in profits.

In the third edition of *On the Principles of Political Economy and Taxation,* Ricardo inserted a new chapter called "On Machinery." This was an interesting addition because it represented a complete change of mind on Ricardo's part, to the consternation of his followers and friends. By raising the possibility of technological unemployment, Ricardo further accentuated the conflict of interests between workers and capitalists.

Ricardo claimed that he had erred when he had previously supported the view that the introduction of machinery would help all three major classes. Their money incomes, he once thought, would remain the same while their real incomes would rise, because with machinery, goods could be produced more cheaply. Even labor would gain because the same labor would be demanded as before mechanization occurred, and therefore money wages would not fall. Even if the number of workers in one industry became excessive, capital would shift to some other industry and increase employment there. The only inconvenience would be the temporary maladjustment which occurs when capital and labor must move from one employment to another.

Having revised his thinking, Ricardo stated that the sudden introduction of machinery would benefit the landlord and the capitalist, as he had believed in the past, but it frequently would be very injurious to labor. If more capital were invested in machinery, less would be available to pay wages. In other words, capital is scarce, and the portion which is diverted to machinery represents a deduction from that which might be used to pay wages. The capitalist could be making the same amount of profit on the same total investment, but the gross output and investment could decline. In the long run, said Ricardo, the introduction of machinery would enable the capitalist to save and invest more. Even though his money profits were to remain the same, the lower cost of the consumer goods he uses would leave a larger portion for investment, ultimately re-employing the redundant population. Technological unemployment was therefore a short-run problem for the workers, but a very real one. "The opinion entertained by the labouring class, that the employment of machinery is frequently detrimental to their interests, is not founded on prejudice and error, but is conformable to the correct principles of political economy." [Vol. I, p. 392]

Rent and the Law of Diminishing Returns

THE theory of rent was developed by four writers and presented in pamphlets, all published early in 1815. Malthus was the first to appear in print with his theory, followed by Edward West, Ricardo, and Robert Torrens, in that order. This is an interesting example of how the questions of the hour called forth a theory developed independently by different people. Ricardo modestly stated that Malthus and West deserved most of the credit.

Rent was an interesting subject in England because tenant farming was widespread. The impending parliamentary debate in 1815 on the corn laws—tariffs on grain imports—was the immediate issue that sparked the development of rent theory. As the Napoleonic wars drew to a close, farmers and landlords feared that grain would pour into Great Britain at ruinous prices. The landowners, who dominated Parliament, clamored for higher protection in the name of the general welfare. The business interests spoke not only against higher tariffs, but also for repealing the existing corn laws. The businessmen could use Ricardo's economics to bolster their position. If workers tended to get the minimum level of subsistence and if bread was cheaper, production costs would be lower, and British goods could compete more effectively in foreign markets. In addition, the manufacturers were aware that the more grain Great Britain imported, the more manufactured goods businessmen could export. They were perfectly willing to sacrifice the interests of the landlords in order to benefit themselves.

It was this background of conflict that brought forth the theory of rent in 1815. While Ricardo did not originate this theory, he developed it most clearly and completely. He also integrated rent theory with the theory of wages and profits, and with economic changes.

"Rent," said Ricardo, "is that portion of the produce of the earth, which is paid to the landlord for the use of the original and indestructible powers of the soil." He modified this definition by including also long-run capital investments which were amalgamated with the land and increased its productivity.

No one pays rent in a newly settled country in which fertile soil is abundant. But

When in the progress of society, land of the second degree of fertility is taken into cultivation, rent immediately commences on that of the first quality, and the amount of that rent will depend on the difference in the quality of these two portions of land.

When land of the third quality is taken into cultivation, rent immediately commences on the second, and it is regulated as before, by the difference in their productive powers. At the same time, the rent of the first quality will rise, for that must always be above the rent of the second, by the difference between the produce which they yield with a given quantity of capital and labour. With every step in the progress of population, which shall oblige a country to have recourse to land of a worse quality, to enable it to raise its supply of food, rent, on all the more fertile land, will rise. [Vol. I, p. 70]

Marginal land will pay all the expenses of production and the average rate of profit on the investment in labor and capital. The value of farm produce depends on the labor required per unit of output on the least productive land in use. The better land produces a surplus which is taken by the landowner as rent. This explains rent as measured at the extensive margin of cultivation.

Rent also arises from the intensive cultivation of land because of the law of diminishing returns. If successive units of labor and capital are added to a piece of land while technology remains constant, each added unit of investment will add less to the output than previous units. If this were not so, the food for all the world could be grown in a flower pot. The last unit of labor and capital must pay for itself, including an average rate of profit. Earlier units yield a surplus return, which is rent.

Ricardo was also aware that rent can originate through differences in location. If lands of equal fertility are situated at varying distances from the market, the farthest land worked must pay the normal returns to labor and capital. The more favorably located land will yield extra returns because of smaller transport costs, and these returns constitute rent.

Rent is both a differential return and a surplus above costs. Rents are high because the prices of farm products are high. But it is not true that farm product prices are high because rents are high. These propositions are based on the limited supply of the best land, on the law of diminishing returns, and on land having no alternative uses. If we consider the shifting of land among different uses, both agricultural and non-agricultural, then rent is a cost that enters into price. Ricardo, looking at agriculture as a whole, did not consider land as having alternative uses. Therefore rent is price-determined and not price-determining.

The average rate of profit at any time is determined by the rate of profit on marginal land. No rent is paid on this land, and the total product is divided between the employing farmers and the laborers. If wages rise, profits will fall, and vice versa. If the rate of profit in industry were higher than in farming marginal land, capital would flow from agriculture to industry, and a better grade of land would become the new marginal land. If agriculture were more profitable than industry, capital would flow toward agriculture, and the next worse grade of land would become the marginal land worked.

As stated in the previous section, Ricardo saw a conflict of interests between workers and capitalists. An even more basic conflict exists, he said, between landlords and the rest of society. As population increases, the increased demand for food will raise its price. Poorer land will be brought into cultivation, and better land will be worked more intensively. Rents will therefore rise. As wages also will rise to give the workers their minimum of subsistence, profits will fall. "All classes, therefore, except the landlords, will be injured by the increase in the price of corn."

Improvements in agriculture and imports of cheap grain would partially counteract the tendency toward rising rents and falling profits. Therefore Ricardo opposed the corn laws. By repealing the tariffs and other restrictions on the import of grain, society's interests would be promoted at the expense of the landlords. Nevertheless, the long-run trend was unmistakably gloomy.

Adam Smith thought the rate of profit would fall because of growing competition among entrepreneurs, and this development he welcomed. Ricardo thought that the rate of profit would fall because of the increasing difficulty of growing food for an increasing population, and this he deplored. Falling profits, he thought, would curb the accumulation and investment of capital, and ultimately the stationary state would prevail. This state would be reached when new investment ceased; population could no longer expand because the limits of food production had been reached, and every available surplus had been appropriated as rent.

Obviously this diagnosis of the fate of capitalism was erroneous. The stationary state has seldom appeared anywhere, nor has it remained stationary for long. Improvements in farming have more than kept pace with the growth of population in advanced countries, so that the percentage of the labor force in agriculture has tended to decline. Rents have not absorbed an increasing percentage of the national income. Agriculture, an ever declining sector almost everywhere, cannot govern the rate of profit in the whole economy. It might only if Ricardo's implicit assumptions were correct: perfect competition, complete mobility of the factors of production within a country, unchanging technology in agriculture, etc. Ricardo was unaware that the proportionate increase in rents and prices for urban land would exceed by far the increases for farm land.

Accused of considering landlords the enemies of society, Ricardo denied the allegation. "High rent and low profits, for they invariably accompany each other, ought never to be the subject of complaint, if they are the effect of the natural course of things." [Vol. IV, p. 21]

Laissez faire was the ideal policy, Ricardo thought, not only in foreign trade but also in domestic affairs. Wages should not be regulated, nor should poor relief be given to the indigent.

Like all other contracts, wages should be left to the fair and free competition of the market, and should never be controlled by the interference of the legislature.

The clear and direct tendency of the poor laws, is in direct opposition to those obvious principles: it is not, as the legislature benevolently intended, to amend the condition of the poor, but to deteriorate the condition of both poor and rich; instead of making the poor rich, they are calculated to make the rich poor. [Vol. I, pp. 105–06]

Ricardo overemphasized the role of diminishing returns. This law is correct only if other factors, including the level of technology, are kept constant. But with improvements in agriculture, historically there have been increasing returns per unit of labor in the most advanced, progressive countries. Nor was he correct in emphasizing that landlords as a whole were never interested in increased productivity in agriculture. Land that could not support the people who worked on it could not be tilled. Improvements permitted poorer land to be worked, thereby increasing the surplus available for rent. Only if improvements in agriculture were not accompanied by an increased demand for farm products would rent fall.

Ricardo's idea of opposing interests, this germ of the concept of class conflict, was not forgiven by adherents of the neoclassical school who later appeared on the scene. The idea of labor as the source of all value led to the socialist concept that the worker deserved the whole product. To this Marx added the doctrine of class struggle.

The Theory of Comparative Cost

SMITH advocated foreign trade without impediments in order to widen markets and remove surpluses; trade was based on differences in absolute costs—everybody buying in the cheapest market. Ricardo made a brilliant and lasting contribution to economic thought by developing the theory of comparative cost. If one country is more efficient than another in producing all commodities, trade between the two nevertheless would be of mutual advantage. The more efficient country should export those commodities in which her comparative cost is lowest, and she should import those whose comparative cost is highest. This is the basis for Ricardo's free-trade policy for manufactured goods. As we saw above, the significance of free trade in agricultural products was to keep down the cost of food, wages, and rent, thereby keeping profits high and promoting investment. But the actual trade in farm produce also would be based on comparative cost.

Using Ricardo's example, Portugal could produce a certain quantity of wine with 80 man-years of labor, and cloth with 90 man-years. England could produce the wine with 120 man-years, and the cloth with 100. Portugal required one-third less labor than England to produce wine, and one-tenth less labor for cloth. She should therefore export wine and import cloth. By producing and exporting wine, Portugal would obtain cloth for 80 man-years of labor which otherwise would cost her 90. England, by producing and exporting cloth, would get wine for 100 man-years of labor which otherwise would cost her 120.

Ricardo explicitly assumed that capital and labor were immobile between countries. Otherwise both wine and cloth would be made in Portugal. He also implicitly assumed constant costs rather than increasing costs as output expanded. Otherwise specialization would not be carried on to its fullest extent.

Suppose, said Ricardo, England improved her manufacture of wine, so that it still paid to ship cloth from her to Portugal, but it no longer was profitable to ship wine in the opposite direction. The Portuguese importer would have to pay more for the pound sterling he bought in England to pay for the cloth. This might cut off imports entirely. But if the premium on British currency were less than the profit from importing cloth, gold or silver would flow to England in payment for cloth. The declining money supply in Portugal would cause falling prices there, and the rising money supply in England would cause rising prices in that country. This would bring about a new equilibrium in foreign trade. Here is Hume's price specie-flow mechanism once again.

Ricardo has been criticized for basing his theory of comparative cost on the labor theory of value, and for implicitly assuming a full-employment economy. If there were unemployment in Portugal, would it not pay her to produce wine and cloth both for her own use and for export to England? Actually Ricardo's labor theory of value is not crucial to his international trade theory. It is possible to compare money costs of domestic and foreign goods, based on foreign exchange rates. If both Portuguese cloth and wine were cheaper in Portugal than the British goods that might be imported, no imports could be sold if cost were the only consideration. Exchange rates would vary, however, to the point where British cloth in Portugal would become cheaper than domestic cloth. The theory of comparative cost really helps explain international trade, although the problems are more complicated than in Ricardo's simplified model. Nor did he attempt to explain what determines the ratios of exchange between commodities traded internationally, although his theory did define the limits within which the ratios could fluctuate.

We shall end this chapter with Ricardo's powerful plea for laissez faire in foreign trade. This was based on his concept of a harmony of interest, which he applied to international affairs, although not to rent, wages, and profit in domestic matters.

Under a system of perfectly free commerce, each country naturally devotes its capital and labour to such employments as are most beneficial to each. This pursuit of individual advantage is admirably connected with the universal good of the whole. By stimulating industry, by rewarding ingenuity, and by using most efficaciously the peculiar powers bestowed by nature, it distributes labour most effectively and most economically: while, by increasing the general mass of productions, it diffuses general benefit, and binds together by one common tie of interest and intercourse, the universal society of nations throughout the civilized world. It is this principle which determines that wine shall be made in France and Portugal, that corn shall be grown in America and Poland, and that hardware and other goods shall be manufactured in England. [Vol. I, pp. 133–34]

CHAPTER 7

The Classical School:

THOMAS ROBERT MALTHUS

Thomas Robert Malthus (1766–1834) was a curate, a writer, and a professor of history and political economy in the East India College in England. His *An Essay on the Principle of Population*, which first appeared in 1798, established his enduring fame; it went through six editions during twenty-eight years. He also published *Principles of Political Economy* in 1820.

Malthus and Ricardo enjoyed a warm, close friendship in spite of the fact that they disagreed about almost every aspect of political economy except Malthus' analysis of population. Through frequent personal visits and through correspondence which began in June 1811, they subjected each other's views to merciless scrutiny. Neither ever persuaded the other, as Ricardo observed in his last letter to Malthus, written August 31, 1823, eleven days before Ricardo's unexpected death. "And now my dear Malthus I have done. Like other disputants after much discussion we each retain our own opinions. These discussions however never influence our friendship; I should not like you more than I do if you agreed in opinion with me."

The two outstanding contributions of Malthus were his theories of population and of market gluts. While he fits into the classical tradition, Malthus is sufficiently at variance with some basic classical principles to merit an analysis of the background and significance of his ideas. Therefore the five questions we use in analyzing each school will be applied to him.

Overview of Malthusian Theories

The social background of Malthusian theories. By 1798 many of the evil effects of the industrial revolution were showing themselves. Unemployment, poverty, and disease were already problems that called for remedial treatment. Tax rates for poor relief were burdensome to property owners. The ferment of the French Revolution radiated outward to infect the poorer classes in other countries; the reaction of the British propertied classes was to deny any responsibility for widespread poverty. The landlords were under attack as people who loved to reap where they did not sow, as Adam Smith had phrased it. Their political power was challenged by the rising merchant and industrial capitalists and their followers.

The immediate cause that provoked Malthus' pessimistic outlook on man's prospect was his father's optimistic belief in the perfectibility of man and society. The faith of his father was based on the works of Godwin and Condorcet. Young Malthus assumed the task of demolishing their philosophies.

William Godwin (1756–1836), father-in-law of the poet Shelley, was a minister, novelist, and political philosopher who turned anarchist and atheist. He published his influential book, *An Enquiry Concerning Political Justice and Its Influence on General Virtue and Happiness* in 1793. This work was among the first to formulate the philosophy of anarchism. Godwin was an extreme individualist who opposed not only all coercive action by the state, but also collective action by the citizens. He would rely entirely on the voluntary good will and sense of justice of individual men guided by the ultimate rule of reason. The human race is perfectible through a continuous advance toward higher rationality and increased well-being. As men's characters depend on the social environment instead of being immutable and determined by heredity, a more perfect society will produce more perfect people. The major obstacles to progress, he said, are private property, economic and political inequality, and the coercive state. On population, his thought was that when the limit of population is reached, men will refuse to propagate themselves further to the point of overpopulation. Godwin's regret was that his optimism helped evoke what he thought was the evil genius of Malthusian pessimism about overpopulation and the hopelessness of man's future.

The Marquis de Condorcet (1743–94) was an eminent French mathematician of an aristocratic family who was elected to the Academy of Science at the age of twenty-six, and to the French Academy at thirty-nine. He was a skeptic in religion, a democrat in politics, a physiocrat in economics, and a pacifist. Among his friends were Turgot, Voltaire, Thomas Paine, Thomas Jefferson, Benjamin Franklin, and Adam Smith. After the outbreak of the French Revolution, which he greeted with enthusiasm, he and Paine founded the journal *Le Républican*.

Condorcet favored universal suffrage for men and women. He vigorously opposed the provisions of the French Constitution of 1791 that established property qualifications for voting and election to office. The fierce party strife of the Revolution left him isolated, and he was ordered to be arrested in 1793. Friends hid him for nine months, after which he deliberately left his refuge in order not to endanger further the woman who sheltered him. After several days of wandering in disguise, he was arrested as a suspect, imprisoned, and was found dead in prison the morning after his arrest, from either exposure or suicide by poison.

While in hiding, Condorcet wrote his most important work, *Sketch of the Intellectual Progress of Mankind*. In spite of his persecution by the Revolution that he had welcomed so ardently, his theme was the idea of social progress based on three fundamental principles: (1) equality among nations; (2) equality of individuals within a nation; and (3) the perfectibility of mankind. Ultimately the equality of nations would abolish war "as the greatest of plagues and as the greatest of crimes," he wrote. A permanent league of nations would maintain peace and the independence of every nation. The equality of individuals would be won when the differences in wealth, in inheritance, and in education were wiped out. He favored the wide distribution of property, social security, and universal, free education for men and women. The natural order tends toward economic equality, but existing laws and institutions encourage inequalities. Equality would overcome the social evils of the day and lead to men becoming perfect. The only inequalities that should be permitted, he thought, are those based on natural abilities. Population would increase as a result of these beneficent reforms, but the food supply would increase even more rapidly. If the problem of subsistence eventually could not be solved in this way, Condorcet thought that birth control would limit the growth of population.

These were the ideas against which young Malthus rebelled. The vices and misery which plague mankind are due, he said, not to evil human institutions, but to the fecundity of the human race. The abolition of war which Condorcet dreamed of would merely remove one of the essential remedies for overpopulation. The Frenchman's welfare programs would vitiate a second limiting factor controlling population—hunger. Godwin's equalitarian, communistic society would mean more food for the masses and therefore a more massive growth of population. Godwin and Condorcet seemed to stand for all the excesses of the French Revolution. Malthus' voice appealed to conservatives as representing sanity and an able defense of the status quo.

The essence of the Malthusian population theory. In the first edition of his *An Essay on the Principle of Population*, Malthus presented his "law of population." Population, when unchecked, increases in a geometrical ratio; subsistence increases at best only in an arithmetical ratio. That is, population tends to increase every twenty-five years at the ratio of one, two, four, eight, sixteen, thirty-two, etc., while subsistence increases at best as one, two, three, four, five, six. He pointed to America (the India or China of his day with respect to rate of population growth) for proof of his propositions.

It has been stated frequently that Malthus was a rash young man in 1798, overenthusiastic and too extreme in presenting his theory; in his more mature writing he is supposed to have relinquished the idea of mathematical ratios. Let us look, therefore, at his *A Summary View of the Principle of Population*, which appeared in 1830. This work was published even later than his sixth and last edition of *An Essay on the Principle of Population*. In *A Summary View*, published thirty-two years after the first edition of the *Essay* and four years before his death, Malthus wrote:

It may be safely asserted, therefore, that population, when unchecked, increases in a geometrical progression of such a nature as to double itself every twenty-five years. . . . If, setting out from a tolerably well peopled country such as England, France, Italy, or Germany, we were to suppose that, by great attention to agriculture, its produce could be permanently increased every twenty-five years by a quantity equal to that which it at present produces, it would be allowing a rate of increase decidedly beyond any probability of realization. . . . Yet this would be an arithmetical progression, and would fall short, beyond all comparison, of the natural increases of population in a geometrical progression.

Malthus perceived certain checks to population growth. These he classified as preventive checks, which reduced the birth rate, and positive checks, which increased the death rate.

The preventive check that Malthus approved was moral restraint. People who could not afford children should either postpone marriage or they should never marry; conduct before marriage should be strictly moral. The preventive check that Malthus disapproved of was vice. This included prostitution and birth control, both of which reduced the birth rate.

The positive checks to population were those that increased the death rate: famine, misery, plague, war. These were elevated to the position of natural phenomena or laws, necessary evils, which were required to limit the population. Positive checks were the punishments for people because moral restraint was not practiced. If the positive checks could somehow be overcome, people would face starvation as a rapidly growing population pressed upon a food supply that at best would grow slowly. Here is how Malthus pictured the positive checks to population in the sixth edition of his *Essay:*

It is an evident truth that, whatever may be the rate of increase in the means of subsistence, the increase of population must be limited by it, at least after the food has once been divided into the smallest shares that will support life. All the children born, beyond what would be required to keep up the population to this level, must necessarily perish, unless room be made for them by the deaths of grown persons. . . . To act consistently therefore, we should facilitate, instead of foolishly and vainly endeavouring to impede, the operations of nature in producing this mortality; and if we dread the too frequent visitation of the horrid form of famine, we should sedulously encourage the other forms of destruction, which we compel nature to use. Instead of recommending cleanliness to the poor, we should encourage contrary habits. In our towns we should make the streets narrower, crowd more people into the houses, and court the return of the plague. In the country, we should build our villages near stagnant pools, and particularly encourage settlements in all marshy and unwholesome situations. But above all, we should reprobate specific remedies for ravaging diseases; and those benevolent, but much mistaken men, who have thought they were doing a service to mankind by projecting schemes for the total extirpation of particular disorders. If by these and similar means the annual mortality were increased . . . we might probably every one of us marry at the age of puberty, and yet few be absolutely starved. [Bk. IV, Ch. 5]

According to Malthus, then, poverty and misery are the natural punishment for the "lower classes," which did not restrain their multiplication. From this view followed his highly significant policy conclusion: there must be no government relief for the poor. To give them aid would cause more children to survive, thereby ultimately worsening the problem of hunger. This is the way he phrased it in the second (1803) edition (but he withdrew the following statement from later editions) of his Essay:

A man who is born into a world already possessed, if he cannot get subsistence from his parents on whom he has a just demand, and if the society do not want his labour, has no claim of right to the smallest portion of food, and, in fact, has no business to be where he is. At nature's mighty feast there is no vacant cover for him. She tells him to be gone, and will quickly execute her own orders, if he do not work upon the compassion of some of her guests. If these guests get up and make room for him, other intruders immediately appear demanding the same favour. . . . The order and harmony of the feast is disturbed, the plenty that before reigned is changed into scarcity.

No wonder Thomas Carlyle, after reading Malthus, called political economy the "dismal science."

Malthus opposed contraception, which he classified under the heading of vice, as a preventive check to population. During his lifetime the English reformer Francis Place and others were popularizing birth control. In the appendix to the fifth (1817) edition of his Essay, Malthus wrote:

Indeed I should always particularly reprobate any artificial and unnatural modes of checking population, both on account of their immorality and their tendency to remove a necessary stimulus to industry. If it were possible for each married couple to limit by a wish the number of their children, there is certainly reason to fear that the indolence of the human race would be very greatly increased; and that neither the population of individual countries, nor of the whole earth, would ever reach its natural and proper extent.

While opposing the preventive check to population that could work, he endorsed moral restraint, the check that would not work. His concern about the indolence of the human race might lead one to think that he was more interested in a large, hard-working, poorly paid population than he was in really effective measures for the limitation of human reproduction.

While Ricardo endorsed the population theory of Malthus, he was not as dogmatic. True apostle of economic growth, he wrote in his *On the Principles of Political Economy and Taxation:*

It has been calculated, that under favourable circumstances population may be doubled in twenty-five years; but under the same favourable circumstances, the whole capital of a country might possibly be doubled in a shorter period. In that case, wages during the whole period would have a tendency to rise, because the demand for labour would increase still faster than the supply. [Ch. 5]

In a lighter vein Ricardo wrote in a letter:

Now that I am a grandfather I should be puzzled, even with the assistance of Mr. Malthus, and Major Torrens, to calculate the accelerated ratio at which my progeny is increasing. I am sure that it is neither arithmetical nor geometrical. I have some notion of consulting with Mr. Owen on the best plan of establishing one of his villages for me and my descendants, admitting only in addition a sufficient number of families to prevent the necessity of celibacy.

Malthus, who married at thirty-nine, had three children but no grandchildren. Ricardo, married at twenty-one, had eight children and twenty-five grandchildren. Had this progression continued, England would have been overrun with Ricardos.

The essence of the Malthusian theory of gluts. In Book II of his *Principles of Political Economy*, Malthus developed his theory of the inadequacy of effective demand to maintain full employment. There is an unlimited human desire for goods. But if the individual who wishes to buy has nothing to sell that others want, goods will remain unsold. If a person has only his labor to sell, the employer will not hire him unless he produces a value greater than that which he receives; that is, there must be a profit.

As the worker cannot buy back the total output, others must. The profit cannot be turned over to the workers, because in a free-enterprise, private-property economy, production and employment cease if profits disappear.

Full employment can be maintained if investment is high enough to absorb the surplus. Spending on capital goods stimulates production and employment about as much as spending on consumption goods. But, said Malthus, the consumption by workmen employed in productive labor can never alone furnish a sufficient motive to the accumulation and employment of capital. And if landlords and capitalists agree to be parsimonious in order to add to their capital, goods will remain unsold.

Who will consume the surplus? Workers cannot, or profits would disappear. Capitalists have the power to consume their profits, but it is not their habit to do so. The great object of their lives is to save a fortune, and they are too busy in the countinghouse to consume it all.

There must therefore be a considerable class of persons who have both the will and power to consume more material wealth than they produce, or the mercantile classes could not continue profitably to produce so much more than they consume. In this class the landlords no doubt stand pre-eminent; but if they were not assisted by the great mass of individuals engaged in personal services, whom they maintain, their own consumption would of itself be insufficient to keep up and increase the value of the produce, and enable the increase of its quantity more than to counterbalance the fall of its price. Nor could the capitalists in that case continue with effect the same habits of saving. [Bk. II, Ch. 1, sec. 9]

While Malthus favored unproductive consumption by landlords, including the hiring of large numbers of menial servants, he opposed excessive unproductive consumption financed by government. Statesmen, soldiers, sailors, and those who live from interest on the national debt necessitate higher taxes, which might stop the increase of wealth. Society should consider private property as sacred and it should not allow the redistribution of wealth through excessive taxation. Nor is a growing government debt desirable, for the inflation it promotes will hurt the receivers of fixed incomes.

War, wrote Malthus in *Principles of Political Economy*, offers another type of stimulus that can eliminate gluts in highly productive economies.

England and America . . . suffered the least by the war, or rather were enriched by it, and they are now suffering the most by the peace. It is certainly a very unfortunate circumstance that any period should ever have occurred in which peace should appear to have been, in so marked a manner, connected with distress. [Bk. II, Ch. 1, sec. 10]

He defended the corn laws, which would continue to enrich landlords and thereby promote unproductive consumption. For times of acute distress, he recommended government spending for public works.

It is also of importance to know that, in our endeavours to assist the working classes in a period like the present, it is desirable to employ them in those kinds of labour, the results of which do not come for sale into the market, such as roads and public works. The objection to employing a large sum in this way, raised by taxes, would not be its tendency to diminish the capital employed in productive labour; because this, to a certain extent, is exactly what is wanted; but it might, perhaps, have the effect of concealing too much the failure of the national demand for labour, and prevent the population from gradually accommodating itself to a reduced demand. This however might be, in a considerable degree, corrected by the wages given. [Bk. II, Ch. 1, sec. 10]

Ricardo's answer to Malthus was based on his refusal to admit the possibility of chronic unemployment:

A body of unproductive labourers are just as necessary and as useful with a view to future production, as a fire, which should consume in the manufacturers warehouse the goods which those unproductive labourers would otherwise consume. . . . In what way can a man's consuming my produce, without making me any return whatever, enable me to make a fortune? I should think my fortune would be more likely to be made, if the consumer of my produce returned me an equivalent value.*

What groups of people did Malthusian doctrines serve or seek to serve? His population theory served the wealthy by absolving them from any responsibility for poverty and its alleviation; the poor had only themselves to blame for their condition. His opposition to the poor laws would reduce taxes on property at a time when property ownership was concentrated among relatively few people. His defense of the corn laws and unproductive consumption promoted the interests of the landlords, that group which had long been dominant but was rapidly losing its political power and social prestige. It was with some amazement that he wrote in his *Principles of Political Economy:* "It is somewhat singular that Mr. Ricardo, a considerable receiver of rents, should have so much underrated their national importance; while I, who never received, nor expect to receive any, should probably be accused of overrating their importance." [Bk. I, Ch. 3, sec. 9]

How were Malthusian doctrines valid, useful, or correct in their time? They were useful insofar as they served the wealthy, the property own-

* Piero Sraffa, ed., *The Works and Correspondence of David Ricardo,* Vol. II (Cambridge, 1951), pp. 421–22.

ers, and the landlords. The theory of gluts showed the earliest awareness of the problem of unemployment. Malthus argued strongly that the economic system is not self-adjusting. His population theory was understandable when rising birth rates and falling death rates caused phenomenal increases in population. Widespread poverty required an explanation, and Malthus developed what appeared to be a plausible theory to explain it.

Yet the theory of gluts was less useful in 1820 than it is today. In the nineteenth century capitalism was expanding rapidly. Investment was booming both in England and overseas. Depressions were milder and affected fewer people in the early decades of the century than later. Only in recent decades has the problem of unemployment awakened new interest in Malthus.

How did the Malthusian doctrines outlive their usefulness? The theory of population was based on the law of diminishing returns. Malthus treated this as a historically valid principle. As population would grow over the years, more workers would be required to grow more food, and the average and marginal yield per worker would decline. But this law is valid only under static conditions, with technology remaining unchanged. Historically fewer workers in agriculture grow more food than ever. Malthusian pessimism resulted from underestimating the possibilities of increasing agricultural production.

Nor did Malthus foresee sharply reduced birth rates in those societies where urbanization, education, and rising standards of living became important.

Malthus and his theory of population are still useful to those who wish to attribute poverty and war to excessive and indiscriminate breeding among the world's impoverished people. Mankind has not yet been persuaded that war, instead of being a cure for overpopulation and poverty, is one of the greatest causes of poverty ever devised.

The Malthusian theory of gluts, while it was the first attempt to explain unemployment, was not a theory of business cycles. It dealt with the tendency toward chronic depression because of underconsumption, but not with the ups and downs of business activity. The concept of unproductive consumption can be observed today in huge military budgets. But modern societies have tried to alleviate the problem of gluts by moderate redistribution of income, which Malthus opposed. The many fiscal and monetary controls that can reduce the amplitude of fluctuations were unknown in his day. The history of industrial society has shown his theory of gluts to have been a brilliant insight into a major problem of a capitalistic economy. But he used it to defend agriculture against the advance of industrialization. His was a backward-looking bias, justifying the big landlords—the heroes of a bygone era.

CHAPTER 8

The Classical School:

BENTHAM, SAY, SENIOR, and MILL

Bentham

THE LIFE span of Jeremy Bentham (1748–1832) overlapped the publication of David Hume's economic essays, Adam Smith's *Wealth of Nations*, the works of David Ricardo and Thomas Robert Malthus, and the early writing of John Stuart Mill. Not only was Bentham an enthusiastic adherent of the classical school, but he made some original contributions to its philosophy and economics. Bentham boasted, "I was the spiritual father of [James] Mill, and Mill was the spiritual father of Ricardo: so that Ricardo was my spiritual grandson."

Bentham, a precocious child, read history and studied Latin at four. He matriculated at Queen's College, Oxford, at twelve and took his degree at fifteen. After that he studied law as his father wished. But he soon deserted the legal profession for a scholarly life, relying on his indulgent and admiring father for support. Most of his writing has never been published. He gathered around him a circle of congenial friends and ardent disciples who promoted his ideas.

Bentham's body, in accordance with his wishes, was dissected in the interest of science. He left his entire estate to the University of London, with the stipulation that his remains be present at all meetings of its Board. His skeleton, stuffed and dressed, is seated in a chair, with cane in gloved hand. The head on the body is wax, but his actual head, preserved in the manner of South American head hunters, rests between his feet.

The central and most controversial theme of Bentham's thought has been called utilitarianism, or the greatest happiness principle. The underlying philosophy, going back to the Greeks of antiquity, was that of hedonism: Each man seeks his own greatest happiness. Utilitarianism superimposed on hedonism the ethical doctrine that conduct should be directed toward promoting the greatest happiness of the greatest number of persons. The extremely individualistic outlook of hedonism was moderated by utilitarianism, which at least recognized that organized society has a role to play. If an individual pursues only his own pleasure, will that necessarily promote the general happiness? Not necessarily, thought Bentham. Society, however, has its own methods of compelling individuals to promote the general happiness. There are political sanctions through the rule of law to punish individuals who harm others excessively in their own pursuit of pleasure. There are moral or social sanctions, of which ostracism is an example. Even theological sanctions, such as fear of punishment in the hereafter, would help reconcile the individualistic self-interest of hedonism with the greatest happiness for the greatest number of people of utilitarianism.

Using utilitarianism as his foundation, Bentham developed a system of philosophy, economic policy, and reform. We can let Bentham speak for himself on the principle of utility, as he did in the first chapter of *An Introduction to the Principles of Morals and Legislation,* first printed in 1780.

Nature has placed mankind under the governance of two sovereign masters, *pain* and *pleasure.* It is for them alone to point out what we ought to do, as well as to determine what we shall do. On the one hand the standard of right and wrong, on the other the chain of causes and effects, are fastened to their throne. They govern us in all we do, in all we say, in all we think: every effort we can make to throw off our subjection, will serve but to demonstrate and confirm it. In words a man may pretend to abjure their empire: but in reality he will remain subject to it all the while. The *principle of utility* recognises this subjection, and assumes it for the foundation of that system, the object of which is to rear the fabric of felicity by the hands of reason and of law. . . .

By the principle of utility is meant that principle which approves or disapproves of every action whatsoever, according to the tendency which it appears to have to augment or diminish the happiness of the party whose interest is in question: or, what is the same thing in other words, to promote or to oppose that happiness. I say of every action whatsoever; and therefore not only of every action of a private individual, but of every measure of government.

By utility is meant that property in any object, whereby it tends to produce benefit, advantage, pleasure, good, or happiness, . . . or . . . to prevent the happening of mischief, pain, evil, or unhappiness to the party whose interest is considered: if that party be the community in general, then the happiness of the community: if a particular individual, then the happiness of that individual.

. . . The community is a fictitious body, composed of the individual persons who are considered as constituting as it were its *members.* The interest of the community then is, what?—the sum of the interests of the several members who compose it.

It is in vain to talk of the interest of the community, without understanding what is the interest of the individual. A thing is said to promote the interest . . . of an individual, when it tends to add to the sum total of his pleasures: or, what comes to the same thing, to diminish the sum total of his pains.

An action then may be said to be conformable to the principle of utility . . . when the tendency it has to augment the happiness of the community is greater than any it has to diminish it.

A measure of government . . . may be said to be conformable to or dictated by the principle of utility, when in like manner the tendency which it has to augment the happiness of the community is greater than any which it has to diminish it.

Two conclusions can be drawn from Bentham's doctrines. First, in their time they promoted progress, reform, wider democracy, and the amelioration of social conditions. Second, they led to insoluble contradictions and confusions; these doctrines could not provide a firm basis for developing a system of economics, philosophy, or aesthetics.

First, on the positive side: Bentham lived and wrote at a time when common men, the "labouring poor," had no voice and no vote in managing social and political affairs. They were expected to be subservient, docile, and hard working. Their toil and sacrifices enhanced the power of the nation, the glory of its rulers, the wealth of the industrial and commercial moneyed class, and the indolent ease of the aristocrats. Yet here was a philosopher who said that a man is a man regardless of his social position. If something adds to a commoner's pleasure more than it detracts from the pleasure of an aristocrat, it is commendable. If government intervention enhances the happiness of a community more than it diminishes it, the intervention is justified.

Bentham emphasized that legislators ought to augment the total happiness of the community. Instead of people serving the state, the state should serve the people. He concluded that most existing state controls and regulations are harmful, and his slogan for government was "Be quiet." But he did not worship laissez faire as a dogmatic principle to be accepted blindly. If special reasons existed, government ought to intervene. He thought the state should monopolize the issue of paper money, thereby saving interest on its borrowing. It should operate life and annuity insurance and tax inheritances, monopolies, etc. Where men's interests are not naturally harmonious, let the state establish an artificial harmony of interests that promotes the greatest happiness of the greatest number.

The utilitarian philosophers hoped to establish morals as an exact science.

If only pleasure and pain could be measured quantitatively and compared among different individuals, every law and every act could be judged by balancing one against the other. Money, Bentham concluded, is the instrument that measures the quantity of pleasure or pain. "Those who are not satisfied with the accuracy of this instrument must find out some other that shall be more accurate, or bid adieu to politics and morals."*

In *The Philosophy of Economic Science* Bentham argued that wealth is a measure of happiness, but that wealth has diminishing marginal utility as it increases:

Of two persons having unequal fortunes, he who has most wealth must by a legislator be regarded as having most happiness. But the quantity of happiness will not go on increasing in anything near the same proportion as the quantity of wealth:—ten thousand times the quantity of wealth will not bring with it ten thousand times the quantity of happiness. It will even be matter of doubt, whether ten thousand times the wealth will in general bring with it twice the happiness. The effect of wealth in the production of happiness goes on diminishing, as the quantity by which the wealth of one man exceeds that of another goes on increasing: in other words, the quantity of happiness produced by a particle of wealth (each particle being of the same magnitude) will be less and less at every particle; the second will produce less than the first, the third than the second, and so on.†

This is an argument for egalitarianism that the welfare economists later wrestled with. If you take income from the hundred-thousand-pounds-a-year man, said Bentham, and give it to the ten-pounds-a-year man, more happiness will be gained by the poor man than will be lost by the wealthy one. But he was not *that* radical. By marshaling new arguments against the redistribution of income, he was able to repudiate the conclusions of his own theory. Equalizing incomes, he thought, would destroy happiness by alarming the rich and depriving them of a feeling of security, by taking away from them the enjoyment of the fruits of their work, and by destroying all inducement to labor. When security and equality are in opposition, said Bentham, equality should give way.

Bentham's devotion to the greatest good for the greatest number led him to study and advocate many democratic reforms. He defended universal manhood suffrage, equal electoral districts, annual parliaments, and vote by secret ballot. He opposed the monarchy and the House of Lords, arguing that only in a democracy do the interests of the governors and the governed become identical. At a time when there was little enthusiasm for education, Bentham was urging a system of national education, even for

* W. Stark, *Jeremy Bentham's Economic Writings*, Vol. 1 (New York, 1952), p.117.
† *Ibid.*, p. 113.

pauper children. "Frugality Banks," he suggested, should be organized to stimulate saving by the poor. Public works should provide employment for unemployed workers during slack times. He endorsed free trade, competition, and legal reforms. An elaborate plan for a model prison was designed to reform criminals rather than punish them. No wonder Bentham and his circle, including James and John Stuart Mill and David Ricardo, were called "philosophical radicals."

Benthamite economics is not altogether satisfactory. He had to assume that people are rational in calculating their own interests, with each individual being the best judge of his own interests. One can doubt the complete validity of this assumption. He sought an exact, quantitative measure of utility, yet his problem was compounded by introducing the concept of the diminishing marginal utility of wealth. It is difficult enough to compare precisely the increases in happiness of two people who receive equally increased incomes. But it is even more difficult when the two people start at different levels of wealth and income. His outlook, further, was steeped in a tradition of individualism. But increasingly, collective activity was required in pursuing society's goals of increasing the production of goods and services and distributing them in a satisfactory manner.

The idea that "the interest of the community . . . is . . . the sum of the interests of the several members who compose it" is not necessarily true. Each individual may be uninterested in conservation if the cost is greater than the present value of the expected future income resulting from conservation measures. But society may favor conservation because it must think in terms of the needs of future generations, or because it wants a make-work scheme during depressed times. Again, each individual might rather not pay taxes to promote flood control, but it is in the interest of society to tax itself for such a purpose. Each manufacturer might gain if he alone would lower wages, but if all were to do that they might sell fewer goods. Illustrations of Bentham's "fallacy of composition" can be multiplied endlessly.

Utilitarianism is also deficient as a philosophy. Bentham, abjuring all value judgments on qualities of pleasures, stated that "quantity of pleasure being equal, push-pin is as good as poetry." He playfully described the difference between prose and poetry: *"Prose* is where all the lines but the last go on to the margin—poetry is where some of them fall short of it." If Mickey Spillane's detective stories gave more joy to more people in a recent decade than Shakespeare, Bentham would say that Spillane's contribution to mankind during that time was greater. Yet qualitative measures of happiness may be more significant than quantitative. Shakespeare explored all aspects of life; he portrayed characters in a comprehensive manner and showed how they change under the forces of changing circumstances. He can be reread with pleasure and with increased understanding of the many facets of life he pictured. We gain deeper insights into people and how they act and react in different circumstances. By reading Spillane we can easily form the wrong ideas about how blondes behave!

Understanding the world may be preferable to enjoying it. Being of service to humanity may be a higher aim than selfishly seeking one's own happiness, although this idea may sound quaintly old-fashioned today. The utilitarian would say, "If you feel so strongly about serving humanity, this gives you the greatest personal pleasure and conforms to our principle of happiness." This line of reasoning reduces hedonism to an empty tautology. Even if you risk your life rescuing a child in the river, you must be doing it for your own pleasure at being a hero. But if we say that serving society is preferable to pursuing one's own narrow self-interest, we contradict the utilitarian, for we are ranking happiness qualitatively, not quantitatively, on a preference scale. Our value judgments in aesthetics and our philosophy of the good life aim at more than happiness. As John Stuart Mill said, "It is better to be a human being dissatisfied than a pig satisfied; better to be Socrates dissatisfied than a fool satisfied."

There are widely held explanations of human behavior that dispute the hedonistic view of men motivated solely by the desire to maximize pleasure and minimize pain. Early experimental psychologists, for example, studied the association of stimulus and response in the learning process. The behaviorists added the idea of the conditioned reflex. Freudian psychiatry claimed that the fundamental driving force governing human behavior was the conflict between opposing forces deep within the personality. Students of cultural anthropology pointed out that society, one way or another, imposes on the individual its system of ideas, patterns of behavior, and way of living. These ideas questioned the pleasure-pain principle as the guiding force explaining the behavior of man.

Bentham's utilitarianism as an ethical system also has had rival systems to dispute its claims. The idea that every society and every government should promote the greatest happiness for the greatest number of people has been denied by many. Plato taught that pleasure is subordinate in value to knowledge, and it should be a by-product of effective achievement. The Stoics favored disciplining the appetites of the body, for passion and desire are a morbid condition of the soul. Various religions preached resignation to the inescapable sufferings of this world as the key to the good and worthy life, or mortification and self-denial to overcome impulses to sin, or the performance of Christian duty as leading toward salvation. Thomas Hobbes (1588–1679) held that man has a fundamentally depraved nature that drives him toward war, strife, and the selfish appropriation of all things he can lay hands on; therefore a strong and absolute government is required to keep him in check. John Locke (1632–1704), who did not think every good was a moral good, found a social principle in man and a sense of obligation that would bind where no constraint of law existed. Modern fascists glorify the strong state as the supreme good, and communists place the advancement of class interests above the individual quest for happiness. Advocates of all these ethical systems, which are alternatives to utilitarianism, would claim that they too seek the greatest happiness of the greatest number of people. Nevertheless, Benthamism erected the greatest happiness principle as the most immediate guide and directing force; the others would approach this goal by indirection, either in this world or in the next, either in the present or in some vague and undefined future.

Bentham's concept of human nature became the foundation for the economic systems of Ricardo, Mill, and the early marginalists, especially William Stanley Jevons. Underlying the marginalist theory of demand was the concept of marginal utility, which assumed that each person would compare the intensity of satisfactions received from a great variety of goods. Man was considered to be perfectly rational and carefully calculating. Labor was believed to be painful. To get the maximum happiness, one would work just up to the point where the marginal utility of his earnings was equal to the marginal disutility of his labor. The entrepreneur, in determining his volume of output, would always try to maximize his money income or minimize his losses. Later marginalists have argued, however, that their analysis does not depend on the extreme form of utilitarianism that Bentham presented. Economic theory can take other motives and other behavior patterns into account.

Say

JEAN BAPTISTE SAY (1767–1832) was a Frenchman who popularized Adam Smith on the continent. His major work, *Traité d'Économie Politique* (*A Treatise on Political Economy*) was published in 1803. Say's career was temporarily blocked because Napoleon was displeased with his extreme laissez faire views. Some time after Waterloo, he became a professor of political economy, after having spent years as a businessman.

Say opposed the labor theory of value of the classical school. In its place he substituted supply and demand, which in turn were regulated by cost of production and utility. He added the entrepreneur to land, labor, and capital as a fourth factor of production. But his chief claim to fame rests on the theory that general overproduction is impossible. This doctrine came to be known as Say's Law of Markets. In the work cited above, he wrote:

Should a tradesman say, "I do not want other products for my woollens, I want money," . . . he may be told, . . . "You say, you only want money; I say, you want other commodities, and not money. For what, in point of fact, do you want the money? Is it not for the purchase of raw materials or stock for your trade, or of victuals for your support? Wherefore, it is products that you want, and not money." [Ch. 15]

Here Say adds a cheerful footnote:

Even when money is obtained with a view to hoard or bury it, the ultimate object is always to employ it in a purchase of some kind. The heir of the lucky finder uses it in that way, if the miser do not: for money, as money, has no other use than to buy with.

Apparently a possible lag of a whole generation between the receipt of money and its expenditure was not at all disturbing to him.

Say continued his exposition:

It is worth while to remark, that a product is no sooner created, than it, from that instant, affords a market for other products to the full extent of its own value. When the producer has put the finishing hand to his product, he is most anxious to sell it immediately, lest its value should vanish in his hands. Nor is he less anxious to dispose of the money he may get for it; for the value of money is also perishable. But the only way of getting rid of money is in the purchase of some product or other. Thus, the mere circumstance of the creation of one product immediately opens a vent for other products. . . .

But it may be asked, if this be so, how does it happen, that there is at times so great a glut of commodities in the market, and so much difficulty in finding a vent for them? Why cannot one of these superabundant commodities be exchanged for another? I answer, that the glut of a particular commodity arises from its having outrun the total demand for it in one of two ways; either because it has been produced in excessive abundance, or because the produce of other commodities has fallen short.

Though refuted by Sismondi and Marx, Say's law continued to dominate economic thinking until Keynes relegated it to a position of minor importance. Uncritical acceptance of the Law of Markets appears to have delayed the study of business cycles many decades.

Senior

NASSAU WILLIAM SENIOR (1790–1864) was the oldest son of a country clergyman who had ten children. He became the first professor of political economy at Oxford in 1825. The government appointed him a member of several royal commissions that investigated important social problems. In his economic thinking Senior departed significantly from classical economics and moved toward the neoclassical position that triumphed after 1870.

Senior wished to separate the science of political economy from all value judgments, all policy pronouncements, all efforts to promote welfare. The economist should concern himself with wealth, not happiness.

But his conclusions, whatever be their generality and their truth, do not authorize him in adding a single syllable of advice. That privilege belongs to the writer or the statesman who has considered all the causes which may promote or impede the general welfare of those whom he addresses, not to the theorist who has considered only one, though among the most important, of those causes. The business of a Political Economist is neither to recommend nor to dissuade, but to state general principles.*

The exchange value of goods, according to Senior, depends on demand and supply. Underlying demand is the concept of the diminishing marginal utility of goods as more units are acquired. Supply depends on cost of production. But cost is subjective, a sum of sacrifices required to use nature's agents to produce useful goods. The costs of production are the labor of the workers and the abstinence of the capitalists. "Abstinence" is the term that Senior contributed to the lexicon of political economy.

But although Human Labour, and the Agency of Nature, independently of that of man, are the primary Productive Powers, they require the concurrence of a Third Productive Principle to give them complete efficiency. . . . To the Third Principle, or Instrument of Production, without which the two others are inefficient, we shall give the name of *Abstinence:* a term by which we express the conduct of a person who either abstains from the unproductive use of what he can command, or designedly prefers the production of remote to that of immediate results. . . . *By the word Abstinence, we wish to express that agent, distinct from labour and the agency of nature, the concurrence of which is necessary to the existence of Capital, and which stands in the same relation to Profit as Labour does to Wages.*†

Abstinence implied a value judgment about the sacrifices undertaken by the capitalist in postponing (or even foregoing forever) the consumption of his wealth. Marx and the German state socialist Ferdinand Lassalle made great sport of this concept. The latter wrote scornfully of the abstinence of a Baron Rothschild and the profligate wastefulness of the English laborer who squandered all his income of a few shillings a week on consumption.

* Nassau William Senior, *An Outline of the Science of Political Economy* (New York, 1951), p. 3. [Originally published in 1836.]
† *Ibid.*, pp. 58–59.

Alfred Marshall later redesignated the function of saving as "waiting"—postponing consumption. This term was both less colorful and less controversial. It did not imply any suffering or sacrifices by the rich while they were accumulating wealth.

The socialist critics who ridiculed the concept of the irksomeness of saving overlooked one crucial point: As the idea of the margin finally developed and matured, the sacrifice of foregoing consumption was measured at the margin; the sacrifice was not intended to represent the total supply of saving. It is likely that the millionaire could save ten thousand dollars with far less agonized tightening of the belt than a poor man could save a dollar. Let us consider, however, that portion of the saving that is made at the borderline of uncertainty as to whether to save an extra sum or spend it on consumption. At that margin, the sacrifice of postponing consumption may well be large enough to require remuneration in the form of interest to compensate for the sacrifice. The widest discrepancy exists between the sacrifice, *on the average*, of the rich man who saves a dollar and that of a poor man who does; but the discrepancy is narrowed considerably if we consider the sacrifice of saving a *marginal* dollar in the two cases.

Senior disagreed with Adam Smith, who thought that the producers of services are all unproductive. Lawyers, doctors, and teachers, he said, are productive because they promote the increase of wealth. Where a soldier must protect the husbandman, both are productive. Suppose a thousand men are constantly employed in forging bars and bolts to keep out thieves; if one hundred of them can achieve the same purpose as watchmen, is wealth diminished by the conversion from "productive" to "unproductive" workers? To Senior the proper distinction was not between productive and unproductive labor, but rather between productive and unproductive consumption. The latter category includes lace, embroidery, jewelry, tobacco, gin, and beer. Their consumption diminishes the mass of commodities without adding to workers' capacities to produce.

Senior served on the Poor Law Commission appointed in 1832. He wrote the bulk of the report resulting in the harsh Poor Law Amendment Act of 1834, which sought to discourage applications for relief by people physically able to work.

As a passionate champion of laissez faire, freedom as he saw it, and mobility of labor, Senior was unequivocally opposed to the trade union movement. Among his proposals were prohibition of all conspiracies and restraints of trade by labor; severe punishment for all solicitations to form unions; prohibition and severe punishment for all picketing; confiscation of funds owned by unions; compensation from public funds for people who were injured in resisting unions.

In 1837 Senior published a pamphlet opposing the English Factory Acts,

which at the time limited the working day to twelve hours in those factories where children were employed. While he endorsed the principle of
regulating child labor, he opposed laws limiting the hours of adults. In calculating the economic effect of a shorter working day, Senior made no
allowance for reduced outlays on raw materials, heating, lighting, depreciation, etc. He also ignored the probability of an increased output per man-
hour because the working day was reduced. His confused and erroneous
reasoning led to the conclusion that all profit was derived from the last
hour of work. If the working day were shortened by more than an hour,
capitalists would actually lose money, and England would be ruined in
competition with foreign producers. His major concern was to attack the
"ten-hours agitation" of his time.

Senior did not heed his own prescription that economists should never
offer a single syllable of advice. In his long career in public life, he never
explained the status of his recommendations at the time they were offered,
whether they had all the weight of economics behind them or not.

Mill

JOHN STUART MILL (1806–73) was the last great economist of the classical
school, undoubtedly the greatest since the death of Ricardo in 1823. He
made some significant original contributions, in addition to systematizing
and popularizing the whole body of economic thought of his predecessors.
The classical school already was in decline during Mill's mature years. He
himself departed from some of the key concepts built into the classical
structure by Smith and Ricardo. Before his death neoclassical economics
had appeared on the scene, ultimately to displace its classical forebears.
Mill's great *Principles of Political Economy*, first published in 1848 and reprinted in the United States as late as 1920, was the leading textbook in the
field at least until the publication of Alfred Marshall's *Principles of Economics* in 1890. The popularity of Mill's book for so long may be due to
two causes: it was well written, and there is a cultural lag that permits
books to linger on in the classroom even after they are antiquated.

Mill reported his amazing upbringing in his *Autobiography*, published
shortly after his death. His father, James Mill, was the man who urged Ricardo to write, publish, and sit in Parliament; he popularized Bentham's
ideas, and he helped found the group known as philosophic radicals, which
pushed political reforms in Great Britain. A strict disciplinarian, James
Mill himself supervised the education of John, the oldest of his nine children. The boy began to learn Greek at three, and he wrote apologetically
that "I learnt no Latin until my eighth year." By then he was reading the
Greek philosophers in the original, but not always understanding them. At

eleven he read the proofs of his father's *History of India* and was greatly impressed. He mastered algebra and elementary geometry and began studying differential calculus by the time he was twelve; he had by then written a history of the Roman government—which was not published. From then on he studied logic, and at thirteen he began the study of political economy. Between the ages of fifteen and eighteen Mill edited and published five volumes of Bentham's manuscripts. At nineteen he was publishing original, scholarly articles, and at twenty he had a well-earned nervous breakdown.

John Stuart Mill wrote in his *Autobiography* that his father made him read and give a verbal account of books in which he had no interest. There were few toys or children's books permitted. He was not allowed to take holidays or associate much with other boys, lest the habit of work should be broken and a taste for idleness acquired. "But my father, in all his teaching, demanded of me not only the utmost that I could do, but much that I could by no possibility have done." No wonder Mill wrote of his father that "the element which was chiefly deficient in his moral relation to his children was that of tenderness."

The boy was taught that he was quite ordinary, and any special abilities he had were due to the special advantages of being James Mill's son. Therefore late in life John Stuart Mill could write in his *Autobiography*:

What I could do, could assuredly be done by any boy or girl of average capacity and healthy physical constitution. . . . If I thought anything about myself, it was that I was rather backward in my studies, since I always found myself so, in comparison with what my father expected from me.

It was when John was fourteen and about to leave home for a long absence that his father broke the news to him that he had been taught much more than the average educated youth his age, but it should not go to his head.

He wound up by saying, that whatever I knew more than others, could not be ascribed to any merit in me, but to the very unusual advantage which had befallen to my lot, of having a father who was able to teach me, and willing to give the necessary trouble and time; that it was no matter of praise to me, if I knew more than those who had not had a similar advantage, but the deepest disgrace to me if I did not.

The son was more modest than the father!

Mill met Mrs. Harriet Taylor (1807–58) when he was twenty-four years old. There followed a warm friendship and association between them, even to taking vacations together on the continent and in the English country-side. Twenty years later, after Mr. Taylor died, they were married. Mill at-tributed to her his humanitarianism, his hope for and faith in human progress, his love of liberty, and his passionate defense of the rights of women. He tried to persuade the world that his whole intellectual develop-ment other than his technical competence in economics was due to Mrs. Taylor. He called his writings both before and after their marriage the joint product of their minds, with her share constantly increasing as the years advanced; it did not matter which of them held the pen.

Mill, raised in the Benthamite tradition, finally rejected the latter's nar-row and dogmatic utilitarianism. He regarded as too limited Bentham's view that human beings are motivated in their conduct by nothing more than self-love and the desire for self-gratification. He charged Bentham with neglecting motives that involved the search for perfection, honor, and other ends, entirely for their own sakes.

Mill's *Principles of Political Economy with Some of Their Applications to Social Philosophy* is divided into five Books: "Production," "Distribu-tion," "Exchange," "Influence of the Progress of Society on Production and Distribution," "Of the Influence of Government."

In the first book he analyzed the three productive factors—land, labor, and capital. Wealth is defined as including all useful things that possess ex-change value; only material objects are included, because only they can be accumulated. Productive labor includes only those kinds of exertion that produce utilities embodied in material objects. But labor that yields a ma-terial product only indirectly is also held to be productive. Thus educators and government officials are productive because their services create the conditions required for the output of material goods. Unproductive labor is that which does not terminate in the creation of material wealth. Exam-ples are labor that ends in immediate enjoyment without any increase of the accumulated stock or permanent means of enjoyment; saving a friend's life is unproductive unless the friend is a productive laborer who produces more than he consumes; missionaries or clergymen are unproductive unless they teach the arts of civilization in addition to religious doctrines. Unpro-ductive labor may nevertheless be useful.

Capital, the result of saving, is the accumulated stock of the produce of labor, and its aggregate amount limits the extent of industry. Every in-crease of capital is capable of giving additional employment to labor with-out limit. This eliminates the necessity of unproductive expenditure by the rich to give employment to the poor. Mill assumed that everything saved through the abstinence of the capitalist would be invested. If capitalists spent less on luxury consumption and more on investment, the demand for labor would rise. If population increased, the increased demand for necessities by wage-earners would offset the decreased demand for luxuries by capitalists. If population did not increase in proportion to the growth of capital, wages would rise and luxury consumption by workers would supplant luxury consumption by their employers. This is the optimistic world of full employment. "Thus the limit of wealth is never deficiency of consumers, but of producers and productive power. Every addition to capital gives to labour either additional employment, or additional remuneration; enriches either the country, or the labouring class." [Bk. I, Ch. 5]

What are the obstacles to increasing production? Lack of labor is not one of them, said Mill, for population has the power of increasing in a geometrical ratio. That it does not is due to impulses superior to mere animal instincts. People do not propagate like swine, but are capable of being withheld by prudence from multiplying beyond the means of subsistence. Population is restrained by the fear of want, rather than by want itself.

The increase of capital depends on two things—the surplus product after the necessities are supplied to all engaged in production, and the disposition to save. The greater the profit that can be made from capital, the stronger is the motive for its accumulation. The inclination to save also varies from person to person and from country to country.

The limited extent of land and its limited productiveness are the real barriers to the increase of production. Mill recognized increasing returns to scale in industry; that is, the larger the enterprise within certain limits, the more efficient it became. He thought agriculture exhibited decreasing returns to scale. But he applied the law of diminishing returns only to agriculture. That is, if the supply of land is constant, adding labor will not add to the product in the same proportion. He did not concern himself with the proposition that the same would be true in industry if capital were kept constant. The reason for his differentiating between the two is obvious: the supply of capital can be increased easily, while land cannot.

Population therefore must be restrained, not because of inequality of property, but because of the niggardliness of nature. An unjust distribution of wealth does not even aggravate the evil of overpopulation but, at most, causes it to be felt somewhat earlier.

In Book II, "Distribution," Mill began with his famous, far-reaching pronouncement:

The laws and conditions of the production of wealth, partake of the character of physical truths. There is nothing optional or arbitrary in them. . . . It is not so with the Distribution of Wealth. That is a matter of human institution solely. The things once there, mankind, individually or collectively, can do with them as they like.

He did not see that production and distribution are interrelated, and that interference with one involves interference with the other. The "things" are not there as a mass of goods already produced. They appear as a continuous flow that can be reduced or completely interrupted if the distribution is unfavorable to the maintenance of production. While both his propositions are exaggerations, with them Mill opened the prospect of a greater role for government in economic affairs. It can be said, to Mill's credit, that he abandoned Ricardo's idea of inexorable "laws of distribution," with man being helpless beneath them. He flung a challenge at the classical school's belief in the universality and permanence of natural law.

Mill immediately entered into a discussion of communism. The judgment expressed in the fifth edition of his book follows:

If, therefore, the choice were to be made between Communism with all its chances, and the present state of society with all its sufferings and injustices; . . . all the difficulties, great or small, of Communism, would be but as dust in the balance. But to make the comparison applicable, we must compare Communism at its best, with the régime of individual property, not as it is, but as it might be made. The principle of private property has never yet had a fair trial in any country.

Mill called himself a socialist. From his *Autobiography* we can see that he leaned toward utopian socialism (a set of beliefs that will be discussed in the following chapter). This was half a century after these ideas had developed and spread throughout Europe.

We [Mill and Mrs. Taylor] saw clearly that to render any such social transformation either possible or desirable, an equivalent change of character must take place both in the uncultivated herd who now compose the labouring masses, and in the immense majority of their employers. Both these classes must learn by practice to labour and combine for generous, or at all events for public and social purposes, and not, as hitherto, solely for narrowly interested ones. . . . The deep-rooted selfishness which forms the general character of the existing state of society, is *so* deeply rooted, only because the whole course of existing institutions tends to foster it. . . . We regarded all existing institutions and social arrangements as being . . . merely provisional, and we welcomed with the greatest pleasure and interest all socialistic experiments by select individuals (such as the Co-operative Societies).

Mill continued his discussion of distribution in Book II of *Principles of Political Economy* with a defense of the limitation of inheritance. He favored a broader diffusion of property, with a reduction of the very large heritable fortunes.

Mill, like Senior, Malthus, and James Mill before him, accepted what has been called the wages-fund theory. Wages, he said, depend mainly upon the demand and supply of labor. The demand for labor depends on that part of the capital that is set aside for the payment of wages. The supply of labor depends on the number of people seeking work. Under the rule of competition, wages cannot be affected by anything other than the relative amounts of capital and population. Wage rates cannot rise, except by an increase of the aggregate funds employed in hiring laborers, or a diminution in the number of workers for hire. Nor can wage rates fall except either by a diminution of the funds devoted to paying labor, or by an increase in the number of laborers to be paid. The wages-fund theory therefore presupposed a unitary elasticity of demand for labor; no matter what the wage rate, the same sum is expended for labor.

It follows then, according to Mill, that government cannot fix a minimum wage above the equilibrium level. With a wages fund of a fixed size, some workers have to become unemployed. To remedy this condition, the government can increase the size of the wages fund by forced saving through taxation, using the proceeds to overcome the unemployment that it created with minimum-wage laws. Then there is no restraining influence on the procreation of the poor. "But no one has a right to bring creatures into life, to be supported by other people."

The wages-fund doctrine provided a basis for opposing unionism, although Mill did not use it for this purpose as others did. Workers cannot raise their incomes through collective action. If one group raises its wage rate, wages must fall elsewhere. Mill, passionately devoted to liberty, urged that workers should have the right to combine to raise their wages even though he thought unions are seldom effectual, and when effectual are seldom desirable.

The wages-fund concept was erroneous in that there is no predetermined proportion of capital that must go to labor. Capital can be shifted from one employment to another, and more or less can be spent on labor. The idea of a fund arose because the harvest of one season was used to provide subsistence for labor for the following year. But after a business gets under way wages are paid, not from an advance fund of capital, but from a flow of income to the enterprise that the worker helps generate. The relative sizes of the rivulets into which the income stream is subdivided can be altered within certain limits.

Mill finally repudiated the wages-fund doctrine in a book review he published in *Fortnightly Review* in 1869. He recognized that there is a considerable range in the wage rate that economic conditions allow; therefore unions may raise wages to a certain extent. The price of labor, he said, instead of being determined by the size of a given wages fund, itself determines the size of the fund. If the employer has to pay more for labor, his own income will be reduced. The real limit to the rise in wages comes at the point where the employer would be ruined financially or driven to abandon his business.

Profit, said Mill, resolves itself into three parts: interest, insurance, and wages of superintendence. These are the rewards for abstinence, risk, and exertion implied in the employment of capital. Allowing for differences in risk, attractiveness of different employments, and natural or artificial monopolies, the rate of profit in all spheres of employment tends toward equality.

In "Exchange," Mill confidently stated the following:

Happily, there is nothing in the laws of Value which remains for the present or any future writer to clear up; the theory of the subject is complete: the only difficulty to be overcome is that of so stating it as to solve by anticipation the chief perplexities which occur in applying it. [Bk. III, Ch. 1]

Price expresses the value of a thing in relation to money; the value of a commodity is its general power of purchasing other commodities. There can be a general rise of prices, but not a general rise of values, for all things cannot rise relatively to one another.

The value of a commodity cannot rise higher than its estimated use value to the buyer. Effectual demand—desire plus purchasing power—is therefore one of the determinants of value. But different quantities are demanded at different values. If demand depends partly on value, and value depends on demand, is this not a contradiction? asked Mill. He resolved it by introducing the concept of a demand schedule. Demand means quantity demanded; the quantity is not fixed, but varies according to the value. The interaction of demand and supply results in a market value.

Mill definitely had an understanding of elasticity of demand:

Let us suppose that the demand at some particular time exceeds the supply, that is, there are persons ready to buy, at the market value, a greater quantity than is offered for sale. Competition takes place on the side of the buyers, and the value rises: but how much? In the ratio (some may suppose) of the deficiency: if the demand exceeds the supply by one-third, the value rises one-third. By no means: for when the value has risen one-third, the demand may still exceed the supply; there may, even at that higher value, be a greater quantity wanted than is to be had; and the competition of buyers may still continue. If the article is a necessary of life, which, rather than resign, people are willing to pay for at any price, a deficiency of one-third may raise the price to double, triple, or quadruple. Or, on the contrary, the competition may cease before the value has risen in even the proportion of the deficiency.

A rise, short of one-third, may place the article beyond the means, or beyond the inclinations, of purchasers to the full amount. At what point, then, will the rise be arrested? At the point, whatever it be, which equalizes the demand and the supply. [Bk. III, Ch. 2]

The minimum exchange value is cost of production; otherwise the commodity will not continue to be produced. Under competition, if output of the commodity can be expanded indefinitely, this minimum value will also be the maximum. If price is above cost of production, capital will rush in to share in the extra gain. In other words, the exchange values of things depend on cost of production if they can be indefinitely increased. If they cannot be indefinitely increased, supply and demand determine value.

Mill accepted Ricardo's Law of Rent and Say's Law of Markets. To Ricardo's endorsement of free international trade because of the Law of Comparative Cost, Mill added the Law of International Values, one of his important original contributions to economic analysis. He sought to discover how the benefits of international trade were divided among the trading nations.

Within a country, where capital flows freely, the values of commodities depend on their costs of production; but the value of an imported product depends on the cost of production of the thing that is exported to pay for it. The terms of international exchange depend on the strength and elasticity of demand for each product in the foreign country.

Suppose ten yards of cloth made in England cost as much as fifteen yards of linen, and in Germany as much as twenty. If there were no transport costs, the limits of the terms of trade between the two countries would be ten yards of cloth for between fifteen and twenty yards of linen.

Now suppose that Germany increases the efficiency of producing linen, so that she produces thirty yards with the same effort that formerly produced twenty. How will these gains be divided between the two countries? If ten yards of cloth formerly exchanged for seventeen yards of linen, would they now exchange for twenty-five and a half yards? This would hold only if the elasticity of demand for linen in England were unitary, so that she would spend the same portion of her income on linen as formerly. But if the demand for linen in England were elastic (greater than one), she would buy up linen even before its price fell by the full amount indicated by its reduced cost of production; the ratio of exchange might settle at ten yards of cloth for twenty-one of linen, and Germany would get most of the benefits of her increased efficiency in producing linen. If, however, the English demand for linen were inelastic, the price would have to fall considerably to induce England to buy the increased output which Germany could produce with the same effort. Germany would have to offer more than twenty-five and a half yards of linen for ten yards of cloth, and most of the gains would go to England. Mill implicitly assumed that under any given technological conditions, output could be changed without altering unit costs of production.

The first three books of his *Principles*, said Mill, covered the economic laws of a stationary and unchanging society in equilibrium. This he called Statics. In the final two books he added a theory of motion, of progressive changes and ultimate tendencies—Dynamics. In Book IV, "Influence of the Progress of Society on Production and Distribution," Mill forecast increasing production and population; continuing growth of man's mastery over nature; increasing security of person and property; a growing role for corporations. Improvements in industrial production would be offset by diminishing returns in agriculture and mining as population would continue to grow.

Mill, like Smith and Ricardo, thought that the rate of profit would continue to fall, but for different reasons.

There is at every time and place some particular rate of profit, which is the lowest that will induce the people of that country and time to accumulate savings, and to employ those savings productively. This minimum rate of profit varies according to circumstances. It depends on two elements. One is, the strength of the effective desire of accumulation; the comparative estimate made by the people of that place and era, of future interests when weighed against present. This element chiefly affects the inclination to save. The other element, which affects not so much the willingness to save as the disposition to employ savings productively, is the degree of security of capital engaged in industrial operations. [Bk. IV, Ch. 4]

Social progress tends to diminish the minimum acceptable rate of profit. More security, less destruction by war, reduced private and public violence, improvements in education and justice—all these reduce the risks of investment, and thereby also reduce the minimum necessary rate of profit. In addition, mankind will show more forethought and self-control in becoming more inclined to sacrifice present indulgence for future goals. This too will promote accumulation at lower rates of profit. Reduced risk and increased providence will lower profits and interest in Mill's happy world of the future.

The growth of capital would not cause a glut on the market, for Say's Law of Markets keeps the economy operating at full employment; but the rate of profit would decline. Counteracting forces to this tendency are the waste and destruction of capital values during crises, improvements in production, the inflow of cheap commodities from abroad, and the outflow of capital into colonies and foreign countries.

The final result of progress, Mill thought, was a stationary state. But why, he wondered, must we have a rapid rate of progress? Why not settle for a large production and a more equitable distribution of wealth?

I cannot, therefore, regard the stationary state of capital and wealth with the unaffected aversion so generally manifested towards it by political economists of the old school. I am inclined to believe that it would be, on the whole, a very considerable improvement on our present condition. I confess I am not charmed with the ideal of life held out by those who think that the normal state of human beings is that of struggling to get on; that the trampling, crushing, elbowing, and treading on each other's heels, which form the existing type of social life, are the most desirable lot of human kind, or anything but the disagreeable symptoms of one of the phases of industrial progress. . . . It is only in the backward countries of the world that increased production is still an important object: in those more advanced, what is economically needed is a better distribution, of which one indispensable means is a stricter restraint on population. [Bk. IV, Ch. 6]

As the working classes increase their intelligence, education, and love of independence, their good sense will grow correspondingly. Their habits of conduct will then lead to a population that will diminish in relation to capital and employment. Profit-sharing business and cooperative enterprises, operating within a competitive milieu, will further ameliorate conditions. This is preferable, Mill argued, to a full-blown socialism which, by deprecating competition, would promote monopoly.

In "On the Influence of Government" Mill defended laissez faire and then introduced enough exceptions to smother the idea.

In all the more advanced communities, the great majority of things are worse done by the intervention of government, than the individuals most interested in the matter would do them, or cause them to be done, if left to themselves. The grounds of this truth are expressed with tolerable exactness in the popular dictum, that people understand their own business and their own interests better, and care for them more, than the government does, or can be expected to do. [Bk. V, Ch. 11]

Mill then pointed out that individuals, operating in a market economy, are not necessarily the best judges of how much education society should provide. Child labor should be regulated. Natural monopolies such as gas and water companies should be operated by municipal authorities, or their rates regulated by the state. Where individuals are good judges of their own interests, the government may act to give effect to that judgment; for example, if the workers would gain from reducing the working day from ten hours to nine, it might require government action to win the point. If people are to receive charitable aid, it is desirable that such help come from public authorities rather than from casual and uncertain private charity. Legislators should supervise and regulate colonization schemes—this from a man who was employed all his working life by the East India Company, which controlled British trade with and colonization in India from 1600 to 1858. Government also should do those things that serve the general interests of mankind but which are not profitable to individuals, such as undertaking geographic or scientific exploration. Finally,

In the particular circumstances of a given age or nation, there is scarcely anything, really important to the general interest, which it may not be desirable, or even necessary, that the government should take upon itself, not because private individuals cannot effectually perform it, but because they will not. At some times and places there will be no roads, docks, harbours, canals, works of irrigation, hospitals, schools, colleges, printing presses, unless the government establishes them. [Bk. V, Ch. 11]

John Stuart Mill must appear prominently in any intellectual history of man. His importance was not limited to his being the last great economist of the classical school, the greatest of the orthodox economists during the two generations between Ricardo and Marshall. His first important book was *System of Logic* (1843), which established him as a leading logician. The essays he published, including "On Liberty" (1859), "Considerations on Representative Government" (1861), and "Subjection of Women" (1869), showed him to be an outstanding political scientist, social philosopher, and able champion of the democratic way of life. He looms large as a man of courage and honesty in his trenchant criticisms of the status quo, his support of reforms that were radical in his day, his defense of an idealistic utopian socialism, and his repudiation of the wages-fund doctrine. Cynics may scorn his belief in progress through the development of man's intellectual and moral faculties, but it cannot be denied that he had a noble vision of the perfectibility of man. Mill's warmth, his humanitarianism, his empathy for the poor and lowly, are unusual for a leading theoretician in a science which some people feel is too coldly objective and even dismal.

We take leave of John Stuart Mill to turn to the socialists, who were less compromising.

CHAPTER 9

The Rise of Socialist Ideologies

Hints of socialistic ideas can be found in antiquity. The concepts we are considering are quite recent, however, arising in the early 1800's. Although socialists disagree violently among themselves, three strands of thought characterize them. First, they all repudiate the idea of laissez faire and a harmony of interests among different classes. Second, they advocate collective action and public ownership of enterprise to ameliorate conditions for the masses; public ownership can be undertaken by the central government, local governments, or cooperative enterprises. Third, they all optimistically believe in the perfectibility of man; given the proper environment, the nobility of man will shine in all its glory.

Overview of Socialism

The social background of socialism. The industrial revolution did not lead to the millennium. The security of the old agricultural-village-handicraft economy was shattered. The new industrialism erected large factories, with the workers living crowded around them in noisome and pestilential slums where vice, crime, disease, hunger, and misery were a way of life. Industrial accidents brought scant or no compensation for the families of the maimed and the killed. There were no political rights for wage-earners, and their unions were proscribed. Every ill wind that reduced production and employment compounded the misery of the proletariat. Every new triumph of industrialization threw additional tens of thousands of impoverished handicraft workers onto the labor market. The poverty of the masses seemed increasingly oppressive as great fortunes multiplied. As George Crabbe wrote in *The Village* in 1783:

> Where Plenty smiles, alas! she smiles for few,
> And those who taste not, yet behold her store,

Are as the slaves that dig the golden ore,
The wealth around them makes them doubly poor.

No wonder John Stuart Mill, a century after the beginning of the industrial revolution in England, believed that "Hitherto it is questionable if all the mechanical inventions yet made have lightened the day's toil of any human being. They have enabled a greater population to live the same life of drudgery and imprisonment, and an increased number of manufacturers and others to make fortunes."

The rise of Marxian socialism was given additional force by the failure of the utopian socialists to persuade capitalists to join in humanitarian movements.

The essence of socialism. Here we shall define the various forms of socialism, and of capitalism which it sought to replace.

Capitalism has as its essential characteristics private ownership of capital and land, and the predominance of the profit motive operating as a guiding force in a market system. In free-enterprise, laissez faire capitalism, competition rather than monopoly or oligopoly prevails, and there is a minimum of government regulation; prices, freely formed in the market, guide production and distribution. But capitalism can also be controlled or regulated either by government or by monopolistic organization in business and in the labor market through unions. Then it might be called a *private*-enterprise economy rather than a *free*-enterprise economy. But it is still capitalism.

State capitalism means that a government in a capitalist milieu owns and operates industries for maximum profit or minimum loss, as a private entrepreneur would. The state is the entrepreneur, operating an island of public enterprise in the surrounding sea of private enterprise. When Bismarck had the state take over the railways in Germany, he was a state capitalist, not a socialist. When the New York City government took over the bankrupt and obsolete private subway systems (at a price that caused the stock of the subways to rise on the exchanges), that was an example of state capitalism.

State socialism occurs when a government, existing in a capitalistic framework, undertakes to own and operate sectors of the economy for over-all social objectives rather than for profit. Examples in the United States would be the federal social security system, the Tennessee Valley Authority, and the publicly owned canals. Historically the state socialists were those who considered the state an impartial power that could be influenced to favor the working class if the vote were extended and the workers educated and organized. Then the state would take over enter-

prises and become the employer, or it could foster and subsidize cooperatives. Louis Blanc, to be discussed later, was a state socialist. So was
Ferdinand Lassalle, who is alleged to have made a secret agreement with
Bismarck to support his expansionist policies in return for an extension of
the vote to wage earners; Lassalle urged the organization of cooperative
producers' associations under the benevolent guidance of the state, with
the government using its public credit for raising the necessary capital.

The present British economic system, according to these definitions,
would be mixed—predominantly capitalist, but including elements of state
capitalism and state socialism. In the United States the admixture of the
latter two would be smaller; in India, larger.

Utopian socialism dates from about 1800 on, with the Compte de Saint-
Simon, Charles Fourier, and Robert Owen as the founders. They developed their ideas at a time when the industrial workers were still weak,
unorganized, demoralized by the rapid changes of the industrial revolution, deprived of the franchise, and not yet aware of their latent power.
The utopian socialists regarded the competitive capitalist market economy
as unjust and irrational. They worked out in their minds perfect social
arrangements and then appealed to the whole world to adopt them. They
preached universal brotherly love rather than class struggle, and they
looked to the capitalists to cooperate with and finance their schemes. Model
cooperative communities were elaborated in their imagination, and some
were actually tried, usually unsuccessfully.

Christian socialism developed in England and Germany after 1848, with
Charles Kingsley a leading advocate of this idea in England. It arose after
the defeat of radical movements in both countries. The workers were offered the solace of religion to assuage their pain and to give them hope.
The Bible was to form the manual of the statesman, the employer, and the
worker. God's order was mutual love and fellowship. Property owned by
the rich was to be held in trust for the benefit of everybody. This movement, repudiating violence and class struggle, advocated sanitary reform,
education, factory legislation, and cooperatives.

Anarchism, with Pierre-Joseph Proudhon as one of its early proponents,
holds that all forms of government are coercive and should be abolished.
As Mikhail Bakunin (1814–76) said, "The State is the root of the evil."
Anarchists do not conceive of a society without order, but of an order
arising out of self-governing groups through voluntary or associative effort. Human nature, they contend, is essentially good if not corrupted by
the state and its institutions. Private property also should be eliminated,
being replaced by collective ownership of capital by cooperating groups.
Anarchists envisioned communities engaging in production and carrying
on trade with other communities, with associations of producers con-

trolling agricultural, industrial, and even intellectual and artistic production. Associations of consumers were expected to coordinate housing, lighting, health, food, and sanitation. For specific purposes, still wider groups might embrace a whole country, or possibly several countries. Mutual understanding, cooperation, and complete liberty would characterize anarchist society. Individual initiative would be encouraged, and every tendency to uniformity and centralized authority would be effectively checked. Although the methods for achieving their goals differ, the ideal anarchist community resembles the final aim of other socialists.

Marxian socialism resuscitated Ricardo's labor theory of value and added to it a theory of exploitation of the wage earners by the capitalists. It is based on the materialist conception of history: In every historical epoch, the prevailing method of production and exchange and the social organization following from it form the basis for legal, political, cultural, and intellectual superstructures. As each social system develops its productive forces, the relations of production become a barrier to further progress. Then the system has to be changed, revolutionized, so that the new productive relations among men permit the higher development of the forces of production. The mechanism for overthrowing old societies is the class struggle. Thus slavery, the earliest form of class society, developed the productive forces to the maximum possible under that system, and then was followed by feudalism. This system was superseded by capitalism, which in turn inevitably will be overthrown by the proletariat, who will establish socialism. The state was viewed as an instrument of force used by one class against another. The capitalist state oppresses the workers. The working class, in overthrowing the bourgeois state, will establish its own dictatorship of the proletariat to destroy the bourgeoisie as a class.

Under socialism private property in consumer goods is permitted. But the capital and land are publicly owned by the central government, local authorities, or cooperatives promoted and regulated by the state. Production is planned, as is the rate of investment, with the profit motive and the free market eliminated as guiding forces for the economy.

Communism is the next higher stage of society, according to Marxism. The socialist slogan is "From each according to his ability, to each according to his work." Under communism it will be "From each according to his ability, to each according to his need." This presupposes a superabundance of goods, the elimination of money payments based on work performed, and a devotion to society as selfless as a person's loyalty to his family is at present. The state will wither away when antagonistic classes disappear, and the government over men will be replaced by the administration over things such as large railway systems and coal-iron-machinery complexes.

The so-called communist countries have established socialism or are in the process of establishing it. Communism exists nowhere except as small cooperative communities, usually motivated through a common religious or other crusading fervor, where people work together, pool their earnings, and draw from the common fund the things they need.

Revisionism, with Eduard Bernstein a leading advocate, followed the rise of Marxism in Germany. In England the Fabian socialists were revisionists, but they never had adhered to Marxism to any significant degree as had the German left-wing movement. Revisionism abjured the class struggle, denied that the state is a class institution, and pinned its hope on education, electioneering, and gaining control of government through the ballot. The government was to regulate monopolies, control factory working conditions, take over some public utilities, and gradually extend its ownership of capital. As the revisionists, and especially the Fabian branch, favored municipal ownership of public utilities, it has sometimes been called "gas and water socialism."

Syndicalism was promoted and popularized in labor circles in the Latin countries of Europe by Georges Sorel (1847–1922). Syndicalists were antiparliamentarian and antimilitarist. They believed that socialism deteriorates into bourgeois beliefs when it engages in political and parliamentary activity. If represented in parliament, the movement will degenerate into opportunism to gain political influence. What the workers require is one big union that will not play the bourgeois game of seeking social reform and the amelioration of conditions. The union must not dabble in strike and insurance funds, union contracts, union treasuries, or piecemeal reform. Strikes must be fomented to stir up the revolutionary consciousness and militancy of workers; frequently sabotage was advocated by the syndicalists as a weapon in the class struggle. Eventually the general strike of the one big union will overthrow capitalism. Then each industry will be organized as an autonomous unit managed by the workers, and these units will be combined in a federation which will become the administrative center. The syndicalists expected coercive government to disappear.

Apparently syndicalism differed from anarchism in that the former relied exclusively on revolutionary unionism and the general strike for the overthrow of government. But both favored the abolition of private property and the extinction of political government. The Industrial Workers of the World, organized in the United States in 1905, was an example of a syndicalist union.

Guild socialism's major advocate was G. D. H. Cole (1889–1959), a professor of economics at Oxford University. It remained primarily a British movement, a movement of gradualism and reform, which reached its height around the time of World War I. The guild socialists accepted the state as a necessary institution for the expression of the general interests of citizens as consumers. The actual management of industries was to be entrusted to the employees (the producers) organized in their industrial guilds, rather than to the government. But the government was to develop over-all economic policy on behalf of the whole community, not merely for the workers. Every worker would have the status of a partner in the enterprise for which he worked; this was the essence of the "industrial democracy" that guild socialists favored. The nation would no longer be divided into opposing camps of capital and labor; instead, it would be divided into producers and consumers, with each having its national association—the guild and the government. They would form a partnership of equals.

What groups of people did socialism serve or seek to serve? The more moderate groups (utopian and Christian socialism) claimed to represent everybody's interests, with primary emphasis on the needs and interests of the workers. They did serve the workers by arousing the conscience of society and inspiring middle-class reformers, thereby promoting reform legislation. To the extent that they diverted workers from organizing unions and political parties to promote their own interests, they served the employers and landowners. Christian socialism arose at a time when socialist doctrines were gaining ground among the workers. Its adherents felt that the radical movement must be Christianized or Christianity would lose its appeal.

The more extreme socialist groups (Marxists, anarchists, and syndicalists) proclaimed class warfare against the rich; they aimed at promoting the interests of the working class. Their agitating and organizing helped win concessions from the capitalists through vigorous trade union activity, parliamentary pressure, or the threat of revolts.

How was socialism valid, useful, or correct in its time? Workers had legitimate grievances against laissez faire capitalism as it developed in its early decades. In the early 1800's utopian socialism expressed the disturbed conscience of humanity. Marxian socialism offered an involved theoretical dissection of contemporary society that exposed and perhaps exaggerated all its evils. But it and other socialist criticisms had a certain validity in their time. The two problems of poverty and recurring business depressions were not faced squarely by the spokesmen for the status quo. The socialists performed a real service by concentrating their fire on these unsolved problems. Marx also correctly predicted the growth of monopoly. He contributed the evolutionary approach to the study of society and social problems, strengthening the idea that social institutions grow and change historically and are relative to their environment. His theory of economic development was impressive at the time. His ideas won considerable popularity in Europe where class lines were clearly drawn and the working class was at the bottom of the social and economic ladder, where the dominant classes fully intended to keep them.

Socialism played a historically useful role by promoting factory acts, sanitary reforms, cooperative associations, unions, pensions, workmen's compensation laws, and so on.

How did socialist doctrines outlive their usefulness? They have not, in a sense. One-third of the people of the world live under regimes basically guided by Marxian economics. Perhaps another third of the people either live under governments that are guided to a considerable extent by socialist aspirations (India, Indonesia, Sweden), or they are large socialist minorities in a non-socialist milieu (Japan, Italy, France).

Socialists who sought reforms have outlived their usefulness to the extent that non-socialist groups have instituted the changes they advocated. Had the social programs and labor's position of today been proposed in 1850 in Great Britain and the United States, it would have looked like a bloody revolution. The socialists' minimal demands have been more than fulfilled. The capitalist system undertook reforms without giving up its property because the workers grew stronger, because of the fears that if a little was not given much more would be taken, because the system grew richer and could afford to offer more, because middle-class reformers worked for reforms, and because capitalists as a group can give up what one capitalist could not because it would weaken his competitive position.

Revolutionary socialism made a number of remarkably accurate predictions, but enough of its forecasts turned out to be incorrect to vitiate its role and function. Marx extrapolated into the future the trends of the past. He believed that the absolute impoverishment of the working class would continue, meaning that the standard of living would continue to fall. It is difficult to see how the terrible conditions of the wage earners even in mid-nineteenth-century Britain, which Marx pictured so well by quoting official government reports, could have become much worse. He had a better case for the relative impoverishment of the workers, which he also predicted; this means that if workers' incomes rise, the capitalists' incomes rise even faster. There is a sound basis for this belief, for it is well known that the second million dollars is much easier to acquire than the first. But Marx did not foresee that unions, political action, and government intervention could curb this tendency.

Marx predicted the disintegration and decline of the middle class. The upper echelons would merge with the bourgeoisie, while the lower strata would be ground down into the ranks of the proletariat. This would mean a polarization of the whole population into two opposing classes. Marx's typical middle-class man was the small businessman who owned his own capital. The belief that small business would be overcome in competition with big business was a brilliant economic forecast. But he did not foresee that a new middle class would arise—self-employed professional people, salaried scientists, engineers, teachers, salesmen, advertisers, administrators, etc.

The hard-bitten, grasping capitalists, according to Marx, would exploit labor to the utmost of their ability, thereby driving the workers into revolutionary activity. This was not due to any inherent meanness or other defect of the capitalist mentality. It was an inexorable law of the social system. In the competition among capitalists, the generous or easy-going or incompetent employer would go under. The state, which acted as the executive committee of the bourgeoisie as a whole, would guarantee those conditions that would perpetuate wage slavery. Marx did not believe that the state could be influenced to ameliorate conditions. Nor did he understand that the interests of the capitalist class as a whole do not necessarily coincide with those of each individual among them. Thus, it is in the interest of a single employer to cut wages; but if all cut wages, their market for goods is reduced. Therefore the class as a whole can live with minimum wage laws. Again, a capitalist may resist to the utmost the granting of pensions. But when all have to grant them under identical terms, the burden is not so great as when only one must sacrifice his competitive position by incurring such a cost. Unions frequently negotiate pensions, with the employer paying the difference between the federal social security pension and the negotiated benefit; in such situations, employers frequently join their employees in pressing for larger government pensions to reduce their own payments. Such class collaboration is very un-Marxian.

Marx predicted a falling rate of profit and ever worsening crises, which would make the capitalist system untenable. While he recognized certain counteracting tendencies to the falling rate of profit, he underestimated their importance. And he did not foresee massive government intervention in the economy to reduce the severity of fluctuations.

Marx erred in expecting revolutions first in the most advanced industrial countries and in many countries simultaneously or in rapid succession. He and Engels underestimated the force of nationalism when they ended *The Communist Manifesto* (1848) with "The proletarians have nothing to lose but their chains. They have a world to win. Workingmen of all countries, unite!" The tentacles of imperialism, it was believed, would not be disengaged from the colonies except with fire and sword; yet we have seen political freedom obtained with only a moderate degree of violence by India, Gold Coast, French Guinea, and other colonies. Capitalism has not demonstrated the bull-headed obstinacy assumed by Marx, and has indicated a greater ability to adjust to new circumstances than he thought possible.

Many socialists of various persuasions have been disappointed with the way the system developed in Soviet Russia. The reorganization of society was, hopefully, to represent a new flowering of freedom, of collective activity for the common good, of better standards of morality and justice, of greater security for the individual, of a cultural renaissance. During the Stalin dictatorship these dreams turned to gall and wormwood among millions of dreamers of a socialist utopia. Even with the post-Stalin thaw in the Soviet Union, one wonders how much room there is for independent thinking and for dissent from orthodoxy when the state is the dominant employer. One wonders whether the state as an instrument of force has thwarted the growth of democracy and individuality. And one cannot help wondering if the all-powerful state will ever wither away.

The socialist principle of "From each according to his ability, to each according to his work" is difficult to apply equitably. It is feasible within a particular trade that lends itself to a piece-rate system. If one worker sews twice as many buttonholes as another, he will get twice the pay. But how much more productive is a factory superintendent than a tool-and-die-maker? How many times more money should a poet get than a worker on an automated assembly line? In the Soviet Union, income payments are quite arbitrary, helping to create a group of loyal, highly paid intellectuals and administrators, and an impoverished mass of unskilled workers. The inequality of incomes among a Russian factory's employees probably is greater than among those in an American factory, if we consider the incomes of factory employees only from the superintendent level on down.

Socialism presents formidable problems, not only in the sphere of income distribution, but in the allocation of productive resources as well. How much should go for consumption goods, and how much for investment? Which consumption goods should be produced, and how many of each? What are the alternatives if the only supplier of a good offers shoddy wares? How can the masses of people make their voices heard and their wishes known to the top government planners who make decisions that vitally affect the humblest individual in the farthest corner of the land? The socialist regimes and their populations are beset with stupendous problems which their leading theoreticians of the past and present have not solved successfully.

Saint-Simon

THE COMPTE DE SAINT-SIMON (1760–1825) came from an impoverished family of the nobility. He fought on the colonial side in the American Revolution. During the early stages of the French Revolution he renounced his title. At the height of the Revolution he became a big speculator in the nationalized land of the Church and of the *emigrés,* buying on credit and later paying in rapidly depreciating *assignats.* He served a term in prison but was released after the fall of Robespierre. Later he abandoned the role of financier to become a philosopher and prophet. With reckless extravagance he entertained and subsidized promising young scientists, artists, and scholars. This prodigality soon left him penniless, and he lived for several years at the home of a former servant. On the death of his mother, Saint-Simon surrendered his rights of inheritance in return for a small pension from his family. Being in a desperate financial position in 1823, he fired seven pistol bullets at his head but survived with the loss of an eye.

Saint-Simon, a utopian socialist, developed his ideas before the political movement of the working class in France had taken shape. He therefore made no appeal to the working class to struggle against their employers. Regarding idleness as a sin, he made a religion of work and industry. An industrial parliament, he wrote, should consist of three chambers—invention, review, and execution. The first, composed of artists and engineers, would plan public works. The second chamber, run by scientists, would examine the projects and control education. The third chamber would consist of the leaders of industry who would carry out the projects and control the budget. This was one of the earliest attempts to work out a centrally planned economy governed by an educated elite.

Saint-Simon rejected the fundamental assumption of the classical economists that the interests of the individual automatically coincided with the general interest. He insisted that a new ethic was required to restrain the antisocial egoism of the rich and an anarchic uprising of the poor. Humanitarian concern for the working class was a dominant theme in his later writings.

Saint-Simon's attack on idlers led his followers to oppose the laws of inheritance and urge the collective ownership of property. They organized a school after his death which became almost a religion. The Saint-Simonian enthusiasm for large-scale industry helped inspire big banks, railways, highways, the Suez Canal, and huge industrial undertakings.

A few selections from Saint-Simon's works will illustrate his ideas.*

The sole aim of our thoughts and our exertions must be the kind of organization most favourable to industry—industry understood in the widest sense, including every kind of useful activity, theoretical as well as practical, intel-

* F. M. H. Markham, ed., *Henri Comte de Saint-Simon, Selected Writings* (Oxford, Blackwell, 1952) pp. 70–74, 77–80. By permission of Basil Blackwell.

lectual as well as manual. . . . Our desire is that men should henceforth do consciously, and with better directed and more useful effort, what they have hitherto done unconsciously, slowly, indecisively and too ineffectively. . . . Now, in my opinion, the time has come when the general revolution common to all civilized peoples in every land will come about. Governments will no longer order men about; their functions will be limited to ensuring that useful work will not be hindered. They will no longer have more than a small amount of power or money, for these functions will not require much. The money required for useful undertakings on a small or large scale will be supplied by voluntary subscription, and the subscribers will themselves supervise the spending and administration of their own money.

Suppose that France suddenly lost fifty of her best physicists, chemists, physiologists, mathematicians, poets, painters, . . . engineers, . . . bankers, . . . business men, . . . farmers, . . . miners, . . . metal-workers, . . .; making in all the three thousand leading scientists, artists, and artisans of France.

These men are the Frenchmen who are the most essential producers, those who make the most important products, those who direct the enterprises most useful to the nation, those who contribute to its achievements in the sciences, fine arts and professions. They are in the most real sense the flower of French society; they are, above all Frenchmen, the most useful to their country, contribute most to its glory, increasing its civilization and prosperity. The nation would become a lifeless corpse as soon as it lost them. . . . It would require at least a generation for France to repair this misfortune. . . .

Let us pass on to another assumption. Suppose that France preserves all the men of genius that she possesses in the sciences, fine arts and professions, but has the misfortune to lose in the same day Monsieur the King's brother [and other members of the royal household]. . . . Suppose that France loses at the same time all the great officers of the royal household, all the ministers (with or without portfolio), all the councillors of state, all the chief magistrates, marshals, cardinals, archbishops, bishops, vicars-general, and canons, all the prefects and subprefects, all the civil servants, and judges, and, in addition, ten thousand of the richest proprietors who live in the style of nobles.

This mischance would certainly distress the French, because they are kind-hearted, and could not see with indifference the sudden disappearance of such a large number of their compatriots. But this loss of thirty-thousand individuals, considered to be the most important in the State, would only grieve them for purely sentimental reasons and would result in no political evil for the State.

In the first place, it would be very easy to fill the vacancies which would be made available. There are plenty of Frenchmen who could fill the function of the King's brother as well as can Monsieur. . . . The ante-chambers of the palace are full of courtiers ready to take the place of the great household officials. . . . As for the ten thousand aristocratic landowners, their heirs could need no apprenticeship to do the honours of their drawingrooms as well as they.

The prosperity of France can only exist through the effects of the progress of the sciences, fine arts and professions. The Princes, the great household officials, the Bishops, Marshals of France, prefects and idle landowners contribute nothing directly to the progress of the sciences, fine arts and professions. Far from contributing they only hinder, since they strive to prolong the supremacy existing to this day of conjectural ideas over positive science. They inevitably harm the prosperity of the nation by depriving, as they do, the scientists, artists, and artisans of the high esteem to which they are properly entitled. They are harmful because they expend their wealth in a way which is of no direct use to the sciences, fine arts, and professions: they are harmful because they are a charge on the national taxation, to the amount of three or four hundred millions under the heading of appointments, pensions, gifts, compensations, for the upkeep of their activities which are useless to the nation. . . . Society is a world which is upside down. The nation holds as a fundamental principle that the poor should be generous to the rich, and that therefore the poorer classes should daily deprive themselves of necessities in order to increase the superfluous luxury of the rich.

Saint-Simon was arrested and tried for this heresy in 1819, but was acquitted.

The richest and most powerful men have an interest in the growth of equality, since the means of satisfying their wants increases in the same proportion as the levelling of the individuals composing the community. . . . Scientists, artists and industrialists, and the heads of industrial concerns are the men who possess the most eminent, varied, and most positively useful ability, for the guidance of men's minds at the present time. . . . They . . . are the men who should be entrusted with administrative power. . . .

The community has often been compared to a pyramid. I admit that the nation should be composed as a pyramid; I am profoundly convinced that the national pyramid should be crowned by the monarchy, but I assert that from the base of the pyramid to its summit the layers should be composed of more and more precious materials. If we consider the present pyramid, it appears that the base is made of granite, that up to a certain height the layers are composed of valuable materials, but that the upper part, supporting a magnificent diamond, is composed of nothing but plaster and gilt.

The base of the present national pyramid consists of workers in their routine occupations; the first layers above this base are the leaders of industrial enterprises, the scientists who improve the methods of manufacture and widen their application, the artists who give the stamp of good taste to all their products. The upper layers, which I assert to be composed of nothing but plaster, which is easily recognizable despite the gilding, are the courtiers, the mass of nobles whether of ancient or recent creation, the idle rich, the governing class from the prime minister to the humblest clerk. The monarchy is the magnificent diamond which crowns the pyramid.

Here are revolutionary implications indeed! Despite these extreme statements, Saint-Simon misses being a socialist in one respect: He did not advocate the appropriation of private property, though some of his disciples did.

Fourier

CHARLES FOURIER (1772–1837) was an eccentric utopian socialist who slowly acquired a large and devoted following late in life and posthumously. He was by no means a revolutionary. His appeals usually were addressed to the wealthy or the king. Son of a middle-class merchant family which lost most of its possessions during the French Revolution, he was a clerk in various cloth houses and other businesses. A poor laborer all his life, his education had to be acquired in spare moments in library reading rooms.

Fourier was a critic of capitalism. Unlike Saint-Simon, he disliked large-scale production, mechanization, and centralization in all their forms. Competition, he thought, multiplies waste in selling, and businessmen withhold or destroy commodities to raise their prices. Commerce to him was pernicious and corrupt, and he laid bare the material and moral poverty of the bourgeois world. He denounced a society that "accords its high protection to the agents of famine and pestilence." He criticized the "progress of financiering, systems of extortion, indirect bankruptcy, anticipations of revenue, art of devouring the future." Under "progress of the mercantile spirit" he included "consideration accorded to commercial plundering and knavery. Stock-jobbing raised to a power which scoffs at law, encroaches upon all the fruits of industry, shares in the authority of governments, and propagates everywhere the frenzy of gambling in the public funds."*

Fourier's solution to social problems was to organize cooperative communities called *phalansteries* or *phalanxes*. His love of order, symmetry, and precision drove him to elaborate plans for these communities down to the most insignificant details. Each association would combine three hundred families—eighteen hundred people—on nine square miles of land. Everybody would live in a palace-like dwelling three stories high which he described minutely. Agricultural and handicraft production would predominate. The output of wealth would increase tenfold over incoherent private industry. One large granary would be more economical to build and easier to guard against fire than three hundred small ones. People living together in honor and comfort would eliminate theft and the expense of guarding against it. Collective work would improve climatic conditions, and fewer clothes would be required. The economies of a common kitchen

* Julia Franklin, tr., *Selections from the Works of Fourier* (London, 1901), pp. 93–94.

and apartments rather than separate dwellings were carefully calculated. The *phalanx* would solve the major problem, which was not the inequality of wealth, but its insufficiency.

Who would do the "dirty work" in this utopian colony? The children. Children love dirt, and they love to organize into gangs. Instead of thwarting these natural tendencies, they should be directed into useful social functions, such as doing the most disagreeable work. Meanwhile children should learn a variety of trades, so that as adults they would not be overspecialized and limited to a single task.

After the minimum of subsistence was provided for each member of a *phalanx* regardless of his own contribution to the enterprise, the surplus would be divided five-twelfths to labor, four-twelfths to capital, and three-twelfths to talent and skill. Therefore an appeal could be made to capitalists to finance such a project on the basis of earning a satisfactory return on the investment. In fact Fourier announced to the world that he would be at home every day at noon to await a capitalist who would underwrite an association. For the rest of his life he waited in vain. But many *phalanxes* were started throughout the world by his followers.

In the United States the movement was popularized before the Civil War by Albert Brisbane, Horace Greeley, George Ripley, and others. Of the forty Fourierist *phalanxes* organized in this country, all of which failed, the best known were the North American Phalanx, located near Red Bank, New Jersey, which lasted from 1843 to 1856; and Brook Farm, which was organized in 1841 near Boston. Among its members and interested visitors were Charles A. Dana, Nathaniel Hawthorne, Ralph Waldo Emerson, Amos Bronson Alcott, Margaret Fuller, Theodore Parker, Orestes Bronson, and William Henry Channing. A disastrous fire in 1846 ended the experiment.

Perhaps the closest approach at present to Fourier's *phalanxes* can be seen in the communes of China. They, of course, have gone far beyond him in enforcing centralized control and planning and in promoting large-scale enterprise.

Fourier showed much originality, and his ideas have remained influential even though he is seldom credited with having pioneered over new and uncharted ground. Cooperative living was central in his thinking. This was the way to change the environment in order to generate an entirely new and noble type of man. The *phalanxes* would provide cradle-to-grave or womb-to-tomb social security. As a minimum in the early stages of his ideal society, he advocated "guaranteeism," the assurance that every person would be given a minimum of subsistence, security, and comfort. The idea that gangs of children should do the dirty work was a preview of the process of assigning workers to tasks according to their aptitudes; this is an interesting way of solving, in a non-price society, one of the problems of resource allocation. Fourier's objection to overspecialization anticipated by a hundred years the warning that routine assembly-line work warps and thwarts the individual although it greatly expands his output. The Fourierist *phalanxes*, though failures, were not ignominious failures; they influenced the labor movement at the time, and they inspired much thought on how to eliminate the wastes of private enterprise and on how to promote a better economic system. The cooperative movement is in part a living monument to Fourier.

Sismondi

SIMONDE DE SISMONDI (1773–1842) was a Swiss economist and historian of French descent. He and his family took refuge in England during the revolutionary disturbances of 1793–94. On their return, they sold most of their property and bought a small farm in Italy, which they worked themselves. Sismondi returned to Geneva, where he wrote many scholarly works. Among them was a sixteen-volume *History of the Italian Republics of the Middle Ages*, and a twenty-nine-volume *History of the French*.

Sismondi was among the first to launch a direct attack on classical economics, although he had been an ardent follower of Adam Smith in his earlier years. While he never was a socialist in the modern sense, he paved the way for socialist thought. In 1819, after viewing the appalling conditions in England following his absence of twenty-four years, he published *New Principles of Political Economy*. In this book he stated that unrestricted capitalist enterprise, far from yielding the results that Adam Smith and J. B. Say expected of it, was bound to lead to widespread misery and unemployment. His criticisms of Say's Law of Markets and his denial that a free-enterprise economy tended toward full employment were stated fairly early in the rise of modern industrial society; John Stuart Mill a half century later and the neoclassical economists more than a whole century later were still proclaiming the impossibility of general gluts. Sismondi, raising the possibility of overproduction and crises, was one of the early contributors to business-cycle theory. He thought that when wages are at the subsistence level, more capital funds become available for investment in machines. The output of manufactured goods is thereby increased, while the demand for consumption goods is simultaneously reduced. The consequence is that the system can be maintained only by the periodic crises which liquidate a large part of the capital overinvested in large-scale industry. Bankers, by extending credit, worsen the problem of overproduction and crises. As the concentration of wealth narrows the home market more and more, industry is increasingly compelled to open up foreign markets, which necessarily results in nationalistic wars. Sismondi thus explicitly formulated the charge that economic imperialism is inherent in capitalism.

Only state intervention would insure to the worker a living wage and a minimum of social security. Sismondi denied that the largest possible aggregate production necessarily coincided with the greatest happiness of the people. A smaller output, well distributed, would be preferable. The state, therefore, should enact laws regulating distribution in the general interest. Small-scale family farming, as opposed to tenant farming, would promote a good distribution of income. He also urged small-scale production in the towns to avoid producing more than could be sold. Agriculture should be promoted at the expense of urbanization. He favored inheritance taxes; curbing new inventions by discontinuing patent rights so that "the zeal for such discoveries will grow cold"; compelling employers to provide security for their workers in old age, illness and unemployment; cooperation and solidarity between workers and employers; and profit sharing.

Sismondi was concerned not merely with too large production poorly distributed, but also with too small production, which reflected the conflict between the individual and the social interest. The peasant, he thought, tries to increase his gross product, while the large landowner is concerned only with his net revenue. Suppose, he said, a well-cultivated piece of land produces a total output of 1000 shillings of which 100 go to the proprietors as rent. If the land is let out as pasture, it would yield 110 shillings rent. The proprietor would therefore dismiss his tenants in order to gain 10 shillings, while the nation loses 890 shillings.

Sismondi introduced the term "proletary." They were the men in the Roman republic who had nothing, paid no taxes, and who could contribute only their offspring, the "proles," to the country.

Sismondi was relatively modern in his prescription for curing a glut in a particular industry:

The government ought, in fact, to come to the assistance of men, and not of industry; it ought to save its citizens, and not business. Far from making advances to the master manufacturer, to encourage him to manufacture to a loss, it ought largely to contribute funds to take the operatives from an employment which increases the embarrassment of all their fellow citizens. It ought to employ them in those public works whose products do not bear upon the markets, and do not increase the general glut. Public edifices, town-halls, markets, public walks, are native wealth, though not of a kind that can be bought and sold. . . .

But in assisting the workmen in any depressed industrial business by public works, government must adhere principally to the following rules:—not to compete with an existing business, and thus bring fresh disturbances into the markets; not to make of those works which it orders and pays for a permanent occupation, to which will be attached a new class of day-labourers—*proletarii* —but to make them perceive how long it will last, and where it will end, that they may not marry in this precarious state. . . .

On whatever side we look, the same lesson meets us everywhere, *protect the poor,* and ought to be the most important study of the legislator and of the government. . . . Protect the poor, that they may keep . . . that share of the income of the community which their labour ought to secure to them; protect the poor, for they want support, that they may have some leisure, some intellectual development, in order to advance in virtue; protect the poor, for the greatest danger to law, public peace and stability, is the belief of the poor that they are oppressed, and their hatred of government; protect the poor, if you wish industry to flourish, for the poor are the most important of consumers.*

Sismondi was not exactly a socialist so much as a social critic and a dissenter from classical theory. His strong interest in the business cycle and his humanitarian views set him apart from the orthodox economists of his day and inspired the socialists; but he made no fundamental attack on the institution of private property.

Owen

ROBERT OWEN (1771–1858) was the most spectacular and the most famous of the utopian socialists. Son of a Welsh shopkeeper, he attended school only two years. At nine he went to work in a neighboring store as a shop-boy, and later he was employed in dry-goods stores. At eighteen he borrowed a hundred pounds and set up a partnership with a mechanic who could make the revolutionary new textile machinery. When his partner left him, Owen set himself up in business, using the machines he had on hand. He was successful, but a better opportunity came his way; he became manager of one of the largest and best-equipped spinning mills in Lancashire while still under twenty, with five hundred workers under him. Owen was the first spinner in Britain to use American sea-island cotton. His employer offered him a partnership, but instead he started a new company for the manufacture of yarn. Again highly successful, at twenty-nine he bought the New Lanark Mills in Scotland from David Dale, whose daughter he married soon afterward; the spinning mills became the largest and best equipped in Scotland.

By examining Owen's ideas, we can see what led him to become a factory reformer, pioneer socialist, advocate of cooperatives, trade union

* Simonde de Sismondi, *Political Economy and the Philosophy of Government* (London, 1847), pp. 220, 221, 223. [Originally published from 1826 to 1837.]

leader, founder of utopian communities, and theorist in the field of education. His central thesis was that human nature is molded, for better or worse, by the environment. Man cannot form his own character; it is, without a single exception, formed for him. As character is made by circumstances, men are therefore not responsible for their actions, and they should be molded into goodness instead of being punished for being bad. All of Owen's theories, dreams, and programs, like Fourier's, were based on the belief that providing better conditions would produce better people. And one should try to serve the community and thereby achieve one's own highest happiness. This was the reverse of classical economics and Benthamite thinking, which held that self-interest will serve society.

In an essay published in 1813, Owen wrote:

Any general character, from the best to the worst, from the most ignorant to the most enlightened, may be given to any community, even to the world at large, by the application of proper means; which means are to a great extent at the command and under the control of those who have influence in the affairs of men. . . .

The happiness of self, clearly understood and uniformly practised . . . can only be attained by conduct that must promote the happiness of the community. . . .

These plans must be devised to train children from their earliest infancy in good habits of every description (which will of course prevent them from acquiring those of falsehood and deception). They must afterwards be rationally educated, and their labour be usefully directed. Such habits and education will impress them with an active and ardent desire to promote the happiness of every individual, and that without the shadow of exception for sect, or party, or country, or climate. They will also ensure, with the fewest possible exceptions, health, strength, and vigour of body; for the happiness of man can be erected only on the foundations of health of body and peace of mind.*

Owen proceeded to convert the New Lanark Mills into a model community, a show place inspected by distinguished visitors from all over the world. On arriving there, he found five hundred pauper children living in the factory boarding house, serving seven- to nine-year apprenticeships. They started working at six years of age, and their working day, summer and winter, was twelve hours, six days a week. There also was a factory village to house families of workers, who lived in poverty, crime, debt, sickness, and misery. Yet David Dale, the former owner, was far more humanitarian than most employers.

Owen introduced his reforms to prove that character could thereby be

* Robert Owen, *A New View of Society and Other Writings* (London, 1927), pp. 16, 17, 20.

reshaped for the better. He discontinued the use of pauper children. Youngsters were not admitted into the factory until they were ten, and free schooling was available to them between the ages of five and ten. For the preschool children he founded an infant school or nursery, the first in Britain. He wanted children to grow up happily in a healthy environment. Comfortable houses were built for the families who worked at New Lanark. Food, fuel, and clothing were sold to the workers at cost. The working day was reduced to ten and a half hours, and wages were high. He paid his employees during slack times and sickness, gave them old age insurance, and provided adult educational and recreational facilities. Fines and punishments, so characteristic of the time, were abolished. Owen reformed his employees, who worshipped him, and still he made good profits. But his partners objected to such extravagance. Twice he had to buy out his partners and acquire new ones. This third and last partnership, formed in 1814, included Jeremy Bentham. They agreed to limit their dividends to 5 per cent on invested capital and to use all surplus revenue in the interests of the employees. Owen withdrew from his business in 1829.

This great textile manufacturer shocked the world when he denounced all established religions because they taught that men were responsible for their evil ways, instead of attributing evil to bad environment. He preached social rather than moral reformation. Even he himself was a mere product of forces over which he had no control:

Causes, over which I could have no control, removed in my early days the bandage which covered my mental sight. If I have been enabled to discover this blindness with which my fellow-men are afflicted, to trace their wanderings from the path which they were most anxious to find, and at the same time to perceive that relief could not be administered to them by any premature disclosure of their unhappy state, it is not from any merit of mine; nor can I claim any personal consideration whatever for having been myself relieved from this unhappy situation. But, beholding such truly pitiable objects around me, and witnessing the misery which they hourly experienced from falling into the dangers and evils by which, in these paths, they were on every side surrounded,—could I remain an idle spectator? . . .

No! The causes which fashioned me in the womb,—the circumstances by which I was surrounded from my birth, and over which I had no influence whatever, formed me with far other faculties, habits, and sentiments. These gave me a mind that could not rest satisfied without trying every possible expedient to relieve my fellow-men from their wretched situation, and formed it of such a texture that obstacles of the most formidable nature served but to increase my ardour, and to fix within me a settled determination, either to overcome them, or to die in the attempt.*

* *Ibid.*, p. 108.

Owen always did things for the people instead of relying on their own initiative. He pleaded with his brother manufacturers to follow his example. Why not care for your living machines as well as your inanimate machines? he asked. If you will help the workers, he said, you will increase your own happiness and intellectual enjoyment. He appealed to the government to enact factory legislation, and was mainly responsible for the Factory Act of 1819, although he repudiated it as being far weaker than he wished. During the slump following the end of the Napoleonic Wars, Owen urged that the government should employ the poor in "villages of cooperation," modeled after his own establishment at New Lanark. Having failed to persuade either capitalists or government to follow his example, he himself promoted a model cooperative community to show the way. In 1825 he established the New Harmony colony on thirty thousand acres in Indiana, which he bought from the Rappites; that sect did not have much of a future, as its followers believed in celibacy. This type of organization, Owen thought, would sweep away capitalism and the competitive system. While Fourier had allowed profit on the capital invested in utopian colonies, Owen favored only a fixed rate of interest until the owners of capital voluntarily gave it up, as he believed they would. Within three years the colony failed and Owen had lost four-fifths of his $250,000 fortune. Other villages of cooperation, established later in Great Britain, also failed.

Owen now found himself at the head of a growing army of working class disciples. The modification of the British anti-union laws in 1825 was followed by the considerable growth of trade unionism. Workers also promoted cooperatives as the forerunners of Owen's "villages of cooperation." He placed himself at the head of both movements. In 1832 he founded the National Equitable Labour Exchange as a market where products could be exchanged on the basis of notes representing labor time. His hope was to eliminate money and profit, twin social evils, by bringing producers and consumers into direct contact with one another. Although this experiment failed in two years, his followers founded the Rochdale Pioneers' Co-operative Society in 1844; this was the beginning of a highly successful consumers' cooperative movement in Great Britain, inspired by Owen but far from the producers' cooperatives he had hoped for to replace capitalism.

Disappointment in the Reform Act of 1832, which left the workers voteless, led to an upsurge of unionism and later the Chartist movement. Owen plunged into union activity by promoting the Grand National Consolidated Trades Union in 1833. It soon recruited half a million members. Hasty strikes and bitter lockouts followed. There was internal dissension, with Owen opposing militant action, conflict, and strikes. He suddenly ordered the union dissolved in 1834, after six farm laborers were sentenced to transportation to Australia for seven years for administering secret oaths. But many of the constituent trade unions in the Grand National reorganized themselves as separate societies, living on to become the nuclei of the modern British union movement.

Owen had a significant impact on socialism as well as on cooperation and unionism. The word "socialism" in the modern sense was first used in the Owenite *Co-operative Magazine* in 1827 to designate the followers of Owen's cooperative doctrines. It was formed from the word "social" as opposed to "individual," as applied to the ownership of capital. His sharp criticisms of capitalism, his dream of collective action to organize cooperative communities based on large-scale industry, inspired a whole generation of socialists. He himself at the end of a long life became a spiritualist.

Owen had four sons, all of whom became United States citizens. The oldest, Robert Dale Owen (1801–77) sat in Congress, drafted a bill founding the Smithsonian Institution, represented the United States as ambassador to Italy, and advocated birth control, emancipation for the slaves, women's rights, and free public education.

Blanc

LOUIS BLANC (1811–82), commonly regarded as a founder of state socialism, was a French social reformer, journalist, and historian. He came from a royalist family. His grandfather, a prosperous merchant, was guillotined during the first French Revolution, and the family was impoverished after Napoleon fell. The publication of his *Organisation du Travail* in 1839 brought him fame and a position of leadership in the socialist movement. In the revolution of 1848 he was elected to the provisional government that overthrew the monarchy, the first avowed socialist to be elected to public office anywhere. Under pressure of Blanc and his followers over the issue of the right to work, the government organized National Workshops to give work to the unemployed. This make-work scheme, consisting mostly of common labor on public works, was deliberately mismanaged by Blanc's political enemies. To disperse the National Workshops, the government gave the men employed there the alternative of entering the army or leaving Paris for the provinces. The Paris workmen threw up barricades in revolt, but the army blasted them with artillery. In four days of fighting at the end of June 1848, there were sixteen thousand people killed on both sides, according to the British ambassador. Blanc had to flee to England, returning to France in 1870. He was elected to the National Assembly, where he ended his days as a mild social reforming deputy.

In Blanc's view universal suffrage would transform the state into an instrument of progress and welfare. Uncompromising in his attacks on capitalism and competition which he said would ruin both the laboring class and the bourgeoisie, he was opposed to the doctrine of class war. Even trade unionism was condemned by him, for he saw in strikes the futility of unprepared, isolated action. The solidarity of the entire community would promote state economic planning for full employment, the development of welfare services, government capital for getting national workshops started, and workers' cooperatives financed and promoted by the government. The state should become "the banker of the poor" by establishing a publicly owned bank to distribute credit to cooperatives. Capitalists could join the associations, receiving a fixed rate of interest guaranteed by the state for their capital. He believed that producers' associations aided by the state would attract the best workers and drive the capitalists out of business by superior competitive efficiency. Capitalism would simply fade away.

Blanc's attitude toward the state was expressed succinctly in his little book, *A Catechism of Socialism* (1849):

Q.–How are we to pass from the present order of things to that which you contemplate?
A.–By the intervention of Government.
Q.–What is the Government or State?
A.–It is a body of upright and distinguished men, chosen by their equals to guide us all on our way to liberty. . . .
Q.–Does not the word Government or State imply an idea of tyranny?
A.–Yes; wherever power is something distinct from the people.

In his *Organization of Work*, Blanc wrote:

Who would be blind enough not to see that under the reign of free competition the continuous decline of wages necessarily becomes a general law with no exception whatsoever? . . . The population increases steadily; command the mothers of the poor to be sterile and blaspheme God who made them fruitful; for if you do not command it, the space will be too small for all strugglers. A machine is invented; demand it to be broken and fling an anathema against science! Because if you do not do it, one thousand workmen, whom the new machine displaces in the workshops will knock at the door of the next one and will force down the wages of their fellow-workers. A systematic lowering of wages resulting in the elimination of a certain number of laborers is the inevitable effect of free competition. . . .

The government ought to be considered as the supreme regulator of production and endowed for this duty with great power. This task would consist of fighting competition and of finally overcoming it. The government ought to float a loan with the proceeds of which it should erect *social workshops* in the most important branches of national industry. . . . It would use competition as a weapon, not to destroy private industries without consideration, which would be to its own interest to avoid, but to guide them imperceptibly into the new system. Soon, indeed, workmen and capitalists would crowd to every industrial sphere where social workshops are opened, on account of the privileges they offer to their members. . . . Everybody, irrespective of position, rank or fortune, is interested in the creation of a new social order.*

Blanc's foremost contribution was to popularize the socialist ideas that arose before he appeared on the scene. He rejected the self-contained and diversified Owenite and Fourierist communities which were to undertake cooperative consumption as well as production. Instead, he favored cooperative producers' societies in each trade, with the workers operating their specialized workshops and selling their products to the rest of society. The large-scale enterprise he envisaged required large capital investments. Therefore Blanc, unlike other advocates of cooperation, looked to the government to supply the initial capital and the starting impetus.

Kingsley

CHARLES KINGSLEY (1819–75) was a clergyman, poet, novelist, and reformer. He was chaplain to Queen Victoria, professor of modern history at Cambridge, and canon of Westminster. Early in his career he and the other Christian socialists wanted to "socialize the Christian and Christianise the socialist." Kingsley was swept along by the Chartist movement when he went to London during the turbulent times of 1848. He shocked and angered the aristocrats when he announced at a public meeting, "I am a Chartist!" while the workers cheered.

Why was this vehement declaration so shocking to the respectable and the powerful? The Chartists had six demands: equal electoral districts; universal suffrage, including women; voting by secret ballot; parliaments elected annually; no property qualifications for serving in the House of Commons; and payment to members of parliament. By 1928 these demands were all enacted into law except annual parliaments. They no longer seemed terribly radical. What, then, was all the excitement about in 1848? First, reforms are dangerous when they are wrested from the rulers by mass agitation and action; they are much safer when handed down from above. Revolutionary movements are likely to go much further than the reforms that they demand, and small victories simply spur them on. Second, large numbers of Chartists were undertaking military training, preparing for possible insurrection, and they were striking and rioting. Third, Chartists threatened to elect a people's parliament to meet at Birmingham

* Louis Blanc, *Organization of Work*, Maria P. Dickoré, tr. (Cincinnati, 1911), pp. 16, 51–53, 59. [Originally published in 1839.]

with half a million workers to protect it. No wonder Kingsley's declaration was shocking to many.

The Christian socialists issued a weekly journal in 1848 called *Politics for the People*. Kingsley wrote a series of "Letters to Chartists" over the signature "Parson Lot." His second letter included a passionate defense of the poor:

My friends,—If I was severe on some of you in my last letter, believe me, it is not because I do not feel for you. There are great allowances to be made for most of you. If you have followed a very different 'Reformer's Guide' from mine, it is mainly the fault of us parsons: we have never told you that the true Reformer's Guide, the true poor man's book, the true 'God's Voice against Tyrants, Idlers, and Humbugs,' was the Bible. Ay, you may sneer, but so it is; it is our fault, our great fault, that you should sneer—sneer at the very news which ought to be your glory and your strength. It is our fault. We have used the Bible as if it was a mere special constable's handbook—an opium-dose for keeping beasts of burden patient while they were being overloaded—a mere book to keep the poor in order. We have told you that the powers that be were ordained of God, without telling you who ordained the impotences and imbecilities that be, alas, sometimes! We have told you that the Bible preached to you patience, while we have not told you that it promised you freedom. We have told you that the Bible preached the rights of property and the duties of labour, when (God knows!) for once that it does that, it preaches ten times over the *duties of property* and the *rights of labour*. We have found plenty of texts to rebuke the sins of the poor, and very few to rebuke the sins of the rich. You say that we have not preached to you; really I think we have preached to you a great deal more than your fair share. For, for one wholesome rating that we have given the rich, we have given you a thousand. I have been as bad as any one, but I am sick of it.

In his third letter he was more moderate and more typically Christian socialist:

My friends,—and when I say friends, I speak honestly, and from the bottom of my heart, for you and I are, after all, I believe, longing for the same thing —*to see all humbug, idleness, injustice swept out of England;* only I think you are going, if not the wrong road, yet certainly neither the shortest, the safest, nor the wisest road, to gain the good end.

My friends, I have to tell you that in the Bible you will find what you long for, promised more fairly than any man in these days promised it you; that in that book you will find what you want to say, said for you; you will find how much of what you want to see done, God wants to see done. Let me try if I cannot prove my words somewhat.

What are the things which you demand most earnestly? Is not one of them, that no man shall enjoy wages without doing work?

The Bible says, at once, that *"he that will not work, neither shall he eat;"* and as the Bible speaks to rich as well as poor, so is that speech meant for the idle rich as well as for the idle poor. . . .

I entreat you, I adjure you, to *trust the Bible,* to trust my samples from it, and *to read it honestly for yourselves,* and see if it be not the true *Radical Reformer's Guide*—God's everlasting witness against oppression, and cruelty, and idleness.

Elsewhere Kingsley wrote: "God will only reform society on condition of our reforming every man his own self—while the devil is quite ready to help us to mend the laws and the parliament, earth and heaven, without ever starting such an impertinent and 'personal' request."

Kingsley repudiated mass meetings, physical violence, union strikes, and hatred of the rich by the poor. The rich were ignorant, not hostile. His doctrines included love, religion, cooperative associations, sanitary reforms, and education. After a few years he abandoned his intense activities on behalf of Christian socialism except for his continuing interest in the sanitary movement.

Proudhon

PIERRE-JOSEPH PROUDHON (1809–65) promoted anarchism as a mass movement. He was fiercely proud of his humble origins. His father was a poor cooper and brewer, and his mother had been a farm maid. They tried to promote his education as best they could, in spite of extreme poverty. As a young man he became a printer and proofreader, and he experienced his share of unemployment and imprisonment for his writing.

Liberty of the individual and justice were the goals Proudhon proclaimed. The ideal system is anarchism, which means not disorder, but the absence of a master, a sovereign. As he wrote in *What Is Property?* (1840):

In a given society, the authority of man over man is inversely proportional to the stage of intellectual development which that society has reached. . . . As man seeks justice in equality, so society seeks order in anarchy. . . . Every question of domestic politics must be decided by departmental statistics; every question of foreign politics is an affair of international statistics. The science of government rightly belongs to one of the sections of the Academy of Sciences, whose permanent secretary is necessarily prime minister; and since every citizen may address a memoir to the Academy, every citizen is a legislator. But, as the opinion of no one is of any value until its truth has been proven, no one can substitute his will for reason—nobody is king.*

* Pierre-Joseph Proudhon, *What Is Property?* Benjamin R. Tucker, (tr. London, no date), pp. 264–265. [Originally published in 1840.]

In 1851 Proudhon attacked government in the following manner:

Experience, in fact, shows that everywhere and always the Government, however much it may have been for the people at its origin, has placed itself on the side of the richest and most educated class against the more numerous and poorer class; it has little by little become narrow and exclusive; and, instead of maintaining liberty and equality among all, it works persistently to destroy them, by virtue of its natural inclination towards privilege. . . . We may conclude without fear that the revolutionary formula cannot be *Direct Legislation,* nor *Direct Government,* nor *Simplified Government,* that it is NO GOVERNMENT. Neither monarchy, nor aristocracy, nor even democracy itself, in so far as it may imply any government at all, even though acting in the name of the people, and calling itself the people. No authority, no government, not even popular, that is the Revolution. . . . Governing the people will always be swindling the people. It is always man giving orders to man, the fiction which makes an end of liberty.*

"What is property?" asked Proudhon. "Property is theft." By property he really meant large property that permitted its owner to live without working by exacting rent, interest, and profit from the producers. He favored small-property ownership of dwellings, land, tools, and the products of labor by the laborer. Large industries should be owned by associations of workers, with society controlling the associations so that they would charge a just price, as near as possible to cost. Proudhon basically disliked large-scale machinery because he felt it to be incompatible with his small producers' commonwealth. He favored equality of incomes even with inequality of abilities, strength, talents, and output:

Let Homer sing his verse. I listen to this sublime genius in comparison with whom I, a simple herdsman, a humble farmer, am as nothing. What, indeed,— if product is to be compared with product,—are my cheeses and my beans in the presence of his "Iliad"? But, if Homer wishes to take from me all that I possess, and make me his slave in return for his inimitable poem, I will give up the pleasure of his lays and dismiss him. I can do without his "Iliad," and wait, if necessary, for the "Aeneid." Homer cannot live twenty-four hours without my products. Let him accept, then, the little that I have to offer; and then his muse may instruct, encourage and console me.†

To promote individual freedom and equity in exchange, Proudhon proposed that the gold standard should be abolished. Credit, he said, is what blood is to an animal, but the "bankocracy" has monopolized it. Only bank

* Pierre-Joseph Proudhon, *General Idea of the Revolution in the Nineteenth Century,* John B. Robinson, tr. (London, 1923), pp. 108, 126. [Originally published in 1851.]
† Proudhon, *What Is Property?* pp. 142–43.

paper redeemable in merchandise and services should circulate, and French citizens should have the right to establish banks as they do retail shops. He urged that a Bank of Exchange should be organized with a thousand subscribers. The amount of paper it would issue would be in proportion to the business of these people and negotiable only among themselves. As additional people joined, the circulation of bills would grow. Eventually all of France would be under the same system. The circulation could never be inflated because it would be issued proportionately to the delivery of products. The banks would buy goods from members at between 50 and 100 per cent of the cost of production. This transaction would really be a loan on goods for a limited time, for the producer could sell the goods, pay back the loan, and keep the excess revenue. Or, after the loan matured, the bank would sell the consignment at public auction and pay the original seller the excess of the selling price over the loan after deducting a small commission. Thus interest, a tribute which represented exploitation, would be abolished. Every worker or group of workers could get free credit with which to buy capital goods, and the class structure of society would disappear. Property and labor would be reunited.

Proudhon actually succeeded in organizing a "People's Bank" in Paris in 1849. The basic capital of the bank was to be fifteen million francs in five-franc shares of non-interest-bearing stock, and many thousands of shares had been subscribed. His arrest and trial ended the bank before it could get under way.

Proudhon, the philosophical anarchist, appears to be the mildest sort of reformer; yet the ideas he planted came to fruition among his more militant intellectual descendants.

CHAPTER 10

Marxism and Revisionism

K ARL HEINRICH MARX (1818–83) and Friedrich Engels (1820–95) were the founders and leading theoreticians of Marxian or "scientific" socialism. They also organized and actively led a revolutionary movement that they thought would storm and overturn the citadels of capitalism during their lifetimes. In this they were disappointed, but they never despaired of ultimate triumph. Their movement grew in strength, and they lived to see one revolution of the type they advocated: the Paris Commune, which lasted ten weeks in 1871.

Marx was born in Prussia in a Jewish family that converted to Protestantism during his childhood. He studied law, history, and philosophy at the universities of Bonn, Berlin, and Jena, and received the degree of doctor of philosophy at twenty-three years of age. Two years later he married Jenny von Westphalen, the daughter of a baron who occupied a high government office. She was a most devoted companion to Marx during all the vicissitudes of his career.

University positions were closed to Marx because of his radicalism. He turned to journalism, was exiled from Germany, studied French socialism and English political economy in Paris, was exiled from France at the request of the Prussian government, and finally settled in London. Except for brief visits to the Continent, he lived the rest of his life in England. Marx spent days and years in the Reading Room of the British Museum exploring "the confounded ramifications of Political Economy." Tormented by illness, extreme poverty, and the death of several of his children in infancy, he continued to study, write, and organize. He wrote many articles for the *New York Tribune*, whose payments helped him subsist. He organized and led the International Working Men's Association, the "First International," which lasted from 1864 to 1876. In 1867 he published the first volume of his *magnum opus*, *Capital*. After Marx's death, Engels edited his manuscripts and also published Volumes II and III. After Engels died, the remaining Marx manuscripts were left to the leading Marxian of the time, Karl Kautsky, who published another three volumes under the title *Theories of Surplus Value*.

Friedrich Engels, close friend, coworker, and financial supporter of Marx, was the son of a prosperous German cotton manufacturer. He pursued a dual career. From 1842 until his retirement in 1869, he looked after the family manufacturing interests in Manchester, England. At the same time he was a scholar, writer, and revolutionist. During a brief visit to Paris in 1844 he met Marx (whom he had previously known in 1842), and they remained lifelong friends and collaborators. Together the two young men wrote the *Manifesto of the Communist Party* in 1848. Engels once wrote that he was happy to play second fiddle to Marx. Marx wrote to Engels, "You know I am always slow to grasp things, and that I always follow in your footsteps."

The Labor Theory of Value

MARX sought "to lay bare the economic law of motion of modern society." His starting point was the analysis of commodities in capitalist society. A commodity must be capable of satisfying human wants, whether "they spring from the stomach or from fancy." It may satisfy these wants directly as means of subsistence, or indirectly as means of production. Use values constitute the substance of all wealth. Marx did not try to measure use values quantitatively, nor did he consider diminishing utilities with increasing quantities of a commodity. He would therefore say that a large wheat crop represented greater utility, and therefore greater wealth, than a small wheat crop, even though it might have no greater exchange value.

Besides use value, or utility, a commodity has exchange value, commonly abbreviated as value. What determines the value of a commodity? The socially necessary labor time congealed in it, considering normal conditions of production and the average skill and intensity of labor prevalent at the time. The socially necessary labor time includes the direct labor in producing the commodity; it also includes the labor embodied in the machinery and raw materials that are used up and the value transferred to the commodity during the process of production.

Suppose the average labor time contained in a pair of shoes is ten hours. That determines its value. If a worker is incompetent or lazy and takes twenty hours to produce a pair of shoes, its value is nevertheless ten hours. Suppose a worker or his employer leads the field in technological improvement and efficiency, and a pair of shoes is produced with five hours of labor. Its value nevertheless is ten hours, the average labor cost for society as a whole.

The labor time that determines value is simple average labor. Skilled work counts as multiple units of unskilled, average labor. Thus an engineer's hour of productive effort might contribute as much value to a commodity as five hours of simple labor. The equalization of labor time of different skills to one common denominator of unskilled labor occurs in the market.

The market also arrives at prices that are based on the underlying labor cost. One commodity, such as gold, becomes the universal equivalent that reflects all values. One coat will exchange for two ounces of gold because both require the same amount of socially necessary labor time in their production. If two ounces of gold when coined are worth two pounds, then one coat will sell for two pounds. Temporary fluctuations of supply and demand will cause prices to deviate from true values, sometimes rising above value and sometimes falling below. The continual oscillation of prices allows them to compensate each other and reduce themselves to average prices that reflect the values of commodities.

Marx's labor theory of value differed from Ricardo's in that the former held that labor time determined the *absolute* value of goods. Ricardo believed that the *relative* values of different goods were proportional to the labor time embodied in each. Marx's version of the labor theory opened the door to a theory of exploitation by assuming that all value was created by labor, and the owner of capital goods had no legitimate claim to any of the product.

The Theory of Exploitation

MARX assumed that all commodities sell at their value. How, then, does the capitalist receive a profit? He does it by purchasing the one commodity that can create a value greater than its own—labor power. Here we must distinguish carefully between Marx's concepts of labor power and labor time. Labor power refers to man's ability to work; labor time is the actual process and duration of work. Labor power is a commodity, bought and sold in the market; labor time is the ingredient that gives all commodities, including labor power, their value. The value of labor power is determined by the socially necessary labor time required to produce the necessities of life that the worker and his family consume. If the subsistence of the worker and his family could be produced in four hours per day, the value of the commodity labor power would be four hours per day, even if the labor time worked per day were eight hours. If the productivity of labor power doubled, so that subsistence could be produced in two hours per day, the value of labor power would fall 50 per cent, from four hours of labor time to two hours; but the value produced by a day's labor of the same duration as previously would still be eight hours. If the productivity of labor were so low that the worker had to consume values equivalent to his own output, the value of a day's labor power would be a day's labor time. Then there would be no profit, no surplus, no exploitation, and no capitalism. Only when the worker can produce more than he must consume in order to survive and to replenish the labor force through reproduction can exploitation arise, according to Marx. The employer pays the worker the full value of his labor power, but the daily pay equals only part of the worker's daily output, and therefore only part of the value he creates. The labor time that the worker spends at work during the day represents a larger sum of values than the value of his own labor power, the cost of subsistence.

In Volume I of *Capital*, Marx illustrated these ideas with a numerical example. Suppose that six hours of socially necessary labor time are embodied in the commodities a worker and his family must consume each day. Then half of the labor of the twelve-hour day (then customary) forms the value of a day's labor power. If half a day's average socially necessary labor time is incorporated in three shillings, then three shillings is the price corresponding to the value of a day's labor power. If this is the wage rate, the worker receives the full value of the one commodity he sells—labor power. (In this illustration the value imparted to a commodity by an hour of labor can also be represented by half a shilling; that is, an hour of labor will produce a quantity of gold which is designated as half a shilling.)

The capitalist employs the laborer, supplying him with the required machinery and raw materials. Suppose the worker in six hours of labor converts ten pounds of cotton into ten pounds of yarn. Assume that the wear and tear of the spindles amounts to four hours of labor or two shillings during the half-day of labor. To explain this assumption, suppose that all the spindles one worker operates will wear out after ten days of working. Assume also that eighty hours were required to manufacture the spindles. These eighty hours are part of the socially necessary labor time required to manufacture the yarn. As the spindles wear out, their value reappears in the yarn. In half a day, the worker uses up one-twentieth of the value of the spindles and transfers it to the yarn; this is four hours.

On the money side, assume that all the spindles a worker uses cost forty shillings. As they will last ten days, two shillings will be transferred to the value of the yarn during each half-day of use.

Thus we assume that the wear and tear of the spindles amounts to four hours of labor or two shillings, and the cotton used up has a value of twenty hours of labor or ten shillings. The total value of the yarn produced in six hours is thirty hours of labor: six for the labor power, twenty for the cotton, and four for the used-up value of the spindles. The total money cost of production is fifteen shillings: three for the labor power, ten for the cotton, and two for the used-up value of the spindles. If profit does not arise from buying cheaply and selling dearly, if all commodities sell at their value, then the yarn must sell for fifteen shillings.

Our capitalist stares in astonishment. The value of the product is exactly equal to the value of the capital advanced. . . . [He] exclaims: "Oh! but I advanced my money for the express purpose of making more money." The way to Hell is paved with good intentions, and he might just as easily have intended to make money, without producing at all. He threatens all sorts of things. He won't be caught napping again. In future he will buy the commodities in the market, instead of manufacturing them himself. But if all his brother capitalists were to do the same, where would he find his commodities in the market? And his money he cannot eat. He tries persuasion. "Consider my abstinence; I might have played ducks and drakes with the fifteen shillings; but instead of that I consumed it productively, and made yarn with it." Very well, and by way of reward he is now in possession of good yarn instead of a bad conscience. . . . Our friend, up to this time so purse-proud, suddenly assumes the modest demeanour of his own workman, and exclaims: "Have I myself not worked? Have I not performed the labour of superintendence and of overlooking the spinner? And does not this labour, too, create value?" His overlooker and his manager try to hide their smiles. Meanwhile, after a hearty laugh, he re-assumes his usual mien. Though he chanted to us the whole creed of the economists, in reality, he says, he would not give a brass farthing for it. He leaves this and all such like subterfuges and juggling tricks to the professors of political economy, who are paid for it. He himself is a practical man; and though he does not always consider what he says outside his business, yet in business he knows what he is about.*

The answer to the riddle that Marx posed about the source of profit lies in the fact that the worker is required to work another six hours without being paid for it. The ten pounds of yarn produced in the second half-day also are worth fifteen shillings, but they cost the capitalist only twelve. Hence his profit or surplus value. It does not matter that part of the industrial capitalist's profit is turned over to the banker in the form of interest, part to the landlord in the form of ground rent, and part to the merchant capitalist in the form of mercantile profits. All property income arises from the exploitation of labor in the productive process.

Within capitalism, said Marx, all labor appears as paid labor, but this is an illusion. Under slavery an opposite error was made: all labor appeared as unpaid, although subsistence for the slave represented partial payment. Only under feudalism was exploitation obvious, when the serf worked part of the time for himself and part for his overlord.

* Karl Marx, *Capital*, Vol. I (Chicago, 1906), pp. 212–15. [Originally published in 1867.]

That part of the capital invested in machinery and raw materials Marx called constant capital (c). The value of this capital is transferred to the final product without any increase. The capital that goes for wages, for the purchase of labor power, is variable capital (v). It produces a value greater than its own. The extra value that it produces, which the capitalist takes without compensating the worker who produced it, is surplus value (s). The rate of surplus value, or the rate of exploitation, is the ratio of the surplus value to the variable capital, or the ratio of total profit to wages, or the ratio of unpaid labor time to paid labor time, or s/v. The rate of profit is the ratio of surplus value to the total capital invested, or $s/(c+v)$.

In Marx's hypothetical example presented above, the rate of surplus value was 100 per cent. If the working day had been extended to fifteen hours, it would have been 150 per cent. If it had been reduced to nine hours, the rate of exploitation would have been 50 per cent. What is the proper length of the working day?

The capitalist maintains his rights as a purchaser when he tries to make the working day as long as possible, and to make, whenever possible, two working days out of one. On the other hand, the peculiar nature of the commodity sold implies a limit to its consumption by the purchaser, and the labourer maintains his right as seller when he wishes to reduce the working day to one of definite normal duration. There is here, therefore, an antinomy, right against right, both equally bearing the seal of the law of exchanges. Between equal rights force decides. Hence is it that in the history of capitalist production, the determination of what is a working day, presents itself as the result of a struggle, a struggle between collective capital, i.e., the class of capitalists, and collective labour, i.e., the working class.*

Surplus value could be increased even if the working day were not lengthened, by reducing the value of labor power through increasing the efficiency of production. If the worker's necessities could be produced in a shorter time, a larger share of the new value would go to the capitalist. Suppose the working day were shortened from twelve hours to ten; but instead of being divided into six hours of paid labor for the worker and six hours for the capitalist, it was divided into four for the worker and six for the capitalist. The rate of exploitation would rise from 100 per cent to 150.

Value and Price of Production

IN VOLUME I of *Capital*, Marx analyzed the capitalist process as a whole, thrusting aside certain complications that become apparent when the de-

* *Ibid.*, p. 259.

tails of an economic system are examined. In Volume III, he considered the problem that troubled Ricardo. If labor is the source of value, the industry that employs much socially necessary labor and little constant capital will be more profitable than the one that uses much constant capital and little labor. Marx presented a hypothetical table showing five different industries with different ratios of constant capital to labor. He assumed that all of the constant capital is used up during a year and its value is entirely transferred to the product. (See Table 1.)

TABLE 1. Varying Rates of Profit Based on Marx's Labor Theory of Value

CAPITALS	RATE OF SURPLUS VALUE	SURPLUS VALUE	VALUE OF PRODUCT	RATE OF PROFIT
I. 80c + 20v	100%	20	120	20%
II. 70c + 30v	100%	30	130	30%
III. 60c + 40v	100%	40	140	40%
IV. 85c + 15v	100%	15	115	15%
V. 95c + 5v	100%	5	105	5%

SOURCE: Karl Marx, *Capital*, Vol. III (Chicago, 1909), p. 183.

Marx then dropped the assumption that all of the constant capital is used up during one year. The larger the ratio of constant to variable capital, the more slowly is the constant capital likely to be used up. Table 2 illustrates this. The last column, Cost Price, is the sum of the constant capital used up and the variable capital expended, or the value of commodities minus surplus value.

TABLE 2. Varying Rates of Profit, with Constant Capital Lasting More than One Year

CAPITALS	RATE OF SURPLUS VALUE	SURPLUS VALUE	RATE OF PROFIT	USED-UP C	VALUE OF COMMODITIES	COST PRICE
I. 80c + 20v	100%	20	20%	50	90	70
II. 70c + 30v	100%	30	30%	51	111	81
III. 60c + 40v	100%	40	40%	51	131	91
IV. 85c + 15v	100%	15	15%	40	70	55
V. 95c + 5v	100%	5	5%	10	20	15
Total 390c + 110v		110	100%			
Average 78c + 22v		22	22%			

SOURCE: Karl Marx, *Capital*, Vol. III (Chicago, 1909), p. 185.

Permanent variations of the rates of profit for different industries are of course untenable where competitive conditions prevail. Capital will flow out of industry *V*, and prices of that industry's products will rise above their value. As capital flows toward industries *II* and *III*, prices there will fall below their values, as shown in Table 3.

TABLE 3. Conversion of Values into Prices of Production

CAPITALS	SURPLUS VALUE	VALUE	COST PRICE OF COMMODITIES	SELLING PRICE OF COMMODITIES	RATE OF PROFIT	DEVIATION OF PRICE FROM VALUE
I. 80c + 20v	20	90	70	92	22%	+ 2
II. 70c + 30v	30	111	81	103	22%	− 8
III. 60c + 40v	40	131	91	113	22%	−18
IV. 85c + 15v	15	70	55	77	22%	+ 7
V. 95c + 5v	5	20	15	37	22%	+17

SOURCE: Karl Marx, *Capital*, Vol. III (Chicago, 1909), p. 185.

Marx called the selling prices of commodities the prices of production. They are defined as cost of production plus the average rate of profit on the total capital invested. According to him, the labor theory of value holds for the capitalist system as a whole. Individual commodities, however, will sell at prices above or below their value in order to equalize rates of profit for the whole economy. "In short, under capitalist production, the general law of value enforces itself merely as the prevailing tendency, in a very complicated and approximate manner, as a never ascertainable average of ceaseless fluctuations."*

The Falling Rate of Profit

IF VALUE and profit are produced only by labor, should not the capitalist invest more in labor power and less in machinery? Why the drive toward more and more efficiency through mechanization and invention? There are two reasons. First, if one capitalist leads in promoting efficient production through the use of more and better machines, he will receive extra profits; the employer who lags behind the trends in his industry will go under. Second, the greater the efficiency of production, the lower the value of labor power, and the more profit is produced per working day.

The increasing proportion of constant to variable capital means that there is a long-run tendency for the rate of profit to fall, even though the amount of profit rises as the labor force grows. Marx thought that this law demonstrated that capitalist production faced internal barriers to its own

* *Ibid.*, Vol. III (1909), p. 190.

indefinite expansion. As machinery displaces labor, an "industrial reserve army" of unemployed is created which further impoverishes the proletariat by forcing wages downward. Larger capital investments for each individual establishment lead to "a growing concentration of capitals (accompanied by a growing number of capitalists, though not to the same extent)."

Marx perceived certain counteracting forces to the falling rate of profit which make it a long-run tendency rather than an inexorable and invariable law. First, the intensity of exploitation can be increased by speeding up the workers or lengthening the working day. Second, wages may be cut below their value. Third, the constant capital can be cheapened. The ratio of constant capital to labor is a *value* relationship, and as machinery and raw materials become cheaper, the fall of the rate of profit is retarded. Fourth, growing relative overpopulation and unemployment is conducive to setting up new industries that use much labor and little capital. The high rates of profit in such industries enter into the average rate of profit for the system as a whole. Fifth, foreign trade raises the rate of profit by cheapening the elements of both constant capital and the necessities of life. In addition, capital invested in colonies yields higher rates of profit because the ratio of constant capital to variable capital is lower, and because the exploitation of colonial peoples is more intense than the exploitation of wage labor at home.

The falling rate of profit is but one of the insoluble problems of capitalism, according to the Marxian analysis. We shall now examine the over-all trends and consequences of capital accumulation.

Capitalist Accumulation and Crises

MARX attacked Say's Law of Markets, saying that it applied only to simple commodity production. The self-employed small artisan, seeking to acquire use values, produces commodities in order to exchange them for others that he wishes to consume. The weaver produces linen, sells it, and uses the money to buy a Bible. The process can be represented by *C-M-C*, with the linen and the Bible representing commodities with equal exchange values and different use values. Money is simply the medium of exchange.

But even under simple commodity production the possibility of crisis exists.

Nothing can be more childish than the dogma, that because every sale is a purchase, and every purchase a sale, therefore the circulation of commodities necessarily implies an equilibrium of sales and purchases. If this means that the number of actual sales is equal to the number of purchases, it is mere tautology.

. . . No one can sell unless some one else purchases. But no one is forthwith bound to purchase, because he has just sold. Circulation bursts through all restrictions as to time, place, and individuals, imposed by direct barter, and this it effects by splitting up, into the antithesis of a sale and a purchase, the direct identity that in barter does exist between the alienation of one's own and the acquisition of some other man's product. . . . If the interval in time between . . . the sale and the purchase becomes too pronounced, the intimate connexion between them, their oneness, asserts itself by producing—a crisis.*

Under large-scale capitalist production the process of exchange becomes M-C-M, buying in order to sell, instead of selling in order to buy under handicraft production. Money is changed into commodities such as labor power, raw materials, and machinery. The products are then sold for money. The process, however, does not make sense if the two M's are equal. Therefore the correct representation of the capitalist process is M-C-M', where M' is larger than M by the amount of surplus value squeezed out of the productive workers. This is the process of expanding investment. "Accumulate, accumulate! That is Moses and the prophets!"

One result of this trend, said Marx, is to centralize large aggregates of capital into few hands.

Capital grows in one place to a huge mass in a single hand, because it has in another place been lost by many. . . . The battle of competition is fought by cheapening of commodities. The cheapness of commodities depends, *caeteris paribus*, on the productiveness of labour, and this again on the scale of production. Therefore, the larger capitals beat the smaller. It will further be remembered that, with the development of the capitalist mode of production, there is an increase in the minimum amount of individual capital necessary to carry on a business under its normal conditions. The smaller capitals, therefore, crowd into spheres of production which Modern Industry has only sporadically or incompletely got hold of. Here competition rages in direct proportion to the number, and in inverse proportion to the magnitudes, of the antagonistic capitals. It always ends in the ruin of many small capitalists, whose capitals partly pass into the hand of their conquerors, partly vanish. Apart from this, with capitalist production an altogether new force comes into play—the credit system.

In its beginnings, the credit system sneaks in as a modest helper of accumulation and draws by invisible threads the money resources scattered all over the surface of society into the hands of individual or associated capitalists. But soon it becomes a new and formidable weapon in the competitive struggle, and finally it transforms itself into an immense social mechanism for the centralisation of capitals.†

* *Ibid.*, Vol. I, pp. 127–28.   † *Ibid.*, pp. 686–87.

The increase of labor-saving machinery and the growth of big business lead to both absolute and relative impoverishment of the workers. The tendency toward absolute impoverishment means that the standard of living of workers will fall. Relative impoverishment means that even if standards of living remain stationary or rise somewhat, the percentage share the workers receive of the new value they produce declines; workers will grow poorer relative to the capitalists' incomes. With the growing "misery, oppression, slavery, degradation, exploitation" of the workers, their will to revolt also grows. "The knell of capitalist private property sounds. The expropriators are expropriated."

Marx and Engels described crises as early as 1848.

Modern bourgeois society with its relations of production, of exchange and of property, a society that has conjured up such gigantic means of production and of exchange, is like the sorcerer who is no longer able to control the powers of the nether world whom he has called up by his spells. For many a decade past the history of industry and commerce is but the history of the revolt of modern productive forces against modern conditions of production, against the property relations that are the conditions for the existence of the bourgeoisie and of its rule. It is enough to mention the commercial crises that by their periodical return put the existence of the entire bourgeois society on trial, each time more threateningly. In these crises a great part not only of the existing products, but also of the previously created productive forces, are periodically destroyed. In these crises there breaks out an epidemic that, in all earlier epochs, would have seemed an absurdity—the epidemic of over-production. . . . And how does the bourgeoisie get over these crises? On the one hand by enforced destruction of a mass of productive forces; on the other, by the conquest of new markets, and by the more thorough exploitation of the old ones. That is to say, by paving the way for more extensive and more destructive crises, and by diminishing the means whereby crises are prevented.*

Later, in analyzing the causes of crises, Marx held that accumulation of capital leads to overproduction relative to "needs with capacity to pay." There is a piling up of improvements, an accumulating development of productive powers. The market expands more slowly than production because of the limited purchasing power of the workers. Crises occur because the profitability of production temporarily disappears, not because the needs of the people are adequately met. The workers *cannot* buy the flood of consumer goods that follows a period of rapid capital investment; and the capitalists *will not*. The falling rate of profit is another aspect of the same problem. Capital accumulation and growing productivity of labor cause both a falling rate of profit and periodic crises.

* Karl Marx and Friedrich Engels, *Manifesto of the Communist Party* (New York, 1948), pp. 14–15.

If accumulation proceeds rapidly enough, the demand for laborers may exceed the supply, and therefore wages may rise. If "the stimulus of gain is blunted," the rate of accumulation is lessened and the price of labor falls as the economy goes into a slump. Crises are therefore inevitable, and rising wages "leave intact the foundations of the capitalistic system."

The system, however, recovers from each crisis, even though the way is paved for more severe crises in the future. How does it recover? Some capital values are destroyed; some factories close; prices of commodities fall; credit contracts; wages fall. The fall in prices and the competitive struggle give every capitalist an impulse to raise profits "by means of new machines, new and improved working methods, new combinations." The depreciation of the value of constant capital tends to raise the rate of profit. "The present stagnation of production would have prepared an expansion of production later on, within capitalistic limits."

After the death of Engels in 1895, revisionism—an offshoot of Marxist orthodoxy—won favor among many socialists throughout the world. We shall now consider two important cases of modifications of Marxian doctrines in the two most significant revisionist movements in Europe: England and Germany.

Fabian Revisionism: The Webbs

IT MAY seem odd to classify the Fabians, who never claimed to be followers of Marx, as revisionists. They preferred to base themselves on Bentham, Ricardo, Mill, and Jevons. Yet their thinking and program influenced Marxian groups almost everywhere, and especially in England and Germany.

The British Fabian Society was organized in 1884, a year after Marx's death in London. It was named after Quintus Fabius Maximus, surnamed Cunctator (the Delayer), the Roman general who did everything hurtful to the enemy except to fight on the field of battle in the war against Hannibal. Though never very large, the society was most influential in the British Labor Party, in government circles, and among intellectuals. It attracted such luminaries as George Bernard Shaw, Sidney Webb, Beatrice Webb, Graham Wallas, H. G. Wells, John Galsworthy, Bertrand Russell, R. H. Tawney, and Harold Laski.

The Fabians undertook prodigious research and educational activities. They favored trade unionism, factory acts, extension of the ballot, tax reform, consumer cooperatives, government regulation of industry, social legislation, and the nationalization of key industries. Repudiating the doctrines of class struggle and revolution, they worked to introduce significant reforms by influencing government leaders, forming alliances with liberal groups, and promoting the Labor Party. Ultimately an enlightened electorate would, in the name of social justice, slowly and peacefully socialize the basic means of production, with local, regional, and national agencies managing industries.

In international affairs the Fabians were imperialists. They supported the British side in the Boer War and in World War I. In *Fabianism and the Empire,* written by George Bernard Shaw and revised and published in 1900 by the Fabian Society as its official position, imperialism was explicitly endorsed. Great Britain should become the nucleus of one of the world empires of the future rather than stupidly lose its colonies and be reduced to a tiny pair of islands in the North Sea. A Great Power must govern in the interests of civilization as a whole.

Sidney Webb (1859–1947), the son of lower-middle-class parents, became a government clerk several years after completing his college education at sixteen. Later he was admitted to the bar. He possessed a very orderly mind, a prodigious memory, a passion for social justice, and an unusual skill in maneuvering people in high places to promote his program of social reform. Public administration was far more interesting to him than economic and social theory. He served in Parliament and as a cabinet minister in successive Labor governments. His wife Beatrice (1858–1943) was the daughter of a big financier and railway magnate. Her interest in social problems was intensified during a month's visit with her Lancashire cousins who were impoverished factory workers. Her independent income enabled Sidney to leave the civil service after they were married. Together they formed a brilliant research team which she called "the firm of Webb."

The Webbs founded the London School of Economics and Political Science (now a part of the University of London). They also helped organize the influential weekly *New Statesman.* This indefatigable pair published forty-five volumes, in addition to numerous pamphlets, articles and essays. For their books on trade unionism, they ransacked the archives of all important unions throughout Great Britain. In their research on local government, they examined the records of hundreds of villages and towns and attended meetings of local government bodies. To see how a sweatshop industry looked from the inside, Beatrice Webb learned tailoring and obtained employment as a "plain trouser hand."

The Webbs believed that consumers' cooperatives and unions would ultimately replace capitalism with the "Cooperative Commonwealth." They had no faith in producers' cooperatives, such as agricultural credit banks and creameries. Such organizations seek more profit and are therefore a part of the capitalist system. They exclude their own employees from membership. When agricultural cooperatives unite with capitalist combinations in monopolizing the distributive trades, they become a public danger. Producers in different industries (and even within the same industry) have diverse interests, but consumers are united. Farm organizations should sell to consumer cooperatives, and the latter should compete with municipalities and national government organizations in manufacturing.

As a result of the disillusionment that followed World War I, the Webbs in 1923 came forth with a sharp indictment of capitalism in *The Decay of Capitalist Civilization*. Following the great crash and depression, they published in 1935 a eulogy of the Soviet Russian system in their two-volume work, *Soviet Communism: a New Civilization?*

German Revisionism: Bernstein

THE German Social Democratic Party was the largest Marxist party in the world before World War I. It operated vigorously in a country that produced the two founders of "scientific socialism," where the conditions of laborers were worse than in France and England. Yet, in spite of the party's dogmatic enthusiasm for Marx's doctrines, it turned increasingly toward revisionism.

The leading advocate of this new and moderate approach to socialism was Eduard Bernstein (1850–1932). He was a political exile from Germany from 1881 to 1901 because of Bismarck's Anti-Socialist Laws. In Switzerland he was coeditor of the *Sozialdemokrat*, the organ of his party which was smuggled into Germany in large numbers. When that country expelled him in 1888, he went to London where he was associated with Engels in his last years, and with the Fabians, whose approach to politics appealed to him. After returning to Germany, he served in the Reichstag for eighteen years.

Beginning in 1896, a year after Engels' death, Bernstein began urging the revision and modernization of Marx. He argued that social conditions did not sharpen class conflicts as Marx and Engels had predicted in *The Manifesto of the Communist Party* in 1848. The common interest would increasingly gain an ascendancy over the private interest. The severity of crises had diminished. The middle classes did not disintegrate and disappear. The concentration of capital did not occur in all branches of production. Shareholdings were being diffused among increasing numbers of people. In all technically advanced countries the privileges of the capitalists were yielding to democratic institutions. Working-class organizations were growing stronger. Factory acts, democracy in local government, freeing trade unions and cooperatives from legal restrictions, humane labor conditions in work undertaken by public authorities—all these characterized the new, evolutionary approach toward the amelioration of capitalism. Bernstein denied the Marxian concept that socialism is the necessary outcome of an objective historical process. Instead he substituted the idea of socialism as the goal of civilized mankind, free to choose its future to conform to higher ethical and moral standards.

Bernstein repudiated the anti-imperialism and working-class internationalism of the Marxists.

But has social democracy, as the party of the working classes and of peace, an interest in the maintenance of the fighting power? From many points of view it is very tempting to answer the question in the negative, especially if one starts from the sentence in the *Communist Manifesto:* "The proletarian has no fatherland." This sentence might, in a degree, perhaps, apply to the worker of the 'forties without political rights, shut out of public life. To-day in spite of the enormous increase in the intercourse between nations it has already forfeited a great part of its truth and will always forfeit more, the more the worker, by the influence of socialism, moves from being a proletarian to a citizen. The workman who has equal rights as a voter for state and local councils, and who thereby is a fellow owner of the common property of the nation, whose children the community educates, whose health it protects, whom it secures against injury, has a fatherland without ceasing on that account to be a citizen of the world. . . .

Just as little as it is to be wished that any other of the great civilised nations should lose its independence, just as little can it be a matter of indifference to German social democracy whether the German nation, which has indeed carried out, and is carrying out, its honourable share in the civilising work of the world, should be repressed in the council of the nations.

. . . The Imperial Government will think ten times before venturing on a war which has social democracy as its determined opponent. . . . But . . . where really important national interests are at stake, internationalism can be no reason for a weak yielding to the pretensions of foreign interested parties. . . .

If we take into account the fact that Germany now imports yearly a considerable amount of colonial produce, we must also say to ourselves that the time may come when it will be desirable to draw at least a part of these products from our own colonies. . . . If it is not reprehensible to enjoy the produce of tropical plantations, it cannot be so to cultivate such plantations ourselves. . . . Only a conditional right of savages to the land occupied by them can be recognised. The higher civilisation can ultimately claim a higher right.*

Bernstein's views were voted down at Social Democratic Party congresses in 1899 and 1901. Yet in practice the party became increasingly revisionist. It supported the fatherland in World War I and voted for military appropriations in the Reichstag. Bernstein himself voted for war credits twice in 1914, abstained twice in 1915, and finally voted against additional funds for the military.

* Edward Bernstein, *Evolutionary Socialism*, Edith C. Harvey, tr. (New York, Huebsch, 1909), pp. 169–71, 178–79.

Eduard Bernstein died at eighty-two, six weeks before Hitler became chancellor. But his ideas lived on and triumphed once again in West Germany. In November 1959 the German Social Democratic Party voted officially to bury its Marxist past. It renounced class struggle, extended a friendly hand to organized religion, endorsed private property of capital goods, favored parliamentary democracy, and declared for "free competition in a free economy." The old socialist demand for the socialization of industry was replaced by the principle that "effective public controls" must prevent "misuse of the economy by the powerful." National defense was declared to be the duty of every citizen.

CHAPTER II

The German Historical School*

THE GERMAN historical school arose in the 1840's, with major publications by Friedrich List and Wilhelm Roscher. It ended by World War I, when Gustav Schmoller died. By then the ideas of this school, along with its methodology, had been modified and absorbed into the marginalist and institutionalist schools.

Overview of the German Historical School

The social background of the school. The peace treaty after the Napoleonic wars left Germany divided into thirty-nine separate states, most of them monarchical, almost all of them undemocratic. The victorious great powers of Europe manipulated Germany to promote their own ulterior purposes. Austria wanted Germany weak and divided. Britain wanted a strong Prussia to thwart a future resurgent France. Russia wanted the rest of Poland not yet seized by Germany or Austria.

The German struggle against Napoleon had aroused patriotic and nationalistic emotions. Many Germans demanded unification and constitutional reforms. The quest for national unity was frustrated for about half a century. The aspirations toward democracy remained unrealized for over a century, and then were achieved only briefly under the most adverse conditions, as the result of a lost war.

In 1815 the Holy Alliance of Prussia, Austria, and Russia was organized as a means of defeating revolution wherever it might threaten. Minor revolutionary outbursts in Germany from 1830 to 1832 were repressed, and the major upheavals of 1848 were crushed by Prussian and Austrian troops.

Prussia, the largest, richest, most militaristic, and most powerful state

* This chapter has benefited substantially from Professor Jack C. Myles's unpublished Ph.D. thesis at Princeton University, *German Historicism and American Economics*, 1956.

in Germany, dominated the country. Foreign intrigue promoted Prussia as a powerful ally. Foreign and native conservatism saw in Prussia a bulwark against democracy and socialism. Native nationalists relied on Prussia to forge a unified Germany. Prussians dominated the German government and armed forces. A series of successful wars further strengthened nationalism under Prussian hegemony. Advanced social legislation, enacted by Bismarck, revealed the paternalism of the monarchy and evoked further loyalty and patriotism among the German workers. Bismarck bragged that in Germany the kings made the revolutions.

Some key economic institutions of nineteenth-century Germany differed substantially from those in Britain. Therefore the same economic ideology could not apply to both countries. Mercantilistic regulations persisted in Germany at least until the formation of the Empire in 1871, long after they disappeared from the British scene. Competition and freedom of enterprise, which the classicists took for granted in their economic analyses, were severely restricted. Because of the large bureaucracy that administered and regulated manifold phases of economic life, the science of public administration was highly developed. British theories were obviously inapplicable to the German situation. The historical school defended and rationalized the German way of life by questioning the historical relevance of economic doctrines.

The Germany that gave birth to the historical school had been divided, weak, and primarily agricultural. Nationalism, patriotism, militarism, paternalism, devotion to duty, hard work, and massive government intervention all combined to change the pattern and promote industrial growth. Germany was far behind England in the development of industry, and she required government assistance to help her catch up.

The essence of the German historical school. There were four principles that were basic in the thinking of this school.

1. The historical school was evolutionary in its study of society. It concentrated on cumulative development and growth. An analogy was sometimes drawn to Darwin's evolutionism in biology: the social organism is born, develops and grows, and finally decays and dies. Society is constantly changing. Therefore what is relevant economic doctrine for one country at a particular time may be inappropriate for another country or another age. This approach was especially useful in attacking classical economics as being suitable for England but not for Germany.

2. The historical school was nationalistic, while classical economics was individualistic and cosmopolitan. If the social organism is the center of study, if it is the force for dynamic movement, then society and the state rather than the individual occupy the center of the stage. In Germany it

was the state that fostered industry, transportation, and economic growth. In the process of defending a unified economy, it was easy to develop an ardent nationalistic glorification of the state. The historical school gave great prominence to the role of the state and the need for its intervention in economic affairs. It was felt that the community had interests of its own that were quite distinct from those of the individual.

3. The economists of the historical school emphasized the importance of historical research. They criticized the abstract, deductive, static, unrealistic, and unhistorical qualities of classical and marginalist methodology. They undertook massive inductive studies, using primary source material, studying changing social institutions. The school professed to study, with its historical method, *all* the forces of an economic phenomenon, *all* the facets of economic behavior, and not merely the economic logic of it. Some of the historical economists became antitheory, denying that there were any valid economic laws, with one exception. They believed that patterns of development were discernible in history and could be generalized into "laws of development."

4. The historical economists were reformers, although of a conservative persuasion. They thought the German state should be entrusted with ameliorating conditions for the common man. This would strengthen loyalty to the state while it safeguarded the health, well-being, and efficiency of the factory workers. Reforms, they hoped, would also divert the working class away from socialistic ideology. The advocates of moderate social changes were dubbed "Socialists of the Chair," a reference to the academic positions they held.

What groups did the German historical school serve or seek to serve? First, its members served themselves. They enjoyed close and friendly relations with government officials, and they rose to a dominant position in academic life, with the government controlling most universities. Schmoller, known as the "professor maker," controlled most academic appointments in Germany through his influence at the Prussian Ministry of Education. His students and followers were placed in academic posts while the German adherents of the Austrian marginalist school were excluded from university positions.

This school also served the German imperial government well by defending its role and functions in a nationalistic state.

The historical economists served the dominant business, financial, and landowning groups by promoting moderate reforms which frustrated the drive for a more radically democratic transformation of society. Instead of the poor and lowly fighting and winning their own battles for improvements, concessions were handed down to them by a paternalistic state. As a result, servility, nationalism, and loyalty to the regime were more wide-spread in Germany than almost anywhere else.

How was the German historical school valid, useful, or correct in its time? The evolutionary approach to society and to economic thought provided a necessary antidote to the static, timeless thinking of the classical and marginalist schools. How else could one attempt to explain Great Britain's adherence to laissez faire in the nineteenth century, and her considerable departure from it in the twentieth? If universal economic principles are appropriate everywhere and for all time, why are many underdeveloped countries refusing to rely exclusively on free enterprise to build their economies? Some, devoted to a never changing world, say that departures from once-reliable doctrines represent colossal errors. Obviously we must familiarize ourselves with changing history and changing environments, with economic and social evolution, in order to understand the present world. For this, inductive factual studies are required. New theories and new ideas must be evoked if we are to understand new situations. This was the lasting contribution offered by the German historical school.

This school promoted, through its nationalism and the glorification of the state, the unification of Germany and her economic growth.

The historical economists were the leaders in the attack on laissez faire. This theme was the trend of the future. They were astute enough to know that unrestricted free enterprise does not necessarily produce the best possible results for society as a whole. They were right in their belief that reform can be a substitute for worse upheavals, which might occur if the class struggle were allowed to develop and sharpen.

How did the German historical school outlive its usefulness? Its task was completed when the economists of various persuasions agreed that historical, empirical studies are required to explain the present, to test old theories, and to develop new ones. The historical-inductive method has become generally acceptable as complementary to the abstract-deductive approach; changing times and methodological controversies have forced them into a kind of uneasy but tolerably placid marriage.

The attempts to promote the economic growth and power of Germany have been successful. Germany has surpassed Great Britain, and she no longer needs protection and paternalism as she once did. Since World War II there is more laissez faire in Germany than in Britain. The historical school's analyses of their country's situation have become antiquated through the process of change, which they themselves recognized in economic affairs. Of course this does not imply that historical analysis is less applicable in Germany today than in the past.

The condemnation of economic theorizing by the adherents of the historical school was sterile. They failed to demonstrate the ability of the historical method to produce theory. Their antitheoretical position has been decisively rejected by all types of economic schools other than the American institutionalists.

The German nationalism advocated by the historical economists overreached itself as it evolved into militarism run amok. Academic men are likely to be rather shamefaced about chauvinism—except in time of war. During the century ending in 1914, the hope was rising that the world could win peace, international cooperation, and universal harmony. The German historical economists struck a strident note of nationalism that jarred these internationalist sentiments of good will. Their ideas seemed to lead logically to the holocaust of World War I. Theirs was the more realistic tone in a world of hatred and conflict, but they offered little hope and few dreams of good will to which men could cling.

List

FRIEDRICH LIST (1789–1846), a forerunner of the historical school, was inclined neither toward formal study in school nor toward his father's occupation of tanner. He became a government clerk and by 1816 had risen to the post of ministerial undersecretary. A year later he accepted a professorship of administration and politics at the University of Tübingen, but his dissident political views caused his dismissal in 1819. He became active in promoting a strong political and commercial union of German states. Elected to his state legislature, List advocated administrative and financial reforms. These views were regarded as treasonable, and he served eight months in prison, after which he was deported. From 1825 to 1832 List lived in the United States, where he became a farmer, a journalist, and a business promoter, making and losing a fortune in coal mining. He gained much more popularity in the United States than in Germany with his protectionist ideas.

List was an ardent advocate of a railway network for Germany. In a pamphlet published in 1833, he sketched in nearly all the lines as they were afterwards built. He also was a driving force behind a German customs union, the *Zollverein*, which was established in 1834. The plans he presented for a German postal system and a national patent law were realized more than twenty years after his death. Ill health, financial difficulties, and despair over the delay in German unification darkened his later days, and he committed suicide in 1846.

In 1819 List presented a petition for a customs union to the Federal Assembly on behalf of the association of merchants and manufacturers that he had organized.

Thirty-eight customs boundaries cripple inland trade, and produce much the same effect as ligatures which prevent the free circulation of the blood. The merchant trading between Hamburg and Austria, or Berlin and Switzerland must traverse ten states, must learn ten customs-tariffs, must pay ten successive transit dues. Any one who is so unfortunate as to live on the boundary-line between three or four states spends his days among hostile tax-gatherers and custom-house officials; he is a man without a country.*

While List advocated free trade within Germany, he championed a high tariff against imports of manufactured goods to protect infant industries. He opposed protection for agriculture because this was an old and mature industry, and manufacturing required cheap food and raw materials. Besides, the development of large industry through protection would enlarge the home market for agriculture. List severely condemned Adam Smith and classical economics for claiming universality for doctrines that were well suited for England but were inappropriate for underdeveloped countries. Heavy emphasis was placed on what history teaches us, and the importance of the state was stressed. He popularized the idea of stages of economic growth, and he urged that the government actively assist a people who wished to pass from a lower stage to a higher against the competition of more advanced nations. Only after a country reached industrial maturity could it revert to free trade.

In the introduction to his famous work, List referred to himself in the third person.

The author will begin, as theory does not begin, by interrogating History, and deducing from it his fundamental principles. . . . For greater clearness, we give here a cursory view of the principal results of his researches and meditations: The association of individuals for the prosecution of a common end, is the most efficacious mode towards ensuring the happiness of individuals. Alone, and separated from his fellow-creatures, man is feeble and destitute. The greater the number of those who are united, the more perfect is the association, and the greater and the more perfect is the result, which is the moral and material welfare of individuals. The highest association of individuals now realized, is that of the state, the nation; and the highest imaginable, is that of the whole human race. . . .

A nation may by war be deprived of its independence, its wealth, its liberty, its constitution, its laws, of its own special features, of that degree of culture and national well-being to which it may have attained; it may be wholly en-

* Margaret E. Hirst, *Life of Friedrich List and Selections from His Writings* (London, 1909), p. 139.

slaved. Nations are thus the victims of each other, and selfish policy is continually disturbing and delaying the economical development of nations. To preserve, to develop, and to improve itself as a nation is consequently, at present, and ever must be, the principal object of a nation's efforts. . . .

In the economical development of nations, it is necessary to distinguish the following principal stages: the savage state, the pastoral state, the agricultural state, the agricultural and manufacturing state, and finally, the agricultural, manufacturing, and commercial state. . . . A nation that greatly values its independence and its safety, must make a vigorous effort to elevate itself as fast as possible, from an inferior to a higher state of civilization, uniting and perfecting as quickly as possible, its own agriculture, manufactures, navigation, and commerce. . . . The elevation of an agricultural people to the condition of countries at once agricultural, manufacturing, and commercial, can only be accomplished under the law of free trade, when the various nations engaged at the time in manufacturing industry shall be in the same degree of progress and civilization; when they shall place no obstacle in the way of the economical development of each other, and not impede their respective progress by war or adverse commercial legislation.

But some of them, favored by circumstances, having distanced others in manufactures, commerce, and navigation, and having early perceived that this advanced state was the surest mode of acquiring and keeping political supremacy, have adopted and still persevere in a policy so well adapted to give them the monopoly of manufactures, of industry and of commerce, and to impede the progress of less advanced nations or those in a lower degree of culture. . . . The anterior progress of certain nations, foreign commercial legislation and war have compelled inferior countries to look for special means of effecting their transition from the agricultural to the manufacturing stage of industry, and as far as practicable, by a system of duties, to restrain their trade with more advanced nations aiming at manufacturing monopoly. . . .

Experience teaches us, it is true, that the wind carries with it the seeds of one country to another, and that desert places have thus been changed into heavy forests. But would it be wise for the proprietor of waste land to wait for the wind to perform this office of planting and transformation during the lapse of centuries? Is it folly in him to force nature by planting his uncultivated lands, that he may attain his object in a score of years? . . .

The doctrine of Adam Smith in regard to international commerce, is but a continuation of that of the physiocrats. Like the latter, it disregards nationality; it excludes almost entirely politics and government; it supposes the existence of perpetual peace and universal association; it depreciates the advantages of national manufacturing industry, as well as the means of acquiring it; it demands absolute free trade.*

List denied Smith's harmony of interests between the individual and society. He believed that the immediate private interest of the separate mem-

* Frederick List, *National System of Political Economy*, G. A. Matile, tr. (Philadelphia, 1856), pp. 70–73, 181, 420. [Originally published in 1841.]

bers of the community does not necessarily lead to the highest good of the whole. A nation may suffer, for example, from an absence of manufacturing industry, but some people may flourish in selling foreign manufactures. An individual may grow rich by extreme parsimony, but if a whole nation follows his example, there will be no consumption and, in consequence, no support of industry. National unity, which is the result of past development, is necessary to the individual whose interests should be subordinated to the preservation of this unity.

List thought that only the temperate zone would develop manufacturing, for only there could one find the appropriate intellectual and physical efforts. The tropics should remain on a free-trade basis and should continue to supply tropical products in exchange for manufactured goods. He saw this as the true foundation for the international division of labor and world trade.

Military preparations, wars, and war debts, said List, may in certain cases contribute immensely to increase the productive powers of a country. He pointed to England as an example. War expanded her productive power so much that the increased values she received annually far exceeded the interest on her enlarged war debts. The whole of her war expenditure was carried, in the form of manufactured articles, to the theater of war, which ruined foreign manufacturers and assured England's industrial supremacy.

Judging from his writing, we might guess that List would have welcomed Germany's participation in the free-trade association of the European Common Market. He would have deplored, however, the current drive of the former colonial areas for industrialization.

Roscher

WILHELM ROSCHER (1817–94) was one of the founders of the "older historical school." This group wanted to supplement classical theory, while the younger school wanted to supersede it entirely with historical studies and policy considerations. Roscher became professor of political economy at Göttingen and later at Leipzig. His ideas on the role of the state and on historical method follow.

By the science of national, or Political Economy, we understand the science which has to do with the laws of the development of the economy of a nation, or with its economic national life. . . . National life, like all life, is a whole, the various phenomena of which are most intimately connected with one another. Hence it is, that to understand one side of it scientifically, it is necessary to know all its sides. But, especially, is it necessary to fix one's attention on the following seven: language, religion, art, science, law, the state and economy. . . .

If, by the public economy of a nation, we understand economic legislation and the governmental guidance or direction of the economy of private persons, the science of public economy becomes, so far as its form is concerned, a branch of political science, while as to its matter, its subject is almost coincident with that of Political Economy. . . . Just as clear, is the close connection between politics and Political Economy, in the case of the science of finance, or of the science of governmental house-keeping, otherwise the administration of public affairs. . . . As the physiologist cannot understand the action of the human body, without understanding that of the head; so we would not be able to grasp the organic whole of national economy, if we were to leave the state, the greatest economy of all, the one which uninterruptedly and irresistibly acts on all others, out of consideration. . . .

The thorough application of this [the historical] method will do away with a great number of controversies on important questions. Men are as far removed from being devils as from being angels. We meet with few who are only guided by ideal motives, but with few, also, who hearken only to the voice of egotism, and care for nothing but themselves. It may, therefore, be assumed, that any view current on certain tangible interests which concern man very nearly, and which has been shared by great parties and even by whole peoples for generations, is not based only on ignorance or a perverse love of wrong. The error consists more frequently in applying measures wholesome and even absolutely necessary under certain circumstances, to circumstances entirely different. And here, a thorough insight into the conditions of the measure suffices to compose the differences between the two parties. Once the natural laws of Political Economy are sufficiently known and recognized, all that is needed, in any given instance, is more exact and reliable statistics of the fact involved, to reconcile all party controversies on questions of the politics of public economy, so far, at least, as these controversies arise from a difference of opinion. It may be that science may never attain to this, in consequence of the new problems which are ever arising and demanding a solution. It may be, too, that in the greater number of party controversies, the opposed purposes of the parties play a more important part even than the opposed views. Be this as it may, it is necessary, especially in an age as deeply agitated as our own, when every good citizen is in duty bound to ally himself to party, that every honest party-man should seek to secure, amid the ocean of ephemeral opinions, a firm island of scientific truth, as universally recognized as truth as are the principles of mathematical physics by physicians [physicists?] of the most various schools.*

Roscher added that the historical method does away with feelings of self-sufficiency, and the higher civilizations will not look down with contempt on the lower. Societies are continually evolving from immature forms to the mature, which may be considered the most perfect. These then in their turn decline and decay.

Roscher showed his affinity for economic theory by including a simpli-

* William Roscher, *Principles of Political Economy*, Vol. I, John J. Lalor, tr. (New York, 1878), pp. 87–88, 91–92, 112–13. [Originally published in 1854.]

fied version of English classical price theory in his *Principles of Political Economy*. Instead of disdaining abstract theory, he sought to discover its historical basis. He asserted that the study of contemporary facts and opinions was an essential adjunct to the classical deductive method.

Schmoller

GUSTAV SCHMOLLER (1838–1917), leading figure of the "younger historical school," was professor of political science at Halle, Strasbourg, and Berlin. He taught many generations of students and administrative officials and wielded great influence in academic and government circles. The task of accumulating historical and descriptive factual materials he considered as prior to and far more important than deductive theorizing. He engaged in a famous controversy with Carl Menger over whether inductive or deductive analysis was most fruitful. In the end this *Methodenstreit* seemed to resolve itself in the belief that both are important.

Schmoller believed that ethical value judgments were not to be disparaged. Justice in the economic system was to be realized through a paternalistic policy of social reform furthered by the state and all social groups. The guiding principle of social reform, he said, was a more equitable distribution of income. Social science was to be the guide for the attainment of the objectives of social policy.

What are economic institutions but a product of human feelings and thought, of human actions, human customs and human laws? . . .

If in the economic order we could recognize only the ruling of blind forces, of selfish interests, natural masses and mechanical processes, it would be a constant battle, a chaotic anarchy. . . . No, harmony does not exist *per se;* selfish impulses combat each other, natural masses tend to destroy each other, the mechanical action of natural forces interferes relentlessly still to-day; the struggle for existence is to-day still carried on in the struggle of competition. . . . While struggle and strife never cease they do not preserve the same character throughout the course of history. The struggle which ended in annihilation, in subjugation, turns into a peaceful contest which is decided by an umpire. The forms of dependence grow milder and more human. Class government grows more moderate. Every brutal strength, every undue assertion of superior force is made punishable by law. Demand and supply, as they confront each other in the different systems of custom and law, are quite different in their results. . . .

There is no worse delusion than that of the older English economists that there are a number of simple and natural legal and economic institutions which have always been as they are and will always remain so; that all progress of civilization and wealth is simply an individual or technical one; that this is simply a question of increased production or consumption which will and can be accomplished on the basis of the same legal institutions. This faith in the stability of economic institutions was the result of the naive overweening confidence of the older economists in the omnipotence of the individual and of the individual life. Socialism then has perhaps over-estimated the significance of social institutions. Historical economics and the modern philosophy of law have given them their due position by showing us that the great epochs of economic progress are primarily connected with the reform of social institutions.*

Schmoller was so antagonistic to deductive economists that he declared publicly that members of the "abstract" school were unfit to teach in a German university. When he received a pamphlet written by Carl Menger, founder of the abstract Austrian marginalist school, for review in his journal, he printed an announcement that he was unable to review it because he had immediately returned it to the author. He also printed the insulting letter which he sent to Menger along with the pamphlet.

Schmoller accused the older historical school of attempting to apply the lessons of history too quickly. He called for much more historical study in order to establish an empirical basis for national economic theory. Despite innumerable massive historical studies which he and his disciples published, they failed to produce economic theory. Their major contribution lay in the area of economic history.

Weber

MAX WEBER (1864–1920) established himself in Berlin in the legal profession. After publishing several scholarly works, he became a professor of political economy and sociology at Freiburg, and later at Heidelberg and Munich. He considered himself an intellectual descendant of Schmoller.

Weber aroused a lively controversy that has persisted through the years over the relationship between Protestantism and the rise of capitalism. He rejected the Marxian idea that religious doctrines are merely ideological manifestations of particular economic conditions. Ideas for him were, at least in part, autonomous entities with a power to affect social changes. It seemed to him that capitalism was a result rather than a cause of the Reformation. He believed that Calvinist theology in particular contained certain elements that were exceedingly conducive to rationalized, individualistic economic activity undertaken for profit. Speaking of Protestantism, Weber wrote:

The religious valuation of restless, continuous, systematic work in a worldly calling, as the highest means to asceticism, and at the same time the surest and

* Gustav Schmoller, *Idea of Justice in Political Economy* (Philadelphia, no date), pp. 22, 26, 27, 37.

most evident proof of rebirth and genuine faith, must have been the most powerful conceivable lever for the expansion of that attitude toward life which we have here called the spirit of capitalism. When the limitation of consumption is combined with this release of acquisitive activity, the inevitable practical result is obvious: accumulation of capital through ascetic compulsion to save. The restraints which were imposed upon the consumption of wealth naturally served to increase it by making possible the productive investment of capital.*

R. H. Tawney and others have disputed Weber's analysis. Religion of course influenced men's outlook on society, but economic and social changes acted powerfully on religion. Weber, it has been said, emphasized the first point, but he touched the second point only in passing. The rise of business enterprise induced the middle class to do away with Catholicism, which condemned usury, suspected economic motives, and took a dim view of private fortunes. Besides, the Catholic Church was the largest feudal landowner, and it sought to perpetuate such feudal institutions as the just price, primogeniture, entail, and mortmain. Because the Reformation struck a powerful blow at authority, it loosened the hold of tradition on men's minds. Because it called into question ideas that had long held sway, it strengthened the temper of rationalism. Calvinism endowed economic activities and the accumulation of wealth with a new sanctification. Tawney argued that economic changes such as the great geographic discoveries and the expansion of commerce were ultimately responsible for the transformation of the Christian ethic from the sixteenth century onward. Both Calvinism and the spirit of capitalism, he said, were produced by those changes in economic organization and social structure.

We should not overlook the facts that Luther's doctrines were permeated with a feudal aura, and that Catholicism was adaptable to the new world of business enterprise. Apparently the adaptation was hastened by the threat posed by the Reformation. Early capitalist manifestations were discernible in the late medieval cities in Catholic Italy, and in Catholic France before the Revolution. A notably powerful motive for the revolt against Rome, especially among people who had no interest in business enterprise, was the prospect of plundering wealthy Church organizations. Peasants who had grievances against their feudal overlords also were swept into the Protestant movement. The rising nationalist spirit found itself in opposition to the internationalism centered in Rome.

In the complex interrelations of Protestantism and the rise of capitalism, it is difficult to disentangle cause from effect with any high degree of assurance. Did Protestantism produce capitalism, as Weber said? Or did ris-

* Max Weber, *The Protestant Ethic and the Spirit of Capitalism*, Talcott Parsons, tr. (London, 1930), p. 172. [Originally published in 1904–05.]

ing capitalism accept Protestantism as a more suitable credo for its business activities, as his opponents believe? Or is there some truth in both positions?

Sombart

WERNER SOMBART (1863–1941), German economic historian, was the son of a prosperous farmer who was elected to the Reichstag and settled in Berlin. The son studied in Pisa and Berlin and taught at the Universities of Breslau and Berlin. His encyclopedic researches into the origins and evolution of capitalism revealed the intellectual influence of Marx, and also of the German historical school, especially Schmoller. As a student at the University of Berlin, Sombart absorbed from Schmoller a nationalistic outlook, hostility to classical economics, and antipathy toward liberal individualism. Although the German historical school may be said to have ended by World War I, Sombart lived beyond that time to carry on the school's methodology and perspectives. As a critic of the capitalistic form of economic organization, Sombart started his adult life as a socialist; he ended it as a nazi.

Sombart sought to explain the rise and growth of capitalism. The foundations of this revolutionary system of economic organization, he wrote, rested on the business enterpriser, the modern state, and the machine process. The enterpriser, a new type of man, assumed the direction of economic activities. Because a handful of men were smitten with a passion to make money, society has been changed completely. An important role in this process has depended on historical accidents, such as the discovery of great gold deposits, and the existence of virgin resources awaiting exploitation. Sombart questioned Max Weber's thesis that puritanism had a large share in forming the capitalistic spirit of businessmen. Instead, he stated that "those parts of the Puritan dogma which appear to be of real importance for the formation of the spirit of capitalism, are borrowed from the realm of ideas of the Jewish religion." It was the Jews who gave to capitalism its impersonal, rational, and materialistic qualities. Puritanism, said Sombart, did help discipline the workers to the new way of life. Great difficulties had been experienced in adapting workers to the technical requirements of capitalism. To overcome the irregular habits of the workers, they had to be inspired with the desire to get on in the world through capitalistic ideals. The desire for gain, instead of being an inborn trait of human nature, had to be deliberately inculcated in order that capitalism might flourish.

It is interesting to note that Sombart assigned to the Jews a decisive role not only in the development of capitalism, but also of socialism. Early in his life, when he leaned toward Marxism and was critical of capitalism, Sombart emphasized the role of the Jews in the development of capitalism. After World War I, when he developed a strong antipathy toward Marxian socialism, he found that socialism was strongly influenced by Jewish thought.

Sombart divided capitalism into three stages of development: early capitalism, which dated from about 1400 to 1760; high capitalism, which lasted from 1760 to 1914; and late capitalism, from 1914 on. The phenomenon of capitalism, he said, must be studied as a part of cultural history. The appearance and growth of capitalism meant not only changes in technology, but also economic, political, military, psychological, religious, and intellectual changes which dissolved the medieval social order.

The period of high capitalism, according to Sombart, marked the ascendancy and the decline of the system. Symptoms of the decline were revealed when business leaders became fat, rich, and complacent; they lost the spirit of adventure. Risk-taking became subordinate to a policy of caution and routine business methods. Economic life was increasingly stabilized and regulated by the state. The scope for aggressive and energetic enterprise was decreased by cartels and other monopolistic arrangements. The decline of the rate of population growth and the narrowing of investment opportunities further increased capitalism's difficulties. By 1914, when the period of late capitalism set in, these decadent tendencies had become quite pronounced.

Sombart predicted the eventual rise of a new economic organization. He expected capitalism to endure indefinitely, but it would continue to change in the future as it had changed in the past. Public control and conscious planning for satisfying needs rather than for making money would increasingly come to the fore. Small craftsmen, shopkeepers, and farmers would continue to survive along with capitalistic enterprises, cooperatives, and public regulation. The farmers would grow in importance with the continued growth of world population.

By 1933 Sombart had become a full-fledged supporter of the nazi philosophy. Germany under Hitler, he thought, was the new, dynamic system that would overcome capitalist decadence. He glorified German racism and nationalism as welcome alternatives to the debilitated society that they vanquished.

The results of the economic age show, first of all, that in public life there is in fact but one basis and one measure of success, that of wealth in money; and only one order of rank, that of money or income. . . . An intellectual person obtains neither standing nor approval in society until he has a large income. . . . Wealth has become an object of admiration, whereas earlier—at least in the case of private persons—it was rather an object of contempt or scorn unless its bearers were possessed of other values, such as culture or noble lineage. . . .

"Comfortism," the name I have given to this practical materialism, which means the deviation of the direction of human life toward amenity-values, brings the whole body of people to decay. . . . The necessity, touched upon above, of filling the void created in the materialistic soul after each enjoyment by a new enjoyment, has led to the chase in which modern man spends his life. The capitalistic economic system was here the pacemaker in so far as it urged, in accordance with its nature, the acceleration of the tempo, so that the future would be continually anticipated by the present. . . .

With every new generation there is a new-born capacity to be bearers of culture, which is lost only through racial degeneracy—a danger which wise precaution can prevent. . . .

For us there is only one aim—Germany. For the sake of Germany's greatness, power and glory, we will gladly sacrifice every "theory" and every "principle," whether it bears a liberal or any other stamp. . . .

If, finally, we are to understand that our own [artistic and literary] creations should be influenced by foreigners, this kind of relation would constitute a great danger to German culture which really has no need of such inspiration from without.*

Sombart, like other members of the German historical school, neglected value and distribution theory in favor of history. He believed that the "laws" of capitalism, like all economic laws, are neither final nor universal. They are valid only for capitalism. In describing the evolution of capitalism, he tried to explain economic behavior in a type of theory, but not of the conventional kind. According to Wesley C. Mitchell, Sombart's chief weakness as a scientific inquirer was that he did not restudy and enrich his preconceived notions as he gathered and assimilated his data. His greatest strength was that his encyclopedic studies and the frequently provocative conclusions he drew from them stimulated further research.

* Werner Sombart, *A New Social Philosophy*, Karl F. Geiser, tr. (Princeton, 1937), pp. 22–23, 34, 147, 152, 187.

CHAPTER 12

The Rise of the Marginalist School:

GOSSEN and JEVONS

THE MARGINALIST school developed in several countries and through the work of different people working, at first, independently of each other. Among the pioneers were Hermann Heinrich Gossen in Germany, Carl Menger in Austria, Léon Walras at Lausanne, Switzerland, and W. Stanley Jevons and Alfred Marshall in England. Here is another interesting case of new ideas arising almost simultaneously in different places and through different people, when enough dissatisfaction had developed over old doctrines, and when the need was felt strongly enough for the new.

By the 1870's marginalism was well on its way toward displacing classical economics over a hundred years after the latter's birth. Marginalism reigned supreme in Western economic thought until it was suddenly shocked by the Keynesian onslaught in 1936. Since then both types of economic analysis have continued to flourish side by side, living in a sort of symbiotic relationship. Marginalism, having adapted itself to new ideas and new situations, has changed considerably from its earliest presentation. It is still the dominant school in microeconomic or partial analysis. Almost every elementary college textbook uses marginal economics to analyze the single firm and its behavior, the individual in his productive and consumptive activities, the market for a single good, the formation of individual prices. In this sense marginalism has remained triumphant for almost a hundred years. It had to move aside, however, to allow Keynesian economics its macroeconomic sphere—the analysis of the economy as a whole, including general price movements, levels of business activity, and the role of government.

Overview of the Marginalist School

The social background of the school. Serious social problems remained unsolved even a hundred years after the beginning of the industrial revolution. There were problems of widespread poverty even though increasing productivity was making magnificent progress. There were problems of the extremely uneven distribution of wealth and income, which created much dissatisfaction even while average levels of living were rising. Business fluctuations affected many people adversely, and the individual could no longer depend exclusively on his own initiative and ability to overcome conditions that were thrust upon him. Farmers and farm laborers had their difficulties; many drifted to the cities, attracted by the carrot of better opportunities, and also driven by the club of rural poverty. The hazards of industrial accidents meant serious hardships on workers and their families before adequate workmen's compensation laws were enacted. Long hours of labor, dangerous and unhealthy working conditions, a preponderance of economic power on the side of employers in bargaining with workers, usury, the rise of monopolistic business, insecurity in old age—these and many other problems caused people to seek solutions beyond the narrow confines of classical economic thinking.

The trend of the nineteenth century in Europe was to develop three lines of attack on pressing social problems, and all three flouted classical economic precepts. Movements arose to promote socialism, trade unionism, and government action to ameliorate conditions by regulating the economy, eliminating abuses, and redistributing income. The marginalist economists opposed all three trends. They theorized with seemingly Olympian impartiality, and came up with the conclusion that this was the best of all possible worlds. They defended laissez faire, deplored government intervention, denounced socialism, and sought to discourage labor unionism as either ineffective or pernicious.

To the leading early marginalists, classical economic theory was especially pernicious because it seemed to conclude that economic rent was an unearned income, and because of its labor theory of value. The first idea was seized and expanded by Henry George, and the second by Karl Marx. If classical economics could be made to say what its creators never intended—namely, that rent was immoral and labor created all values—then the science of wealth was ripe for a thoroughgoing revision.

The essence of the marginalist school. The basic ideas of marginalism can be condensed into ten major principles, listed below. They will be amplified in the discussion of seven leading marginalist economists presented in the latter part of this chapter and in the two following chapters.

1. This school concentrated on the margin, the point of change where decisions are made, to explain economic phenomena. They extended to all of economic theory the marginal principle that Ricardo developed in his theory of rent.

2. The approach was microeconomic rather than macroeconomic. The individual moves to the center of the stage. Instead of considering the aggregate economy, they considered individual decision-making, market conditions and prices for a single type of goods, the output of a single firm, etc.

3. The method of this school was abstract and deductive, as was the method of the classical school.

4. The world of the marginalists is one of pure competition, with an occasional nod toward monopoly at the other extreme. In this world of small, individualistic, and independent entrepreneurs there are many buyers, many sellers, homogeneous products, uniform prices, and no advertising. No one person or business has enough economic power perceptibly to influence market prices. Individuals can adapt their own actions to demand, supply, and price as worked out in the market through the interactions of hundreds and thousands of people. Each person is such a tiny operator in the huge anthill of the market that no one will note his presence or absence.

5. Demand becomes the primary force in price determination. The classical school had emphasized cost of production, supply, as the sole determinant of value. The early marginalists swung to the opposite extreme and emphasized demand to the virtual exclusion of supply. Alfred Marshall synthesized both into what may be called neoclassical economics, which is basically marginalism with a judicious recognition of the surviving contributions of the classical school.

6. Economics becomes subjective and psychological. Demand depends on marginal utility, which is a psychic phenomenon. Costs of production involve the sacrifices and irksomeness of working, managing a business, and saving money to form a capital fund.

7. The marginalists believed that economic forces are generally working toward equilibrium, toward a balancing of opposing tendencies. Whenever disturbances cause dislocations, new movements toward equilibrium occur.

8. The tendency developed to deprecate Ricardo's rent theory. The uncomfortable idea had gotten around that rent is an unearned income and an unnecessary payment in order to insure the use of land. Marginalist theory generally merged land with man-made capital goods, and coupled the reward to the landowner with interest theory.

9. The marginalists assumed that men are rational in balancing pleasures and pains, in their knowledge of marginal utilities of different goods, in balancing present against future needs. They also assumed that rational behavior is normal and typical, for the random abnormalities will cancel each other out. Their approach was hedonistic, assuming that the dominant drives among men are to maximize pleasure and minimize pain.

10. The marginalists continued the classical school's defense of laissez faire as being the most desirable policy. There should be no interference with natural economic laws if maximum social benefits are to be realized.

What groups of people did the marginalist school serve or seek to serve? This was the economics of conservatism. It favored all those whose interests committed them to the status quo, who resisted the currents of change. This type of theory favored employers (even though most of them did not really understand it) by opposing unions, and by attributing unemployment to wages that were inflexible on the downward side. It defended landowners against Ricardian rent theory. This school favored the wealthy, who generally were opposed to government intervention which might tend to redistribute income.

How was the marginalist school valid, useful, or correct in its time? It developed new and powerful tools of analysis, especially through the use of geometrical diagrams and mathematical techniques. Economics became a more nearly exact science, thanks to the marginalists. Conditions of demand were given importance as one set of determinants of prices of both final goods and factors of production. The school emphasized the forces that shape individual decisions; this was valid in a world where such decisions were significant in determining the course of economic activities. Fundamental assumptions underlying economic analysis, which were lurking in the background of classical thinking, were ultimately brought out into the open and clearly stated by the marginalists. The methodological controversies they aroused finally led to a separation of those principles which are objective and verifiable based on the stated assumptions, from those which depend on value judgments and philosophical outlook.

The method of partial analysis can be justified on the ground that it enables us to investigate complex phenomena, taking one step at a time. We allow one variable at a time to change, assuming that everything else remains constant. The problems of our immensely complicated society with its countless variables can thereby be simplified and penetrated in an orderly and systematic manner. As we introduce successive variables, we approach more realistic situations. Assuming that everything remains unchanged except the one factor we allow to vary is a technique used everywhere all the time. If you say, "I am going to the movies tonight," you are implicitly making hundreds of assumptions about other things not changing unexpectedly. For example, you are assuming that you will not break a leg or die of a heart attack during the day; that the theater will not burn down; that a flood or an earthquake will not cut the highway to town; that something more interesting will not come along before evening.

How did the marginalist school outlive its usefulness? In a sense it did not, as it still dominates the field along with Keynes, and on the world scene both share the field with socialism. However, marginalism as it remained from 1870 to 1930 had to be modified considerably before it could continue as a viable set of ideas. Nevertheless some of the weaknesses which permeated its structure then probably still persist.

The microeconomic approach, while it has its uses, introduced the famous fallacy of composition that led to erroneous conclusions. The fallacy develops with the belief that what is true for one is necessarily true for all, or what is true for part of a situation is therefore, on that account alone, true for the whole situation. If you were to get to your destination two hours early, you would find a parking place for your automobile; but if everybody were to get there early, would everybody solve his parking problems? If one employer were to cut wages, he could expand employment by selling more goods at lower prices. The decline in the ability to buy among his own employees would not affect him, as they would normally buy only a negligible portion of his output. However, if all employers were to cut wages, they might find their markets shrinking rather than expanding. Yet the eminent marginalist economist Lionel Robbins could write as late as 1934 that wage reductions were one of the necessary cures to overcome the great depression.

In the United States the word went forth that consumers' purchasing power must at all costs be maintained. President Hoover pledged the leaders of big industry to make no reduction of wage rates. Until the summer of 1930 no serious reduction of wage rates took place. At the same time special efforts were made to maintain rates of dividends for shareholders. In Germany, too, throughout 1930 wage rates were well maintained. Now this policy was the reverse of what was needed. . . .

The very fact, therefore, that there was unemployment on this scale is a proof that, in some parts of the labour market, the rates charged were too high. . . . Wage rates in Great Britain were more or less constant from 1924 onwards. All that happened was that, in the face of a tendency to a decline in the demand for labour, wage rates were not lowered.*

The assumption of pure competition was a reasonable abstraction looking backward from the 1870's. But it was too unrealistic to be useful as

* Lionel Robbins, *The Great Depression* (New York, 1935), pp. 69, 82, 83.

competition declined after the 1870's. In large sectors of the economy pure competition is completely irrelevant. Even today, the elementary theory of market price is typically expounded to exclude monopoly elements.

The subjective, psychological, individualistic equilibrium approach to economic analysis has several serious weaknesses. One is revealed by Marshall's opening paragraph in the chapter headed, "Temporary Equilibrium of Demand and Supply."

The simplest case of balance or equilibrium between desire and effort is found when a person satisfies one of his wants by his own direct work. When a boy picks blackberries for his own eating, the action of picking is probably itself pleasurable for a while; and for some time longer the pleasure of eating is more than enough to repay the trouble of picking. But after he has eaten a good deal, the desire for more diminishes; while the task of picking begins to cause weariness, which may indeed be a feeling of monotony rather than of fatigue. Equilibrium is reached when at last his eagerness to play and his disinclination for the work of picking counterbalance the desire for eating. The satisfaction which he can get from picking fruit has arrived at its *maximum:* for up to that time every fresh picking has added more to his pleasure than it has taken away; and after that time any further picking would take away from his pleasure more than it would add.*

Is it really true that a person always stops putting forth effort at the exact point of his own individual equilibrium? In a footnote 197 pages later, Marshall admitted that a man might have to work a standard day even though the disutility of the last hour of labor might be greater than the utility of the earnings from that hour. "But such cases are rare," he added. More significant than Marshall's berry-picking boy was the post-World-War-II case of the Seventh Day Adventist who refused to work overtime on Saturday in a shoe plant. Obviously the marginal utility of her earnings for the week was far less than the marginal disutility of her work on the seventh day of the week. Yet the arbitrator in her case agreed to her being dismissed because she violated the union-management contract. Again, one of the issues in a strike of the Teamsters Union against the A. & P. food chain in 1959 was the right of individual workers to refuse overtime work. Apparently historical and institutional factors are more important in determining the length of the working day than is the equilibrium of the individual. The discipline of the factory time clock, worked out through collective agreements, is more relevant to the length of the work-

* Reprinted with permission of Macmillan & Co. Ltd., The Macmillan Company of Canada Limited, and The Macmillan Company from *Principles of Economics*, 8th ed., by Alfred Marshall (London, 1920), p. 331. [Originally published in 1890 and first published in the United States in 1948.]

ing day than the whims of the employee acting in isolated contemplation of his maximum welfare; and the fact that he can always quit his job is scant consolation. Individualism remained triumphant in economic theory despite a world of growing collective action.

The early marginalists held that a laissez faire regime produced the best possible results. Economic laws seemed to them to be natural laws that must not be tampered with. At a time when government intervention was growing, they generally denied its desirability, because the economy was supposed to be self-regulating, served unwittingly by each individual who sought to serve himself. They believed that what was good for General Motors was good for the country. This was exactly what the classical economists believed. But, one might ask, how does an individual or a group promote the social interest when output is restricted and prices raised? The classical economists relied on competition to thwart and curb the selfish interests of the individual. In their day competition was widespread enough to produce reasonably good results. That is, no General Motors then existed. But with the decline of competition, laissez faire became increasingly untenable. Recognition of monopolistic trends, however, would have undermined faith in individualism.

The marginalists assumed a positive time preference, which means that people prefer present to future spending. A rate of interest is therefore required to induce people to postpone consumption. Interest is the reward for abstinence or waiting. This idea assumed that rational man is in this case irrational, for he underestimates his future needs and therefore refuses to save unless he receives a monetary inducement. The drive toward the accumulation of wealth as a means to power and prestige was overlooked in considering saving a sacrifice. The marginalist theory of saving might have some applicability in a world of small business and small savers; but it is less relevant when the bulk of the saving is done through corporate decisions, the expansion of bank credit, and government taxation. The rate of interest rather than the level of income is made the prime reason for saving. If interest is the reward for the sacrifice of waiting, there should be no persistent problem of unemployment. As soon as unemployment appears, the rate of interest falls; owners of wealth increase their consumption spending, for they refuse to suffer through abstinence or waiting at the lower rate of return. A rise in consumption spending should therefore offset any drop in investment. But it does not happen that way.

The neglect of rent theory by the marginalists makes sense from the individual viewpoint. To the man who buys land and machinery, there is no significant theoretical difference between them. To the man who pays rent, the payment is necessary to win the land away from competing uses. Land is a part of his cost of production, and the selling price must cover that cost. It is only from the total social viewpoint that land is sufficiently different from other means of production to merit separate treatment. The total supply of land, unlike that of man-made goods, is almost completely inelastic, even though the supply of land for any one use is quite elastic. From society's point of view, land has no alternate uses and therefore rent is not a necessary payment. Rent does not enter into cost of production; high rents are a consequence of high prices, not a cause. Rent is an unearned income from society's viewpoint because land costs society nothing. To the individual who bought the land, however, it represents a very real cost. The marginalists, in condemning Ricardian rent theory, generally failed to consider the alternative point of view on which that analysis was based. And by predicating a stationary state, they assumed that the supply of capital also was fixed; the differences between land and capital were thereby obliterated.

The marginalist analysis originally was static, timeless, and unhistorical. There were few attempts at inductive verification of theories; in fact, hypotheses were framed in ways that excluded testing. Business cycles were generally ignored in the firm conviction that J. B. Say was right when he said that supply creates its own demand and therefore full employment is normal. The school failed to explain economic growth, and its theory was inadequate for underdeveloped countries. Marginalists tried to stem the tide of social change that threatened to engulf their concepts. Finally, floundering helplessly during the great depression of the 1930's, they merged forces with the Keynesians and salvaged something from the wreckage.

Gossen

HERMAN HEINRICH GOSSEN (1810–58) left his employment as a minor German government official to spend four years in seclusion writing a book. Published in 1854, the book's title may be translated as *Development of the Laws of Exchange Among Men*. Like many authors, he was filled with hope that his work would move the world. He claimed to have done for economic science what Copernicus did for astronomy. Hardly a copy was sold, however, perhaps because the treatment was heavily mathematical. Gossen recalled the printed copies and had them destroyed. Shortly afterward he died of consumption, a disappointed and neglected man. His exposition of the foundations of marginalism remained unknown until after Jevons developed the same ideas independently. After Jevons published the first edition of *The Theory of Political Economy*, he discovered Gossen's book and was disappointed to learn that his theory had been anticipated by another. He gave full credit to Gossen in subsequent editions of his own book; fame arrived belatedly to the deceased pioneer theorist, whose book was reprinted in German in 1889. (Jevons' own works on economics were not best-sellers. The first edition of his *The Theory of Political Economy* sold a thousand copies in seven years.)

Gossen based his economic system on hedonism—man tries to maximize his pleasure and minimize his pain. His first law, stated in modern terms, may be called the law of diminishing marginal utility. It states that the marginal utility of a good for a person diminishes with every increase in the amount of it he already has. This law explains how an exchange of equivalents between two people can result in a gain of utility for both.

Gossen's second law relates to the balancing of marginal utilities through rational consumption spending in order to secure maximum satisfaction. Rational man will spend on each commodity up to the point where the last unit of money spent on any good gives equal satisfaction with the last unit of money spent on any other good.

Gossen's third principle was that the utility of any product must be estimated after deducting the pains of labor required to produce it. He held that we will carry on labor to the point at which the utility of the product equals the pain of effort in production.

Jevons

WILLIAM STANLEY JEVONS (1835–82) in his youth spent five years in Australia as an assayer at the mint. There he earned enough to return to England to continue his studies. Great was his disappointment and bitterness when he failed to win a prize in political economy at University College, London. He attributed this to the prejudice of his professor against the new ideas Jevons was developing. He published several books on logic, and became professor of logic, political economy, and philosophy, first in Manchester and later at University College, London. An invention of his was a logic machine, exhibited before the Royal Society in 1870; it could yield a conclusion mechanically from any given set of premises. Jevons also was famous as a historian of science, and he made outstanding contributions to the development of index numbers.

At forty-seven, Jevons drowned while swimming.

Jevons called Ricardo "that able but wrong-headed man" who "shunted the car of Economic science on to a wrong line." Mill pushed the car further toward confusion. Malthus and Senior were much more to Jevons' taste.

On the first page of his *The Theory of Political Economy*, Jevons stated, "Repeated reflection and inquiry have led me to the somewhat novel opinion, that *value depends entirely upon utility*." In dismissing the labor theory of value, he did agree that labor often indirectly determines value by varying the degree of utility of the commodity through an increase or limitation of the supply. Elsewhere in the same work Jevons formulated his theory of value this way:

> Cost of production determines supply;
> Supply determines final degree of utility;
> Final degree of utility determines value.*

Why, therefore, does not cost of production determine value? Jevons, in refuting the labor theory of value, argued that labor cannot be the regulator of value because labor itself is of unequal value; it differs infinitely in quality and efficiency. "I hold labour to be *essentially variable*, so that *its value must be determined by the value of the produce, not the value of the produce by that of the labour.*"†

Labor itself is a subjective, pyschological cost, a "painful exertion." The problem of economics is "to satisfy our wants with the least possible sum of labour." His own formulation should have led him to concede that cost of production also plays a significant role in determining value.

The keystone of the whole theory of exchange, said Jevons, lies in this proposition: "The ratio of exchange of any two commodities will be the reciprocal of the ratio of the final degrees of utility of the quantities of commodity available for consumption after the exchange is completed."‡

Suppose, Jevons explained, one trading body possesses only corn and another only beef. Exchange will increase total utility, but will cease when, at the margin, a pound of beef has as much utility as ten pounds of corn and exchanges for ten pounds of corn. If, however, to the trading body that possesses corn, ten pounds of corn are less useful than one of beef, that body will desire to carry the exchange further. Should the other body possessing beef find one pound less useful than ten pounds of corn, it will also desire to continue the exchange. Exchange will thus go on until each party has obtained all possible benefit, and loss of utility would result if more were exchanged.

In other words, Jevons' proposition amounts to this: If a pound of steak costs ten times as much as an ice cream cone, each person will consume both up to the point at which the steak has ten times the marginal utility of the ice cream cone.

Jevons presented graphically the equilibrium between the pain of work and the pleasure of the earnings. (See Figure 1.) The line *OX* represents the potential working day. The height of points above the line *OX* denotes

* W. Stanley Jevons, *The Theory of Political Economy*, 4th ed. (London, 1911), p. 165. [Originally published in 1871.]

† *Ibid.*, p. 166. ‡ *Ibid.*, p. 95.

pleasure, and depths below it pain. At the beginning of the working day labor is usually more irksome than later in the day when one adjusts to it. Thus there is neither pleasure nor pain at *b* and *c*, and there is actual pleasure from working between those two points. Beyond *c*, however, the pain of additional work increases.

FIGURE I. Jevons' Equilibrium Between the Pain of Work and the Pleasure of Earnings

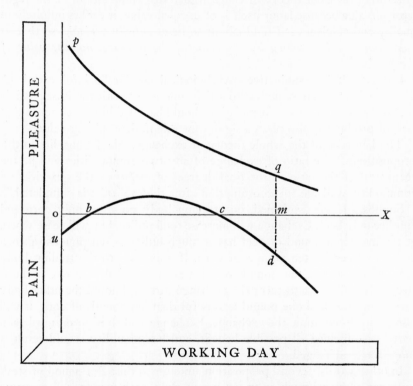

SOURCE: W. Stanley Jevons, *The Theory of Political Economy*, 4th ed. (London, Macmillan, 1911), p. 173.

The utility of the product (it would have been more appropriate to call it the utility of the earnings) is shown by the line *pq*. Its downward slope reflects the law of diminishing marginal utility. At *m*, where *qm* = *dm*, the pleasure gained is exactly equal to the pain of the labor endured. The laborer will cease working at point *m*. Jevons did indicate that "it is not always possible to graduate the work to the worker's liking."

Jevons rejected any attempt to compare intensity of pleasures among different people. Even for one person, total utilities cannot be compared. But a person can compare his own utilities and disutilities which are of approximately the same order of magnitude at the margin. For example,

> The whole amount of pleasure that a man gains by a day's labour hardly enters into the question; it is when a man is doubtful whether to increase his hours of labour or not, that we discover an equality between the pain of that extension and the pleasure of the increase of possessions derived from it.*

Yet later in the same work Jevons did compare marginal utilities among different people. By extending the principle of diminishing marginal utility to money, he gave a theoretical justification for the welfare economists' argument that redistributing income from rich to poor might increase total happiness. Jevons himself did not draw this conclusion from his theory.

> What, for instance, is the utility of one penny to a poor family earning fifty pounds a year? . . . Its utility is equal to the utility of the quantity of bread, tea, sugar, or other articles which they could purchase with it, this utility depending upon the extent to which they were already provided with those articles. To a family possessing one thousand pounds a year, the utility of a penny may be measured in an exactly similar manner; but it will be much less, because their want of any given commodity will be satiated or satisfied to a much greater extent, so that the urgency of need for a pennyworth more of any article is much reduced. . . . In Economics we regard only commercial transactions, and no equalisation of wealth from charitable motives is considered. . . . So far as is consistent with the inequality of wealth in every community, all commodities are distributed by exchange so as to produce the maximum of benefit.†

Jevons' law of diminishing marginal utility solved the paradox of water and diamonds which puzzled some of the classical economists. Adam Smith believed that utility had nothing to do with the *magnitude* of exchange value, because water was more useful than diamonds, but diamonds were more valuable than water. The principle of diminishing marginal utility reveals that while the total utility of water is greater than the total utility of diamonds, the marginal utility of diamonds is far greater than the marginal utility of water. We would rather have all the water in the world

* *Ibid.*, pp. 13–14.   † *Ibid.*, pp. 140–41.

and no diamonds than the other way around; but we would rather have an additional diamond than an extra unit of water.

Basing himself on the diminishing marginal utility of money, Jevons showed that gambling does not pay and insurance does. Assuming that there is no pleasure attached to gambling itself other than in winning, the money we may lose has a higher marginal utility than an equal amount of money we may gain. In the case of insurance, the small sums we pay out for premiums have, dollar for dollar, less utility than the large sums we may lose without insurance coverage.

Jevons did not fully develop a general theory of distribution based on marginal productivity. Nor did he adequately explain the law of diminishing returns on which such a theory of distribution can be built. Yet he did hit on the rudiments of both ideas, as shown by Figure 2. Successive

FIGURE 2.   Jevons' Determination of Interest Rates Through Diminishing Returns to Capital

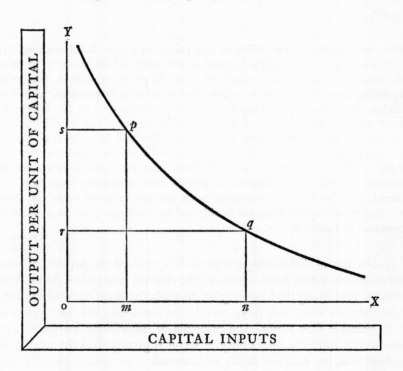

SOURCE: W. Stanley Jevons, *The Theory of Political Economy*, 4th ed. (London, Macmillan, 1911), p. 258.

units of capital investments, he said, are less productive than earlier units. Hence the tendency toward a falling rate of profit. The rate of interest tends toward uniformity at any one time. Distances along the line OX in Figure 2 represent quantities of capital employing a fixed number of laborers in any industry. The area under the curve pq denotes the whole product of labor and capital. With capital On, the total product is measured by the area between the vertical lines OY and qn. A small increase of capital at that point will add qn to the product, and that is all the entrepreneur can pay for that portion of the capital. With uniform interest rates, the total interest on capital will be On times qn, or the area of the rectangle $Onqr$. The remainder of the product, $rqpY$, will belong to the workers. Were capital available, say Om, its rate of interest would be pm, total interest $Omps$, and only spY would remain for labor. Interest, he said, is one of three components of profit, the other two being wages of superintendence and insurance against risk.

Jevons accepted Ricardian rent theory, which is based on a marginal analysis. He did not apply a similar approach to labor. To him wages are a residual after other claims are met. "The wages of a working man are ultimately coincident with what he produces, after the deduction of rent, taxes, and the interest of capital." It was John Bates Clark who formulated the best exposition of the law of diminishing returns and the marginal productivity theory of distribution.

The problem of business cycles attracted Jevons' attention. He believed that the sun-spot cycle influences the weather, which in turn affects the size of crops. Large crops occur when sun spots are at a minimum, and the resulting low prices of agricultural products stimulate the economy. The effects may manifest themselves internationally; a large crop and cheap food in India will leave the wage-earner surplus income for clothing, thereby promoting prosperity for the cotton mills of Manchester.

Jevons favored free public museums, concerts, libraries, and education. Child labor should be restricted by law, and health and safety conditions in factories should be regulated. He approved of trade unions as benefit or friendly societies, for their insurance functions keep men off public relief. But unions should leave the rate of wages to the operation of natural laws. If they obtain wage increases, it is at the expense of other workers or from the population in general through higher prices. "The supposed conflict of labour with capital is a delusion. The real conflict is between producers and consumers." Profit-sharing is preferable to union efforts to raise wages, and workers should save to improve their lot.

Jevons opposed regulating the hours of labor of adult males. He advocated excluding mothers with children below school age from factories and workshops for the sake of their children. Free hospitals and medical charities of all kinds were deplored because they "nourish in the poorest classes a contented sense of dependence on the richer classes for those ordinary requirements of life which they ought to be led to provide for themselves." He opposed government conservation measures to check the waste of coal because such modes of interference "break the principles of industrial freedom, to the recognition of which, since the time of Adam Smith, we attribute so much of our success."

Jevons supported a cautious extension of sanitary legislation, but was undecided if imprisonment for debt should be abolished. Moderate government regulation of railways won his approval. Consumption taxes such as the match tax are most desirable because industry is not adversely affected; besides, all people above the rank of actual paupers should contribute to the state in the proportion of their incomes. Basing himself on hedonism, he advocated the greatest happiness principle. No laws, no customs, no rights of property, he said, are so sacred that they must remain if it can be proven that they stand in the way of the greatest happiness. But, he asked, how can we prove that a certain change will increase the sum of happiness? Without conclusive evidence, "the present social arrangements have the considerable presumption in their favour that they can at least exist, and they can be tolerated."

CHAPTER 13

The Marginalist School:

THE AUSTRIANS and CLARK

Menger

CARL MENGER (1840–1921), a professor at the University of Vienna, published his path-breaking treatise on marginalist economics in 1871, the same year that Jevons' major book appeared. During the last three decades of his long life Menger published very little. He had wished to produce a systematic work on economics and also a comprehensive treatise on the character and methods of the social sciences in general. His interests and the scope of his projects continued to expand in wider and wider circles, and he resigned his professorship in 1903 in order to devote himself entirely to his work. He was never satisfied with his writing, and at his death he left voluminous manuscripts which were fragmentary and disordered.

Menger's exposition of diminishing marginal utility and the balancing of marginal utilities included a table which is reproduced here (see Table 4). The most important requirement for consumption is food, and the first unit of food consumed is assumed to have a utility of ten, as shown in Column I. If a second unit of food were consumed in the same day, its utility would be nine. With ten units of food available, the last unit would give a satisfaction of one. An eleventh unit of food would add nothing to total satisfaction.

Tobacco, less urgently needed, is shown in Column V. The first unit consumed gives a satisfaction of only six, and beyond five units no increased satisfaction can be obtained through increased consumption. If an individual obtained four units of food, his utility per unit would fall from ten through seven. He would then find that a fifth unit of food would afford the same satisfaction, six, as the first unit of tobacco. However, if one could afford to buy only three units, he would buy two of food and one of the commodity represented in Column II. Menger did not state that an implicit assumption of his table is that each unit of each commodity represents the same expenditure of money or effort or sacrifice. Otherwise, if a unit of tobacco could be obtained with ten cents or five minutes of work, and a unit of food could be obtained with twenty cents or ten minutes of work, the first unit of tobacco would be more desirable than even the first unit of food.

TABLE 4.   Diminishing Marginal Utility According to Menger

I (food)	II	III	IV	V (tobacco)	VI	VII	VIII	IX	X
10	9	8	7	6	5	4	3	2	1
9	8	7	6	5	4	3	2	1	0
8	7	6	5	4	3	2	1	0	
7	6	5	4	3	2	1	0		
6	5	4	3	2	1	0			
5	4	3	2	1	0				
4	3	2	1	0					
3	2	1	0						
2	1	0							
1	0								
0									

SOURCE: Carl Menger, *Principles of Economics*, James Dingwall and Bert F. Hoselitz, trs. and eds. (Glencoe, Free Press, 1950), p. 127. By permission of The Macmillan Company (New York).

Menger then drew an interesting conclusion from his table. Suppose an individual could afford only seven units of food. He would then satisfy only those of his needs for food that ranged in importance from ten through four, and the other needs, ranging in importance from three to one, would remain unsatisfied. What would be the usefulness to him of seven units of food? Jevons would have answered this question by adding the utility of each unit, from ten through four, and the answer would be forty-nine. Menger's answer would be twenty-eight—the marginal utility of the last unit (four) times the number of units (seven). Why? Because all units are alike. If a man had only one unit of food per day, his state of semi-starvation would attribute high utility to that unit. But if he had seven units, no one unit of food would give him more satisfaction than the marginal unit would.

Menger thereby identified exchange value with total utility, unlike Jevons who equated exchange value with marginal utility. Jevons would say that in Table 4, Column I, ten units of food have greater total utility than five units, but a smaller marginal utility; similarly, a large wheat crop offers more total utility than a small wheat crop, even if it sells for less money. According to Menger, five units of food offer more satisfaction for the individual ($5 \times 6 = 30$) than ten units ($10 \times 1 = 10$); a small wheat crop is more satisfying to consumers than a large one if it sells for more money.

Menger originated the idea of imputation in pricing factors of production. The marginalists emphasized the importance of consumer demand, especially in its subjective, psychological aspects, in determining price. The concepts of marginal and total utility refer to consumers' wants; therefore they apply only to consumer goods and services. What governs the prices of goods used in production, such as machinery, raw materials, land, and so on? Menger, in his theory of imputation, held that such goods also yield satisfactions to consumers, though only indirectly, by helping to produce things that do satisfy consumer wants directly. The consumer's marginal utility for a piece of iron is governed by the marginal utility of the final product that is made from that iron, say, a thimble; the iron has usefulness imputed to it by the usefulness of the thimble. The principle of marginal utility is thereby extended to the whole area of production and distribution. The rent received by landowners, for example, is governed by the utility of the products grown on that land. The factors or agents of production are assigned use values that govern their exchange values. The present value of the means of production is equal to the prospective value (based on marginal utility) of the consumer goods they will produce, with two deductions: first, a margin has to be subtracted "for the value of the services of capital" (interest); second, there must be a reward for entrepreneurial activity (profit).

Menger considered the problem of monopoly in a manner which anticipated several important concepts which were more fully developed later by others.

The monopolist is not completely unrestricted in influencing the course of economic events. As we have seen, if the monopolist wishes to sell a particular quantity of the monopolized good, he cannot fix the price at will. And if he fixes the price, he cannot, at the same time, determine the quantity that will be sold at the price he has set. He cannot, therefore, sell large quantities of the monopolized good and at the same time cause the price to settle at as high a level as it would have reached if he had marketed smaller quantities. Nor can he set the price at a certain level and at the same time sell as large a quantity as he could sell at lower prices. But what does give him an exceptional position in economic life is the fact that he has, in any given instance, a choice between determining the quantity of a monopolized good to be traded or its price. He makes this choice by himself and without regard to other economizing individuals, considering only his economic advantage. . . .

A monopolist will therefore raise his price, within the limits between which exchange operations have economic character, if he anticipates a greater economic gain from selling small quantities of the monopolized good for a high price. He will lower his price if he finds it more to his advantage to market larger quantities of the monopolized good at a lower price. . . . Under some circumstances, he may even have occasion to abandon part of the quantity of the monopolized good at his disposal to destruction instead of bringing it to market, or, with the same result, to leave unused or to destroy part of the corresponding means of production of the monopolized good. . . .

It would be entirely erroneous to assume that the price of a monopolized good always, or even usually, rises or falls in an *exactly* inverse proportion to the quantities marketed by the monopolist, or that a similar proportionality exists between the price set by the monopolist and the quantity of the monopolized good that can be sold. If, for example, the monopolist brings 2,000 instead of 1,000 units of the monopolized good to market, the price of one unit will not necessarily fall from six florins, for example, to three florins. On the contrary, depending upon the economic situation, it may in one case fall only to five florins, for example, but in another to as little as two florins.*

Menger indicated that the monopolist would price his product at that level that would give him the maximum profit.

The theoretical system of this pioneer marginalist was based on a more extreme individualism than was true of his disciple, Wieser.

Wieser

FRIEDRICH VON WIESER (1851–1926), disciple of Menger, was born in Vienna and trained in law and economics. He taught at the University of Prague, and later at the University of Vienna. He also held high posts in the Austrian government, serving at one time as minister of commerce. It was he who introduced the term "marginal utility," although others developed the concept before him without giving it the label that stuck.

Wieser, true to the marginalist doctrine, said that there is no "objective" exchange value, for "its roots are bedded in the subjective estimates of individuals, grouped to determine the result." We might well ask if the marginal price offer really reflects the marginal utility for a good. A well-fed millionaire offers ten dollars for a steak dinner for which a starving beggar will not pay more than fifty cents. Which man has the greater marginal utility for the dinner? Wieser was fully aware of this problem.

* Carl Menger, *Principles of Economics,* James Dingwall and Bert F. Hoselitz, trs. and eds. (Glencoe, Free Press, 1950), pp. 211–13. [Originally published in 1871.] By permission of The Macmillan Company (New York).

In order, however, properly to appraise the service of exchange value in economic life, it must be remembered that it does not contain exactly the same elements as does value in use in the self-contained economy. The latter simply depends upon utility: the former is besides dependent upon purchasing power. . . . Value in use measures utility; exchange value measures a combination of utility and purchasing power.*

Therefore, said Wieser, diamonds and gold stand exceptionally high in price because they are luxuries, valued and paid for according to the purchasing power of the richest classes. Coarser foodstuffs and iron are low in price because they are common goods, whose prices depend primarily on the purchasing power and the valuation of the poor.

Production is ordered not only according to simple want, but also according to wealth. Instead of things which would have the greatest utility, those things are produced for which the most will be paid. The greater the differences in wealth, the more striking will be the anomalies of production. It will furnish luxuries for the wanton and the glutton, while it is deaf to the wants of the miserable and the poor. It is therefore the distribution of wealth which decides how production is set to work, and induces consumption of the most uneconomic kind.†

Wieser then introduced the concept of natural value, which is the resultant of the quantity of goods and their marginal utility.

In natural value goods are estimated simply according to their marginal utility; in exchange value, according to a combination of marginal utility and purchasing power. In the former, luxuries are estimated far lower, and necessaries, comparatively, much higher than in the latter. Exchange value, even when considered as perfect, is, if we may so call it, a caricature of natural value; it disturbs its economic symmetry, magnifying the small and reducing the great.‡

From this Wieser drew a conclusion which was more typically Germanic than marginalist: There is room for limited government intervention in the economy whenever exchange value and natural value diverge too greatly.

People look for something better from a government. This does not, however, in the least involve that the form of undertaking for profit be entirely rejected. It may be retained, but, with the endeavour to obtain the highest business return, must be conjoined, in some way or other, the endeavour to serve the interests

* Friedrich von Wieser, *Natural Value*, Christian A. Malloch, tr. (London, 1893), p. 57. [Originally published in 1889.]
† *Ibid.*, p. 58.   ‡ *Ibid.*, p. 62.

of the public. In particular, where any considerable want is concerned while the power to pay is wanting, the service must be undertaken at limited prices, —that is to say, valuation according to exchange value must be replaced by valuation according to natural value. Thus emerges the "public enterprise."*

Wieser held that the utility of all goods of the same type equals the marginal utility, for any one unit can be considered the marginal unit. Where needs remain the same and the supply increases, the marginal utility must fall; this is his law of supply. The law of demand is shown when needs increase and supply remains the same, thereby increasing the marginal utility. He agreed with Menger that the total utility of a good is the marginal utility times the number of units available. This produces "the paradox of value." Each additional quantity of goods brings with it a diminished increment of utility and therefore a diminished increment of value. Value, and therefore utility, is zero when we have no goods, and when goods become superabundant. At some point, marginal utility times the units of goods gives a declining total. This occurs, although Wieser did not spell it out, where demand turns inelastic. Do we therefore find a larger supply of goods less useful than a smaller supply where the demand is inelastic, because it will sell for a smaller sum of money? Should we convert superfluity into want, and want into a greater want, in order to create and increase value? No, Wieser replied. The highest principle of all economy is utility. Where value and utility come into conflict, utility must conquer. He was confident, however, that human economies move almost entirely in the range where increasing supplies of goods increased both exchange value and total utilities; that is, demands are elastic. "In most things we are so far from having a superfluity that almost every multiplication of goods shows a corresponding increase in the total value," and "value is the form in which utility is calculated." Free competition prevents entrepreneurs from restricting output to raise prices, and any one producer's supply will not lower prices significantly. If there are cases of monopoly that restrict output to raise prices, then government must take over, "but such cases are too few to call for the socialist organization of society." All we need is that the free economic order of society should be "supplemented by suitable interference on the part of governments."

The assumptions of the simple economy are so framed as to demand the domination of the general interest. A paradox that arises in the opposition between personal power and social interest is therefore excluded. Yet even in the simple economy there are such glaring cases of this sort that the semblance of paradox is apt to arise. This mystery is most easily solved if we presuppose the extreme case in which a method of production makes possible an increase of stocks to

* *Ibid.*, p. 225.

the point of superabundance. Let us assume, for example, that by driving an artesian well or opening up a copious mountain spring it is possible to provide a town with pure water in superabundant quantities. If the principle of marginal utility were strictly adhered to, such an enterprise would never be started; a superabundant stock of free goods has a marginal utility of zero. But will such a consideration deter the public from incurring expenses for such an enterprise? Surely not. The undertaking guarantees the greatest possible benefit. The public will realize this benefit irrespective of the fact that the utility which results cannot be computed. It will be seen that the computation according to marginal utility does not simplify matters in this case, as it usually does in others. Rather it leads one astray. Hence the more complicated computation of total benefit will be resorted to.

This is precisely the state of affairs where we examine all other cases of apparent paradox. Whenever the increase of the supply, computed at the marginal utility, leads to a lower numerical expression, the reckoning by marginal utility ceases to simplify and the plan of production must be drafted on the basis of total utility.

Marginal utility may be used as a basis for calculations where the larger stock still gives a larger product. It is inapplicable when the product is smaller. Cases of the first kind are altogether too general; the latter are exceptional.*

That is, private enterprise serves society only when the demand for each firm's output is elastic. This will always be true under competitive conditions.

Wieser is famous for his doctrine which came to be called the opportunity-cost principle or the alternative-cost principle. This concept turned cost of production into a subjective, psychological cost. The entrepreneur who produces something for a market gives up the opportunity to produce and sell alternative commodities.

Whenever the business man speaks of incurring costs, he has in mind the quantity of productive means required to achieve a certain end; but the associated idea of a sacrifice which his efforts demand is also aroused. In what does this sacrifice consist? What, for example, is the cost to the producer of devoting certain quantities of iron from his supply to the manufacture of some specific product? The sacrifice consists in the exclusion or limitation of possibilities by which other products might have been turned out, had the material not been devoted to one particular product. Our definition in an earlier connection made clear that cost-productive-means are productive agents which are widely scattered and have manifold uses. As such they promise a profitable yield in many directions. But the realization of one of these necessarily involves a loss of all the others. It is this sacrifice that is predicated in the concept of costs: the costs of production or the quantities of cost-productive-means

* Friedrich von Wieser, *Social Economics*, A. Ford Hinrichs, tr. (New York, 1927), p. 128. [Originally published in 1914.]

required for a given product and thus withheld from other uses. . . . The business man, comparing the profits of one product with its cost, compares in truth two masses of utility.*

It is generally agreed that the opportunity-cost principle has wide applicability in economic affairs. The cost of producing more automobiles may be producing fewer houses. If school attendance is increased, output is reduced in the near future. Building a school may involve giving up a hospital or giving up command over consumer or investment goods. Buying a pound of tobacco means sacrificing two visits to the cinema. Opportunity costs are involved when the small entrepreneur considers his implicit wage, interest, and rent costs, for he could earn these factor incomes in other employments. It is doubtful, however, if this principle contributes anything fundamental toward explaining value and market price; it seems to offer a chain of circular reasoning.

Böhm-Bawerk

EUGEN VON BÖHM-BAWERK (1851-1914) was the third member of the triumvirate (along with Menger and Wieser) who founded and promoted the Austrian marginalist school. He was a professor of political economy at the University of Vienna, and also had served in the Austrian government as minister of finance. He was married to Wieser's sister.

Böhm-Bawerk's major contribution to economic theory was his analysis of the element of time. Not time in relation to systematic changes in the economy, or in relation to economic growth; to him time was significant as an element in the normal course of economic affairs, influencing all values, prices, and incomes.

How Böhm-Bawerk used the concept of time may be seen in his famous agio theory of interest. He based his theory of interest on three grounds, of which the first two are subjective. First, goods are appreciated more highly in the present than in the future. "We systematically underestimate future wants, and the goods which are to satisfy them." Second, we also are prepared to pay interest for present rather than future goods because we expect to be better off in the future. So far interest is based on consumption. The third basis for interest involves production. The process of production is lengthened, or becomes more roundabout, when more and more capital goods are produced and used to turn out final products. To fish more successfully, one builds a boat; this lengthens the process of production, and the physical product increases more than proportionally. Until Böhm-Bawerk's time, the length of the period of production

* *Ibid.*, pp. 99–100.

was regarded as a technological datum and therefore constant. He turned it into a variable.

From this followed the explanation of interest. It is an agio, or premium, placed on the value and price of present consumer goods. Workers and landowners receive the present value of their productive services. The increments in value, which are due to the more highly productive methods made possible by the passage of time, remain in the hands of the entrepreneur. From him interest flows to the capitalist who made funds available for roundabout or capital-using production. Therefore workers and landowners do receive the value of the product of their services, but the value is discounted to the present time.

In brief, interest *can* be paid by the entrepreneur because the more roundabout the process of production, the more productive and efficient it becomes. Interest *must* be paid because people prefer present to future consumption.

Böhm-Bawerk agreed with the other two leaders of the Austrian marginalist school, that total utility of a good is the marginal utility times the number of units. He also agreed with them that the value of means of production depends on the value of the final goods they produce, which in turn depends on the marginal utility of the final goods. The value of the final product is greater than the value of the services that produce it by the amount of interest over the period of time that elapses.

Böhm-Bawerk, like the marginalists generally, accepted J. B. Say's analysis that the economy normally tended toward full employment. He cited criticism of his belief that if all members of a community simultaneously save one-quarter of their incomes, production will not fall.

The fault in the reasoning [of his critic] is indeed not far to seek. It is that one of the premises, the one which asserts that a curtailment of "consumption for immediate enjoyment" must involve also a curtailment of production, is erroneous. The truth is that a curtailment of consumption involves, not a curtailment of production generally, but only, through the action of the law of supply and demand, a curtailment in certain branches. . . . There will not, however, be a smaller production of goods generally, because the lessened output of goods ready for immediate consumption may and will be offset by an increased production of "intermediate" or capital goods.*

Böhm-Bawerk then quoted his critic as saying that the production of capital goods is also called forth and guided only by the demand for consumer goods; if the demand for consumer goods is reduced by one-quarter,

* This and the following quote are from Eugen von Böhm-Bawerk, "The Function of Saving," *Annals of the American Academy of Political and Social Science*, Publication No. 304 (May 1901), pp. 62–64.

why will more capital goods than formerly be demanded and produced? This is his reply:

The man who saves curtails his demand for *present* consumption goods but by no means his desire for pleasure-affording goods generally. This is a proposition which, under a slightly different title, has already been repeatedly and, I believe, conclusively discussed in our science both by the older writers and in contemporary literature. Economists are to-day completely agreed, I think, that the "abstinence" connected with saving is no true abstinence, that is, no final renunciation of pleasure-affording goods, but . . . a mere "waiting." The person who saves is not willing to hand over his savings without return, but requires that they be given back at some future time, usually indeed with interest, either to himself or to his heirs. Through saving not a single particle of the demand for goods is extinguished outright, but, as J. B. Say showed in a masterly way more than one hundred years ago . . . , the demand for goods, the wish for means of enjoyment is, under whatever circumstances men are found, insatiable. A person may have enough or even too much of a particular kind of goods at a particular time, but not of goods in general nor for all time. This doctrine applies particularly to saving. For the principal motive of those who save is precisely to provide for their own futures or for the futures of their heirs. This means nothing else than that they wish to secure and make certain their command over the means to the satisfaction of their future needs, that is over consumption goods at a future time. In other words, those who save curtail their demand for consumption goods in the present merely to increase proportionately their demand for consumption goods in the future.

Böhm-Bawerk's emphasis on the productivity of capital, his defense of interest, and his support of Say's Law of Markets probably were partly a reaction to the growing influence of Marxism in his time. He produced a famous criticism of Marx in 1896, which was published in English translation with the title, *Karl Marx and the Close of His System.*

Clark

JOHN BATES CLARK (1847–1938), with a world reputation, represented America's great contribution to marginalist economics. He was born in Rhode Island, studied at Amherst and in Germany, and taught at Carleton, Smith, Amherst, Johns Hopkins, and Columbia. Thorstein Veblen was Clark's student at Carleton College, and his later fame was a source of great pride to Clark. The latter was undisturbed by the fact that much of that fame rested on criticisms of the kind of economic theory Clark had developed.

Clark seems to have thought out independently the concept of marginal utility and its influence on exchange value, around 1880; apparently he had not read Jevons. He not only invented the term marginal productivity, but he presented the clearest and best analysis up to his time of the marginal productivity theory of distribution. This was based on the law of diminishing returns, which Clark applied to all factors of production.

In the opening paragraph of the preface to his most important book, Clark summarized his analysis of distribution and his conclusions.

It is the purpose of this work to show that the distribution of the income of society is controlled by a natural law, and that this law, if it worked without friction, would give to every agent of production the amount of wealth which that agent creates. However wages may be adjusted by bargains freely made between individual men, the rates of pay that result from such transactions tend, it is here claimed, to equal that part of the product of industry which is traceable to the labor itself; and however interest may be adjusted by similarly free bargaining, it naturally tends to equal the fractional product that is separately traceable to capital. At the point in the economic system where titles to property originate,—where labor and capital come into possession of the amounts that the state afterwards treats as their own,—the social procedure is true to the principle on which the right of property rests. So far as it is not obstructed, it assigns to every one what he has specifically produced.*

Clark's theory of distribution was based on the law of diminishing returns, which he first presented in a paper read at the third annual meeting of the American Economic Association in 1888. This law was originally applied to agriculture. In modern terms, it states that as more of any variable factor of production is added to fixed factors, the output beginning at some point increases less than proportionally. In essence this law means that factors of production are not perfect substitutes for each other. The underlying assumption is that all other things remain unchanged, especially technology, while one factor is varied. Thus, if capital, land, and entrepreneurship are kept constant while labor is added, ultimately the average output per worker must fall even though total output continues to increase. Similarly, if capital is added while the other factors remain fixed, the average return per unit of capital must finally fall.

Clark stated the law as follows:

The last tool adds less to man's efficiency than do earlier tools. If capital be used in increasing quantity by a fixed working force, it is subject to a law of diminishing productivity. . . . The diminishing productivity of labor, when it is used in connection with a fixed amount of capital, is a universal phenomenon. . . . This action of the general law . . . becomes the basis of a theory of distribution.†

* John Bates Clark, *The Distribution of Wealth* (New York, 1899), p. v.
† *Ibid.*, 48–50.

Clark recognized that increasing returns to the variable factor might occur at first, if additional units caused a better division of labor or a more perfect organization of work. However, additional units of the variable factor will be employed until the range of diminishing returns has been entered. Equilibrium will occur where the marginal productivity of the variable factor is equal to the cost, or the earnings, of the factor. All units of the factor receive what the marginal unit produces, because all units are assumed to be homogeneous, and the surplus produced by the earlier units goes to other productive factors.

The gross earnings of society are separated into three shares: wages, interest, and profits. These sums represent the earnings of labor, capital, and entrepreneurship separated from the ownership of capital. The rent of land is merged with interest. Profits are a residual share after wages and interest are paid according to the marginal productivity of labor and capital. In a perfectly competitive society profits tend to disappear at both ends of the productive process. "By bidding against each other in selling goods, employers make the prices smaller; and by bidding against each other in hiring labor and capital, they make wages and interest larger." In a zero-profits economy goods sell at cost of production. The businessman will get wages for whatever labor he may perform, and interest for any capital that he may furnish.

Clark claimed that his theory was static, best suited to be a purely analytical instrument. (Since his time "static" seems to have become a term of opprobrium in economics.) He assumed that all changes cease. Toward what level would prices, wages, and interest tend if labor and capital were to remain fixed in quantity, improvements in methods of production ceased, and wants of consumers never altered? We study static laws separately in order to understand what goes on in a dynamic society, he said. The truth that the world is dynamic does not invalidate the conclusions of a static theory, for static laws are nevertheless real laws which reassert themselves after every dynamic change in the economy. Clark did not develop any dynamic (historical) theories. He relied almost exclusively on what is now known as the method of comparative statics, for he compared different stationary equilibria.

In the real world, said Clark, a legal monopoly might secure to an entrepreneur a permanent profit. Labor and capital would be prevented from moving into the favored industry, though economic forces, if they had been left unhindered, would have caused them to move to it. This condition, however, is not a true static state. Like a body of tranquil water, a static state has perfect fluidity but no flow. Factors of production have perfect mobility but no motion. A monopoly represents an element of obstruction or friction that prevents the working out of static economic laws.

Capital is productive, and therefore interest exists. "Paying interest is buying the product of capital, as paying wages is buying the product of labor." Interest furnishes a motive for abstinence. The motive for accumulating productive wealth is to get an income that will never cease. Abstinence leads to new capital goods, but no additional abstinence is required to maintain the existing capital stock. Accumulation, said Clark, is a part of economic dynamics. In the real world capital is increasing faster than the supply of labor. Therefore its rate of earnings, interest, declines. Tools are employed in the order of their productivity, so far as men judge productivity correctly. The rudest hatchet will enormously increase man's power to get firewood. Later, better tools will increase productivity by a smaller percentage.

As accumulation proceeds, there are always made costlier machines, representing more capital; and the product that comes from using them is a smaller fraction of their cost. The straightening of the curves in railroads is one of the ways in which capital may find investment. This may cost as much as the first making of the corresponding parts of the road themselves; but it does not liberate as much labor, in proportion to its cost, as did the building of the old and crooked road. . . . Everywhere do the forms of the capital show differences in earning power; and the owners choose first the most productive forms, and later the less productive. To this fact is due the present low rate of interest. We are utilizing the opportunities for investment that stand late in the series and are low in the scale of productivity.*

Most marginalists agree on the tendency for the rate of interest (or profit) to fall.

Clark's over-all conclusion was that the division of the social income into wages, interest, and profit is, in principle, equitable. Society is not at liberty to violate the "fixed laws of distribution." If every man receives all that he creates, the different classes of men who combine their forces in industry have no grievances against each other. Private property is ethically justified because it is based on an ethical distribution of income.

In 1896 Clark was quite sanguine about business monopolies.† Their high prices attract new competitors, and their large profits are reinvested and thereby promote progress. The exaction of the trust works arithmetically when it takes from the public a definite sum. Progress, however, works geometrically through accumulation and reinvestment by forever multiplying the fruitfulness of industry. As giant trusts invade each other's

* *Ibid.,* pp. 185–86.

† John Bates Clark, "The Theory of Economic Progress," *Economic Studies,* American Economic Association, Vol. I, No. 1 (April 1896), pp. 11–15.

fields, they are driven to be efficient, and large firms are naturally more efficient than small ones.

In 1907, however, in his book dealing with what he called economic dynamics, Clark turned gloomy over the trust problem. Trusts are a product of economic dynamics. Fierce and costly strife among them induces them to take the final step in organization, thus bringing competition to an end. Goods become scarcer and dearer.

No description could exaggerate the evil which is in store for a society given hopelessly over to a régime of private monopoly. Under this comprehensive name we shall group the most important of the agencies which not merely resist, but positively vitiate, the action of natural economic law. Monopoly checks progress in production and infuses into distribution an element of robbery. It perverts the forces which tend to secure to individuals all that they produce. It makes prices and wages abnormal and distorts the form of the industrial mechanism. . . . Prices do not conform to the standards of cost, wages do not conform to the standard of final productivity of labor, and interest does not conform to the marginal product of capital. The system of industrial groups and subgroups is thrown out of balance by putting too much labor and capital at certain points and too little at others. Profits become, not altogether a temporary premium for improvement,—the reward for giving to humanity a dynamic impulse,—but partly the spoils of men whose influence is hostile to progress.*

Clark favored government regulation of monopolies to preserve competition. We would thereby ride roughshod over laissez faire to gain the end that doctrine had in view, namely, a system activated by the vivifying power of competition.

Clark was optimistic over the outcome of economic dynamics if monopolies could be curbed. He saw five types of trends that are tending to promote industrial progress: (1) Population is increasing. (2) Capital is accumulating. (3) Technical processes of industry are improving. (4) Modes of organizing labor and capital are becoming more efficient. (5) The wants of mankind are becoming multiplied and refined. Population will increase less rapidly than capital, and therefore most of the benefits of progress will accrue to the wage-earning classes. His conclusion was that economic harmony, based on competition, should and will prevail.

* John Bates Clark, *Essentials of Economic Theory* (New York, 1907), pp. 375, 377.

CHAPTER 14

The Marginalist School:

ALFRED MARSHALL

ALFRED MARSHALL (1842–1924), the greatest figure in the marginalist school, was the son of a cashier in the Bank of England. The father was a rather tyrannical gentleman, author of a tract called *Man's Rights and Woman's Duties*. He overworked Alfred at his studies, made him promise never to play chess because it was a waste of time, and tried to banish mathematics from the boy's life for it was irrelevant to the ministry, which the father had picked for the son's career. Young Marshall, however, rejected a scholarship at Oxford which would have led to the church, rejected the ministry, rejected the study of "dead languages," and devoted himself to mathematics and physics, and later to economics, at Cambridge. He was aided by a well-to-do uncle, for his father was too poor to pay his tuition when he abandoned the Oxford scholarship.

Marshall was a hypochondriac about his health and hypercritical about his writing. Much of what he wrote he threw into the wastepaper basket. Many of his major ideas he worked out a decade or more before they appeared in print in 1890 in the first edition of his *Principles of Economics*. In successive editions of that work he introduced so many qualifications, exceptions, and hesitations into his system as to weaken the clear and definite principles on which many people love to lean. Marshall criticized Jevons for rushing into print before he was ready. He himself kept portions of his book *Industry and Trade* (1919) in printed proofs fifteen years before publication. Because he was slow in publishing, his ideas seemed commonplace by the time they appeared in print. Yet he was the most influential economic theorist of his day, and undoubtedly the greatest of his generation. As long ago as 1888 it was said that half the economic chairs in the United Kingdom were occupied by his former students.

Marshall was the founder of modern diagrammatic economics—the bane of beginning students—which really helped elucidate certain fundamental principles. Although he was an expert mathematician, he was skeptical of the value of mathematics in economic analysis. He also was the great synthesizer, seeking to combine the best of classical economics with marginalist thinking; hence the name "neoclassical," which is sometimes used synonymously with marginalism. In many of his footnotes and appendices can be found hints of ideas of which he was aware, but which were worked out in greater detail by others decades and generations later.

Marshall defined his subject as follows: "Political Economy or Economics is a study of mankind in the ordinary business of life; it examines that part of individual and social action which is most closely connected with the attainment and with the use of the material requisites of wellbeing."*

Economists, he said, like other scientists, collect facts, arrange and interpret them, and draw inferences from them. They seek knowledge of the interdependence of economic phenomena, of cause-and-effect relationships. Every cause has a tendency to produce some definite result if nothing occurs to hinder it. Economics is not a body of concrete truth, but an engine for the discovery of concrete truth.

We seek to discover economic laws. Any law is a general proposition or statement of tendencies, more or less certain, more or less definite. Social laws are statements of social tendencies. Economic laws, or statements of economic tendencies, are those social laws that relate to human conduct in which the strength of the major motives can be measured by a money price. Economics is less exact than other sciences, but progress is being made toward greater precision.

The implications of Marshall's approach and definitions are interesting. Economic laws are not natural laws that are necessarily beneficient. It is not imperative, although it may be desirable, that they be allowed to work themselves out without any restraining hand. It is not true that "we cannot repeal the law of supply and demand," as is frequently said by the uninformed. Economic laws are not like political laws, which may be broken only at the risk of suffering a penalty. The relationships among supply, demand, and price tend to produce certain results if they are allowed to work themselves out, and if other changes do not intrude to alter the tendencies. But society can influence the outcome if it so desires. During wars, for example, it can control prices and thwart the tendency for them to rise. This does not violate any sacrosanct law. Marshall was far less

* Reprinted with permission of Macmillan & Co. Ltd., The Macmillan Company of Canada Limited, and The Macmillan Company from *Principles of Economics*, 8th ed., by Alfred Marshall (London, 1920), p. 331. [Originally published in 1890 and first published in the United States in 1948.]

dogmatic than most other marginalists, and his thinking left room for cautious reform, for modest departures from laissez faire.

Marshall had little to say about business cycles. This is partly understandable in view of his microeconomic approach. The narrower the sector we consider, the less important is the cycle. To a small retail business, the death of a competitor or the opening of a supermarket next door are far more important events than nationwide business fluctuations. To individuals, events other than cycles are important. The fortunes of a huge corporation, however, are likely to be linked closely to the level of aggregate business activity. Marshall and others who dealt with individuals and small representative firms found it easy to ignore fluctuations. Only aggregative economics grappled with such problems.

Marginal Utility and Demand

DEMAND is based on the law of diminishing marginal utility and the balancing of marginal utilities. The subjective, psychological approach of the Marshallian system dealt with pleasures and pains, desires and aspirations, incentives to action. How can we measure such intangibles? With money. Other marginalists said that the strength of a person's motives determines the money payments. Marshall said that money payments measure the force of a person's motives. The definite and precise money measurement of the motives in business life makes economics the most exact of the social sciences, just as the chemist's fine balance has made chemistry more exact than most physical sciences. This measuring device of economics, rough and imperfect as it is, is the best device we have to gauge man's psychological drives as expressed in the market place.

We cannot directly compare the pleasures that two persons derive from smoking. Nor can we compare the pleasure that one person gets from smoking at two different times. However, if we find a man in doubt whether to spend a few cents on a cigar, or a cup of tea, or on riding home instead of walking, we may say that he expects from them equal pleasures. Money measures utility at the margin.

If then we wish to compare even physical gratifications, we must do it not directly, but indirectly by the incentives which they afford to action. If the desires to secure either of two pleasures will induce people in similar circumstances each to do just an hour's extra work, or will induce men in the same rank of life and with the same means each to pay a shilling for it; we then may say that those pleasures are equal for our purposes, because the desires for them are equally strong incentives to action for persons under similar conditions.*

* *Ibid.*, pp. 15–16.

Two people with equal incomes will not necessarily derive equal benefit from their use. Take one pound from each of them, and the intensities of the satisfaction given up may not be nearly equal. But when many people are involved, the personal peculiarities of individuals tend to counterbalance one another. Then we can say that the money that people of equal incomes give to obtain a benefit or avoid an injury is a good measure of the benefit or injury.

Obviously a unit of goods has greater marginal utility to a poor man than to a rich man, because he has fewer units. Money also has greater marginal utility for poor people than for the wealthy. How, then, can we generalize about progress, happiness, and the effects of taxation if wealth and income have such wide differences of marginal utility for people in different income groups? Here again the answer lies in large numbers. If we take whole cross sections of the income groups of society, money becomes an acceptable measuring rod.

By far the greater number of the events with which economics deals affect in about equal proportions all the different classes of society; so that if the money measures of the happiness caused by two events are equal, it is reasonable and in accordance with common usage to regard the amounts of the happiness in the two cases as equivalent. And, further, as money is likely to be turned to the higher uses of life in about equal proportions, by any two large groups of people taken without special bias from any two parts of the western world, there is even some *prima facie* probability that equal additions to their material resources will make about equal additions to the fulness of life, and the true progress of the human race.*

Let us measure, then, said Marshall, the strength of motives by means of money. Let us ascertain how much money a particular group is just willing to pay as the price of a certain thing that it desires, or how much money must be offered to induce a group to undergo a certain effort or abstinence that it dislikes.

Marshall, unlike the Austrian marginalists, asserted that the total utility of a good was the sum of the successive marginal utilities of each added unit. Therefore the price that a person pays for a thing can never exceed, and seldom comes up to that which he would be willing to pay rather than go without it. Only at the margin will price generally come up to a person's willingness to pay. Considering a person's total purchases of a good, the satisfaction he gets exceeds that which he gives up in paying for the goods. The surplus of satisfaction Marshall called consumer's surplus.

As an illustration of this idea, take tea. Suppose a man would buy one pound annually if the price were twenty shillings. At fourteen shillings he

* *Ibid.*, p. 20.

would buy two pounds, at ten shillings three pounds, at six shillings four pounds, at four shillings five pounds, and at three shillings six pounds. If the price is actually two shillings, he buys seven pounds of tea annually. He gets all seven pounds at two shillings each, even though the first pound gives him twenty shillings worth of satisfaction. His consumer's surplus is eighteen shillings on the first pound, twelve shillings on the second, and so on, for a total of forty-five shillings. Consumer's surplus shows the benefits we get from living in a productive social environment that cheapens goods by producing them more efficiently. As an individual reaches equilibrium lower on his demand curve (for he will buy more goods as they become cheaper), his consumer's surplus grows. Referring again to the "paradox of value," Marshall would say that a large wheat crop is more useful than a small one. If we pay less for the larger crop, our consumer's surplus is larger.

The idea of consumer's surplus is more applicable to Marshall's partial equilibrium analysis than it would be to aggregative problems. His selection of tea as an illustration is especially appropriate because it requires only a very small part of a person's total outlay on consumer goods. The price of tea is made to vary while all other prices are kept constant. If we consider total consumption spending, there would be multiple counting of the consumer's surplus. Surely you would give, if you had to, half your income for food; and half for shelter; and of course half for clothing if the alternative were to have absolutely none; and why not half for drugs and doctors, if your life depended on them? It could be argued that from the viewpoint of a person's total consumption spending, the consumer's surplus is approximately equal to his current saving. If he now saves 10 per cent of his income, he might save nothing if prices rose much higher. Therefore he gets goods now for which he would be willing and able to pay only 10 per cent more, no matter how crucial they were to his survival. If he has a good credit rating, or if he has accumulated wealth from past saving, he could pay more than an additional 10 per cent for the goods he wants, and his consumer's surplus would exceed his current saving. The concept of consumer's surplus is not as useful in macroeconomics as it is in Marshall's microeconomic analysis.

Marshall was far superior to his predecessors in handling elasticity of demand. He analyzed the subject verbally, diagrammatically, and mathematically. The only universal law pertaining to a person's desire for a commodity, he said, is that it diminishes, other things being equal, with every increase in his supply of that commodity. It follows, therefore, that the lower the price, the more he will buy; the higher the price, the less he will buy. That is why the demand curve slopes downward to the right. Elasticity of demand tells us whether the diminution of desire is slow or rapid as the quantity increases. It relates the percentage drop in price with the percentage increase in quantity demanded, which of course is based on the diminishing marginal utility of the good. The numerical coefficient of the elasticity of demand is the percentage change of quantity divided by the percentage change in price.

The principle of elasticity of demand is useful over a wide range of economic problems and policies. Governments, for example, tax commodities with inelastic demands (cigarettes) rather than those with elastic demands (canned peaches). Monopolistic prices are likely to be set at higher levels where demand is inelastic (antibiotics versus cola soft drinks). Restrictions of agricultural output result in greater gross revenue to farmers if the demand for the product is inelastic, and smaller revenue if the demand is elastic (wheat versus strawberries).

Supply and Market Prices

SUPPLY is governed by cost of production. Marshall conceived of supply as a curve rather than a point, a whole series of quantities that would be forthcoming at a whole series of prices. Cost of production is measured in terms of money, but behind money costs lie the psychological sacrifices, the irksomeness of working and the sacrifice involved in putting off consumption. The latter Marshall called "waiting" rather than "abstinence." Assuming that the efficiency of production depends solely upon the exertions of the workers, the supply curve will slope upward and to the right; the higher the price, the larger the quantity supplied.

What determines market price? The cost of production of the supply, said the classical economists, meaning objective labor-time cost and the sacrifice of abstinence. Demand, said the early marginalists. Both supply and demand, said Marshall, the great synthesizer. Behind supply lie costs, subjective costs. Behind demand lie utility and diminishing marginal utility.

We might as reasonably dispute whether it is the upper or the under blade of a pair of scissors that cuts a piece of paper, as whether value is governed by utility or cost of production. It is true that when one blade is held still, and the cutting is effected by moving the other, we may say with careless brevity that the cutting is done by the second; but the statement is not strictly accurate, and is to be excused only so long as it claims to be merely a popular and not a strictly scientific account of what happens.*

Here Marshall introduced the time element into economic analysis. As a general rule, he said, the shorter the period, the greater is the influence of

* *Ibid.*, p. 348.

demand on value. The longer the period, the more important is the influence of cost of production on value. The reason is that the influence of cost of production takes a longer time to work itself out than does the influence of changes in demand. Market value is influenced by passing events, but in long periods these irregular causes neutralize each other.

For purposes of exposition, Marshall divided time into the immediate present, the short run, and the long run. Market prices refer to the present, with no time allowed for adaptation of supply to changes of demand. It may be the market for a "day." The quantity offered cannot be increased immediately, and it cannot be decreased except through sale and removal from the market. If there were a run on shoes in a city, the messages to increase production and shipments would be flashed back to the distributors and the manufacturers. Shoes would not arrive in the retail stores, however, until a lapse of a certain amount of time, perhaps a day or two. The market period is defined as that period during which the supply cannot be increased in response to a suddenly increased demand. Nor can supply be decreased immediately in response to a decline of demand, because it takes time for production to be curtailed and inventories reduced.

If a good is perishable, and if we assume that the businessman is trying to maximize his profit or minimize his losses, the market supply curve is a vertical straight line. He would rather sell his fresh fish for one cent a pound than let it spoil. If the good is not perishable, the sellers have reservation prices below which they will not sell. Some sellers, however, will sell at prices well below cost of production, perhaps because they have pressing bills to pay. The market supply curve therefore slopes upward and to the right until it encompasses the total quantity on the market. Then it becomes vertical, for no matter how high the market price, by definition no greater supply can be forthcoming during the market period. Therefore demand is the most important determinant of market price. The market supply curve is not based on cost of production, for the costs, being already incurred, are not necessarily recoverable.

To analyze the short-run period, Marshall divided costs into two types which he called prime and supplementary costs, and which we now call variable and constant costs. Variable costs are those that can change over the short run with a changing scale of output, such as those for labor and raw materials. Constant costs are fixed or overhead costs such as depreciation of the plant and top executives' salaries; they cannot be changed in the short run. In fact, the short-run period is defined as that period during which the variable inputs can be increased or decreased, but the fixed plant cannot be changed. In the short run all variable costs must be covered, but some of the fixed costs may not be. For example, a railroad will continue to be operated in the short run even if part of the fixed investment is never recovered. Its losses would be greater if it went out of business, for the scrap value of a railroad is rather small. Demand and supply are both important in this period in determining price, and the supply curve is based on variable costs.

In the long-run period, all costs are variable and they must all be covered if the firm is to continue in business. If price rises above total cost of production, more capital will enter the industry, typically by the entry of new firms. If price falls below cost of production, capital will withdraw, probably by the exit of firms. In the long run, therefore, cost of production is the most important determinant of price and value, and it is the underlying force that determines the location of the supply curve. In a stationary state, with monetary aberrations ruled out, cost of production would govern price and value. In a changing world, however, with adaptations to change that are imperfect and take time, both demand and supply are important.

An increase in the amount demanded generally raises the short-period supply price. As more workers are added to a plant of a fixed size, the principle of diminishing returns to labor asserts itself. Perhaps less efficient workers are hired. In the long run, however, more factories can be built and more workers attracted to the industry and trained. An increased supply could then be produced with no increase in price, or perhaps a decrease in price if there are certain economies in large-scale production.

Marshall defined long-run normal price as that price which in the long run would exactly balance supply and demand, and which would be equal to long-run total cost of production. The normal price changes with every change in the efficiency of production. Market prices tend to fluctuate around normal prices, but it is only by accident that they will be equal. There are very gradual or secular movements of normal price caused by the gradual growth of knowledge, population, capital, and the changing conditions of demand and supply from one generation to another.

Marshall's masterly handling of the element of time was one of his many significant contributions to economic thinking.

Distribution

THE distribution of income in a laissez faire economy is determined by the pricing of factors of production. The businessman, said Marshall, must constantly compare the relative efficiency of every agent of production that he employs. He must also consider the possibilities of substituting one agent for another. Horse power can replace hand power, and steam power replaces horse power. At the margin of indifference between two substitutable factors of production, their prices must be proportionate to their efficiency, or their cost must be proportionate to the money value they add to the total product. The most striking advantage of economic freedom is manifest when a businessman experiments, at his own risk, to find the combination of factor inputs that will yield the lowest costs for producing the output. The entrepreneur must estimate how much net addition to the value of his total product will be contributed by an extra unit of any one factor of production. He will employ each agent up to that margin at which its net product would no longer exceed the price he would have to pay for it. Marshall based this analysis on the diminishing returns which result from the "disproportionate use of any agent of production."

If we take labor as an example, wages are not determined by the marginal productivity of labor, said Marshall. Marginal productivity is the basis for the demand for labor, which is a derived demand depending on the demand by consumers for the final products. Wages, like the return to any factor of production, depend on both demand and supply. If the supply of labor increases, other things remaining constant, the marginal productivity of labor will fall, and wages will fall. If the supply of labor is reduced, the marginal productivity of labor will rise, and therefore wages will rise. Marginal productivity by itself therefore does not determine wages, because there are many possible marginal productivities as we vary the number of workers. It is correct, however, to say that wages measure and are equal to marginal productivity, given the supply of labor. To each individual employer the wage rate is fixed, and he varies the number of workers employed, reaching equilibrium employment in his business when wages equal the marginal productivity of labor.

Another distributive share to be considered is interest. A rise in the rate of interest diminishes the use of machinery, for the businessman avoids the use of all machines whose net annual surplus is less than the rate of interest. Lower interest rates increase capital investments. The demand for the loan of capital is the aggregate of the demands of all individuals in all trades. As with final commodities, the higher the price, the less capital is demanded; the lower the price, the more is demanded. This relationship is based on diminishing marginal productivity as the quantity of a factor increases, just as the demand for consumer goods is based on diminishing marginal utility as the quantity increases.

The diminishing marginal productivity of capital as more units are acquired constitutes the demand for capital, with prices recorded in terms of rates of interest. The demand curve for capital therefore slopes down and to the right. The supply of capital is determined by saving, which depends mainly although not entirely on the rate of interest. It might seem like circular reasoning to say that the supply of saving depends on the rate of interest, and the rate of interest depends on the supply of saving. But Marshall speaks of the supply as being a whole series of quantities that would be offered at different prices, just as the demand is a series of quantities that would be taken at different prices. With saving, as with other factors of production, the price (the rate of interest in this case) settles at the point of intersection of the demand and the supply curves.

The main motive for saving is positive time preference, people preferring present to future consumption.

Human nature being what it is, we are justified in speaking of the interest on capital as the reward of the sacrifice involved in the waiting for the enjoyment of material resources, because few people would save much without reward; just as we speak of wages as the reward of labour, because few people would work hard without reward.

The sacrifice of present pleasure for the sake of future, has been called *abstinence* by economists. But this term has been misunderstood: for the greatest accumulators of wealth are very rich persons, some of whom live in luxury, and certainly do not practise abstinence in that sense of the term in which it is convertible with abstemiousness. What economists meant was that, when a person abstained from consuming anything which he had the power of consuming, with the purpose of increasing his resources in the future, his abstinence from that particular act of consumption increased the accumulation of wealth. Since, however, the term is liable to be misunderstood, we may with advantage avoid its use, and say that the accumulation of wealth is generally the result of a postponement of enjoyment, or of a *waiting* for it.*

Marshall recognized that other motives for saving might also be important. He mentioned family affection, force of habit, miserliness, magnitude of the income, and prudence in wishing to provide for the future. Some saving might therefore occur even if interest were zero or negative. If a man wanted a certain annuity for his old age, he might save less at a high rate of interest than at a low rate. But these are all exceptional cases. A fall in the interest rate will in general induce people to consume a little more in the present, and a rise will induce them to consume a little less.

Thus interest tends toward an equilibrium level that equalizes the aggregate demand for capital in a market with the aggregate supply forthcoming at that rate.

Normal profits, according to Marshall, include interest, the earnings of management, and the supply price of business organization. Interest we have already discussed. The earnings of management are a payment for a specialized form of labor. Profits as the supply price of business organization are a reward to entrepreneurship, that fourth factor of production which was added to the three of the classical school—land, labor, and capital.

* *Ibid.*, pp. 232–33.

Marshall incorporated Ricardian rent theory into his system.

The amount of . . . rent . . . is itself governed by the fertility of land, the price of the produce, and the position of the margin: it is the excess of the value of the total returns which capital and labour applied to land do obtain, over those which they would have obtained under circumstances as unfavourable as those on the margin of cultivation. . . . The cost of production on the margin of the profitable application of capital and labour is that to which the price of the whole produce tends, under the control of the general conditions of demand and supply: it does not govern price, but it focusses the causes which do govern price.*

From the point of view of the individual producer, said Marshall, land is but a particular form of capital. There is not much difference between land and buildings. Both are subject to diminishing returns as their owner tries to force more and more from them. From the point of view of society, however, the supply of land is permanent and fixed. If one person has possession of land, there is less for others to have. In contrast, if one were to invest in improvements of land or in buildings on it, he would not appreciably curtail the opportunities of others to invest capital in similar improvements.

In the short run, Marshall wrote, land and man-made capital goods are similar because the supplies of both are fixed. Therefore the return to old capital investments is something akin to rent, and Marshall called it quasi-rent. Interest is the earnings of "free" or "floating" capital or on new investments of capital; quasi-rent is the earnings on old capital investments in the short run. Even if part of the economic rent of land is taxed away, the landowner will continue to let his land, assuming that he wishes to maximize his returns instead of withdrawing his land from use in a fit of pique. Similarly, a tax on part of the earnings on fixed capital will not interfere with production *in the short run*, because it is better to lose part of one's normal profits than to lose everything beyond the scrap or salvage value. This assumes that the capital is specialized and has no alternative uses. In the long run, of course, quasi-rent disappears, for a normal return to the fixed capital investment is essential if the investment is to be renewed and the business perpetuated.

This is another way of saying that only variable costs influence prices in the short run. Prices in turn determine the earnings of the fixed investment. In the long run, however, both variable costs and normal returns on the fixed investment must be covered, and they both enter into price.

To sum up the whole in a comprehensive, if difficult, statement:—Every agent of production, land, machinery, skilled labour, unskilled labour, etc., tends to

* *Ibid.*, pp. 427–28.

be applied in production as far as it profitably can be. If employers, and other business men, think that they can get a better result by using a little more of any one agent they will do so. They estimate the net product (that is the net increase of the money value of their total output after allowing for incidental expenses) that will be got by a little more outlay in this direction, or a little more outlay in that; and if they can gain by shifting a little of their outlay from one direction to another, they will do so.

Thus then the uses of each agent of production are governed by the general conditions of demand in relation to supply: that is, on the one hand, by the urgency of all the uses to which the agent can be put, taken together with the means at the command of those who need it; and, on the other hand, by the available stocks of it. And equality is maintained between its values for each use by the constant tendency to shift it from uses, in which its services are of less value to others in which they are of greater value, in accordance with the principle of substitution.*

Increasing and Decreasing Cost Industries

MARSHALL introduced the concept of the representative firm for reasons that will be discussed below. It was the typical nineteenth-century small sole proprietorship.

We may read a lesson from the young trees of the forest as they struggle upwards through the benumbing shade of their older rivals. Many succumb on the way, and a few only survive; those few become stronger with every year, they get a larger share of light and air with every increase of their height, and at last in their turn they tower above their neighbours, and seem as though they would grow on for ever, and for ever become stronger as they grow. But they do not. One tree will last longer in full vigour and attain a greater size than another; but sooner or later age tells on them all. Though the taller ones have a better access to light and air than their rivals, they gradually lose vitality; and one after another they give place to others, which, though of less material strength, have on their side the vigour of youth.

And as with the growth of trees, so was it with the growth of businesses as a general rule before the great recent development of vast joint-stock companies, which often stagnate, but do not readily die. Now that rule is far from universal, but it still holds in many industries and trades. Nature still presses on the private business by limiting the length of the life of its original founders, and by limiting even more narrowly that part of their lives in which their faculties retain full vigour. And so, after a while, the guidance of the business falls into the hands of people with less energy and less creative genius, if not with less active interest in its prosperity. If it is turned into a joint-stock company, it may retain the advantages of division of labour, of specialized skill and machinery: it may even increase them by a further increase of its capital;

* *Ibid.*, pp. 521–22.

and under favourable conditions it may secure a permanent and prominent place in the work of production. But it is likely to have lost so much of its elasticity and progressive force, that the advantages are no longer exclusively on its side in its competition with younger and smaller rivals.

When therefore we are considering the broad results which the growth of wealth and population exert on the economies of production, the general character of our conclusions is not very much affected by the facts that many of these economies depend directly on the size of the individual establishments engaged in the production, and that in almost every trade there is a constant rise and fall of large businesses, at any one moment some firms being in the ascending phase and others in the descending. For in times of average prosperity decay in one direction is sure to be more than balanced by growth in another.*

Marshall's representative firm served at least three major purposes in his analysis. First, in speaking of the normal cost of producing a commodity, he referred to the expenses of a representative producer who was neither the most efficient nor the least efficient in the industry. Second, this analytic device showed that an industry could be in long-period equilibrium even though some firms were growing and others declining; they simply neutralized each other. Third, even though the representative firm did not inherently increase its efficiency, it could experience falling costs of production as the industry expanded.

Marshall thought that an increased volume of production in an industry would generally increase the size and therefore the internal economies possessed by a representative firm; it would always increase the external economies to which the firm had access; and therefore the cost of production in terms of labor and sacrifice would fall if the volume of output of an industry expanded.

Internal economies depend on the efficiencies introduced by an individual firm. As it grows larger, it can enjoy more specialization and mass production, using more and better machines to help lower the cost of production. There also are economies in buying and selling as a firm's size increases. Larger firms can secure credit on easier terms, and high-grade managerial ability can be utilized more effectively.

External economies are external to the firm; they depend on the general development of the industry. To use our own example: The first automobile plant located in Detroit is far less efficient than the fiftieth plant, even if technology remains constant. The first entrepreneur has to train his labor force. He may draw steel from Pittsburgh, rubber tires from New Orleans, and glass from southern California. The fiftieth plant draws its labor from a pool of skilled workers, already trained, living in the area. Suppliers build

* *Ibid.,* pp. 315–17.

plants nearby to serve an expanding automotive industry, so that steel, rubber tires, and glass are at hand; these supplies become cheaper both because smaller transport costs are involved, and because they are mass produced in industries that grow to meet the growing needs of the automobile industry. Perhaps, in addition, railroad, highway, and water transportation facilities are expanded as the volume of traffic between Detroit and the rest of the country expands. These are typical external economies that a growing industry will experience.

Another external economy arises when a coal mine requires less water to be pumped from its shafts as the number of mines operating in the neighborhood increases. As water is removed from each mine, the underground water level is lowered for all, thereby reducing the pumping costs for everybody.

The external economies are available to all firms in an industry. However, if internal economies grow with the size of the firm, how can competition be maintained? If the larger the firm grows, the more efficient it becomes, will this not lead to monopoly? Marshall's concept of the representative firm provided the answer. The decline and death of the entrepreneur will lead to the decline and death of his firm. Businesses, he thought, will typically not last long enough to realize all the benefits of an ever increasing scale of production. New entrepreneurs will elbow their way into the business arena and renew the process of increasing the size and efficiency of their firms.

We have already seen that Marshall had a sound grasp of the principle we call the law of diminishing returns. Basing himself on this principle, he held that agriculture was subject to diminishing returns in the long run. An increase in the capital and labor applied in the cultivation of a fixed supply of land will cause a less than proportionate increase in the product, unless agricultural improvements counteract this tendency. He felt certain that the latter force was the weaker. Eventually, increased applications of capital and labor to land must result in a diminution of the extra produce that can be obtained by a given extra amount of capital and labor. The principle of diminishing returns should, of course, be applied to every factor of production assuming that the others are kept constant. This idea Marshall did not develop except in an offhand way, in discussing other matters. When he did discuss it, he treated it as a historic law. One should not, however, assume the law implies change, for it has validity only in a static, timeless world, with technology in particular remaining constant. This does not imply any doubt about the truth or usefulness of the law of diminishing returns.

Marshall used increasing and diminishing returns in industry in another sense: If all factors of production used in an industry expand, will the cost per unit of output rise or fall? (We now call this decreasing and increasing returns to scale.) He thought that we generally have increasing returns in industry; as labor and capital expand, the organization of work is improved and efficiency is increased. Only when man relies heavily on nature, as in agriculture, do we have diminishing returns. Where the actions of the laws of increasing and diminishing returns are balanced we have the law of constant returns: expanded output is obtained by both labor and the sacrifice of waiting, expanding in the same proportion. With enlarged blanket output, for example, the increasing cost of wool due to the need to bring poorer land into use to obtain this extra wool may be exactly counterbalanced by the growing efficiency of manufacturinig blankets, and we will have constant returns. In most manufacturing, Marshall thought, the cost of raw materials counts for little, and the law of increasing returns acts almost unopposed.

Marshall drew an optimistic conclusion from this analysis. While there may be certain disadvantages resulting from a rapid growth of population, the final outcome is likely to be favorable. The collective efficiency of a people can be expected to increase out of proportion to their increased numbers.

If an industry obeys the law of constant returns, an increased demand for its product will in the long run not affect the price. If it is an industry with diminishing returns, an increase in demand will raise its price; more will be produced, but not so much more as if it obeyed the law of constant returns. If the industry is one of increasing returns, an increase of demand will ultimately cause the price to fall, and more will be produced than if it were an industry of constant returns.

This analysis led Marshall to some interesting policy conclusions. An industry of increasing returns, especially in a new country, would produce more cheaply if it expanded under tariff protection—the "infant industry" argument. The difficulty, he said, was that power politics might wrench this policy from its proper uses. He did recommend that industries of diminishing returns should have their products taxed. By restricting their output in this way, their unit costs of production exclusive of the tax would fall. The revenue received should be used to subsidize the industries of increasing returns. As their output expanded, their unit costs and selling prices would fall. The consumers would thereby benefit from such taxes and subsidies.

The implication of this argument is that competitive prices and laissez faire do not necessarily result in the maximum satisfaction to the community. Marshall was very much aware of this. If producers were very much poorer than consumers, he said, restricting the supply and raising prices would increase aggregate satisfaction; conversely, if consumers were poorer than producers, expanding production and selling commodities at a loss would increase total satisfaction. Again, if an individual spent his income in such a way as to increase the demand for the services of the poor and thereby increase their incomes, he would add something more to the total happiness than if he added an equal amount to the incomes of the rich. If a person spent his income on things which obeyed the law of diminishing returns, he would make those things more expensive for his neighbors, thereby lowering their real incomes.

These conclusions, it will be observed, do not by themselves afford a valid ground for government interference. But they show that much remains to be done, by a careful collection of the statistics of demand and supply, and a scientific interpretation of their results, in order to discover what are the limits of the work that society can with advantage do towards turning the economic actions of individuals into those channels in which they will add the most to the sum total of happiness.*

At Marshall's death in 1924, John Maynard Keynes proclaimed him the "greatest economist in the world for a hundred years." One cannot help wondering if Keynes in later years would have subscribed to his earlier judgment. Few would doubt, however, that Marshall was the most influential economic theorist of his day. Most economists would include him in a list of the four greatest figures of the classical and marginalist schools during the last two hundred years; the other three are Adam Smith, David Ricardo, and John Stuart Mill.

* *Ibid.*, p. 475.

CHAPTER 15

Mathematical Economics

THE TERM "mathematical economics" refers to those economic principles and analyses that are formulated and developed using mathematical symbols and methods. The use of graphs and mathematical symbols to supplement verbal explanations is common practice. Mathematical economics therefore does not constitute a separate school of economic thought, but rather a distinct method. Theorists from all schools may use mathematical language, if they have the ability, to assist in expressing in a clear and consistent way the definitions, postulates, and conclusions of a theory.

We will now consider a number of topics relating to mathematical economics.

Econometrics

"ECONOMETRICS," a branch of mathematical economics, combines theoretical, mathematical and statistical analysis. It is a science that deals with the determination by statistical and mathematical methods of concrete quantitative laws occurring in economic life. With this tool kit we can obtain conclusions that may be used to test the realism of a theory. The input-output analysis and linear programming, discussed below, are examples of the applications of econometrics. A kind of econometric approach goes back hundreds of years. Sir William Petty's follower, Charles Davenant, defined "Political Arithmetick" as "the art of reasoning by figures upon things related to government." Quesnay, the French physiocrat, also did genuinely econometric work.

The name "econometrics" was introduced in 1926 by the Norwegian economist and statistician, Ragnar Frisch. He modeled the term on the expression "biometrics" which appeared late in the nineteenth century to denote the field of biological studies employing statistical methods.

Econometrics as a separate method of studying economic life developed with particular speed immediately after World War I. The Econometric Society, which publishes the journal called *Econometrica*, was founded in 1930.

Econometrics developed in response to changing conditions in economic life. Business cycles became of increasing concern both to private enterprises and to society as a whole. A large enterprise, if it could forecast business fluctuations with a reasonable degree of accuracy, could to some extent insulate itself from their adverse effects. Also, only a large corporation, not small businesses, could employ the staff required to make such forecasts. Society as a whole, operating through government and through private non-profit research organizations, also was interested in forecasting business trends in order to control, ameliorate, or counteract them. Growing government intervention in the economy therefore stimulated econometric research, with national governments becoming the world's greatest agencies for gathering statistics.

Econometric analysis is important in market studies for big corporations, including elasticities of demand faced by monopolistic enterprises which they try to influence. Unions, in negotiating the terms of sale of labor services, are concerned with the elasticity of demand for labor and the products labor helps produce. In contrast, the nineteenth-century world had little need for econometric research, and few funds available for it. Unions were then weak, businesses were small, there was minimal government intervention, and no one individual had much market power.

Deductive economic theorizing required an empirical element to test its validity and to make it more applicable to the real world. Even a very elaborate theory of saving derived from the most up-to-date psychology of consumers' behavior cannot deduce the specific fact that American families with an annual disposable income of five thousand dollars tend to spend on the average x dollars and save the rest. Many economic processes can be explained only in terms of the actual magnitudes of consumers' propensities to save, elasticities of demand, workers' responses to wage changes, farmers' decisions based on market prices and forecasts, and other factual relationships of a similar kind.

With inadequate knowledge of the facts, theorists resorted to conditional statements of the "if, then" variety. Instead of describing the effects of a million dollars' worth of additional investment, they said that if the propensity to consume is of a certain magnitude, then national income will increase by a certain amount. Intricate relationships can thus be set up and studied without referring to the actual magnitudes of the unknown elements involved. The work of deductive theorists was therefore frequently replete with abstract models containing algebraic symbols representing quantities of unknown magnitudes. Economic theory had begun to lose its contact with reality. Econometrics was an attempt to establish a new contact with the real world.

General Equilibrium

GENERAL equilibrium analysis, in contrast to Alfred Marshall's partial equilibrium, considers the interrelationships among the many variables in the economy as a whole. One of the originators of this approach was the Frenchman at Lausanne, Switzerland, Léon Walras (1834–1910); he was also one of the founding fathers of marginalism, for he independently arrived at the basic marginalist principles, which appeared in his book published in 1874.

Just as a stone dropped into a pond causes ever widening circles of ripples, so any change in the economy causes further changes that radiate outward with gradually diminishing force. Take, for example, an increase in the price of butter. If we assume that everything else remains unchanged, a reduced quantity of butter will be bought, and that is an end of the matter; this is the partial equilibrium approach. But let us consider a few of the further ramifications that enter into general equilibrium economics. The quantity demanded of a substitute good such as margarine will rise, and perhaps its price will rise. The quantity demanded of a complementary good such as bread may fall as butter consumption decreases, and perhaps the price of bread will fall. In a sense all goods are substitutes for each other, directly or indirectly, for they all compete for the consumers' dollars. If less is spent on butter plus margarine, perhaps more will be spent on books. If the production of books is subject to decreasing costs as output expands, their prices may fall a little, thereby further increasing consumer purchases. With these changes in the markets for consumer goods, factors of production will shift their employment. Less labor will be required in the industries producing bread and butter, and more in margarine and books. Capital will also shift, and land use will change from dairy feed and pasture to soybeans and pulpwood. Meanwhile the changed cost of living will influence wage demands, which will in turn determine to what extent machinery will be substituted for labor. At this point we would need a high-powered microscope to detect the further changes brought about by the original disturbance.

Thus general equilibrium theory presents an over-all framework of the basic price and output interrelationships for the economy as a whole, including both commodities and factors of production. Its purpose is to demonstrate mathematically that all prices and quantities produced can adjust to levels which are mutually consistent. Its approach is static, assuming that certain basic determinants remain unchanged, such as consumer preferences, production functions, forms of competition, and factor supply schedules. Changes over time are generally excluded from the analysis.

An awareness of the interdependence of economic phenomena is important; without it we might go astray. A person who loses his employment because of cheaper imported goods might very reasonably conclude that imports cause general unemployment; this is an example of partial equilibrium analysis that assumes that everything else remains unchanged. However, if we study the repercussions of increased imports, and if we find that exports increase in response, then our conclusion may well be that imports do not cause any over-all increase in unemployment.

General equilibrium theory, however, has contributed little to our understanding of economic growth and other changes over time. Nor can the theory predict precise quantitative results of various changes and policies. In the example given above, we simply do not know enough about our economy to predict the changed output of butter, margarine, bread, and books as a result of a 10 per cent increase in the price of butter. The variables are too numerous, too changeable, and too uncertain to work out precisely even with modern electronic computing equipment.

Prices in a market economy can be determined mathematically in a theoretical way, taking cognizance of the interrelatedness of all prices. The quantity demanded of a good varies with its price. That is, the price is the independent variable, and the quantity demanded is the dependent variable. The quantity demanded of any one good, however, includes as variables the prices of all other commodities. A consumer will not decide how much of one good he will buy until he knows the prices of all other goods. If there are a total of n commodities, the total demand for any one of them is determined by the prices of all of them. The aggregate demand for each commodity can be represented by $D_1, D_2 \ldots D_n$. The prices are $p_1, p_2 \ldots p_n$. An equation can be set up for each commodity showing that demand is a function of all prices:

$$D_1 = F_1 (p_1, p_2 \ldots p_n)$$
$$D_2 = F_2 (p_1, p_2 \ldots p_n)$$
$$\cdot \quad \cdot \quad \cdot \quad \cdot \quad \cdot \quad \cdot \quad \cdot \quad \cdot \quad \cdot \quad \cdot$$
$$D_n = F_n (p_1, p_2 \ldots p_n)$$

The demand for any particular commodity, in a state of equilibrium, equals its supply. Therefore $D_1 = S_1, D_2 = S_2 \ldots D_n = S_n$. If supply is substituted for demand in the three equations above, we have:

$$S_1 = F_1 (p_1, p_2 \ldots p_n)$$
$$S_2 = F_2 (p_1, p_2 \ldots p_n)$$
$$\cdot \quad \cdot \quad \cdot \quad \cdot \quad \cdot \quad \cdot \quad \cdot \quad \cdot \quad \cdot \quad \cdot$$
$$S_n = F_n (p_1, p_2 \ldots p_n)$$

We assume that supply is given and fixed. With n commodities, there are n prices that are the unknowns. As we have an equation for each commodity, there are n simultaneous equations, which are sufficient for determining the n unknown prices. As soon as all prices are known, the aggregate demand for any particular commodity can be calculated. Since the demand is satisfied at the prices so calculated, the problem of the distribution of the available commodities is solved.

This kind of analysis illustrates the idea of general equilibrium, with all prices influencing the demand for any one commodity. The analysis does not, however, provide a framework for actual price determination. We do not know all the data that go into the equations; and even if we did, conditions change so quickly that the solution of tens of thousands of simultaneous equations would have to be reworked continually.

Indifference Curves

THE use of indifference curves to analyze consumer demand originated with the Englishman Francis Ysidro Edgeworth (1845–1926) and the Italian Vilfredo Pareto (1848–1923). Its aim was to avoid measuring utility quantitatively and exactly. According to standard marginalist theory, if you spend $15 on a pair of shoes and 10¢ on an ice cream cone, the shoes are 150 times as useful to you as the cone. This numerical precision is questionable. Perhaps we should compare small increments of utility at the margin. Suppose you have the choice between a $14 or a $15 pair of shoes, and you choose the latter. Then the increased satisfaction you obtain from acquiring the more expensive rather than the cheaper shoes is exactly ten times the satisfaction you get from an ice cream cone. Such measurement of the magnitude of utility seems unrealistic and unsatisfactory.

The indifference curve approach avoids any quantitative measurement of marginal utility. All we require is that for any two goods a consumer can determine the various combinations yielding the same total satisfaction. An indifference curve is analogous to a line on a contour map that joins all points of equal altitude. If satisfaction may be considered as the third dimension of the altitude, an indifference curve joins all points that represent equal satisfaction.

One extreme case is that of two goods that are perfect substitutes for each other. Let us consider nickels and dimes, shown in Figure 3. Each of

FIGURE 3.   Indifference Curves with Perfect Substitutes

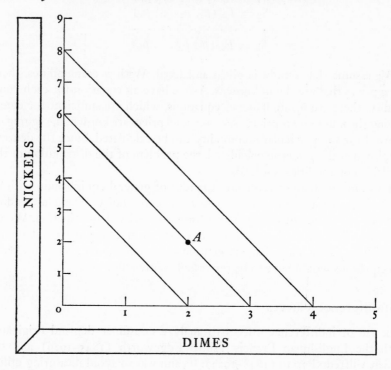

the three lines represents a separate indifference curve with a different level of satisfaction. The farther the curve is from the point of intersection of the two axes, the greater the satisfaction. Taking the middle curve, the person represented feels equally well off regardless of which combination of goods he has as indicated at any point on the curve. At the highest point he has 6 nickels and no dimes. At the lowest point he has 3 dimes and no nickels. At point *A* he has 2 dimes and 2 nickels. He is indifferent, or equally satisfied, among these alternatives. The curve shows nothing, however, about the absolute amounts of satisfaction obtained.

Now we shall consider the case of no possibility of substituting between goods, as with left and right shoes, shown in Figure 4. A person is better off as he moves from the curve closest to the origin to the middle curve. But once he settles on the middle curve, perhaps because of a lack of adequate income to buy more shoes, he is equally well off with any combination of the two goods represented along that curve. At point *A* he has 5 left and 2 right shoes; at *B* he has 2 of each; and at *C* he has 2 left and 5 right shoes. According to our assumptions, he is indifferent and equally well off whichever of the three combinations of shoes he has.

FIGURE 4.   Indifference Curves with No Substitutability

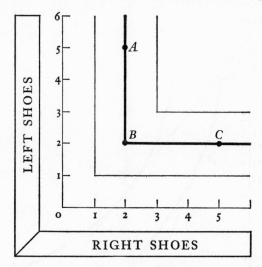

Figure 5 shows the more usual case of two products that are partly but not perfectly substitutable for one another. Curves 1 and 2 are indifference curves. At their upper ends, they show that the person represented would give up a large quantity of potatoes to acquire a small quantity of meat, and he would still feel equally well off. The reason is that the former is abundant and the latter scarce. At the lower end of the curve, as potatoes become scarce relative to meat, he would give up fewer potatoes to acquire another pound of meat.

Line 3 is a price line. Suppose this person has budgeted $2 a day for meat and potatoes, and the prices are 50¢ and 10¢ per pound respectively. Line 3 shows the various quantities of both commodities which can be bought for $2. At the upper end, one can buy 20 pounds of potatoes and no meat; at the lower end, 4 pounds of meat and no potatoes; at point C, 3 pounds of meat and 5.5 pounds of potatoes.

We could draw countless indifference curves, and line 3 could intersect many of them. One of the curves will be tangent to line 3. That will be the curve of greatest satisfaction within the realm of a $2-per-day expenditure on meat and potatoes—curve 1. Point A, with 1.5 pounds of meat and 12.5 pounds of potatoes, gives the greatest satisfaction. We have determined the quantities of each commodity the consumer will demand, given his indifference schedule, the sum he has to spend on both commodities, and their prices.

If the price of meat were cut in half, the individual could buy 8 pounds of meat with $2, and line 4 would be the new price line. He could move to

FIGURE 5. Indifference Curves with Some Substitutability

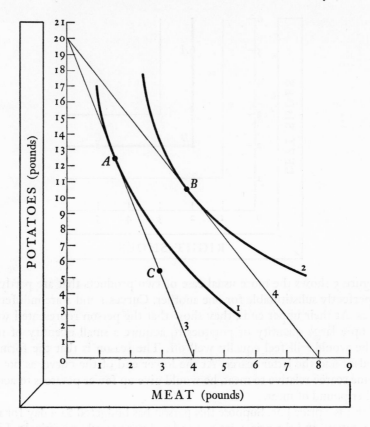

a higher indifference curve, and at point *B* he would demand 3.7 pounds of meat and 10.5 pounds of potatoes. We see how the two commodities are partial substitutes for each other, and how quantities demanded change with changing prices. We have begun, in fact, to derive a demand schedule.

The test of validity for economic theory is not whether it is abstract or concrete. Rather, if abstraction is introduced, is it significant, illuminating, and a reflection of the real world? It is doubtful whether the indifference curve analysis would measure up to these criteria.

Input-Output Analysis

INPUT-OUTPUT analysis is largely the creation of the Russian-born American economist Wassily W. Leontief (born 1906), and is reminiscent of Quesnay's *Economic Table*, discussed above in Chapter 3. He originally sought to present the essence of general equilibrium theory in a simplified form suitable for empirical study. Interest in this type of inter-industry relationship spread as a result of World War II. The planned expansion of war industries created certain bottlenecks that made continued expansion more difficult. The increased output of airplanes, for example, required greater allocations of steel, aluminum, housing for workers, engines, and certain machine tools and other capital goods. Input-output analysis tried to anticipate these requirements, and to plan for the expansion of industries that supplied the things used in the final product whose increase was desired.

Leontief worked out a grid that was expanded by the federal Bureau of Labor Statistics. The input-output grid sums up statistical information about the economy. It shows the sources and the amounts of materials and their destinations. This reveals the relationship of each segment of the economy to every other segment. Every row in an input-output table shows the sales made by one economic sector to every other sector; every column shows what each economic sector purchased from every other sector.

A portion of the grid is reproduced in Table 5. We can see that in 1947 agriculture and fisheries sold $10.9 billions of their output to themselves (feed, seed, breeding livestock, etc.). Another $15 billions were sold to food processors. These data provide the raw materials for computing how a change in one industry will affect all the others. An expansion of the iron and steel industry, for example, will require an expansion of nonferrous metals, which in turn will mean more purchases of agricultural and iron and steel products.

This type of analysis is based on three simplifying assumptions. First, coefficients of production are assumed to be fixed; that is, constant quantities of each factor are necessary to produce a unit of output. Second, production functions are assumed to be linear, with no increasing or decreasing efficiencies as an industry expands or contracts; a certain percentage change in the output of one product entails the same percentage change in the inputs of the various factors used to produce it. Third, input-output assumes given factor supplies, consumer demands, and prices; prices are not variables in the system, which is concerned solely with output adjustments recorded as physical quantities.

These assumptions are rather unrealistic. Increases in output frequently do not require proportionate increases in input, mainly because various factors are indivisible. For example, one might increase the ton-miles of freight hauled by railroad 5 per cent without increasing the supply of locomotives and freight cars at all. The assumption of fixed production coefficients precludes the possibility of factor substitution.

TABLE 5. Input-Output Relations in the United States, 1947 (Millions of dollars. Portion of 50-industry table.)

INDUSTRY PURCHASING

INDUSTRY PRODUCING

	(1) AGRICULTURE AND FISHERIES	(2) FOOD AND KINDRED PRODUCTS	(3) NONFERROUS METALS	(4) IRON AND STEEL	(5) MOTORS AND GENERATORS	(6) MOTOR VEHICLES	(7) TOTAL
(1) AGRICULTURE AND FISHERIES	10,856	15,048	11	..	..	..	44,263
(2) FOOD AND KINDRED PRODUCTS	2,378	4,910	*	3	..	..	37,636
(3) NONFERROUS METALS	..	..	2,599	324	366	176	6,387
(4) IRON AND STEEL	6	2	33	3,982	118	196	12,338
(5) MOTORS AND GENERATORS	..	..	..	..	317	..	1,095
(6) MOTOR VEHICLES	111	3	*	*	..	4,401	14,265
(7) TOTAL	44,263	37,636	6,387	12,338	1,095	14,263	769,248

* Less than $500,000.

SOURCE: Wassily Leontief and others, *Studies in the Structure of the American Economy*, (New York, Oxford University Press, 1953), p. 9. By permission of Oxford University Press.

Technological changes make the grid obsolete rather quickly, and it is a tremendous task to revise the forty thousand entries that went into the two-hundred-industry table for 1947. The grid may give an impression of a system in equilibrium, but that is not necessarily so. There may be serious business-cycle problems that are not revealed by this conceptual framework. This type of analysis probably is more useful in a socialist economy than in one based primarily on private enterprise. Total economic planning requires the allocation of materials by the planning body, and the anticipation of future needs. Industries must expand in step with one another if serious bottlenecks are to be avoided. Because consumer preferences are subordinated to the over-all plan, consumers' whims and desires need not interfere with the desired outcome of economic activity; in other words, in a completely socialized economy a sudden increase in the desire for automobiles will not divert steel away from, say, the machine-tool industry. A socialist economy is more likely to operate at or near full capacity on a sort of forced-draft basis. Shortages of equipment and raw materials are therefore more serious than in an economy that operates at 80 per cent of capacity. It is more difficult to increase the output of steel or trucks on short notice in Soviet Russia than in the United States. They therefore have to plan more carefully; their belated interest in mathematical economics in general and Leontief's grid in particular indicates that these analytical approaches may be more useful to them than to us.

Linear Programming

LINEAR programming was developed during and after World War II, with one of its earliest applications being in connection with the planning activities of the United States Air Force. This method is used by the firm in allocating scarce resources so as to maximize the attainment of some predetermined objective. The lowest-cost diet for animals can be discovered, or the cheapest way to ship goods to market, or the most profitable product mix, or the best combination of factor inputs. Costs can thereby be minimized and profits maximized. Both mathematical and geometrical techniques are used. Linear programming helps solve practical problems for businessmen that the marginal analysis cannot do very effectively.

Two elementary examples will illustrate linear programming.

Suppose a man needs at least 15 grams of an iodine salt and 15 grams of an iron salt per month to stay healthy. He cannot buy either of these in a pure form, but must buy them as a trade-marked patent medicine. There are two available: Nostrum 12 contains 1 gram of iodine and 2 grams of iron per ounce and costs \$1 per ounce. Quackstuff 31 contains 3 grams of iodine per ounce and 1 gram of iron, and costs \$2. In what combination should he take the two preparations to get the required medication at the lowest cost?

If he takes x ounces of Nostrum 12 and y ounces of Quackstuff 31, he will get $x + 3y$ grams of iodine and $2x + y$ grams of iron. As each element must total 15 grams, we get two equations:

$$x + 3y = 15$$
$$2x + y = 15$$

These can be plotted on a graph as straight lines. In the first equation, if $x = 0$, $y = 5$; if $y = 0$, $x = 15$. These two points locate a line in Figure 6. In the second equation, if $x = 0$, $y = 15$; if $y = 0$, $x = 7.5$. The second line can now be drawn.

FIGURE 6.   Linear Programming with Two Variables

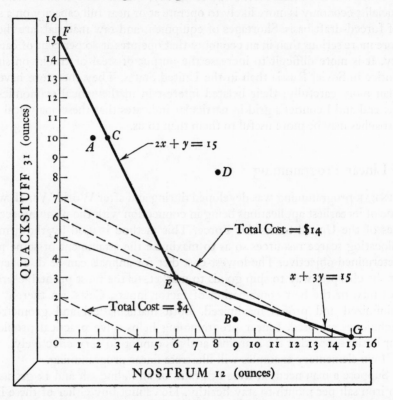

Any combinations of medicines lying to the left and below either line will not give the minimal requirements of iodine and iron. Thus, point A, with 2 ounces of Nostrum 12 and 10 ounces of Quackstuff 31, gives 32 grams of iodine but only 14 grams of iron. Point B, showing 9 ounces of Nostrum 12 and 1 ounce of Quackstuff 31, gives 19 grams of iron and only 12 of iodine. Therefore the proper combination will lie on or northeast of the heavy line FEG. Thus at point C, with 3 ounces of Nostrum 12 and 10 ounces of Quackstuff 31, more than enough iodine and iron will be obtained. Likewise at point D, with 8 ounces of each.

Which of the acceptable combinations will cost the least? Suppose $4 were available to be spent on the two medicines. If the whole sum were spent on Nostrum 12, 4 ounces could be bought at $1 per ounce. If it were all spent on Quackstuff 31, 2 ounces could be bought at $2 per ounce. A straight line connecting 4 on the X axis with 2 on the Y axis will show all the combinations of the two products which could be bought with $4. This is an equal-cost line. If $14 were available for spending on the two products, the equal-cost line joins the 14 on the X axis with the 7 on the Y axis. All equal-cost lines are parallel. The lowest-cost line that will provide the required iodine and iron will go through point E where the two equation lines intersect. Twelve dollars is the lowest cost of acquiring 15 grams of each element. Three ounces of Quackstuff 31 will be bought, and 6 ounces of Nostrum 12. Any other combination will give less than the minimal dosage of medicine, or it will cost more than $12.

Another example:* A cattle producer wishes to fatten steers most economically. He can choose various mixtures of hay and cottonseed cake, both of which contain the four required nutrients: protein, minerals, vitamins, and carbohydrates.

In Figure 7, any point on or to the right of line PP is assumed to satisfy the minimum protein requirement in the ration; the slope of the line reflects the relative proportions of the protein in the two feeds. The minimum mineral requirement is met by diets represented by points on or to the right of line MM. The minimum vitamin requirement is indicated by line VV, and the carbohydrate requirement by line CC. All points on or to the right of the heavy line abcde represent combinations of cottonseed cake and hay that satisfy all four of the minimum nutritional requirements simultaneously. Any point to the left of the heavy line represents a combination of feeds that fails to provide one or more of the minimum requirements.

The parallel dashed lines are equal-cost lines, with each line representing the various combinations of the two feeds that can be bought with a given outlay. The lowest-cost combination of feeds is at point d. If cottonseed cake were to become more expensive, the equal-cost lines would be steeper, and the lowest-cost combination might then be at c or b.

Linear programming is still in its infancy. Obviously it is a powerful tool and will become increasingly important in business planning and decision-making. The larger and more complex the business, the more useful is this technique. It does not, however, represent an advance into the realm of economic theory.

* Based on John F. Due and Robert W. Clower, *Intermediate Economic Analysis*, 4th ed. (Homewood, Irwin, 1961), pp. 471–73. By permission of Richard D. Irwin, Inc.

FIGURE 7. Linear Programming with Four Variables

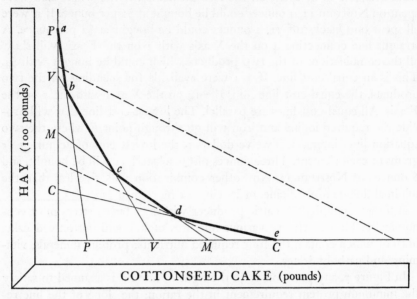

SOURCE: John F. Due and Robert W. Clower, *Intermediate Economic Analysis,* 4th ed. (Homewood, Irwin, 1961), p. 472. By permission of Richard D. Irwin, Inc.

Game Theory

GAME theory as applied to economic problems is based on *Theory of Games and Economic Behavior* (1944), written by the mathematician John von Neumann (1903–57) and the economist Oskar Morgenstern (born 1902). The theory is complex and heavily mathematical, and only a few general remarks will be made here and a simple example given.

Game theory is applicable to situations analogous to games of strategy, such as chess and poker. There are conflicting interests, with each side using its ingenuity to outwit the other. A businessman, in reaching decisions, has to consider the probable response of others. If he is considering a cut in the price of his product, for example, it makes a world of difference whether or not other producers of similar products will also cut their prices. Some business decisions are made openly, such as publicly posted price changes, changes in advertising campaigns, and the manufacture of new products; these moves are analogous to chess, where all moves are known by both sides. Other decisions are secret, such as *sub rosa* price discounting, undertaking new research projects, and planning the invasion of new markets. This is analogous to poker. If a company can place a spy (such as a janitor) in its rival's business to ferret out secrets, this is like playing poker with a marked deck of cards. If businessmen get together in monopolistic agreements, they must still plan strategy to outwit the public and the government's "trust-busters." There is an implication in game theory that economic relations are based on economic warfare, and what one gains is at the expense of another. This perhaps is the logical culmination of the individualistic approach.

The underlying logic of game theory can be seen from a simplified example.* Among games of strategy we can distinguish between games of pure chance and games with strategic uncertainty. Dice-shooting is a game of pure chance unless the dice are loaded. Whether a player wins or loses, and how much, depends only on his own choices and on luck. In a game with strategic uncertainty, such as poker, an additional factor enters: What will the other fellow do?

Assume that Jones and Smith play the following game: Jones is to choose one of the three letters *A*, *B*, or *C*. Smith is to choose one of four Roman numerals *I*, *II*, *III*, or *IV*. Each writes his choice on a slip of paper and then the choices are compared. Each player wins or loses according to the particular combination of his own with his opponent's choice at each "turn." Winning is therefore contingent on strategic uncertainty. A payment is made according to Table 6. The figure zero means that neither pays. A positive number means that Smith pays that amount to Jones; a negative number, that Jones pays Smith. Thus if Jones picks *A* and Smith *II*, Smith pays Jones $100.

TABLE 6. Theory of Games

		Smith's choice			
		I	II	III	IV
Jones'	A	−200	100	300	−2
choice	B	0	−1,000	1,000	0
	C	1	2	3	4

SOURCE: Leonid Hurwicz, "Game Theory and Decisions," *Scientific American*, Vol. 192, No. 2 (February 1955), p. 81. By permission of *Scientific American*.

Let us see how Jones will make a rational choice. He will conclude that Smith will never pick *III*, for every time he will lose from $3 to $1,000. Nor will he pick *IV*, because no matter which letter Jones picks, Smith is better off picking *I* rather than *IV*. If Jones picks *A*, Smith's pick-

---

* Taken from Leonid Hurwicz, "Game Theory and Decisions," *Scientific American*, Vol. 192, No. 2 (February 1955), pp. 78–83. By permission of *Scientific American*.

ing *I* will give him winnings of $200, but he will win only $2 if he picks *IV*. If Jones picks *B*, Smith will neither win nor lose, no matter whether he picks *I* or *IV*. If Jones picks *C*, Smith loses $1 if he picks *I*, and he loses $4 if he picks *IV*. In every case, Smith is equally well off or better off if he picks *I* rather than *IV*.

Jones therefore concludes that Smith will pick *I* or *II* every time. He may conclude that the chances are even that Smith will play either *I* or *II*. If Jones plays *A*, his expectation will be to lose $50 on each play on the average, for on two plays he will lose $100, which is $50 per play. If he plays *B*, he can expect to lose $500 per play on the average. If he plays *C*, he can expect to gain $1.50 per play. Therefore *C* is the best choice.

Suppose Jones had no idea that Smith would never choose *III* and *IV*. Instead, suppose he thought the chances were even that Smith would pick any of the four Roman numerals. In that case, Jones' expectation for *A* would be

$$\frac{-200 + 100 + 300 - 2}{4} = 49.5.$$

His expectation for *B* would be 0, and for *C*, 2.5. Therefore *A* would be his best choice.

If Jones is an incorrigible optimist, he will choose *B*, because it offers the opportunity for the largest payoff ($1,000). If he is a conservative man, he will always choose *C*, because he must then win between $1 and $4 on each play.

From Smith's point of view, optimism will lead him to pick *II*, and pessimism will favor *I*. If Smith knows that Jones is an optimist and will pick *B*, Smith should pick *II* and collect $1,000. If, however, Jones gets wind of this reasoning by Smith, he will switch to *A* and collect $100. If both are pessimists, Jones will play *C* and Smith *I*, with Smith paying $1 to Jones. Whereupon Smith will probably quit the game and go home.

CHAPTER 16

Early American Economists

AMERICAN contributions to economic thought were quite modest during the colonial period and the first century of independence. The founding fathers developed a world-shaking political philosophy and a new and viable type of government; but the contributions to economics remained small until Henry George, John Bates Clark, and Thorstein Veblen appeared on the scene in the late 1800's to win international reputations.

Why was this so? Several factors may explain this intellectual lag. From the sixteenth century on, economic thought at first concentrated mainly on commerce, and later on industry. As America was an underdeveloped area, it did not win an important position in either of these fields before the Civil War, and therefore did not lead in theorizing about them. We were accustomed to getting our economic ideas, along with our science and technology, from England. Moreover, we developed a pragmatic approach to life. With a continent to conquer, action was more important than theory. With our contempt for education, and with the small group that entered higher education, we did not develop independent, original thinking in economics. We were diverted from economic questions by major social and political issues that had a higher priority. While Englishmen were debating laissez faire versus government regulation, tariffs or free trade, and the convertibility of currency into gold, we were concerned first about freedom from England, and later about slavery, Indian affairs, a homestead act, etc. These involved questions of economics, to be sure, and we were also concerned about more purely economic issues. But a comparison of legislative debates, journals, newspapers, and contemporary books would show that the British were much more aroused over purely economic issues than were the Americans.

There were, however, interesting economic ideas appearing on the American scene. These ideas were generally more optimistic than the prevailing thought in Great Britain, for we had seemingly limitless resources to promote a better life. There also were less rigid class lines, so that people could "get ahead" more readily than they could in Europe. A society in flux is less likely to defend the status quo, and movement creates ever renewed hope for better things to come.

Franklin

BENJAMIN FRANKLIN (1706–90) was a man of learning, wisdom, and action. Although his formal education ended at ten years of age, he won world renown and respect as a scientist, an inventor, a philosopher, a journalist and publisher, a statesman, and a diplomat. He founded a public library, a hospital, a mutual fire-insurance company, a philosophical society, a fire-fighting company, and an academy of learning (later the University of Pennsylvania). He invented an improved stove, a lightning rod, bifocal spectacles, and a popular glass harmonica. He advocated crop insurance and daylight-saving time to save candles. His experiments and observations on electricity, heat and light, earthquakes, chimneys, weather, climate, botany, and medicine won the admiration of contemporary scientists everywhere. In the last years of his life he published several papers against slavery, and he served as president of the Pennsylvania Society for Promoting the Abolition of Slavery.

In 1829, at the age of twenty-three, Franklin published a pamphlet called *The Nature and Necessity of a Paper-Currency*. In it he relied heavily on his reading, especially on Sir William Petty's work, but he showed the ability to apply others' ideas to current problems in language easily understood by his Pennsylvania readers. In taking over Petty's labor theory of value, Franklin attacked one of the key themes of mercantilism.

By Labour may the Value of Silver be measured as well as other Things. As, Suppose one Man employed to raise Corn, while another is digging and refining Silver; at the Year's End, or at any other Period of Time, the compleat Produce of Corn, and that of Silver, are the natural Price of each other; and if one be twenty Bushels, and the other twenty Ounces, then an Ounce of that Silver is worth the Labour of raising a Bushel of that Corn. Now if by the Discovery of some nearer, more easy or plentiful Mines, a Man may get Forty Ounces of Silver as easily as formerly he did Twenty, and the same Labour is still required to raise Twenty Bushels of Corn, then Two Ounces of Silver will be worth no more than the same Labour of raising One Bushel of Corn, and that Bushel of Corn will be as cheap as two Ounces, as it was before at one; *caeteris paribus*. Thus the Riches of a Country are to be valued by the Quantity of Labour its Inhabitants are able to purchase, and not by the Quantity of Silver and Gold they possess.*

* Leonard W. Labaree, ed., *The Papers of Benjamin Franklin*, Vol. I (New Haven, 1959), p. 149.

In the same pamphlet, Franklin pointed out that a certain quantity of money is required to carry on a country's trade. Too much is of no advantage, and too little raises interest rates and cheapens land, both of which are bad. If interest rates are low, more money will be invested in land instead of being lent out, and rising land values will "enliven Trade." In addition, plentiful currency will raise prices and encourage agriculture, trade, shipbuilding, and handicrafts. Franklin was trying to remedy a serious colonial problem. Efforts by the colonies to import more goods and services than they could export caused continual shortages of specie.

Franklin disapproved of the overissue of paper money because it would cause a rapid depreciation of its value. In a letter written in 1779 he deplored one aspect of the overissue of paper during the Revolutionary War. However, he could not help marveling at the usefulness of paper money under the exigency of war finance.

The Depreciation of our Money must, as you observe, greatly affect Salary Men, Widows, and Orphans. Methinks this Evil deserves the attention of the several Legislatures, and ought, if possible, to be remedied by some equitable law, particularly adapted to their Circumstances. I took all the Pains I could in Congress to prevent the Depreciation, by proposing first, that the Bills should bear Interest; this was rejected. . . . Secondly, after the first Emission, I proposed that we should stop, strike no more, but borrow on Interest those we had issued. This was not then approved of. . . . When, from the too great Quantity, they began to depreciate, we agreed to borrow on Interest; and I propos'd, that, in order to fix the Value of the Principal, the Interest should be promised in hard Dollars. This was objected to as impracticable. . . .

The *only Remedy* now seems to be a Diminution of the Quantity by a vigourous Taxation . . . ; and the *only Consolation* under the Evil is, that the Publick Debt is proportionably diminish'd with the Depreciation; and this by a kind of imperceptible Tax. . . .

This Currency, as we manage it, is a wonderful Machine. It performs its Office when we issue it; it pays and clothes Troops, and provides Victuals and Ammunition; and when we are obliged to issue a Quantity excessive, it pays itself off by Depreciation.*

In 1751 Franklin wrote a tract, *Observations Concerning the Increase of Mankind, Peopling of Countries, Etc.,* which was read by Adam Smith, David Hume, Turgot, and Malthus. (He met the first three personally while in Europe.) In it he claimed that the easier it is to support a family, the more people will marry, and the earlier in life. Therefore population grows most rapidly where the means of sustenance are most plentiful. In cities deaths exceed births because there are fewer opportunities for employment, the cost of living is greater, and luxuries are more common.

* Albert Henry Smyth, ed., *The Writings of Benjamin Franklin,* Vol. VII (New York, 1907), pp. 293–94.

Population does not increase in fully settled countries either, for wages are low and families can be supported only with difficulty. In America, with plenty of land available, population tends at least to double every twenty years. Our territory is so vast that agriculture and handicrafts will continue to expand and wages will remain high indefinitely. The demand for British manufactures will continue to grow. Not even slavery will enable us to produce manufactured goods more cheaply than the mother country, for slave labor is more expensive than free labor. Interest rates in the colonies are high, and this raises the cost of slave labor. Insurance for the risk of the slave's death also must be included in the cost. There are expenses of his maintenance during illness, and he is not interested in good work for he does not benefit from it.

In a letter written in 1753, Franklin expressed the view that the poor in Protestant countries are more industrious than those of Catholic countries. To relieve the misfortunes of our fellow creatures is godlike; but to encourage laziness and folly is "against the order of God and Nature, which perhaps has appointed want and misery as the proper punishments for, and cautions against . . . idleness and extravagance." The more ample provision for relief of the poor in Catholic countries renders the people less provident, and therefore retards progress.

Franklin, product of an agricultural society, glorified agriculture. On his visits to France he met and established friendly relations with the physiocrats. In 1769 he expressed physiocratic doctrine in the following manner:

There seem to be but three ways for a nation to acquire wealth. The first is by *war*, as the Romans did, in plundering their conquered neighbours. This is *robbery*. The second by *commerce*, which is generally *cheating*. The third by *agriculture*, the only *honest way*, wherein man receives a real increase of the seed thrown into the ground, in a kind of continual miracle, wrought by the hand of God in his favour, as a reward for his innocent life and his virtuous industry.*

Manufacturing was not even mentioned! In a letter written a year earlier, however, he did mention manufacturing. He wrote that "agriculture is truly *productive of new wealth;* manufacturers only change forms . . . so that riches are not *increased* by manufacturing." Yet in 1771 he approved of manufacturing because it would expand the market for agricultural produce, raise the value of land, and keep money within the country which otherwise would be exported. To Franklin the growth of manufacturing output was not an end in itself, but rather a means primarily to promote agricultural prosperity.

* *Ibid.,* Vol. V, p. 202.

Paine

THOMAS PAINE (1737–1809) was born in England, the son of a poor Quaker corset-maker and an Anglican mother. His education ended at thirteen years, and a variety of employments followed. The last position he held in England was in the government tax office. This he lost after trying to organize his fellow employees in order to improve their working conditions. Forced to sell his possessions and threatened with imprisonment for debt, he left England for America in 1774, armed with a letter from Benjamin Franklin recommending him as a clerk, assistant tutor in a school, or assistant surveyor.

In the American Revolution Paine found his *métier*. His passionate political tracts helped defend the revolutionary cause during the darkest days of the war with England. After the war, he went to England in 1787 to demonstrate an iron arch bridge that he had invented, which later proved successful. Other matters, however, attracted his attention. His radical speeches and publications brought the threat of prosecution by the British government, and he sailed for France. There he was welcomed by the Revolution in 1792, which made him a citizen and elected him to the revolutionary National Convention. Paine voted to convict the deposed king of treason, but he opposed his execution. He himself was thrown into prison for almost a year, with a death sentence hanging over him. Finally he was released (after the fall of Robespierre) through the efforts of James Monroe, American minister to France, and readmitted to the National Convention in 1795. In 1802 he sailed for the United States, where he died in poverty and obscurity.

Paine was more of a political philosopher than an economist, but his economic views are interesting. In *Rights of Man*, Part II (1792), he urged disarmament, independence of South America in order to open her up to world trade, progressive taxation, old age pensions, free public education for the needy, and government work for those temporarily unemployed. Commerce, he asserted, is the great civilizing force; it is the means for eliminating war, for it is cheaper to obtain commodities through commerce than through war.

Paine was one of the earliest advocates of a social security system sponsored and regulated by government. In *Agrarian Justice* (1796) he sought to explain the widespread poverty in the most advanced nations. His argument foretold the ideas of Henry George eighty years later.

It is a position not to be controverted that the earth, in its natural, uncultivated state was, and ever would have continued to be, *the common property of the human race*. In that state every man would have been born to property. He would have been a joint life proprietor with the rest in the property of the soil, and in all its natural productions, vegetable and animal. . . .

As it is impossible to separate the improvement made by cultivation from the earth itself, upon which that improvement is made, the idea of landed property arose from that inseparable connection; but it is nevertheless true, that it is the value of the improvement, only, and not the earth itself, that is individual property.

Every proprietor, therefore, of cultivated lands, owes to the community a *ground-rent* (for I know of no better term to express the idea) for the land which he holds; and it is from this ground-rent that the fund proposed in this plan is to issue. . . .

Man did not make the earth, and, though he had a natural right to *occupy* it, he had no right to *locate as his property* in perpetuity any part of it; neither did the Creator of the earth open a land-office, from whence the first title-deeds should issue.*

Paine acknowledged that "the fault" of private land ownership is not in the present possessors, but is in the system, and it should be corrected over successive generations with a minimum of disturbance. This could be achieved, he thought, by a 10 per cent tax on inheritances received by direct heirs, and a 100 per cent tax if there were no direct heirs. In the name of justice, not charity, the funds so raised should be distributed as follows: Every person, on reaching the age of twenty-one, should receive fifteen pounds. After age fifty, every person should receive ten pounds per year for life. Blind and lame persons younger than fifty who are totally incapable of earning a livelihood also should receive ten pounds per year.

The great mass of the poor in all countries are become an hereditary race, and it is next to impossible for them to get out of that state of themselves. It ought also to be observed that this mass increases in all countries that are called civilized. More persons fall annually into it than get out of it. . . .

I have made the calculations stated in this plan, upon what is called personal, as well as upon landed property. The reason for making it upon land is already explained; and the reason for taking personal property into the calculation is equally well founded though on a different principle. . . . Personal property is the *effect of society;* and it is as impossible for an individual to acquire personal property without the aid of society, as it is for him to make land originally. . . .

All accumulation, therefore, of personal property, beyond what a man's own hands produce, is derived to him by living in society; and he owes on every principle of justice, of gratitude, and of civilization, a part of that accumulation back again to society from whence the whole came.

This is putting the matter on a general principle, and perhaps it is best to do so; for if we examine the case minutely it will be found that the accumulation

* Philip S. Foner, ed., *The Complete Writings of Thomas Paine*, Vol. I (New York, 1945), p. 611.

of personal property is, in many instances, the effect of paying too little for the labor that produced it; the consequence of which is that the working hand perishes in old age, and the employer abounds in affluence.

It is, perhaps, impossible to proportion exactly the price of labor to the profits it produces; and it will also be said, as an apology for the injustice, that were a workman to receive an increase of wages daily he would not save it against old age, nor be much better for it in the interim. Make, then, society the treasurer to guard it for him in a common fund; for it is no reason that, because he might not make a good use of it for himself, another should take it.*

Paine has received less attention than he deserves because of his radicalism in religion. His attack on orthodox religious doctrines in *The Age of Reason* (1794–96) resulted in a continuous barrage of epithets and denunciations during the last years of his life and since his death.

Hamilton

ALEXANDER HAMILTON (1755–1804) was a brilliant pamphleteer, statesman, financier, and promoter of American nationalism and economic growth. Born in the British West Indies, he came to mainland America at seventeen years of age. His studies at King's College (now Columbia University) were interrupted by his joining the colonial side when the Revolutionary War began. He distinguished himself in combat and on General Washington's staff. At the Constitutional Convention he was a leading participant, advocating an aristocratic, strongly centralized federal government. He was the first United States secretary of treasury in Washington's cabinet. In spite of his strong antagonism to Thomas Jefferson and his democratic ideas, Hamilton used his influence to have Jefferson rather than that dubious character Aaron Burr elected president in 1800. In 1804 he saw to it that Burr was defeated for the governorship of New York. Burr challenged Hamilton to a duel and killed him on the same spot where three years earlier Hamilton's eldest son, a boy of twenty, also was killed in a duel.

Hamilton was a mercantilist, but this was understandable in an underdeveloped country that could not compete effectively in manufacturing and trade with western Europe. A laissez faire policy, it seemed, would stifle industrial growth. This did not disturb Jefferson, who favored a primarily agrarian society composed of small independent farmers. Hamilton, however, looked toward a powerful industrial-commercial-financial system with the business interests dominating a strong central government. To achieve this, government intervention was necessary. The tremendous economic growth of the United States is a tribute to Hamilton's wisdom and

* *Ibid.*, pp. 619–20.

foresight, just as the growth of our political democracy owes much to Jefferson.

Hamilton, in his *Report on Manufactures* submitted to the House of Representatives in 1791, had little difficulty in demolishing the physiocratic analysis. Simple agricultural labor, he said, is less productive than highly skilled industrial labor even if nature does cooperate in agriculture; besides, nature also cooperates in manufacturing. Farm labor is seasonally unemployed, while manufacturing labor "is constant and regular, extending through the year, embracing, in some instances, night as well as day." Manufacturing is not sterile or barren, for it yields a surplus in the form of profit, which is analogous to both the rent and profit in agriculture.

Hamilton enumerated seven advantages of manufacturing:

1. The division of labor.
2. An extension of the use of machinery.
3. Additional employment to classes of the community not ordinarily at work.

This is the employment of persons who would otherwise be idle, and in many cases a burthen on the community, either from the bias of temper, habit, infirmity of body, or some other cause, indisposing or disqualifying them for the toils of the country. It is worthy of particular remark that, in general, women and children are rendered more useful, and the latter more early useful, by manufacturing establishments, than they would otherwise be. Of the number of persons employed in the cotton manufactories of Great Britain, it is computed that four sevenths nearly are women and children, of whom the greatest proportion are children, and many of them of a tender age.*

4. The promoting of emigration from foreign countries. The government should pay the cost of emigration to this country of foreigners who will be important in promoting our industries.
5. The furnishing of greater scope for the diverse talents and abilities of people.
6. Promoting "the spirit of enterprise."
7. Expanding the market for farm products. The expansion of settlements in this country will expand agriculture. Foreign sales of the surplus are too uncertain, and the domestic market should be developed.

Not only do new industries face disadvantages in this country compared with more developed countries, but other countries grant bounties, premiums and other aids to manufacturers for production and export of their

* Samuel McKee, Jr., ed., *Papers on Public Credit, Commerce and Finance by Alexander Hamilton* (New York, 1934), pp. 193–94.

goods. Therefore if we are to compete successfully with foreigners, "it is evident that the interference and aid" of government are indispensable. To promote manufacturing, Hamilton recommended high protective duties, with the revenues to be given as bounties on domestic manufactures. New inventions and discoveries should be encouraged by the government through pecuniary rewards and exclusive privileges. Not only the authors and inventors but also the introducers should be rewarded.

Good mercantilist that he was, Hamilton favored "judicious regulations for the inspection of manufactured commodities."

This is not among the least important of the means by which the prosperity of manufactures may be promoted. It is, indeed, in many cases, one of the most essential. Contributing to prevent frauds upon consumers at home and exporters to foreign countries, to improve the quality and preserve the character of the national manufactures, it cannot fail to aid the expeditious and advantageous sale of them, and to serve as a guard against successful competition from other quarters. The reputation of the flour and lumber of some States, and of the potash of others, has been established by an attention to this point. And the like good name might be procured for those articles, wheresoever produced, by a judicious and uniform system of inspection throughout the ports of the United States. A like system might also be extended with advantage to other commodities.*

Hamilton, in his *First Report on the Public Credit* (1790) as secretary of treasury, urged that the federal government guarantee full payment on all outstanding state and federal obligations at face value to the current holders of the securities. The securities had been selling at fantastic discounts. The economic elements in his argument are interesting.

The advantage to the public creditors, from the increased value of that part of their property which constitutes the public debt, needs no explanation. But there is a consequence of this, less obvious, though not less true, in which every other citizen is interested. It is a well-known fact, that, in countries in which the national debt is properly funded, and an object of established confidence, it answers most of the purposes of money. Transfers of stock or public debt are there equivalent to payments in specie; or, in other words, stock, in the principal transactions of business, passes current as specie. The same thing would, in all probability, happen here under the like circumstances.†

A sound government debt, said Hamilton, would create a capital fund that would promote trade, manufacturing, and agriculture. Interest rates would be lowered because the quantity of money would be increased and its cir-

Ibid., pp. 244–45.   † *Ibid.,* p. 7.

culation quickened. Land values would increase as money became more plentiful, and loans on land would be obtained more easily.

In the same report, Hamilton recommended taxes and tariffs on such luxuries as wines, whiskey, tea, and coffee. To the extent that this policy would reduce imports, a favorable balance of trade would be promoted. If consumption were reduced, saving would increase.

Hamilton understood the process by which banks create credit through fractional reserve requirements. In his *Report on a National Bank* (1790), he stated that a bank augments the active or productive capital of a country. Gold and silver in a merchant's chest may lie idle or act merely as a means of exchange up to their own value. If the specie is deposited in a bank, however, it will become the basis of a paper circulation. "Banks in good credit can circulate a far greater sum than the actual quantum of their capital in gold and silver," perhaps two or three to one. Though the specie is likely to be withdrawn at any moment, experience proves that "the money so much oftener changes proprietors than place," and if withdrawn will soon be redeposited.

Hamilton denied that the accumulation of precious metals was of overriding importance. Paper could serve as money just as well, and the intrinsic wealth of a nation should be measured, not by the abundance of gold and silver contained in it, but "by the quantity of the productions of its labor and industry." Hamilton had read Smith's *Wealth of Nations*. Appearing on the scene long after mercantilism had passed its zenith, he had to be an enlightened mercantilist, blending those ideas with more modern ones; otherwise his greatness would have been dimmed, and he would not have been acclaimed as enthusiastically on the stage of history.

Carey

HENRY CHARLES CAREY (1793–1879) was the head of the leading publishing house in the United States, which he inherited from his father. Much of his wealth was invested in a wide range of enterprises, including coal mines, paper mills, gas companies, and real estate. Largely self-educated, he retired from active business at forty-two in order to devote the rest of his life to his literary career in social science. His enormous published output, which was rambling, repetitious, and diffuse, included thirteen volumes, about three thousand pages of published tracts, and perhaps an equal quantity of newspaper articles, editorials, and correspondence covering economic and political topics.

Four major themes in Carey's polemics were first, permanent protectionism, for unlike Hamilton and List, he would not settle for temporary tariffs; second, his attempted revision of Ricardian rent theory; third, his harmony-of-interest doctrine; fourth, his opposition to Malthusian pessimism on population. His analysis was dynamic, in marked contrast to that of most of his predecessors, contemporaries, and the first generation or two of successors in the field of economic analysis. His outlook was optimistic, as befitted one who lived in a rapidly expanding country.

Early in his intellectual life, Carey was an admirer of Adam Smith and a supporter of free trade. By 1845 he became an ardent protectionist. Almost all the evils in the world he attributed to international trade, and all the virtues flowed from domestic commerce. Foreign trade annihilates towns and villages, and replaces them with large cities where palaces of merchant princes are surrounded by hovels. It causes soil exhaustion, unemployment, war, and plunder. The people are impoverished while public expenditures increase. The growth of international trade increases enormously the wasteful transportation of goods, and those who control transportation dominate the farmers and the legislatures. The international division of labor limits the range of employment and compels whole populations to scratch the earth, to transport goods, or to engage in the business of trading, with production being neglected. The more people engage in transportation, the worse for society, for the transportation of goods "does least to promote development of the mind or improvement of the heart." The sailor and the wagon driver "are habitually withdrawn from the salutary influence of wives and daughters, while constantly exposed to the baneful one of the grogshop and the brothel." Business crises arise because the great distances between producers and consumers make the exchange of goods slower and more irregular. Even the danger of fires and the rising cost of fire insurance can be attributed to international trade. Self-sufficiency will develop local industry, with stone and iron taking the place of wood in building construction, thereby reducing destruction by fire.

The loss thus resulting from the absence of power to develop the mineral treasures of the earth, and from the consequent waste of property and of labor, *is more than the total value of the merchandise received in the Union from every quarter of the world;* and yet, it is with a view to foster trade that the country pursues a policy which forbids the opening of mines, and the development of the coal and metallic ores that so much abound; and by means of which structures of every kind could be built of materials that would set at defiance the risk of fire.*

Carey disputed Ricardo on rent theory. Ricardo had said that as population increases, men go from better soil to poorer, and rent is based on differentials in productivity measured from the margin. Carey said that

* H. C. Carey, *Principles of Social Science* (Philadelphia, 1888), Vol. II, pp. 247–48. [Originally published in 1858.]

the sequence should be reversed: As population grows and society progresses, men go from poorer soil to better, and therefore rents will fall. The first cultivator, having neither axe nor spade, cannot fell the large trees on the best soil, nor can he drain the swamps of the lowlands. He is forced to seek out the higher lands which are relatively bare of timber, and where the vegetation is sparser because the soil is thin. Perhaps the fear of wild beasts, savage men, and noxious fevers also keeps him on the hillside away from the dense forests. As population increases and tools are acquired and improved, men move into the more fertile lowlands.

The doctrine of Mr. Ricardo is that of increasing dispersion and weakness; whereas under the real laws of nature there is a tendency toward a constant increase of that power of association and combination to which alone man is indebted for the ability to subjugate the more productive soils. As he descends the hills and meets his neighbor man, efforts are combined, employments are divided, individual faculties are stimulated into action, property becomes more and more divided, equality grows, commerce becomes enlarged, and person and property become more secure; and every step in this direction is but preparation for further progress.*

The differences between Carey's analysis and Ricardo's can be explained by their different points of view and the assumptions on which they were based. Ricardo built his rent theory on static conditions, assuming technology as given and constant. He referred to land under cultivation at any one point in time. The historical order of settlement was of no consequence to his theory. If the fertile lowlands could not be worked by primitive man, they were *economically* submarginal even though they were chemically richer. Ricardo assumed that population would increase while technology remained constant; as a result rents would rise and landlords would grow wealthier at the expense of the rest of society. Carey arrived at an opposite position because he looked at the matter historically. Man's mastery over natural forces increased both the supply of land available for cultivation and the average yield per acre. Society would grow richer as the growth in farm output exceeded the growth in population. Ricardo's principle of diminishing returns to labor and capital applied to land is correct as a static law. Nevertheless, Carey's principle of historically increasing returns to labor and capital in agriculture has stood the test of time until now in the more economically advanced countries. Yet even under Carey's scheme, there must be a differential return on different grades of land at any one time; he did not overthrow Ricardian rent theory.

There has been both a clash and a harmony of interests, said Carey, among different groups of people. The strong have always tried to trample the weak, and the latter have combined to set limits to the power of their

* *Ibid.*, Vol. I, p. 138.

oppressors. The feudal landowners, the lords, the tax collectors, the slave-owners, have all advanced their own interests at the expense of their fellows. In modern times, those who stand between the producers and consumers—lawyers, traders, brokers, shippers—profit unduly through their activities. They impede the progress of society. Carey's suspicion of "middlemen" reflects his agrarianism.

Nevertheless, said Carey, the real and permanent interests of all classes of men are the same, although their apparent and temporary interests differ. Individuals and nations, blinded by the idea of present profit and grandeur, pursue them to the exclusion of the common good. In the long run everybody stands to gain as society grows wealthier and more productive.

The workers and the capitalists, said Carey, have common interests. Assume that a worker, using an axe, cuts more wood in a day than he can in a month without it. Suppose the capitalist who lends the worker the axe charges him three-fourths of his product for its use; the worker will still be better off than previously, notwithstanding the large proportion claimed by the capitalist as profit. The actual tendency is for labor's percentage share of the total output to increase while the capitalist's percentage share decreases. Yet both receive increasing *quantities,* and both profit from improvements. The landlord also, like any other capitalist, receives a constantly decreasing proportion of the product of labor but a constantly increasing quantity because of improvements in cultivation.

Such is the great law governing the distribution of labor's products. Of all recorded in the book of science, it is perhaps the most beautiful—being, as it is, that one, in virtue of which there is established a perfect harmony of real and true interests among the various classes of mankind. Still further, it establishes the fact, that, however great may have been the oppressions of the many at the hands of the few—however large the accumulations resulting from the exercise of the power of appropriation—however striking the existing distinctions among men—all that is required for establishing, everywhere, perfect equality before the law, and for promoting equality in social condition generally, is the pursuit of a system tending to establish in the highest degree the power of association and the development of individuality—that system being found in the observance of perfect respect for the rights of others—thus securing the maintenance of peace, and promoting the growth of wealth and population, both abroad and at home. The more rapid the increase of man's control over nature, the greater must be the tendency towards the establishment of power to direct himself—wealth and power travelling, thus, together.*

The harmony of classes will lead to a harmony of nations, with the love of peace diffusing itself throughout the earth.

Carey viewed population trends optimistically. He opposed Malthus on

* *Ibid.,* Vol. III, pp. 113-14.

several grounds. First, the Lord directed mankind to be fruitful and multiply, and surely He did not give false advice. "Is war required to correct an error of the Creator?" asked Carey. Second, as population increases, men's cooperation and mastery of nature will improve, thereby solving the food problem. Third, plants and the lower animals, which provide the necessities of life for humanity, can increase much more rapidly than man. Fourth, as people become more intellectual, their sexual activity and reproduction rate will decline. Fifth, as man's numbers increase, the lower animals tend to diminish; this keeps the carbon dioxide in the atmosphere in correct balance. Increased vegetation decomposes more carbon dioxide given off by animals and men, and liberates more of the oxygen required by human beings. The Divine Plan works harmoniously.

Walker

GENERAL FRANCIS AMASA WALKER (1840–97), a veteran of the Civil War, was superintendent of the United States censuses of 1870 and 1880. He was a professor of political economy at Yale University, and later president of the Massachusetts Institute of Technology. When the American Economic Association was organized in 1885, Walker became its first president. He also served as president of the American Statistical Association.

Walker applied the Ricardian theory of rent to urban as well as to agricultural land. Interest is the reward for abstinence. As wealth accumulates, rent tends to rise and interest to fall. Therefore they have to be treated separately, and not lumped together as J. B. Clark and others proposed.

Walker contributed two major ideas to economic thinking. First, he clearly distinguished between the roles of the capitalist and the entrepreneur. Second, he attacked the wages-fund doctrine, substituting instead the idea that labor is a residual claimant to the value of the output.

The capitalist, said Walker, lends his wealth, and all capital bears the same rate of interest except for differences in risk. The entrepreneur, the captain of industry, is the great engineer of industrial progress, for he directs the efficient functioning of labor and capital. Profit is the reward for his industrial success. He may be the possessor of his own capital, but this is not essential; with his organizing and administrative abilities, he can readily borrow capital.

Walker asserted that profit is analogous to rent, for it neither enters into the price of the product nor causes any diminution of the wages of labor. The price of manufactured goods is determined by the cost of production of that portion of the supply that is produced at the greatest disadvantage.

If the demand for such goods is so great as to require a certain amount to be produced under the management and control of persons whose efficiency in organizing and supervising the forces of labor and capital is small, the cost of production of that portion of the stock will be large, and the price will be correspondingly high, yet, high as it is, it will not be high enough to yield to the employers of this grade any more than that scant and difficult subsistence which we have taken as the no-profits line.

The price at which these goods are to be sold, however, will determine the price of the whole supply, since, in any one market, at any one time, there is but one price for different portions of the same commodity. Hence, whatever the cost of production of those portions of the supply which are produced by employers of a higher industrial grade, they will command the same price as those portions which are produced at the greatest disadvantage. The difference so measured, will go as profits to each individual employer, according to his own success in production.*

Profits do not come out of wages because the marginal, no-profits employer must pay a sufficient wage to attract workers. More capable entrepreneurs pay the same rates of wages, and they receive profit because of their superior abilities. Any cause that brings less competent entrepreneurs into business will raise the profits of the more competent. If the cost of production rises and consequently so do prices, the consumers bear the brunt of it. This will be detrimental to the laboring class as well as to all other consumers. What swells the ranks of incompetent employers? "Shilly-shally" bankruptcy laws, bad money, tariff protection, slavery, and ignorant laborers who can be taken advantage of by their employers. If the least competent employers were driven from the field, all of society would benefit.

Walker's second major idea was concerned with the determination of wages. He denied the validity of the wages-fund doctrine (as had John Stuart Mill and others before him); wages do not depend on the number of workers who must share a fixed wages fund. Instead, wages represent a residual share of the product which workers help produce, after deducting rent, interest, and profit. In this his position was identical with that of Jevons, while he attacked Ricardo's idea that profits are the residual share. Therefore, said Walker, the more efficient and productive the workers become through their own personal development, the higher will wages be.

Under a regime of perfect competition, economic harmony prevails. Where competition is imperfect, however, as when the mobility of labor is impeded, the lowest strata of the population sink even lower, while the rich grow richer because of their advantageous position. Therefore limited state intervention is justified wherever imperfect competition occurs in

* Francis A. Walker, *Political Economy*, 3rd ed. (New York, 1888), p. 240.

order to promote perfect competition, a more equitable division of all burdens, and a diffusion of all benefits throughout society.

Walker discussed Henry George's theoretical views on rent. But of George's practical proposal to tax away all economic rent, Walker asserted: "I will not insult my readers by discussing a project so steeped in infamy."

George

HENRY GEORGE (1839–97) has inspired generations of fervid admirers and followers throughout the world. His formal education ended at fourteen, when he obtained employment as an errand boy, then later as a clerk and a sailor. As a youth of nineteen, he migrated from Philadelphia to San Francisco, where he prospected for gold, became a farm hand, a printer, and a newspaper reporter, editor, and publisher. At times he was unemployed, and there was actual hunger in the George household.

George observed the speculative land craze in San Francisco in 1868 on the eve of the completion of the first transcontinental railroad. As people poured into California, land values rose phenomenally. Generous land grants were handed over to railroad companies throughout the West. Frequently railroads were promoted not to earn operating profits, but rather to profit from the sale of securities and the acquisition of state and federal land as well as cash subsidies and other benefits. Political corruption smoothed the way for the railroad promoters, the monopolists, the profiteers. The great progress visible throughout the West coincided with the impoverishment and degradation of large numbers of people.

Out of this background came Henry George's indignant and zealous work, *Progress and Poverty*, in 1879. He could not find a publisher until he paid for making the plates himself. When D. Appleton and Company finally accepted the book at virtually no risk to themselves, they did not even take the trouble to secure foreign copyrights. A paperback edition was issued in 1881 which outsold the popular novels of the day. In the United States and Great Britain the work ran serially in the newspapers. In the following twenty-five years at least two million copies of *Progress and Poverty* were printed in many languages. The book was especially popular in Great Britain, where antilandlord sentiment had been growing. The Fabian socialist movement received impetus from this work, and both Sidney Webb and G. B. Shaw acknowledged the Fabian debt to the promoter of radical land reform who was clearly opposed to socialism.

Henry George ran for mayor of New York City in 1886 on a labor-party ticket. He wrote the platform favoring taxation of land values, abolition of other taxes, municipal ownership of railroads and the telegraph, and a reformed ballot system. George ran second in a three-way race, ahead of the young Republican candidate, Theodore Roosevelt. It was widely believed that the election was stolen from George by the Democrats. He again ran for mayor of New York City on a third party ticket in 1897, despite his doctor's orders to the contrary. On the Thursday before the election he spoke at four meetings, and he died that night. His son ran for mayor in his place to enable thousands of supporters to vote in memory of Henry George.

The idea of taxing all of the economic rent was based on the Ricardian analysis. Nevertheless Ricardo opposed such a tax on the ground that it is unjust to tax only one class of people, many of whom have bought land with the savings realized from years of toil. George's proposal also resembles that of the French physiocrats, that only economic rent be taxed. But the differences between the two are notable. The physiocrats believed that only the rent of land should be taxed because only that represents the true source of wealth, the economic surplus of society; any other tax should be shifted to rent. Therefore, recognizing what they thought was inevitable, they advocated direct rather than indirect taxes. Nor did they propose to tax away all economic rent and leave nothing for the landowners; they did not wish to undermine private property in land. George, in contrast, considered land rent an unearned income that should be taxed away completely. Moreover, he saw it to be an income that grows as society progresses and that impoverishes all other classes. Yet he never regarded agriculture as the sole source of wealth. In essence, the physiocrats were agrarians while George based himself on the rapid expansion of capitalistic industry.

George stated that labor and capital receive wages and interest; the amount they earn depends on what they could have produced jointly on rent-free land, or the least productive land used. This was the idea that inspired J. Maurice Clark's general law of distribution, that the earnings of any factor of production depend on the marginal productivity of that factor.

George summarized his analysis of distribution as follows:

As Produce = Rent + Wages + Interest,
Therefore, Produce − Rent = Wages + Interest.

Thus wages and interest do not depend upon the produce of labor and capital, but upon what is left after rent is taken out; or, upon the produce which they could obtain without paying rent—that is, from the poorest land in use. And hence, no matter what be the increase in productive power, if the increase in rent keeps pace with it, neither wages nor interest can increase.

The moment this simple relation is recognized, a flood of light streams in upon what was before inexplicable, and seemingly discordant facts range themselves under an obvious law. The increase of rent which goes on in progressive countries is at once seen to be the key which explains why wages and interest fail to increase with increase of productive power. For the wealth produced in every community is divided into two parts by what may be called the rent line, which is fixed by the margin of cultivation, or the return which labor and capital could obtain from such natural opportunities as are free to them without the payment of rent. From the part of the produce below this line wages and interest must be paid. All that is above goes to the owners of land. Thus, where the value of land is low, there may be a small production of wealth, and yet a high rate of wages and interest, as we see in new countries. And, where the value of land is high, there may be a very large production of wealth, and yet a low rate of wages and interest, as we see in old countries. And, where productive power increases, as it is increasing in all progressive countries, wages and interest will be affected, not by the increase, but by the manner in which rent is affected. If the value of land increases proportionately, all the increased production will be swallowed up by rent, and wages and interest will remain as before. If the value of land increases in greater ratio than productive power, rent will swallow up even more than the increase; and while the produce of labor and capital will be much larger, wages and interest will fall. It is only when the value of land fails to increase as rapidly as productive power, that wages and interest can increase with the increase of productive power. All this is exemplified in actual fact.*

The worker and the capitalist, said George, have common interests, and both have interests that are antagonistic to those of the landowners. Wages tend to be minimal because rents increase even faster than society's productive power. Profits and enterprise also are thwarted by rising rents.

Take . . . some hard-headed business man, who has no theories, but knows how to make money. Say to him: "Here is a little village; in ten years it will be a great city—in ten years the railroad will have taken the place of the stage coach, the electric light of the candle; it will abound with all the machinery and improvements that so enormously multiply the effective power of labor. Will, in ten years, interest be any higher?"

He will tell you, "No!"

"Will the wages of common labor be any higher; will it be easier for a man who has nothing but his labor to make an independent living?"

He will tell you, "No; the wages of common labor will not be any higher; on the contrary, all the chances are that they will be lower; it will not be easier for the mere laborer to make an independent living; the chances are that it will be harder."

"What, then, will be higher?"

"Rent; the value of land. Go, get yourself a piece of ground, and hold possession."

* Henry George, *Progress and Poverty* (New York, 1942), pp. 171–72. [Originally published in 1879.]

And if, under such circumstances, you take his advice, you need do nothing more. You may sit down and smoke your pipe; you may lie around like the lazzaroni of Naples or the leperos of Mexico; you may go up in a balloon, or down a hole in the ground; and without doing one stroke of work, without adding one iota to the wealth of the community, in ten years you will be rich! In the new city you may have a luxurious mansion; but among its public buildings will be an almshouse.*

George was opposed to socialistic solutions. Even the mildest of them, he said, a graduated income tax, is objectionable because it represents excessive government regulation, it breeds corruption, and it lessens the incentive to accumulate wealth. Instead, all economic rent derived from land and other natural resources should be taxed. Technically the land would not be confiscated, for the present owners could retain their titles. In essence, however, land would be nationalized without compensation, and it would be rented to the highest bidders. Society creates rising land values, and the unearned increment of land values should belong to it, he said. The owners of land must lose their claims to its income regardless of whether they obtained them recently or in the distant past, perhaps through inheritance. Robbery, said George, is unjustified even if the right to rob was recently purchased out of one's frugal accumulation of savings. Even landowners would gain when justice, love, peace, and plenty triumphed. The present landowners should, however, retain their titles to the improvements on the land, such as buildings, and these should be tax free. They would continue to use the land on which their improvements stand, merely paying to the government the annual value of the use of the land. Just as two men may own a ship without sawing her in half, just as a railroad may be divided into a hundred thousand shares and yet run as if it were the property of a single owner, so all of society may own a piece of land without taking it away from the man who uses and improves it. Land would not lie idle as it does now because speculators hold it for higher prices. No other taxes would be required, hence the idea of a "single tax" on the economic rent of land.

The present method of taxation operates upon exchange like artificial deserts and mountains; it costs more to get goods through a custom house than it does to carry them around the world. It operates upon energy, and industry, and skill, and thrift, like a fine upon those qualities. If I have worked harder and built myself a good house while you have been contented to live in a hovel, the tax-gatherer now comes annually to make me pay a penalty for my energy and industry, by taxing me more than you. If I have saved while you wasted, I am mulct, while you are exempt. If a man build a ship we make him pay for

* *Ibid.*, pp. 293-94.

his temerity, as though he had done an injury to the state; if a railroad be opened, down comes the tax-collector upon it, as though it were a public nuisance; if a manufactory be erected we levy upon it an annual sum which would go far toward making a handsome profit. We say we want capital, but if any one accumulate it, or bring it among us, we charge him for it as though we were giving him a privilege. We punish with a tax the man who covers barren fields with ripening grain, we fine him who puts up machinery, and him who drains a swamp. How heavily these taxes burden production only those realize who have attempted to follow our system of taxation through its ramifications, for, as I have before said, the heaviest part of taxation is that which falls in increased prices. But manifestly these taxes are in their nature akin to the Egyptian Pasha's tax upon date-trees. If they do not cause the trees to be cut down, they at least discourage the planting.*

Recent refutations of George's single-tax proposal have included the idea that, with the growth of government expenditures, it would no longer adequately supply the required revenue. In 1960 total rental payments in the personal-income account of the United States amounted to 12.5 billion dollars, or only 3 per cent of national income and 12 per cent of all local, state and federal taxes. This evidence that economic rent is a minor portion of the nation's revenue is not conclusive. In national-income accounting, rent includes actual payments for the rental of real property and the imputed rental value of owner-occupied dwellings with depreciation, taxes, and interest deducted; most of these rental payments should be excluded if we are to get at the economic rent of land. On the other hand, much economic rent is not included in national-income statistics. If an industrial firm, a railroad, a mining company, or an agricultural enterprise owns the land over or under which it operates, the economic rent of land appears as profit of the enterprise, interest on the debt secured in part by the land, or income of unincorporated enterprise, as is the case with most farmers. As economic rent rises, land values rise proportionately; yet this capital gain does not appear in national-income calculations and rent may not either. These increases in economic rent and in the capitalized value of the land can be quite impressive. To take one extreme illustration, the land under Number One Wall Street, New York City, has sold for $700 a square foot† or $30.5 million an acre. In view of the ever rising trend of urban and mineral land values in particular, Henry George will continue to have disciples, even though his program would be quite disturbing to confidence in existing property rights. We do not really know by how much a single tax on economic rent would fail to meet the more than $100 billion raised in taxes each year. We can be certain, however, that economic rent is larger by far than the national-income accounts indicate.

* *Ibid.*, p. 434.   † *The New York Times Magazine*, May 7, 1961, p. 42.

CHAPTER 17

The Institutionalist School:

THORSTEIN VEBLEN

THE INSTITUTIONALIST school, which represents an outstanding American contribution to economic thought, began in roughly 1900; by then its founder, Thorstein Veblen, had published his first book and many articles and book reviews. It may be said to have ended in 1936, when John Maynard Keynes, creating a more elegant theoretical system, stole its thunder. The three great figures in this school were Veblen, who critically dissected orthodox thinking and provided the theoretical approach of institutional economics; Wesley C. Mitchell, who stimulated inductive research with his own statistical studies; and John R. Commons, who helped persuade the nation of the need for reform through government legislation, and who helped write the new laws.

Overview of the Institutionalist School

The social background of the school. Between the Civil War and World War I, the achievements of American capitalism were impressive. Rapid growth made ours the biggest and most powerful industrial system in the world. The rise in levels of living of the lowest income strata, however, did not keep pace with the rise in national income. The improvements in living conditions of most wage-earners fell far short of their aspirations and of the possibilities. Hours of labor were long; housing was inadequate; security in sickness, unemployment, and old age was negligible; higher education was inaccessible for most workers' children; job security was virtually non-existent; health and safety regulations were inadequate; frequently the employers organized company towns and dominated the workers even in their personal lives; large immigration tended to undermine wage rates; taxation was regressive; usury was widespread; recurring depressions were devastating to those who lost their jobs.

The age of monopoly may be said to have begun in the 1870's, and the movement accelerated around the turn of the century. With unionism still weak, this gave a preponderance of economic and political power to big business. Conservative voices predominated in the schools, in the press, in the pulpits, and in government. The state and federal governments, which proclaimed laissez faire with respect to the workers' interests, were quick to use police and troops against labor in industrial disputes. They were generous in their tariff protection for business and in granting large subsidies to railroads. Political corruption and chicanery were common. Because of passivity, indifference, and conservatism in high places, the Interstate Commerce Act of 1887 and the Sherman Antitrust Act of 1890 were not enforced, and governmental policies allowed the wasteful exploitation of natural resources.

In economic theory and analysis, there was increasing dissatisfaction with the orthodox marginalist doctrines. Besides the socialists, there were a few "respectable" or semirespectable academic economists who disagreed with the postulates, analyses, and conclusions of the dominant school. The assumptions of the marginalists were unrealistic. The defense of laissez faire and the status quo as producing the best of all possible worlds seemed untenable. There was increasing concern about monopoly, poverty, depression, and waste. The operation of modern capitalism was not conforming to expectations based on traditional economic theorizing. The movement for social control and reform was gathering momentum.

Out of this milieu grew institutional economics.

There were two major alternative methods for achieving social change. The first was to reorganize society along socialist lines. This raised the possibility of a sharpening class struggle, militant unionism, and a revolutionary orientation toward existing society. The second method was to achieve social change through social reform. This meant ameliorating conditions through government intervention in the economy. The object was to save capitalism, not to overthrow it, by improving conditions for the masses. Although Veblen kept aloof from socialist movements and was critical of them, he favored a radical reconstruction of society. Nevertheless the institutionalist school that he founded preferred the reformist approach. The changes wrought by the New Deal in the 1930's were in essence the epitome of institutionalism.

While there were certain similarities in methodology between the German historical school and American institutionalism, the latter was less nationalistic and more liberal and democratic in its outlook.

The essence of the institutional school. There are eight key ideas that are basic to this type of economic thinking.

1. The economy as a whole must be studied, rather than examining small parts separately and in isolation from the whole. A complex organism cannot be understood if each segment is treated as if it were unrelated to the larger entity. Economic activity is not merely a summation of the activities of individuals motivated individually and mechanically by the desire for the maximum individual monetary gain. There are patterns of collective action that are more than the sum of the parts.

2. This school emphasized the role of institutions in economic life. An institution is not merely an organization or establishment for the promotion of a particular objective, like a school, a prison, a union, or a federal reserve bank. It is also an organized pattern of group behavior, well established and accepted as a fundamental part of a culture. It includes customs, social habits, laws, modes of thinking, and ways of living. Slavery and a belief in slavery were institutions. Others are beliefs in laissez faire, or unionism, or a government social security system. Going out on New Year's Eve to raise a din and clatter is an institution. So is communist ideology in the Soviet Union and anticommunism in the United States. Economic life, said the institutionalists, is regulated by economic institutions, not by economic laws. Group social behavior and thought patterns that influence them are more germane to economic analysis than the individualism of the prevailing marginal type of theory. The institutionalists of the period from 1900 to 1936 were especially interested in analyzing and reforming the institutions of credit, monopoly, absentee ownership, labor-management relations, social security, and the distribution of income.

3. The Darwinian, evolutionary approach should be used, because society and its institutions are constantly changing. Instead of equilibrium, there is motion. The institutionalists disagreed with the static viewpoint that sought to discover eternal economic truths, without regard to differences of time and place, without concern for changes that were occurring constantly. Instead of asking "What is?" they asked "How did we get here, and where are we going?" The evolution and functioning of economic institutions should be the central theme in economics. This approach required a knowledge not only of economics, but also of history, cultural anthropology, political science, sociology, philosophy, psychology, and social psychology.

4. Maladjustments in economic life are not departures from normal equilibrium, but are themselves normal. The outstanding maladjustment is the business slump. Collective controls through government are necessary to continually correct and overcome these recurring maladjustments.

5. Instead of the harmony of interests that most of their contemporaries

and predecessors deduced from their theories, the institutionalists recognized serious clashes of interest. Man, to be sure, is a cooperative, collective creature. He organizes into groups for the mutual self-interest of the members, which becomes the common interest of the group. There is, however, a clash of interest between groups, such as big business against small business, consumers against producers, farmers against city people, employers against workers, importers against domestic producers, the makers of goods against the makers of money. Here again a representative and impartial government must compromise, reconcile, or override clashing interests for the common good, for the efficient working of the economic system.

6. The institutionalists promoted liberal, democratic reforms for the more equitable distribution of wealth and income. They invariably condemned laissez faire and favored a larger role for government in economic and social affairs.

7. This school favored the inductive rather than the deductive approach. A call went forth for more fact-finding, more statistical studies, a closer examination of the actual working of the system. Abstract theorizing—especially the marginalists'—was condemned as unrealistic and sterile.

8. The institutionalists repudiated the pleasure-pain psychology. They reached out instead for a better psychology, and some of them incorporated Freudian and behavioristic ideas into their thinking.

What groups of people did the institutionalist school serve or seek to serve? This body of thought represented middle-class reform in an era of growing big business and banker capitalism. It represented the needs and interests of agrarian and small business groups, and also labor. Government workers, reformers, humanitarians, leaders of consumers' organizations, and unions were attracted to the institutionalist ideas that, hopefully, might alter the orientation of private business enterprise toward the common good.

How was the institutional school valid, useful, or correct in its time? The institutionalists retarded the development of a rigid orthodoxy in economic thinking. Many of their criticisms of orthodox theory were valid and helped change that type of theory along more defensible lines. The stress on looking at the economy as a whole from the evolutionary point of view and in an institutional setting still has validity. For example, the wages of railroad workers depend more on the development of craft unionism and the procedures of government regulations than they do on the marginal productivity of labor. Again, the widespread interest in national economic growth and development since World War II is a vindication of the institutionalist ideas.

The institutionalists aroused, belatedly, deep and lasting concern over business cycles and monopolies. They promoted a reform movement that remains powerful today. Modest steps toward national economic planning for limited objectives such as conservation and full employment are in line with institutionalist thought. In a world where knowledge is increasingly fragmented and compartmentalized, they urged closer integration of the social sciences. The emphasis on inductive studies reduced the gap between economic theory and practice. It caught on in government circles, among private non-profit research organizations, in business and labor organizations, and among individuals who toil in the field to harvest their mountains of statistical data. The National Bureau of Economic Research, founded by W. C. Mitchell and others in 1920 and guided by him for many years, is a monument to the institutionalist method.

How did the institutional school outlive its usefulness? To a considerable extent, it completed its task when its method and viewpoint became part of the common property of many economists. The rise of Keynesian theory completed the process of submerging institutionalism. There was a certain antitheory bias among institutionalists that was unsatisfactory to those who seek economic laws, or tendencies, and who use the deductive method. The vast ingathering of facts with a minimum of theorizing seemed somewhat futile. The institutionalists, in attacking marginalist theory, offered little to take its place.

Now that reforms and controls have made considerable headway, it has become difficult to reach agreement on what further reforms should be undertaken, and in what order of priority. In 1900 the abuses of unrestricted capitalism and the neglect of social problems were so shockingly visible that reformers could reach some sort of working agreement concerning the necessary changes required to ameliorate conditions. Today, especially with legal protection for unionism, social insurance, built-in stabilizers, and governmental responsibility for full employment, people do not see eye to eye on the necessity for further changes, or in which direction change should go. In addition, an uneasy question arises: How far can reforms be pushed without weakening the incentives to invest?

Economic and social reforms have been displaced from the center of the stage by the great international political issues of the day, such as the cold war, national security, the danger of atomic warfare, and the spread of communism.

We shall now turn to that brooding, enigmatic genius who is considered to be the founder of the school.

Veblen

THORSTEIN BUNDE VEBLEN (1857–1929), the son of Norwegian immigrants, was born on a frontier farm in Wisconsin and raised in rural Minnesota. His undergraduate college education was acquired at Carleton College, where he was a student of J. B. Clark. His graduate work was done at Johns Hopkins, where he failed to obtain a scholarship, and at Yale, where he received a doctor's degree in philosophy. No academic position was available to him, largely because of his agnostic views at a time when a divinity degree was considered a desirable prerequisite for teaching philosophy.

Veblen received fellowships at Cornell and at the University of Chicago to do postdoctoral work. He became the editor of the *Journal of Political Economy* at Chicago, and he also taught economics. He was an instructor there from the time he was thirty-nine until he was forty-three, when many of his classmates were full professors, heads of departments, and later college presidents. Veblen never in his life reached the rank of full professor, in spite of his publishing eleven books and establishing a lasting world reputation. Even his books were not overwhelming successes during his lifetime, and he had to subsidize the publication of several of them himself.

Because of his marital troubles, his indifference to most of his students, his involvements with women, and his poor teaching techniques, he had to move from college to college. After Chicago, he taught at Stanford, the University of Missouri, and at the New School for Social Research. He worked briefly for the Food Administration in Washington, D. C. in 1918, and he served as one of the editors of the journal *The Dial*. A former student aided him financially in his later years. He died in August 1929, a few months before the great stock market crash and the beginning of the depression that he had been predicting.

Veblen was a bitter, skeptical, pessimistic, and lonely man. His books, though written somewhat ponderously and obscurely, are replete with wit, wisdom, and sardonic attacks on middle-class virtues. For example, he wrote about the middle class that lends its conservative, affected, snobbish tone to periodical literature. In a footnote he defined snobbery with a deft twist of his rapier-like wit.

"Snobbery" is here used without disrespect, as a convenient term to denote the element of strain involved in the quest of gentility on the part of persons whose accustomed social standing is less high or less authentic than their aspirations.*

* Thorstein Veblen, *The Theory of Business Enterprise* (New York, 1904), p. 388.

Veblen's first book, and his most popular one, was *The Theory of the Leisure Class,* published in 1899. It was this book that popularized such terms as "leisure class," "pecuniary emulation," and "conspicuous consumption." Veblen held that the leisure class was engaged in the predatory seizure of goods without working. Those who accumulate wealth do so not merely to take care of their physical wants, or even their spiritual, aesthetic, and intellectual wants. Rather, they wish to consume in a way that displays their wealth, for a show of wealth indicates power, prestige, honor, and success in our pecuniary culture. In order to be reputable, such consumption must be wasteful. Poorer people must work in order to subsist, but even their pattern of spending includes an element of wasteful conspicuous consumption. Their outlook on life is imposed on them by the dominant leisure class.

Women are especially useful in displaying the wealth and importance of men. Attired in clothing and shoes that prevent them from doing useful labor, they advertise that they are supported by men. Wearing expensive finery, they indicate that the men to whom they belong are reputably wealthy. Hampered by long fingernails, cumbersome hair styles, delicate skin, or bound and distorted feet, they give constant evidence that they are leisure-class women kept by leisure-class men.

The high gloss of a gentleman's hat or of a patent-leather shoe, said Veblen, has no more intrinsic beauty than a similarly high gloss on a threadbare sleeve. Flowers that are difficult to grow and therefore expensive are not necessarily more beautiful than those that grow wild or with little care. For cropping lawns, pastures, and parks, cows are more useful than deer, and therefore the latter are preferred because they are superior in expensiveness and futility, and they are not vulgarly lucrative.

One can amuse oneself with many modern evidences of conspicuous consumption. To cite but one example, expensive picture windows in living rooms typically face the street where they can be seen. Yet the view across the street may be of other houses with other picture windows staring back, or a cemetery, a dump, or a junk yard. The rear of the house is not favored with an expanse of glass even if the view is magnificent, because the public would not be aware of the lavish expenditure.

Members of the leisure class must avoid useful, productive work. They must indulge only in wasteful or useless tasks if they are to remain reputable.

These occupations are government, war, sports, and devout observances. Persons unduly given to difficult theoretical niceties may hold that these occupations are still incidentally and indirectly "productive"; but it is to be noted as decisive of the question in hand that the ordinary and ostensible motive of the leisure class in engaging in these occupations is assuredly not an increase of wealth by productive effort. At this as at any other cultural stage, government and war are, at least in part, carried on for the pecuniary gain of those who engage in them; but it is gain obtained by the honourable method of seizure and conversion. These occupations are of the nature of predatory, not of productive, employment.*

Force and fraud are present today, Veblen said, as they were among barbarian peoples. We find them in modern warfare, in business, and in sports and games.

Strategy or cunning is an element invariably present in games, as also in warlike pursuits and in the chase. In all of these employments strategy tends to develop into finesse and chicane. Chicane, falsehood, brow-beating, hold a well-secured place in the method of procedure of any athletic contest and in games generally. The habitual employment of an umpire, and the minute technical regulations governing the limits and details of permissible fraud and strategic advantage, sufficiently attest the fact that fraudulent practices and attempts to overreach one's opponent are not adventitious features of the game. In the nature of the case habituation to sports should conduce to a fuller development of the aptitude for fraud; and the prevalence in the community of that predatory temperament which inclines men to sports connotes a prevalence of sharp practice and callous disregard of the interests of others.†

In the same book Veblen asserted that the evolution of social structure has been a process of natural selection of institutions. Progress can be attributed to the survival of the fittest habits of thought and to the enforced adaptation of individuals to a changing environment. Institutions must change with changing circumstances. The development of these institutions is the development of society. Unfortunately there is a conflict between current beliefs and current requirements because of a cultural lag in the process of change.

The situation of to-day shapes the institutions of tomorrow through a selective, coercive process, by acting upon men's habitual view of things, and so altering or fortifying a point of view or a mental attitude handed down from the past. The institutions—that is to say the habits of thought—under the guidance of which men live are in this way received from an earlier time. . . . Institutions are products of the past process, are adapted to past circumstances, and are therefore never in full accord with the requirements of the present. . . . At the same time, men's present habits of thought tend to persist indefinitely, except as circumstances enforce a change. These institutions which have so been handed

* Thorstein Veblen, *The Theory of the Leisure Class* (New York, 1934), p. 40. [Originally published in 1899.]
† *Ibid.*, pp. 273–74.

down, these habits of thought, points of view, mental attitudes and aptitudes, or what not, are therefore themselves a conservative factor. This is the factor of social inertia, psychological inertia, conservatism. . . . The evolution of society is substantially a process of mental adaptation on the part of individuals under the stress of circumstances which will no longer tolerate habits of thought formed under and conforming to a different set of circumstances in the past.*

If any portion or class of society is sheltered from the forces of the environment, it will adapt its views more slowly to the altered general situation, and it will therefore retard the process of social change. The wealthy leisure class is in just such a sheltered position with respect to economic forces that make for change and readjustment. The characteristic attitude of this class is indicated in the maxim, "Whatever is, is right." The law of natural selection, however, as applied to human institutions, asserts that "Whatever is, is wrong." That is, current institutions are wrong to some extent, from the evolutionary standpoint, because they do not change quickly enough to be in tune with the times.

Veblen attacked marginalist economics and the classical school from which it sprang, declaring John Bates Clark's system static and his dynamics essentially a deranged static condition. It was based on the pre-evolutionary ground of normality and natural law. In such a view, no awareness of cumulative change occurs. The hedonism of the dominant economic school would have

a gang of Aleutian Islanders slushing about in the wrack and surf with rakes and magical incantations for the capture of shell-fish . . . to be engaged on a feat of hedonistic equilibration in rent, wages, and interest. And that is all there is to it. Indeed, for economic theory of this kind, that is all there is to any economic situation. The hedonistic magnitudes vary from one situation to another, but, except for variations in the arithmetical details of the hedonistic balance, all situations are, in point of economic theory, substantially alike.†

Hedonism presupposes rational, intelligent people who react quickly and smoothly to the stimuli of anticipated pleasure and pain. They are clear-sighted and farsighted.

The hedonistic conception of man is that of a lightning calculator of pleasures and pains, who oscillates like a homogeneous globule of desire of happiness under the impulse of stimuli that shift him about the area, but leave him intact. He has neither antecedent nor consequent. He is an isolated, definitive human

* *Ibid.*, pp. 190–92.
† Thorstein Veblen, *The Place of Science in Modern Civilization and Other Essays* (New York, 1919), p. 193.

datum, in stable equilibrium except for the buffets of the impinging forces that displace him in one direction or another. Self-imposed in elemental space, he spins symmetrically about his own spiritual axis until the parallelogram of forces bears down upon him, whereupon he follows the line of the resultant. When the force of the impact is spent, he comes to rest, a self-contained globule of desire as before. Spiritually, the hedonistic man is not a prime mover. He is not the seat of a process of living, except in the sense that he is subject to a series of permutations enforced upon him by circumstances external and alien to him.*

Since hedonism came to rule economic science, said Veblen, the science has been in the main a theory of distribution of ownership and income. Consistently with the spirit of hedonism, this theory has centered about a doctrine of price.

The normal economic community, upon which theoretical interest has converged, is a business community, which centers about the market, and whose scheme of life is a scheme of profit and loss. Even when some considerable attention is ostensibly devoted to theories of consumption and production, in these systems of doctrine the theories are constructed in terms of ownership, price, and acquisition, and so reduce themselves in substance to doctrines of distributive acquisition.†

Veblen in effect accused the marginalists of supporting the present scheme of the distribution of wealth and income. Standard theory, he thought, was not truly a theory of anything, but a sort of folklore or theology to justify private property and property incomes. Business economics was developed to defend the business community, and the questions it asked and sought to answer were not relevant to the underlying population. Veblen was concerned with social economics instead of the business economics of price, profit, and ownership.

So much for Veblen's attack on standard theory. What did he offer in its place? He believed that work is not generally irksome, or the survival of the human race would be jeopardized. Man's greatest triumph over the other species in the struggle for survival has been his superior ability to control the forces of environment. It is not a proclivity to effort, but to achievement, that really matters. When not harassed by overwork, man feels not an aversion to work, but an instinct for workmanship that conduces to the material well-being of the race and its biological success. People inherently want to do work, and to do it well. They deprecate waste. Allied with that equally important instinct, the parental bent, the instinct for workmanship impels the current generation to improve life for posterity. We basically try to avoid greed and indolence, we educate and

* Ibid., pp. 73–74.   † Ibid., p. 183.

train our children, we improve technology and we conserve our resources because of our instinct for workmanship and our wish to provide for our descendants. This instinct conflicts with the conventional antipathy to useful effort, but it is the dominant force, especially among the great mass of artisans, farmers, railroad workers, machine-tenders, engineers, and technological experts.

Gradually small-scale handicraft production and trade has given way to large-scale capitalistic enterprises. Formerly the market was narrow and business was managed with a view to earning a livelihood. The modern industrial system has as its dominant features the machine process and investment for profit. The growth of markets and investments has created new opportunities for shrewd manipulation. As the captains of industry enlarge their domain, their interests diverge more and more from those of the rest of the community. Instead of being interested in the production of goods, they are concerned primarily with maximum profit. While the two objectives may coincide, the production of goods is merely the means to profit; where they conflict, the former is sacrificed to the latter. If necessary, coalitions of big businessmen, holding companies, and other types of monopolies are organized to restrict output and raise prices. When making money takes precedence over making goods, the instinct for workmanship is thwarted; it comes to be rated in terms of salesmanship. The absentee owners, who are in control, hamper the increased output of goods that otherwise would occur. Their manipulations prevent prices from falling. They force men and capital into the more competitive sectors of the economy, thus worsening the situation there. They profit from disturbances in the system that may hinder output. If the economy is unstable, the opportunities for profit increase. The shrewd operator can make money as a bull during the upswing of business, and as a bear during the downswing. Progress is hampered by big business, which is more interested in the vendibility of goods than in their serviceability for the needs of mankind. Those who are interested in problems of price rather than in production include business enterprisers and their assistants—salesmen, accountants, advertisers, etc.

The importance of the entrepreneur as a bearer of risks is negligible, Veblen believed. Most of the risks now associated with the production of economic values could easily be eliminated with no reduction of the national income. Risks are associated with the promotion of corporate consolidations, with sales and advertising campaigns, with the establishment of new brand names, with the exploitation of patents and franchises, and with the attempt to capitalize business goodwill. These activities are superb for making money, but they and the risks associated with them can be dispensed with in the production of goods. There are very few real risks

involved in meeting the basic living requirements of the working population. The only risks that the technicians cannot overcome with a high
degree of success are those associated with climate, weather, and the occurrence of natural catastrophes. As these hazards are not a matter of individual responsibility, they could be provided for by the community out
of the net surplus product of industry. No private risk-taking function
would then require remuneration.

Credit has a special role to play in modern business, according to Veblen.
Borrowing money can increase profits as long as the current rate of business earnings exceeds the rate of interest. Under competitive conditions,
what is profitable for one businessman to do becomes compulsory for all
competitors. Those who take advantage of the opportunities afforded by
credit are in a position to undersell those who do not. The recourse to
credit therefore becomes widespread and typical. The competitive earning
capacity of an enterprise comes to rest on the basis of the initial capital
plus such borrowed funds as this capital will support. As aggregate earnings
are only slightly larger than they might have been without credit, the rate
of profit on the total amount invested tends to fall. The competitive use
of credit in extending business operations gives a business concern only
a differential advantage against other competitors; it has no aggregate effect
on earnings or on total industrial output. In fact, aggregate net profits from
industry are reduced by the amount of interest that has to be paid to creditors outside the industrial process.

Why does the expansion of credit have no effect on total earnings or on
industrial output? Is it not true that borrowed funds represent property?
Will not this property be converted to productive use by drawing into the
industrial process, directly or indirectly, the material items of wealth that
these funds represent? No, replied Veblen. While loans may be covered
by property held by the lender, the property may be otherwise engaged.
Real estate may support loans even though it cannot be converted to industrial use. If loans are backed by corporate stock and industrial plants,
this is a duplication of material items that are already a part of the industrial process. Credit created by banks has little real wealth behind it; credit
therefore has only a pecuniary (business) existence and not a material (industrial) one. It represents only fictitious industrial equipment.

From the standpoint of our private-enterprise economy, Veblen neglected the point that bank credit enables a businessman to mobilize a supply
of labor from among those who are unemployed, underemployed, or self-
employed (such as artisans and farmers). The drawing of labor into large
industrial establishments increases the total output. Likewise, credit permits
the mobilization of raw materials and capital equipment, and the expansion
of their supply. It widens the markets and thereby stimulates greater production. His strictures on credit would be valid only on the assumption

that the supplies of factors of production and final products are inelastic and therefore cannot be readily expanded.

It would be unfair to Veblen, however, to criticize him from the standpoint of a private-enterprise economy. He did not accept that frame of reference, and he looked at our society as a detached observer, from the outside. In his analysis of credit, he probably meant that it is not essential in economic life. Primitive societies certainly functioned without it. A modern technological society could dispense with credit if it were organized as some sort of industrial republic run by engineers, or as a socialist society. Taking such a view of things, credit adds nothing to the functioning of an industrial society. In fact, credit detracts from it to the extent that it opens the way to financial manipulation, speculation, increased costs, and greater profits.

Veblen's views on credit led him directly into his business-cycle theory. The extension of credit enables competing businessmen to bid up the prices of the material capital goods used in industry. These goods serve as collateral for the further extension of credit as their dollar value increases. The extension of loans on collateral such as shares of stock or real property has a cumulative character. Credit expands even more with the organization of monopolies, for the costs of the reorganization and the promoters' profits are capitalized in the securities issued. The expected increase in the profits of the monopolies and the imputed goodwill of the new corporations also are capitalized.

This cumulative extension of credit rests on a shaky foundation. Sooner or later a discrepancy arises between the money value of the collateral and the capitalized value of the property computed on expected earnings. In other words, the rise in earnings does not keep pace with the inflation of the nominal capital (capital plus loans). When this discrepancy becomes obvious, a period of liquidation begins. Along with liquidation, the industrial crisis is accompanied by credit cancellations, high discount rates, falling prices, forced sales, shrinkage of capitalization, and reduced output. The creditors take over business properties, thereby further consolidating ownership and control into fewer hands.

Workmen benefit during prosperity, not through higher rates of pay, but through fuller employment. As the general price level rises and spreads, the rising cost of living reduces real rates of wages. Slowly money wages rise in response to rising prices of goods, and this helps bring prosperity to an end, for profit margins shrink and capital values must fall.

Business is the quest of profits, and an inhibition of this quest must touch the seat of its vital motives. Industrial depression means that the business men engaged do not see their way to derive a satisfactory gain from letting the industrial process go forward on the lines and in the volume for which the material equipment of industry is designed. It is not worth their while, and it might even work them pecuniary harm.*

Veblen thought that the discrepancy between capitalization and earning capacity is chronic so long as no extraneous circumstances enter temporarily to set aside the trend of business affairs. Therefore chronic depression, more or less pronounced, is normal to business under the fully developed regime of machine industry. The mitigating factors that temporarily overcome chronic depression are speculative increases of prices, new discoveries of precious metals, and credit expansion. The deliberate promotion of monopoly can restore the profitability of business by restricting output and raising prices, thereby bringing the accepted capitalization into line with the actual earning capacity. If successful, the monopoly will neutralize the cheapening of goods and services effected by current industrial progress.

The decline of profits and chronic depression can be remedied by an increase in the unproductive consumption of goods, in waste, as well as through monopoly. But private wasteful expenditure on a scale adequate to offset the surplus productivity of modern industry is nearly out of the question.

Private initiative cannot carry the waste of goods and services to nearly the point required by the business situation. Private waste is no doubt large, but business principles, leading to saving and shrewd investment, are too ingrained in the habits of modern men to admit an effective retardation of the rate of saving. Something more to the point can be done, and indeed is being done, by the civilized governments in the way of effectual waste. Armaments, public edifices, courtly and diplomatic establishments, and the like, are almost altogether wasteful, so far as bears on the present question. They have the additional advantage that the public securities which represent this waste serve as attractive investment securities for private savings, at the same time that, taken in the aggregate, the savings so invested are purely fictitious savings and therefore do not act to lower profits or prices. Expenditures met by taxation are less expedient for this purpose; although indirect taxes have the peculiar advantage of keeping up the prices of the goods on which they are imposed, and thereby act directly toward the desired end. The waste of time and effort that goes into military service, as well as the employment of the courtly, diplomatic, and ecclesiastical personnel, counts effectually in the same direction. But however extraordinary this public waste of substance latterly has been, it is apparently altogether inadequate to offset the surplus productivity of the machine industry, particularly when this productivity is seconded by the great facility which the modern business organization affords for the accumulation of savings

* Thorstein Veblen, *The Theory of Business Enterprise* (New York, 1904), pp. 213–14.

in relatively few hands. There is also the drawback that the waste of time involved in military service reduces the purchasing power of the classes that are drawn into the service, and so reduces the amount of wasteful consumption which these classes might otherwise accomplish.*

There is conflict, then, between industry, which produces goods, and business, which produces profit; between making goods and making money; between the instinct for workmanship and pecuniary considerations; between the community at large and the absentee owners, the captains of industry; between the need for stability and the extension of credit; between the buyers, who want more goods at lower prices, and the monopolists, who offer fewer goods at higher prices; between the need for social change and the conservatism of people's patterns of thought and action; between meeting the basic needs of people, which is possible, and the desire for conspicuous consumption, which must leave the demand for goods unfulfilled as long as everyone tries to exceed everyone else in wasteful consumption. This disharmony of interest is also revealed in the relations between workers and employers. Recurring unemployment or half-employment is due to considerations of price.

From the like competitive considerations of price, and of gain in terms of price, it has come about that the interests of the employer are not at one with those of the workmen. . . . On the one hand the workmen have no whole-hearted interest in the efficiency of the work done, but rather in what can be got for it in terms of price; on the other hand the employer has none but a humanitarian —said to be quite secondary—interest in the well being, or even in the continued efficiency, of the workmen. From which follow, on the one hand inhibitory trades-union rules, strikes, lockouts, and the like disturbances of the industrial process, and on the other hand an exploitation of the human raw material of industry that has at times taken quite an untoward scope and direction, in the way of over-work, under-pay, unsafe and unwholesome conditions, and so forth.†

What is the solution to the difficulties raised by modern large-scale business enterprise? Veblen was simultaneously critical of and friendly toward socialism, but he definitely was not a socialist himself. Marx's labor theory of value was attacked by him as being at best tautological, and at worst an unproven playful mystification. He denied the socialist claim that the rich are becoming richer and the poor poorer. The existing system, he said, has not made and does not tend to make the workers poorer as measured absolutely; but it does tend to make them relatively poorer as measured in terms

* *Ibid.*, pp. 255–57.
† Thorstein Veblen, *Imperial Germany and the Industrial Revolution* (New York, 1915), p. 120.

of comparative economic importance. Modern society intensifies emulation and jealousy, which leads to unrest and makes for socialism. With the abolition of private property, human nature will find nobler and socially more serviceable activities than emulation. At present, thought Veblen in 1892, we waste half our labor in abstaining from useful work and in conspicuous waste.

Veblen thought that the engineers would make the social revolution and operate industry for the common good. They are the ones to object to ownership, finance, sabotage, credit, and unearned income, because these interfere with technological efficiency and progress. Engineers are the best representatives of the community at large. Capital and labor, bargaining over prices, have become a loose-knit vested interest that seeks its own benefit to the detriment of society. The outcome has been businesslike concession and compromise between them, in the nature of bargain and sale. The two sides play a game of chance and skill, with the industrial system becoming a victim of interference on both sides. Yet the material welfare of the community at large, and more specifically of the workmen, depends on the smooth working of the industrial system without interference. This the engineers can achieve. They promote the community's material welfare and provide free income for the kept classes. Unlike the owners and workers, they are not motivated by self-interest. The technicians are more homogeneous and unified than are the workers. They are the natural leaders of the workers, the officers of the line, the men with a spirit of tangible performance and the best instincts of workmanship. Veblen asserted that a soviet of technicians can solve the nation's problems, but that the chances for it are remote. At present the technical men are docile and harmless, well fed on the whole, and rather placidly content with the "full dinner-pail" allowed them by the vested interests.

In the overview at the beginning of this chapter, the reforming aspect of institutionalism was presented. This definitely does not hold for Veblen. He did not base his hopes on the amelioration of conditions under capitalism. He was so fundamentally opposed to this system that he hoped to see it superseded entirely. The idea that the engineers would make the social revolution was perhaps a fleeting, tentative thought with him. Toward the end of his life he looked quite favorably at the Soviet Russian experiment. Basically, however, he remained a pessimist, taking a dim view of human nature and the future prospect for humanity.

In the following chapter we shall consider two institutionalists who were reformers in different degrees. John R. Commons was the archetype of a reformer. Wesley C. Mitchell seemed to favor reforms, although he failed to emphasize their importance; he seemed to lose himself in a maze of statistical studies without paying much attention to reforms.

CHAPTER 18

The Institutionalist School:

COMMONS and MITCHELL

Commons

JOHN ROGERS COMMONS (1862–1945) was a student of economic institutions in action. He led his college classes in visits to prisons, charitable organizations, mental hospitals, law courts, union halls, factories, and legislative chambers. This approach made him a great synthesizer of the social sciences, for he sought to use and integrate economics, ethics, sociology, psychology, political science, history, and jurisprudence. Commons also became a great reformer, a forerunner of the New Deal. He advocated an increasing role for government to adjudicate and compromise the conflicting interests of many different groups. Instead of a harmony of interests, he detected a clash of interests that had to be curbed in order to have society function in an orderly manner.

Commons was born in Ohio during the Civil War. His antislavery parents had helped run an underground railway for the escape of Negro slaves to Canada. His father was an impoverished newspaper publisher who taught his sons the printing trade. His mother ran a boarding house to help support the family. Commons graduated from Oberlin College at twenty-six, earning his way as a typesetter in a printing office and losing time because of nervous breakdowns. He was an ardent labor unionist, and after reading Henry George's *Progress and Poverty* in his freshman year, he became a "single-taxer." His record as an undergraduate was poor, but he was permitted to graduate because illness was an extenuating circumstance, and because his professors recognized his insatiable curiosity and his persistency.

Commons did two years of graduate work at Johns Hopkins University, but he never earned his Ph.D. because he failed a history examination. He then taught a year at Wesleyan University, but his contract was not renewed. He found employment at Oberlin, at Indiana University, and at Syracuse University. When Commons had an interview with Chancellor James R. Day of Syracuse in the spring of 1895, he decided to tell the whole truth: He labeled himself as a socialist, a single-taxer, a free-silverite, a greenbacker, a "municipal-ownerist," and a member of the Congregational Church. The chancellor replied that he did not care what Commons was as long as he was not an "obnoxious socialist." Commons, with whimsical exaggeration in his autobiography called *Myself*, wrote: "That settled it. I mistakenly thought I was not of the obnoxious kind."

At Syracuse, Commons occupied the chair in sociology established by Mr. Huyler, the candy manufacturer. "I taught ethnology, anthropology, criminology, charity organization, taxation, political economy, municipal government, and other things, all under the name of sociology." His career at Syracuse foundered when he was announced, without prior consultation, as one of the speakers at a mass meeting of all the churches protesting Sunday baseball. Chancellor Day was the chairman and the principal speaker at the meeting. After a hurried investigation of the problem, Commons in his speech opposed professional baseball with admission fees on Sunday. He defended, however, the right of workingmen to play ball on Sunday in view of their having to work six full days a week. In spite of threats of irate parents to withdraw their children from Syracuse unless Commons were dismissed, Chancellor Day defended his right to dissent. It became more difficult for Syracuse to solicit funds successfully because of the baseball episode, and a year or so later the Board of Trustees abolished the Huyler chair in sociology. Commons was once again without a position after four years at Syracuse. He drew some inferences from this experience:

It was not religion, it was capitalism, that governed Christian colleges. Afterwards I sought the fundamental reason, and included it in my historical development of Institutional Economics. The older economists based their definitions of wealth on *holding* something useful for one's own use and exchange. I distinguished a double meaning. The other meaning was, *withholding* from others what they need but do not own. . . . It made possible a distinction of Wealth from Assets which I began to think economists and laity had failed to distinguish. . . .

I figured that a "chair" in political economy was not physically pulled out from under you, it was economically pulled out by withholding the funds. This was such a customary, legal, and quiet way of doing it, under the institution of private property, that everybody, including economists, took it as a part of the Natural Order not needing investigation. At least, I knew, after 1899 at Syracuse, that holding and withholding were not the same, and that the latter was more important. It was the foundation of assets. It converted Chancellor Day from defiance of Protestants to leg-pulling of Plutocrats.*

During the following five years Commons received various subsidies and salaries to engage in research. In 1900 he began publishing the first weekly index of wholesale prices. The index was terminated, along with Commons' salary, when it started to rise in September 1900, to the chagrin of the wealthy Democratic bimetallist who financed the venture; Commons' employer disliked this indication of McKinley prosperity. A second brief period of joblessness led Commons to consider "unemployment the bitterest foe of the capitalist system."

Commons studied immigration for the Industrial Commission of the federal government. He worked for the National Civic Federation, which sought to conciliate labor disputes through collective bargaining and the working out of trade agreements between the opposing parties. In 1904 he went to the University of Wisconsin, where he remained until retirement. As an advisor to Governor Robert M. La Follette, he drafted Wisconsin's civil service law, and also a bill providing state regulation of public utilities. In 1911 he wrote a law combining the objectives of workmen's compensation and accident prevention. In 1921 he developed the idea that the employer should be financially responsible for unemployment, and this was enacted into law in Wisconsin in 1932. To end the "loan shark" evil, he helped get a Small Loans Act passed which limited interest to 3.5 per cent per month. He pioneered in writing labor history, in promoting labor conciliation, and in advocating social legislation.

Commons, like other institutionalists, made the conflict of interests, not the harmony of interests, the starting point of his institutional economics. Each school of economics, he said, arose out of a conflict of interests; yet each rejected the conflict from which it sprang. Economic conflicts, which lead to political and military conflicts, originate in scarcity. Economic classes develop from the similarities of interest in obtaining and retaining ownership of shares of the world's limited supply of wealth. There are not merely two classes, as Marx maintained, nor did Marx identify the major class conflict. Commons held that the major clash of interests was based on the differences between producers and consumers of wealth. These two groups could be broken up into many conflicting classes, such as buyers-sellers, borrowers-lenders, farmers-laborers, capitalists-landowners. These in turn could be broken up into subclasses, such as wheat farmers, livestock farmers, bankers, manufacturers, merchants, skilled and unskilled laborers, mine-owners, railway-owners, and so on. Economic classes organize for concerted action according to similarities in their economic interests. This

* John R. Commons, *Myself* (New York, 1934), pp. 58-59.

results in collective action within the group and conflicts between groups. Out of these conflicts arise a workable harmony of interests, or a stalemate, or an untenable impasse that requires the strong arm of still another collective action—practical politics and war—to bring not harmony but order out of conflict. Besides conflict, there exists mutual dependency and a desire for orderly and stable relations. As social phenomena inherently contain the contradictory elements of conflict, dependence, and order, they are not something analyzed and settled once and forever; instead they are continuously and eternally recurring as problems to be dealt with anew.

The transaction between individuals is the key problem in economics and in jurisprudence. A transaction is surrounded by rules of conduct that give rise to rights, duties, liberties, private property, governments, and associations. These are the reciprocal promises and threats, express or implied, that govern man's relations to man. Every transaction is a meeting of wills, a transfer of commodities, and a determination of their prices.

The transaction is two or more wills giving, taking, persuading, coercing, defrauding, commanding, obeying, competing, governing, in a world of scarcity, mechanism and rules of conduct. The court deals with the will-in-action. Like the modern physicist or chemist, its ultimate unit is not an atom but an electron, always in motion—not an individual but two or more individuals in action. It never catches them except in motion. Their motion is a transaction.

A transaction occurs at a point of time. But transactions flow one into another over a period of time, and this flow is a process. The courts have fully developed the notion of this process in the concept of a "going concern," which they have taken over from the customs of business, and which is none other than a technological process of production and consumption of physical things and a business process of buying and selling, borrowing and lending, commanding and obeying, according to shop rules or working rules or laws of the land. The physical process may be named a "going plant," the business process a "going business," and the two constitute a "going concern" made up of action and reaction with nature's forces and transactions between human beings according to accepted rules.*

Economic theory is therefore concerned with a process of economic relations and behavior, and with working rules that control the conduct of individuals.

Veblen defined an institution as a widely prevalent habit of thought; Commons defined it as collective action in control of individual action. The weakness of the individual has driven him to combine into corporations and unions. Governments have granted to these associations sovereign powers and immunities from higher sovereign power. The state itself interferes with supply and demand through the war power, the taxing power, the

* John R. Commons, *Legal Foundations of Capitalism* (New York, 1924), pp. 7–8.

police power, and the legal-tender power. It encourages or protects certain businesses and occupations rather than others. It restrains certain activities deemed detrimental to the whole. It induces individuals and associations to act in one direction rather than in others.

Collective action means more than mere "control" of individual action. It means liberation and expansion of individual action; thus, collective action is literally the means to liberty. The only way in which "liberty" can be obtained is by imposing duties on others who might interfere with the activity of the "liberated" individual. The American people obtained liberty for the slaves by imposing duties on the slaveowners.*

Commons attached great importance to the meaning of property. Before 1890 the Supreme Court was concerned with corporeal property. Since then the concept of intangible property was added by the Court. Commons interpreted intangible property to mean the right to fix prices by withholding from others what they need but do not own. Court decisions involving reasonable value were concerned with intangible property and the conflicts of interest it engendered.

Veblen, said Commons, was introducing the same idea of intangible property into economics at the same time that he was, and both became known as institutional economists.

But the difference was that Veblen obtained his case material from the testimony of financial magnates before the United States Industrial Commission of 1900, so that his notion of intangible property ended in the Marxian extortion and exploitation. But my sources were my participation in collective action, in drafting bills, and my necessary study, during these participations, of the decisions of the Supreme Court covering the period; so that my notion of intangible property ends in the common-law notion of reasonable value.

On analyzing this notion, not only in Supreme Court cases but also in collective bargaining, labor arbitration and commercial arbitration cases, I discovered that, of course, the decisions of these tribunals began with conflict of interests, then took into account the evident idea of dependence of conflicting interests on each other; then reached a decision by the highest authority, the Supreme Court or the labor and commercial arbitration courts, endeavoring to bring—not harmony of interests—but order out of the conflict of interests, known by the Court as "due process of law."†

Commons contrasted the social and the individual points of view. The social concept of *wealth* depends on use values, on abundance. The individual concept of *assets* depends on scarcity value and is measured by prices.

* John R. Commons, *The Economics of Collective Action* (New York, Macmillan, 1950), pp. 34–35. By permission of The Macmillan Company (New York).
† John R. Commons, *Institutional Economics* (New York, 1934), p. 4.

Capitalism means the double process of creating use value for others and restricting its supply so as to create scarcity value. Hence capitalism requires two units of measurement, the man-hour and the dollar. The first measures the quantity of use value created, the second measures its scarcity value. Man-hours measure wealth and represent a producing society, while dollars measure assets and represent an acquisitive society.

Man's power over nature is productivity, measured by man-hours. His output is augmentation of wealth (use-value). Man's power over others is measured by dollars (scarcity-value). It is the quantity of production relative to the quantity wanted, and restriction of output is augmentation of prices, values, and assets.

It was this confusion of production with productivity that permitted the economists to abandon Ricardo's man-power and substitute the dollar as the measure of efficiency. This confused producing-power with bargaining power. To buy at low prices and sell at high prices became a definition of efficiency, whereas it is a definition of bargaining power. The latter consists in taking advantage of the relative scarcities or abundance of labor and commodities on the markets. The former consists in taking advantage of the relative powers of man over nature's forces on the farm and in the factory.*

At a time when labor unions were not as widely accepted as they are today, Commons defended them as a means of expressing the collective will of workers in bargaining with employers. Through collective bargaining, individual wills meet and become a part of the collective will. While government intervention in the economy was generally deplored in his time, Commons suggested that the state had expanded its powers to curb the abuses of the economic power that flowed from the accumulation of private property. The state, he thought, exists as an impartial force to rectify the imbalances of power. The worker has a property right in his job, and the courts should protect it, just as it protects the businessman's right to a profit.

The progressivism of Commons represented an advanced position in his time, and it won for him denunciations of his radical tendencies. Today, many of his ideas on social reform are generally acceptable, like sound legal tender, and they are compatible with the prevailing new orthodoxy.

Mitchell

WESLEY CLAIR MITCHELL (1874–1948), Veblen's most brilliant student, was the youngest of the three towering figures of the institutionalist school. Veblen's role was to dissect with savage glee what he considered were the absurdities of orthodox theory that defended the status quo; he gave insti-

* *Ibid.*, pp. 285–86.

tutionalism a philosophy and a theory. Commons was the great social reformer who relied on government intervention, under the rule of law, to harmonize and compromise conflicting group interests; he made of institutionalism a crusade for social reform. Mitchell was the great researcher whose most notable work centered on an analysis of business fluctuations; he gave institutionalism its empirical bent. It is at least possible that Mitchell immersed himself in statistical studies in order to avoid an open clash with orthodoxy in economic theory. He was too gentle and discreet to strike at the roots of marginalism with the ferocity of a Veblen, but he did criticize its unrealistic abstractions and its methodology. He felt that Veblen had progressed far beyond contemporary economists because he had a more adequate view of human nature and a broader understanding of cultural processes. Yet Veblen relied too much on speculations that were not tested by empirical verification. Mitchell believed that his statistical studies would provide a firmer foundation for Veblen's pioneer work.

Wesley Mitchell was born in Rushville, Illinois. His father was a country doctor who suffered all his life from a leg that was badly injured during childhood and again in the Union army during the Civil War. His mother insisted that Wesley go to college in spite of the family's financial difficulties. He entered the first class of the newly organized University of Chicago in 1892. Later, as a graduate student, he received a traveling fellowship and spent a winter studying in Germany, but he was not impressed with the state of economic science there. In 1899 he received his Ph.D. at Chicago *summa cum laude*. He took a position in the Census Office in Washington, then he taught and did research at the University of Chicago, the University of California, Columbia University, and the New School for Social Research, with time out for consultation work in Washington throughout the latter part of his life. In 1915 he wrote a monograph for the Bureau of Labor Statistics on *The Making and Use of Index Numbers* that remained a classic over the years. In addition to his studies of business cycles and index numbers, he analyzed the functioning of a money economy, and he directed the work of the National Bureau of Economic Research in launching one of the first comprehensive studies of the amount and distribution of national income.

Economics, said Mitchell, is one of the sciences of human behavior. It has always been a science of human behavior even in the hands of men who defined it as a science of wealth. The future of economics lies in moving toward more research and less theorizing. In his undergraduate article published in the *Journal of Political Economy* in 1896, he wrote, "Deductive reasoning is proverbially likely to lead the inquirer astray, unless its results are checked and corrected by inductive investigation." Social problems should be solved by a scientific investigation of human behavior.

He was a social reformer who never campaigned for immediate action to remedy a specific ill. Instead, he advocated research to promote an understanding of social problems and their interactions. Only after society is thoroughly understood can it be reformed intelligently.

I hope that economics will become a science that explains how men behave in getting their livings. I hope it will deal with living men in the actual world of constant change. I want propositions that can be tested for conformity to fact. I want such tests made. In short, I hope we shall develop a science of economics that has such a definite application to actual behavior that it will be a safe guide in efforts to improve economic organization. . . . Perhaps, and perhaps is all we can say, if we can come to a clearer understanding of how we behave, we can learn how to condition men so that their energies will go less into making one another miserable.*

Perhaps the National Bureau of Economic Research, which Mitchell founded in 1920 and directed for twenty-five years, is the greatest monument to his method. In almost half a century it has published a vast bulk of statistical analyses, and like an iceberg it revealed only a small part of its total mass of material. Yet it has come up with surprisingly little theory and even less in the way of proposed reform.

Scientific discoveries, said Mitchell, have revolutionized the arts of production, but the methods of distributing what is produced have changed relatively little. Yet the two processes of producing and distributing wealth are interdependent in a society whose members get their livings mainly by making and spending money incomes. Economic theorists have concentrated mostly on the production of wealth, which focuses attention on industrial activities for making and using goods. The approach through distribution analyzes business efforts directed at getting and spending money. To understand economic activities, we need both approaches.

Our most grievous economic problem arises from the recurring imbalance between production and distribution. When these processes get out of step with each other, markets are glutted with unsold goods, and men and machines are unemployed. Besides these cyclical contractions, many enterprises remain backward in equipment and methods; few are huge enough to exploit fully the opportunities presented by technological knowledge. We therefore produce less than we might with the same effort even during periods of prosperity.

Our industrial system is still like an army made up of many companies, each commanded by an independent captain who plans his own campaign on the basis of agreements he reaches with other captains. Only in great emergencies

* Quoted in Lucy Sprague Mitchell, *Two Lives* (New York, 1953), pp. 292, 349.

do we mobilize our industries under the direction of a general staff. Our reasons for putting up with such a rudimentary organization are doubtless sound; but they are based upon lack of knowledge. We do not know how to combine full use of our engineering skill with our reliance upon competition to protect the consumer from exploitation. . . .

There is no difficulty in explaining the lag of the social behind the natural sciences. To win understanding of human behavior is far harder than to discover regularities in the behavior of inorganic matter or the simpler forms of life. Not only is man a vastly more complex being than the materials with which the natural sciences deal, and consequently more variable in his responses to given situations, but he is also less susceptible to experimental control by an investigator. . . .

I venture to urge a practical conclusion concerning social policy. If our inability to employ our other resources to the best advantage is due largely to maladjustments among economic processes, and if economics is now applying methods that enable it to deal with actual conditions, then enlightened citizens and public men should do all they can to promote economic research.*

The frequent recurrence of economic crises and depressions, said Mitchell in 1935, is evidence that the automatic functioning of our business system is defective. Our difficulties have increased because of the widening of markets, the growth of combinations, the increasing importance of semidurable goods that people can stop buying when times are bad, the movement of farm people to the cities, and the increasing dependence of farmers on a market. Business planning has not been able to counteract the growth of these factors that make business cycles more serious.

Coordination within an enterprise is the result of careful planning by experts; coordination among independent enterprises cannot be said to be planned at all; rather is it the unplanned result of natural selection in a struggle for business survival. Coordination within an enterprise has a definite aim—the making of profits; coordination among independent enterprises is limited by the conflicting aims of the several units. Coordination within an enterprise is maintained by a single authority possessed of power to carry its plans into effect; coordination among independent enterprises depends on many different authorities which have no power to enforce a common program, except so far as one can persuade or coerce others. As a result of these conditions, coordination within an enterprise is characterized by economy of effort; coordination among independent enterprises by waste.

In detail, then, economic activity is planned and directed with skill; but in the large there is neither general plan nor central direction. The charge that "capitalistic production is planless" therefore contains both an important element of truth and a large element of error. Apart from the transient programs

* Wesley C. Mitchell, "Economic Resources in Economic Theory," *Studies in Economics and Industrial Relations* (Philadelphia, 1941), pp. 12–13, 16.

of economic mobilization adopted under stress of war, civilized nations have not yet developed systematic plans for the sustenance of their populations; they continue to rely on the badly coordinated efforts of private initiative.*

The task, then, is to promote careful social or national planning to overcome the worst features of business fluctuations, while preserving economic liberty and increasing security. Mitchell's reliance on national planning to ameliorate man's condition was based partly on his pragmatic psychology. He believed that the relations between economics and psychology should be more fully and carefully investigated. He rejected the hedonistic preconceptions of classical and neoclassical economics. Instincts did not interest him as they did Veblen because they are not subject to scientific measurement. Human nature can be analyzed from the outside by introducing the subject of social psychology, which can be studied through statistical and historical analysis. We must study social institutions, such as legal and business systems, which influence economic conduct. Human behavior and intelligence are largely social products. To the extent that social institutions are the results of past achievements of human intelligence, they provide a basis of rationality in the individual's behavior. These views led to Mitchell's optimism about social reform. Human nature in the long run is not a barrier to change. Major problems can be solved with intelligence and understanding, for human life changes as our way of life evolves.

Mitchell defended social planning, denying that it was un-American. Our national history, he said, is a history of planning, sometimes successful, sometimes not. The United States Constitution embodied a plan for governing a country. Hamilton had a plan for economic recovery, and from 1917 to 1918 we planned economic mobilization to win the war. The greatest difficulty in social planning has been to agree on what we wish to accomplish. Disunity over goals creates the first and most fundamental obstacle to planning in a democratic community. Unanimity of social aims is attained only on rare occasions.

A second difficulty in planning derives from the truth that social processes are interdependent. Piecemeal planning, detail by detail, often brings unplanned and unwanted results, as illustrated by prohibition that encouraged rum-running and the rise of rich lawbreaking syndicates. Wise social planning must consider the indirect as well as the direct effects of social action.

By following our individual interests, we may produce results that we do not desire as individuals. Certain results cannot be attained by individual

* Wesley C. Mitchell, *Business Cycles: The Problem and Its Setting* (New York, National Bureau of Economic Research, 1927), p. 172. By permission of the National Bureau of Economic Research, Inc.

action. National planning, said Mitchell, is inevitable. The question is, will it be fragmentary and foolish or systematic and technically thorough?

Mitchell's greatest work was in the study of business fluctuations. He called his theory of business cycles a "working hypothesis," because it was tentative and subject to revision in the light of additional evidence. Continuous change was more relevant than equilibrium. His ideas were always checked against observations from real life. Business-cycle theory in his hands approached a tested explanation of experience instead of an exercise in logic. The more intensively Mitchell sought out the facts in explaining fluctuations, the more his explanation broadened into a theory of how our economic system works. Instead of seeking a single decisive cause of the cycle as preceding students of fluctuations had done, he explored the conditions that collectively produce the cyclical movements of the business system. If his ideas seem commonplace now, it is because they are so widely accepted.

Mitchell's study of business cycles led to four major conclusions. First, business fluctuations arise in a money economy. Second, business cycles are not merely fluctuations in aggregate activity, but also fluctuations that are widely diffused throughout the economy. Third, the ebb and flow of activity depends on the prospects of profits, except in times of crisis when the rush toward solvency supplants profits as the main driving force of business enterprise. Fourth, fluctuations are not minor or accidental disruptions of equilibrium, but are systematically generated by the economy itself. Permeating Mitchell's entire work is the evolutionary and dynamic approach. Thus, while each phase of the cycle evolves into its successor, the economy itself gradually undergoes cumulative changes. Therefore, Mitchell believed, the economists of each generation will probably have to recast the theory of business cycles that they learned in their youth.

Crises and depressions have been described as a disease of capitalism. Mitchell preferred to describe them as arising in a society where economic activities are carried on mainly by making and spending money. This is characteristic of capitalism, of course; but that term also stresses other features of less importance from the viewpoint of the business-cycle analyst, such as the character of ownership of the means of production.

It is not until the uses of money have reached an advanced stage in a country that its economic vicissitudes take on the character of business cycles.

This remark does not mean that the economic life of communities with simpler organization is free from crises, or from alternations of good and bad times. On the contrary, life seems to have been more precarious, economic fortune more fluctuating, in a medieval town than in a modern city. But until a large part of a population is living by getting and spending money incomes, producing wares on a considerable scale for wide markets, using credit devices, organizing in business enterprises with relatively few employers and many employees, the economic fluctuations which occur do not have the characteristics of business cycles.*

Business fluctuations are widely diffused throughout the economy because of the interdependence of enterprises. Business firms are bound to each other by industrial, commercial, and financial ties, so that none can prosper or suffer without affecting others. The growth of credit has enhanced financial interdependence. The spread of the corporate form of business organization, with all the interlocking relationships to which it gives birth, organizes many nominally independent enterprises into communities of interest. These bonds are also channels through which the quickening or slackening of activity in one part of the economy spreads to other parts.

Profits, said Mitchell, are the clue to business fluctuations. A business enterprise can serve the community by making goods only on condition that in the long run it makes a profit. The subordination of service to money-making is not grounded in the mercenary motives of businessmen, but is one of the necessary results of a money economy. A public-spirited businessman who disregards profits will be put out of business. Only government and philanthropy can provide services that do not pay.

Anticipated profits are more significant than past profits or losses, for business looks forward more than it looks backward. The prospect of future profits plays the decisive role in determining the direction business expansion will take. Investment reaches its highest point at that stage of the cycle when the anticipated profits are most attractive. Therefore an account of economic fluctuations in a business economy must deal primarily with business conditions, with the pecuniary aspects of economic activity.

According to Mitchell, cycles arise from forces within the economy, with each phase of the cycle generating the next.

An incipient revival of activity, for example, develops into full prosperity, prosperity gradually breeds a crisis, the crisis merges into depression, depression becomes deeper for a while, but ultimately engenders a fresh revival of activity, which is the beginning of another cycle. A theory of business cycles must therefore be a descriptive analysis of the cumulative changes by which one set of business conditions transforms itself into another set.†

Mitchell chose as his starting point that stage of the cycle in which activity begins to quicken after a period of depression. Once started, a revival of

* *Ibid.,* p. 75.
† Wesley C. Mitchell, *Business Cycles and Their Causes* (Berkeley, 1941), p. ix. [Originally published in 1913.]

activity spreads rapidly over a large part, if not all, of the economy along the lines of interconnection among enterprises. Rising wages and higher profits stimulate both consumption and investment demand. Inventories, which have been depleted during dull times, are replenished by retailers and wholesalers. An epidemic of optimism starts and spreads, thereby producing conditions that both justify and intensify it. In the later stages of a revival, prices begin to rise. Anticipations of further price increases stimulate orders for goods. Credit expands as business conditions improve. Profits increase also because wage and overhead costs lag behind rising prices. New investment in capital goods rises.

This, then, is the cumulative upward movement of revival. But why does it culminate in a crisis? Why does prosperity breed depression?

Among the threatening stresses that accumulate within the system during prosperity is the slow but sure increase in the costs of doing business. Overhead costs begin to rise as new capital is invested under conditions of rising cost of capital goods. When new plants are built by new companies, their costs are high in attempting to establish themselves. Sticky costs like rent and interest rise. Less efficient plants and machines, less capable management, and less efficient workers find employment during prosperity, thereby bidding up the prices of materials, labor, and so on. By adding to the supply of goods sent to market, marginal firms make it more difficult to advance selling prices to offset rising costs. Labor costs rise, not only because less capable workers are employed, but also because wages, which have lagged behind rising prices, begin to catch up. Overtime labor during prosperity is more expensive and less productive than normal labor. Labor discipline and productivity decrease as workers are no longer so fearful of losing their jobs as in bad times. Waste in production increases as businessmen grow careless, overoptimistic, and overly busy. This adds to costs of production.

Rising costs encroach on profits, especially as prices of finished goods cannot be raised easily in the later stages of prosperity. The expansion of productive capacity, which promoted the growth of prosperity during its earlier period, adds to the supply of goods and increases the difficulty of raising selling prices. Buyers ultimately resist rising prices because they cannot or will not continually pay more for goods. Certain prices fail to rise in line with costs because of public regulation, contracts, and custom. An actual or even a prospective decline of profits in a few important industries suffices to create financial difficulties in all industries.

These various stresses become more severe the longer prosperity lasts, and they inevitably lead to crisis and depression. The pyramiding of credit ends when creditors become apprehensive. In the crisis and turning point, demands are made on debtors to reduce or pay up their debts. A vast liquidation develops, with prices falling as goods are thrown on the market in desperate attempts to avoid bankruptcy. Expectations of falling prices further reduce the demand for goods and thereby make these expectations come true. With certain costs sticky on the downward side as well as with upward price movements, falling prices squeeze profit margins even more. Gloom spreads, investment spending declines, inventories are reduced, unemployment grows, consumer income and expenditure decline, and the economy sinks into a depression.

Given enough time, a depression generates within itself the forces that produce prosperity. Businessmen cut waste and other costs to the bone. Ultimately, wages, interest, rent, and other sticky costs fall to the point where they are in line with prices of goods. Labor costs also fall because overtime is eliminated, inefficient workers are discharged, and employed workers are driven to greater efforts by the fear of unemployment. Inefficient firms, plants, and machines are allowed to stand idle, thereby tending to reduce overhead costs. While unit overhead costs tend to increase because of the declining volume of sales, sharp competition may force businessmen to price their goods at less than full overhead costs. Reorganization through bankruptcy or the scaling down of debts, interest, or rent will further reduce overhead costs. Even those businesses that never pass through the hands of receivers have their inflated capital values revised downward, thereby justifying a smaller capital charge in fixing selling prices.

As the depression drags on, capital goods wear out and grow obsolete. Prices for new capital goods having fallen, the competitive struggle induces investment in new, more efficient, lower-cost machines that can be financed at low depression rates of interest. Consumers must ultimately replace, if it is at all possible, their durable and semidurable goods that have worn out. Population continues to increase, thereby increasing the demand for all kinds of consumption goods. Inventories, which have been reduced to the barest minimum during depression, must be rebuilt as business expands. Optimism spreads, and the economy is once again on a cumulative upswing.

Mitchell's study of business cycles was a superb contribution to economic analysis. It will be interesting to observe how well each detail of his structure will stand the test of time. So far most of it has stood up fairly well, although a changing economic environment has already caused a number of his observations to become obsolete. Yet even if his work grows increasingly antiquated, it will confirm his prognosis that the economy gradually and continually changes its character. If his work is to be superseded, he will still have laid the foundations that made further progress possible.

CHAPTER 19

Monetary Economics

THERE is no distinct and separate school of monetary economics. Some schools emphasize monetary phenomena more than others. The classical and Marxist schools and the early marginalists, for example, regarded money as a veil that had to be pulled aside to examine the real world; they felt that money and prices were quite secondary to the more basic factors. Others, such as the later marginalists, and also Mitchell and Keynes, combined monetary analysis with their study of the fundamental economic processes. Money in economic theory was destined to grow in importance over the years with the growth of banking, credit, fluctuations, and the increasing importance of monetary policy of the central banks and governments.

The three monetary economists to be discussed in this chapter are all in the neoclassical or marginalist tradition. Their emphasis on the monetary side of economic processes can be explained on three counts. First, they developed an area that had been neglected, that was growing in importance, and that therefore required emphasis. Second, they helped integrate monetary analysis into general economic theory. Third, they may have exaggerated the role of money because it is too easy to overcompensate for past shortcomings, to allow the pendulum to swing too far in the opposite direction.

The monetary economists of the marginalist school were quite different from the nonmonetary theorists in the same school in the sense that they had to deal with aggregative analysis, such as total demand, total income, total saving and investment, and so on. A bifurcation within the school ensued. One branch looked at the individual person's or firm's real sacrifices, income, consumption, saving, and investment. The other branch aggregated these categories for the whole economy, emphasizing monetary factors instead of real factors. It remained for Keynes to fully synthesize monetary and nonmonetary economics, although full credit should be given to Wicksell as an important forerunner of Keynes.

Wicksell

JOHN GUSTAV KNUT WICKSELL (1851–1926) was born in Stockholm of a middle-class family. After studying mathematics, languages, literature, and philosophy as an undergraduate at the University of Uppsala, he took advanced degrees in mathematics and physics. He was elected president of the student body at the university, and he became increasingly active in the philosophical, political, and literary debates and activities of student circles. As a popular lecturer and pamphleteer he covered such social questions as the population problem, birth control, emigration, alcoholism and its causes, prostitution, the future of marriage, the right to universal suffrage, and the need for direct progressive income taxes. He was both a scholar and a social reformer, a combination that in his day was often considered incompatible.

An interest in social problems and reform led Wicksell to a study of economics. From 1885 to 1890 he studied at universities in England, France, Germany, and Austria. His most memorable experience in the study of economic theory was his discovery of Böhm-Bawerk's book on capital theory in a Berlin bookshop soon after its publication in 1888; it had a profound influence on his own economic thinking.

Wicksell obtained a modest government subsidy in 1896 to begin his monetary studies in Berlin. Otherwise, his small and irregular income depended on journalism and popular lecturing on social questions, as well as occasional private tutoring and high school teaching. He received his first small academic appointment in 1896, and he achieved a professorship in 1901 at fifty years of age. In 1909 Wicksell served a brief term in prison for making ironical remarks on Church doctrine.

Wicksell's major contributions to economic thinking were first, an analysis of the role of interest rates either in achieving an equilibrium of prices or in generating cumulative inflationary or deflationary movements; second, the potential contribution of the government and the central bank in retarding or promoting price stability; third, the modern aggregate supply-demand or savings-investment approach to monetary phenomena that was one of the sources for Keynesian economics. Keynes himself complimented Wicksell as an important precursor of his own ideas. Wicksell's objective was to synthesize monetary theory, business-cycle theory, public finance, and price theory into one coordinated system.

Wicksell considered the question, Why do prices rise or fall? as the main problem of monetary theory. To answer the question, he turned to an analysis of interest rates. The money rate of interest, he said, depends on the supply of and demand for real capital that is not yet invested. The supply of capital flows from those who postpone consuming part of their income and thereby save and accumulate wealth. The demand for capital depends on the profits that can be realized from its use, or its marginal productivity.

The rate of interest at which *the demand for loan capital and the supply of savings* exactly agree, and which more or less corresponds to the expected yield on the newly created capital, will then be the normal or natural real rate. It is essentially variable. If the prospects of the employment of capital become more promising, demand will increase and will at first exceed supply; interest rates will then rise and stimulate further saving at the same time as the demand from entrepreneurs contracts until a new equilibrium is reached at a slightly higher rate of interest. And at the same time equilibrium must *ipso facto* obtain— broadly speaking, and if it is not disturbed by other causes—in the market for goods and services, so that wages and prices will remain unchanged. The *sum* of money incomes will then usually exceed the money value of the consumption goods actually produced, but the excess of income—i.e. what is annually saved and invested in production—will not produce any demand for present goods but only for labour and land for future production.*

The above applies only to credit between individuals. Banks, however, complicate matters. They are not, like private persons, restricted in their lending to their own funds or even to the funds placed at their disposal by savers. They create credit, and thereby can extend loans even at very low rates of interest. If they lend money at materially lower rates than the normal or natural rate as defined in the quotation above, saving will be discouraged, and therefore the demand for consumption goods and services will rise. Simultaneously entrepreneurs will seek more capital investments because of the greater net profits to be realized as the cost of borrowing money falls. As investment increases, more income accrues to workers, landowners, the owners of raw materials, etc. The prices of consumption goods therefore begin to rise. As against an increased demand for both consumption and investment goods, there will be an unchanged or even a diminished supply as saving diminishes, assuming that we start at a position of full employment. Anticipations of price increases will cause prices to rise even more. Equilibrium is disturbed, and a cumulative upward price movement has begun. The fundamental cause is a bank or market rate of interest that is below the normal or natural rate that would bring into balance real saving and real investment at constant prices. The natural rate of

* Knut Wicksell, *Lectures on Political Economy*, Vol. II, E. Classen, tr. (London, 1935), p. 193. [Originally published in 1906.]

interest is that rate which is equal to the marginal productivity of capital. Prices will rise without limit so long as the natural rate of interest exceeds the bank rate.

Conversely, prices will fall if the bank rate of interest is above the natural or normal rate. Only when the two rates of interest are equal will the banking and credit system be neutral and will prices remain stable.

Wicksell's analysis of interest rates and his predilection for reform led him to emphasize the role of government and the central bank in promoting stability. He was perhaps the first to advocate stabilizing wholesale prices by controlling discount and interest rates, in his book *Interest and Prices*, published in 1898.

The principal cause of cyclical fluctuations, he said, is the fact that technological and commercial progress has not maintained the same rate of advance as the increase in needs, especially of an expanding population. With rising demand, people seek to exploit the situation by increasing investment; but it takes time to increase the volume of output through new discoveries, inventions, and other improvements. The rush to convert large masses of liquid capital into fixed capital produces a boom. If, however, the technical improvements are already in operation and no new ones promise a profit in excess of the margin of risk, depression occurs.

We have, then, the real cause of business fluctuations, which Wicksell did not pursue in great depth, and the monetary cause, which is the discrepancy between the market and the natural rates of interest. To eliminate the latter factor, we need a rate of interest on loans that is neutral with respect to commodity prices, tending neither to raise nor to lower them. This is the same as the rate of interest that would be determined by supply and demand if money did not exist and all lending were in the form of real capital goods. This would be the natural rate of interest on capital. The natural rate, however, is not fixed or unalterable. It fluctuates with all the real causes of fluctuations in the economy, such as the efficiency of production, the supply of fixed and liquid capital, the supply of labor and land, and so on. An exact coincidence of the two rates of interest is therefore unlikely, unless bankers do something about it.

This does not mean that the banks ought actually to *ascertain* the natural rate before fixing their own rates of interest. That would, of course, be impracticable, and would also be quite unnecessary. For the current level of commodity prices provides a reliable test of the agreement or diversion of the two rates. The procedure should rather be simply as follows: *So long as prices remain unaltered the banks' rate of interest is to remain unaltered. If prices rise, the rate of interest is to be raised; and if prices fall, the rate of interest is to be lowered; and the rate of interest is henceforth to be maintained at its new level until a further movement of prices calls for a further change in one direction or the other.*

The more promptly these changes are undertaken the smaller is the possibility of considerable fluctuations of the general level of prices; and the smaller and less frequent will have to be the changes in the rates of interest. If prices are kept fairly stable the rate of interest will merely have to keep step with such rise or fall in the natural rate as is inevitable.

In my opinion, the main cause of the instability of prices resides in the inability or failure of the banks to follow this rule. . . .

The objection that a further reduction in rates of interest cannot be to the advantage of the banks may possibly in itself be perfectly correct. A fall in rates of interest may diminish the banks' margin of profit more than it is likely to increase the extent of their business. I should like then in all humility to call attention to the fact that the banks' prime duty is not to earn a great deal of money but to provide the public with a medium of exchange—and to provide this medium in *adequate measure*, to aim at stability of prices. In any case, their obligations to society are enormously more important than their private obligations, and if they are ultimately unable to fulfil their obligations to society along the lines of private enterprise—which I very much doubt—then they would provide a worthy activity for the State.*

Wicksell feared that the growing production and stock of gold would provide the basis for an expanding currency that would cause interest rates to fall and prices to rise. Therefore the free coinage of gold should be suspended, and the world should pass over to an international paper standard. Such a standard is usually regarded as a means of meeting a growing scarcity of gold, but it might just as well come into being because of an overabundance.

In any case, such a prospect need not, on closer investigation, provide cause for consternation. On the contrary, once it had come into being it would perhaps be the present system which would sound like a fairy tale, with its rather senseless and purposeless sending hither and thither of crates of gold, with its digging up of stores of treasure and burying them again in the recesses of the earth. The introduction of such a scheme offers no difficulty, at any rate on the theoretical side. Neither a central bureau nor international notes would be necessary. Each country would have its own system of notes (and small change). These would have to be redeemable at par by every central bank, but would be allowed to circulate only inside the one country. It would then be the simple duty of each credit institution to regulate its rate of interest, both relatively to, and in unison with, other countries, so as both to maintain in equilibrium the international balance of payments and to stabilise the general level of world prices. In short, the regulation of prices would constitute the prime purpose of bank rate, which would no longer be subject to the caprices of the production and consumption of gold or of the demand for the circula-

* Knut Wicksell, *Interest and Prices*, R. F. Kahn, tr. (London, Macmillan, 1936), pp. 189–90. [Originally published in 1898.] By permission of Macmillan & Co. Ltd. (London).

tion of coins. It would be perfectly free to move, governed only by the deliberate aims of the banks.*

In discussing the aggregate savings-investment problem, Wicksell analyzed the theory of forced saving. This was not a new idea. Bentham presented this doctrine, which he called "forced frugality," in his *Manual of Political Economy*, written during or before 1804 but published in 1843. In analyzing the role of government in increasing capital, Bentham enumerated taxes and paper money, both of which he called forced frugality. Creating paper money, he said, is a kind of indirect taxation, for it acts as an income tax on those people with fixed incomes. John Stuart Mill in the fourth of his *Essays on Some Unsettled Questions of Political Economy*, "On Profits, and Interest," written in 1829 or 1830, stated that if bankers depreciate the currency, it operates to a certain extent as a forced accumulation. Léon Walras clearly stated the theory of forced saving in 1879. He probably inspired Wicksell, and through him all the later German authors who dealt with the problem.

Wicksell supposed a case in which a new enterprise was financed through a bank loan—pure credit creation—without any corresponding accumulation of real capital. Assuming full employment at the outset, more land and labor would be employed at producing capital goods, leaving less available for turning out consumer goods. Nevertheless the demand for articles of consumption would increase rather than diminish, for entrepreneurs would bid up the prices of land and labor as they expanded investment. With prices rising as a result, entrepreneurs would acquire fewer capital goods than they originally contemplated based on the size of the loans they negotiated. At the same time consumption would be restricted as prices rose. This enforced restriction would in fact constitute the real accumulation of capital that must be achieved if capital investment is to increase. "The *real saving* which is necessary for the period of investment to be increased is in fact *enforced*—at exactly the right moment—on consumers as a whole."

Wicksell took over from the marginalist and classical schools the idea that the normal tendency of the economy is to reach equilibrium at full employment; what is not spent on consumption is normally devoted to investment. To him depressions are primarily monetary phenomena, and secondarily imbalances in real factors as a result of changes in a dynamic economy. It remained for Keynes to deal more adequately with the problems of unemployment. Wicksell's historical significance lies in his combining general and monetary theory, and in developing a theory of the cumulative process of expansion and contraction of business activity.

* *Ibid.*, pp. 193–94.

Fisher

IRVING FISHER (1867–1947) of Yale, a mathematician who turned economist, was a man of many projects. In addition to his vast written output in economics, he published several highly successful mathematical textbooks. Having suffered from tuberculosis as a young man, he turned to diet and health fads; these interests he cultivated all his life, writing several popular books on how to be healthy and live long. He advocated eugenics, and he joined the antiliquor and antitobacco crusades. Long before World War I he proposed a league of nations to preserve peace. He invented many mechanical gadgets, one of which was the visible card-index system that could be mounted on a rotary stand; eventually Fisher received about a million dollars for this, his only commercially successful invention. His and his wife's fortune, which grew to eight or ten million dollars in the stock market, was lost in the crash of 1929.

Fisher restated and amplified the old quantity theory of money based on the equation of exchange. The key question he asked was, What determines the purchasing power of money—or its reciprocal, the level of prices? There are five determinants: (1) the volume of currency in circulation, (2) its velocity of circulation, (3) the volume of bank deposits subject to check, (4) its velocity, and (5) the volume of trade. The branch of economics that handles these five regulators of purchasing power is an exact science, Fisher said, capable of precise formulation, demonstration, and statistical verification.

Fisher's equation of exchange was stated as:

$$MV + M'V' = PT$$

where M is the quantity of currency, V is its velocity of circulation, M' is the quantity of demand deposits, V' is its velocity of circulation, P is the average level of prices, and T is the quantity of goods and services sold, with each unit being counted each time it is sold or resold.

Prices vary directly as the quantity of money (M and M') and their velocity of circulation (V and V'), and inversely as the volume of trade (T). The first of these three relations is the most important, said Fisher, and it constitutes the "quantity theory of money."

Fisher assumed that M', the volume of demand deposits, tends to hold a definite relation to M, the quantity of currency in circulation; that is, deposits are normally a more or less definite multiple of currency. There are two reasons for this: First, bank reserves are kept in a more or less definite ratio to bank deposits. Second, individuals, firms, and corporations maintain more or less definite ratios between their cash transactions and their check transactions, and also between their currency and deposit balances. If the ratio between M and M' is temporarily disturbed, there will come into play a tendency to restore it. Individuals will deposit surplus cash, or they will cash surplus deposits. Transition periods of rising or falling prices also will disturb the relation between M and M', but only temporarily. As long as the normal relation holds in the long run, the existence of bank deposits merely magnifies the effect on the level of prices produced by the quantity of currency in circulation and does not in the least distort that effect.

To propound a cause-and-effect relationship between the quantity of currency and the price level, Fisher also had to assume that the velocity of circulation and the volume of trade are constant. He recognized that both fluctuate over the business cycle, but they always tend to return to an equilibrium level. The tendency toward stability in T also depended on full-employment equilibrium, for with considerable unemployment an increase in M might very well increase T instead of P. The volume of trade also grows in the long run with the change in population, efficiency of production, and so on. Yet in the short run, with a fully employed economy, normally the currency in circulation determines the price level.

We come back to the conclusion that the velocity of circulation either of money or deposits is independent of the quantity of money or of deposits. No reason has been, or, so far as is apparent, can be assigned, to show why the velocity of circulation of money, or deposits, should be different, when the quantity of money, or deposits, is great, from what it is when the quantity is small.

There still remains one seeming way of escape from the conclusion that the sole effect of an increase in the quantity of money in circulation will be to increase prices. It may be claimed—in fact it has been claimed—that such an increase results in an increased volume of trade. We now proceed to show that (except during transition periods) the volume of trade, like the velocity of circulation of money, is independent of the quantity of money. An inflation of the currency cannot increase the product of farms and factories, nor the speed of freight trains or ships. The stream of business depends on natural resources and technical conditions, not on the quantity of money. The whole machinery of production, transportation, and sale is a matter of physical capacities and technique, none of which depend on the quantity of money. . . . We conclude, therefore, that a change in the quantity of money will not appreciably affect the quantities of goods sold for money.

Since, then, a doubling in the quantity of money: (1) will normally double deposits subject to check in the same ratio, and (2) will not appreciably affect either the velocity of circulation of money or of deposits or the volume of trade, it follows necessarily and mathematically that the level of prices must double. . . .

We may now restate, then, in what causal sense the quantity theory is true.

It is true in the sense that one of *the normal effects of an increase in the quantity of money is an exactly proportional increase in the general level of prices.**

If the quantity theory of money is valid, we have a way to stabilize the over-all price level and thereby stabilize the economy: Control the quantity of currency in circulation. This might be achieved with irredeemable paper money, but Fisher took a dim view of that solution before the great depression of the 1930's. Paper money not redeemable in gold tends to arouse public distrust, it is too easily overissued by the monetary authorities, it provokes speculation, and it aligns debtors in a campaign for inflation. The plan he advocated would make paper money redeemable on demand, not in any required weight or coin of gold, but in a quantity of gold that would represent constant purchasing power. The purchasing power of the dollar would therefore remain constant. The more gold in a dollar, the more a dollar would buy, and the lower prices would be, and vice versa.

According to Fisher's plan, we would first abandon gold coinage and use only gold certificates, paper money redeemable in gold bullion. The government would vary the quantity of gold bullion that it would give or take for a paper dollar; that is, it would vary the price of gold, in order to maintain stability in the general price level. If the price index rose 1 per cent, thereby indicating that the purchasing power of the dollar was too low, the weight of the gold dollar would be increased 1 per cent. If the price index were 1 per cent below par, the weight of the gold dollar would be reduced by 1 per cent. If the changed gold content of the dollar did not fully correct the undesirable price change, further changes in the same direction would be called for.

If a flood of gold poured into our circulation from domestic or foreign sources, redundant gold certificates would cause a price rise according to the quantity theory of money. Decreasing the price of gold would reduce the supply of gold certificates for two reasons. First, the deposit of gold with the government would be discouraged. Second, people would exchange their paper money for gold. The currency in circulation would thereby be reduced and prices would be forced downward. If, alternatively, gold were being exported, prices would fall as the money in circulation was reduced. Raising the price of gold would reverse the outflow and thereby restore the previous price level.

The plan would put a stop, once for all, to a terrible evil which for centuries has vexed the world, the evil of upsetting monetary contracts and understand-

* Irving Fisher, *The Purchasing Power of Money* (New York, 1911), pp. 154–57.

ings. All contracts, at present, though nominally carried out, are really tampered with as truly as though false weights and measures were used for delivering coal or grain.*

After the great crash of 1929, Fisher saw in the growth of debts the greatest cause of deflation and depression. Excessive debts lead to liquidation, with the dumping of goods on the markets. Falling prices of goods lead to further pressure for liquidation of debts. Fisher came to believe that fluctuations in demand deposits, based on bank loans, are the greatest cause of business fluctuations. In other words, he lost faith in the stable relationship between currency and demand deposits. He also implicitly accepted a criticism of his earlier stabilization plan: Checking accounts as means of payment are so vast compared to the gold reserves behind them that small changes in the price of gold have little effect on the average price level.

Fisher's solution was to require 100 per cent reserves behind demand deposits, thereby divorcing the process of creating and destroying money from the business of banking. At the beginning of the plan, a government currency commission would offer to buy liquid bank assets for currency, or to lend banks currency on those assets as security, up to 100 per cent of a bank's checking deposits. Then all checkbook money would have actual currency behind it. Thereafter all demand deposits would have to be backed 100 per cent by currency reserves. In other words, demand deposits would literally be deposits, consisting of cash held in trust for the depositor. Banks could lend out only their own money or money put into savings accounts. This would eliminate runs on banks, bank failures, much of the government debt, and most bank earnings. Banks would have to levy service charges on deposits to compensate them for the loss of earnings when their power to create credit was destroyed. The biggest benefit would be to eliminate great inflations and deflations, thereby mitigating booms and depressions.

To stabilize the purchasing power of the dollar, the currency commission would be required to buy securities when the index was below the official par and to sell when above. This now-familiar mechanism of open-market operations of the Federal Reserve System would be a substitute for gold price variations that Fisher had advocated earlier. The country had departed from the gold standard when he began advocating this "100 per cent money" plan, and he did not favor returning to it.

It is apparent that Fisher did not think that business cycles were inherent in the economy. He regarded their causes as almost entirely monetary, and their cure would be effected by stabilizing prices. As late as 1936, Fisher wrote:

* Irving Fisher, *Stabilizing the Dollar* (New York, 1920), p. 108.

As explanations of the so-called business cycle, or cycles, when these are really serious, I doubt the adequacy of over-production, under-consumption, over-capacity, price-dislocation, mal-adjustment between agricultural and industrial prices, over-confidence, over-investment, over-saving, over-spending.

I venture the opinion, subject to correction on submission of future evidence, that, in the really great booms and depressions of the past, each of the above-named factors has played a subordinate role as compared with two dominant factors, namely (1) *over-indebtedness* (especially in the form of bank loans), to start with, and (2) *deflation* (or appreciation of the dollar), following soon after; also that, where any of the other factors do become conspicuous, they are often merely effects or symptoms of these two.

Though quite ready to change my opinion, I have, at present, a strong conviction that these two economic maladies, which may be called the "debt disease" and the "dollar disease" are, in the great booms and depressions, more important causes than all others put together.*

Fisher did outstanding work in mathematical economics, statistics, and index numbers. He was a pioneer in developing the new field of econometrics. With him statistical method was a part of economic theory and no longer a mere adjunct to it. He was honored for his contributions by being elected president of the American Economic Association, the American Statistical Association, and the Econometric Society.

Hawtrey

RALPH GEORGE HAWTREY (born 1879) was a British treasury official who found time to write many books about monetary economics. His main concern was business fluctuations, which he attributed largely to the instability of credit. There might be other causes of fluctuations, he admitted, but they were of minor importance, and they could be controlled by monetary devices.

The key figure in Hawtrey's scheme is not the producer but the wholesale merchant or trader, and the key factor is the rate of interest. If the banks apply credit restrictions, the direct effect on production in agriculture, mining, and manufacturing is likely to be small. The producer's profit depends on his output, and he cannot cut down working capital below the necessary proportion without curtailing output. If the producer relies on temporary borrowing, the interest charge, even at a high rate, will be a minor item among his costs.

The wholesaler, in contrast, is very sensitive to the rate of interest. He borrows money to hold inventories, his markup is quite small, and interest charges are an important component of his costs. Higher interest charges will increase his cost of carrying goods, and he will reduce his inventories.

* Irving Fisher, *100% Money,* 2nd ed. (New York, 1936), pp. 120–21.

Lower interest rates will make it easier to carry large stocks of goods. The merchant takes the initiative in production by increasing or decreasing his orders. His borrowing operations will be influenced not only by the terms on which his banker is willing to lend, but also by the state of demand and the prospects of price movements in the markets in which he deals. If he expects prices to rise, he will wish to increase his inventories to make an extra profit. In doing this, he will have to consider the interest charge for the additional money he must borrow. While the rise in price is more or less speculative, the extra charge for interest is certain.

Why do business fluctuations occur? Because of the inherent instability of credit working through the merchants to upset the rest of the economy in cumulative departures from an unstable equilibrium.

If the banks increase their lending, there will ensue a release of cash and an enlargement of the consumers' income and outlay [on consumption and investment goods]. The increase in the consumers' outlay means increased demand for goods in general, and the traders find their stocks of finished products diminishing. There result further orders to producers; a further increase in productive activity, in consumers' income and outlay, and in demand; a further depletion of stocks. Increased activity means increased demand, and increased demand means increased activity. A vicious circle is set up, a *cumulative* expansion of productive activity.

Productive activity cannot grow without limit. As the cumulative process carries one industry after another to the limit of productive capacity, producers begin to quote higher and higher prices. The vicious circle is not broken, but the cumulative growth of activity makes way for a cumulative rise of prices. The vicious circle of inflation is set up.

Once an expansion of demand has been definitely *started*, it will proceed by its own momentum. No further encouragement from the banks to borrowers is required.

A similar principle applies to a contraction of demand. Suppose that the banks take steps to reduce their lending. There will ensue an absorption of cash and a compression of the consumers' income and outlay [on consumption and investment goods]. Demand falls off, traders' stocks of finished products accumulate, orders to producers are cut down. Decreased activity means decreased demand, and decreased demand means decreased activity.

The vicious circle of depression is the counterpart of the vicious circle of activity, except that it does not encounter any definite limit such as productive capacity interposes in the way of increasing activity. But the decline in activity is certain to be accompanied by a fall in wholesale prices, for producers will make price concessions, each of them endeavouring to get as big a share as possible of the limited amount of demand, in order to keep his plant at work. Here we see the vicious circle of deflation.*

* R. G. Hawtrey, *The Art of Central Banking* (London, Longmans, Green, 1932), pp. 167–68. By permission of Longmans, Green & Co. Limited.

The central bank can regulate credit and thereby promote stability. Sometimes it has merely to modify a tendency to expansion or contraction; at other times it must reverse the tendency. Because the existing tendency possesses a certain momentum, some force is required to reverse it. The greatest danger is that action will be too late, and success therefore more doubtful. If, for example, a vicious circle of inflation has taken hold, there may be such pressure to borrow that only a flat refusal to lend can counteract it. The central bank would thereby abrogate its function as the lender of last resort. Likewise a depression may cause such pessimism among traders that they cannot be induced to borrow.

The appropriate remedies for the instability of credit and therefore of economic activity are central bank open-market operations, changes in the rediscount rate, and varying the reserve requirements of commercial banks. If national income is to be kept steady, then both credit and currency must be allowed to vary. Raising interest rates and restricting bank reserves can curb an inflation, for such policies can always be pushed as far as necessary to the point where they become effective. But the converse is not necessarily true. Cheap money and greater bank reserves may not stimulate revival. When the demand for goods is low, wholesalers seek to reduce their inventories by cutting down their purchases below their sales. If, however, sales fall off more quickly than they expect, their goods in stock will not diminish as much as they intend; in fact, stocks may actually increase. In such a situation, wholesalers cannot be induced to borrow even at very low rates of interest in order to build up their goods on hand. The outcome is what Hawtrey called a complete credit deadlock, stagnation, deep depression, as in the early 1930's.

A deadlock is a rare occurrence, but unfortunately in the nineteen-thirties it came to plague the world, and raised problems which threatened the fabric of civilisation with destruction.*

Hawtrey seemed to lose some of his earlier faith in the effectiveness of lower interest rates in stimulating a revival.

That there are limits to the possibility of evoking an expansion of general demand by reducing the bank rate we have already shown. The reduction of the rate is to be regarded rather as the lifting of a check upon movement than as giving a positive stimulus. Cheap money is *one* of the conditions of revival, but may not be enough by itself.†

The correct solution, Hawtrey decided, lies in proper action during the

* R. G. Hawtrey, *Capital and Employment*, 2nd ed. (London, 1952), p. 79.
† *Ibid.*, p. 112.

previous boom. Early action must be taken to stop any excessive monetary expansion. When the bank rate is raised sufficiently, the boom is reversed. After that occurs, the bank rate must be reduced rapidly in order to avoid a cumulative and vicious deflation.

When we assume that the high bank rate has done its work, that means that it has successfully overcome the vicious circle of expansion and started the vicious circle of deflation. In order to break the latter, it is essential to infuse into the traders a sufficiently concentrated tendency to increase their purchases. At a time when their purchases are still adapted to the restrictive tendencies of a high bank rate, a *sudden* transition to a low bank rate will have this effect. If the transition is delayed and spread over a longer interval, its power at any one time may be insufficient, and the vicious circle of deflation will go on gathering impetus till it becomes irresistible.

Possible though it is to stop this by taking prompt measures to relax credit in time, far better would it be to regulate credit at all times in such a way that neither of the two vicious circles ever gets a serious hold. In quiet conditions credit responds easily to moderate upward and downward movements of bank rate. If these movements were always initiated *in time,* the conditions need never be other than quiet in a monetary sense.*

After the great depression of the 1930's, Hawtrey was more willing to endorse public works expenditures than he had been earlier. If a credit deadlock develops, he said, direct government expenditures may be the only effective way to keep consumption and investment spending from decreasing further. Public works take a long time to get under way, and therefore their effectiveness is limited; yet some benefit may be expected from such deficit spending.

Hawtrey's concept of the merchant as the crucial figure in economic life may have been more appropriate for England than elsewhere, because England was the trader for the world. Her declining position in world trade makes this view less tenable than it formerly was. His uncritical faith in the efficacy of open-market operations made him quite popular in the United States in the 1920's, for the idea then prevailed that the Federal Reserve System could stabilize the economy with that device. Hawtrey's early emphasis on the importance of inventories has received increasing recognition in the United States in recent decades. Fluctuations in stocks of goods have been identified as one of the key factors in the short three- to three-and-a-half-year cycle.

* *Ibid.,* p. 113.

CHAPTER 20

The Departure from Pure Competition

THEORIES concerned with monopoly and with monopolistic or imperfect competition are well within the scope and tradition of the neoclassical school. Although they arose in the early 1930's, they have roots in the more distant past. These new ideas arose because the theory of pure competition was increasingly untenable. Pure competition applied most fully to agriculture, but even there the theory became less suitable under modern conditions. Where only a few buyers offer to purchase farm products in a local market, as in tobacco, meat, grain, and milk, pure competition no longer reigns. In addition, government intervention in agriculture made the conventional analysis of price formation irrelevant to the real world, even if it was useful as a mental exercise and as a construction that would be valid under certain assumed conditions.

In industrial production and in trade the neoclassical theory of pure competition became even less relevant in modern times than in agriculture. The theory presupposes many buyers and sellers all dealing with a perfectly homogeneous product, so that no individual has a perceptible influence in the market; buyers are therefore completely indifferent as to which seller they patronize. This would be a world where every seller can dispose of any quantity of goods he may have at the going market price, and there would be no advertising, no brand names, and no salesmanship required. A rather abstract world!

The methodology of monopolistic and imperfect competition theories with which we shall deal in this chapter showed all the characteristics and predilections of the neoclassical school. It dealt with marginalism and the microeconomic approach in an abstract, deductive, and subjective manner. It was the economics of a rational, static, unchanging world that always tended toward equilibrium. There was nothing in these theories to explain fluctuations, growth, and change as a dynamic process.

These ideas concerning the departure from pure competition showed how monopolies could raise prices above the competitive equilibrium level to yield a permanent monopoly profit. They therefore led toward a greater willingness among economists to accept more vigorous government anti-trust policies and government regulation of the profits of public-utility monopolies. They provided the theoretical rationale for government objectives that had been enacted almost half a century earlier. The hope persisted that vigorous government action to encourage competition would reverse the trend toward big business which can be traced back to the 1870's in the United States, and even earlier in England. The supposed blessings of pure competition that some economists still hope to achieve represent a reaction to monopoly and an exercise in futility. We cannot win back a world that resembles pure competition, and even if we could, it would not be a world of great stability, growth and efficiency. In fact, pure competition as a goal has been largely replaced by "workable competition," which represents a compromise between pure competition and oligopoly.

We learn from these additions to neoclassical theory that under monopolistic competition, even in the absence of the power to realize a monopoly profit, prices are likely to be higher and output less than under pure competition. What can be done about it? The theory has no answer. It offers a better explanation of the world than the theory of pure competition, but as far as a solution or an improvement is concerned, it has nothing to contribute. The new work struck a blow at the widespread idea that a free-enterprise system results in an optimum allocation of productive resources. We are doomed to have too many gasoline stations and grocery stores that operate at less than the most efficient output because of the downward-sloping demand curve facing each entrepreneur.

It is remarkable that the new ideas were fully developed almost simultaneously and independently of each other, by Edward Chamberlin in the United States, Joan Robinson in England, and Heinrich von Stackelberg in Germany. The latter seems to have abandoned all hope for an economic order except as provided by the state as a result of his analysis. If the economic world disintegrates into a wasteful struggle of monopolies without an integrating force, then the force of the state must be called upon to impose order. No wonder von Stackelberg wholeheartedly embraced fascism.

The theory of monopoly goes back almost a hundred years before the work on monopolistic competition was published, to Augustin Cournot in 1838. Others expressed dissatisfaction with and criticized the theory of pure competition. The great gap that Chamberlin and Robinson filled was in the whole range of situations that lie between pure competition and pure monopoly.

Cournot

ANTOINE AUGUSTIN COURNOT (1801–77) was a French mathematician who published treatises in mathematics, philosophy, and economics. He was the first economist to apply mathematics to economic analysis, but his pioneering work was neglected until rediscovered and continued after his death by Jevons, Marshall, and Fisher.

Cournot was the first to visualize the general interdependence of all economic quantities, and he developed a system of equations to depict general equilibrium. He defined and described the downward-sloping demand curve, and he proved that the equilibrium price is established when the quantity supplied equals the quantity demanded. He made a rigorous analysis of pure competition.

In his book published in 1838, Cournot showed that where marginal costs decrease with the expansion of output, a firm's production continues to increase until it has a noticeable impact on the market. In other words, the firm faces a downward-sloping demand curve, and therefore has some monopoly power.

It is, moreover, plain under the hypothesis of unlimited competition, and where, at the same time, the function [of marginal cost] should be a decreasing one, that nothing would limit the production of the article. Thus, wherever there is a return on property, or a rent payable for a plant of which the operation involves expenses of such a kind that the function [of marginal cost] is a decreasing one, it proves that the effect of monopoly is not wholly extinct, or that competition is not so great but that the variation of the amount produced by each individual producer affects the total production of the article, and its price, to a perceptible extent.*

Therefore, said Cournot, with increasing returns or decreasing costs as the scale of an enterprise grows, larger firms will increase their advantage over their smaller competitors; competition leads to monopoly. In his theory of monopoly, Cournot assumed that the monopolist sets the quantity he will sell and observes the reaction of the price in the market. The monopolist is free to sell either more at a lower price or less at a higher price. As he is seeking maximum profit, his decision will be determined by his

* Augustin Cournot, *Researches into the Mathematical Principles of the Theory of Wealth*, Nathaniel T. Bacon, tr. (New York, 1927), pp. 91–92. [Originally published in 1838.]

cost and the elasticity of demand. He will select that combination of price and quantity that yields the greatest profit.

In formulating a theory of duopoly, Cournot assumed that buyers name prices and that the two sellers merely adjust their output to those prices. Each duopolist estimates the total demand for the product and sets his own volume of ouput and sales on the assumption that his rival's output remains fixed. In a step-by-step adaptation of output by each producer, a stable equilibrium is obtained, with the duopolists selling equal quantities at a price that is above the competitive price and below the monopoly price. With other assumptions, of course, other solutions will follow. If, for example, there is collusion among the duopolists, they will charge a monopoly price in order to realize the maximum monopoly profit.

Cournot, in presenting his duopoly case, assumed that two proprietors each own a mineral spring, with the waters of both being perfect substitutes. The price would therefore necessarily be the same for each seller. If p is this price and D is the total sales, then sales are a function of price, or $D = F(p)$. Call D_1 the sales from spring (1) and D_2 the sales from spring (2). Then $D_1 + D_2 = D$. If we assume that there are no costs of production, the respective incomes of the proprietors will be price times sales, or pD_1 and pD_2. Each proprietor independently of the other will seek to make this income as large as possible.

Instead of adopting $D = F(p)$, as above, we can adopt the inverse notation $p = f(D)$, or price is a function of total demand. Then the profits of proprietor (1) can be expressed by $D_1 \times f(D_1 + D_2)$; the profits of proprietor (2) are represented by $D_2 \times f(D_1 + D_2)$. Proprietor (1) can have no direct influence on the determination of D_2. All he can do, when D_2 has been determined by proprietor (2), is to choose for D_1 the value that is best for him. This he will be able to accomplish by properly adjusting his price, except that proprietor (2), seeing himself forced to accept this price and this value of D_1, may adopt a new value for D_2 more favorable to his interests than the preceding one.

Since $D_1 + D_2 = D$, and D is a constant, the above functions are functions of a single variable. Analytically this is equivalent to saying that D_1 will be determined in terms of D_2 by the condition

$$\frac{d\,[D_1 f(D_1 + D_2)]}{dD_1} = 0,$$

and that D_2 will be determined in terms of D_1 by the analogous condition

$$\frac{d\,[D_2 f(D_1 + D_2)]}{dD_2} = 0.$$

The above equations supply the necessary but not sufficient condition for maximizing a function. Here we show proprietors trying to maximize profits, and when the slope of the total profits curve is equal to zero, profits are either at a maximum or at a minimum. For profits to be at a minimum with no costs of production, sales would be zero. The above equations therefore represent the maximum-profits position for each seller.

Using the formula from calculus for the derivative of a product,

$$\frac{d(uv)}{dx} = u\,\frac{dv}{dx} + v\,\frac{du}{dx},$$

the following equations are obtained:

$$(1)\ f(D_1 + D_2) + D_1 f'(D_1 + D_2) = 0$$
$$(2)\ f(D_1 + D_2) + D_2 f'(D_1 + D_2) = 0$$

Subtracting equation (2) from equation (1),

$$D_1 f'(D_1 + D_2) - D_2 f'(D_1 + D_2) = 0$$
$$f'(D_1 + D_2)(D_1 - D_2) = 0$$
$$D_1 - D_2 = 0$$
$$D_1 = D_2$$

That is, the quantities sold by both duopolists will be equal under the assumed conditions.

Cournot worked out his duopoly case geometrically as shown in Figure 8. Equations (1) and (2) can be represented by the two curves in the figure. These are maximum-profit curves. They also are reaction curves, with each seller adjusting his output to the output of the other, each assuming at every point that the rival's output is constant. The horizontal axis represents the sales by proprietor (1), and the vertical axis sales by proprietor (2). Curve $m_1 n_1$ represents equation (1) above, and curve $m_2 n_2$, equation (2). If proprietor (1) sells ox_1 units, proprietor (2) will sell oy_1. Whereupon proprietor (1) will sell ox_2 units, for that gives him the maximum profit when D_2 has the value oy_1. Producer (2) sells oy_2 units, and so on. Equilibrium is established where both curves intersect; at that output, both duopolists sell equal quantities and receive maximum profits.

Cournot has been criticized for his unrealistic assumptions and for omitting many other possible solutions of the duopoly case. In 1897, for example, Francis Y. Edgeworth in his paper "Pure Theory of Monopoly" (originally published in Italy) introduced uncertainty of mutual reactions, concluding that this rendered the duopoly solution indeterminate. In the 1920's, the reaction patterns were made to include sales, costs, quality of product, and service competition. Cournot's assumption that firms never

FIGURE 8.   Cournot's Duopoly Solution

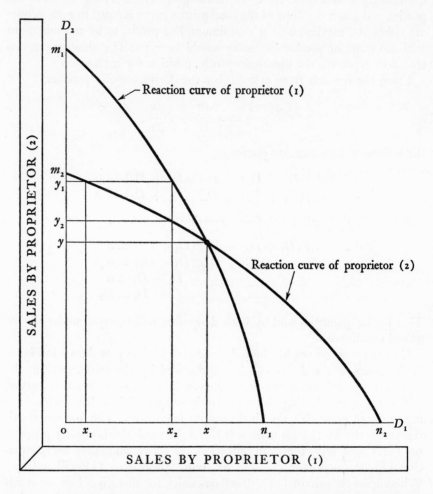

SOURCE: Augustin Cournot, *Researches into the Mathematical Principles of the Theory of Wealth*, Nathaniel T. Bacon, tr. (New York, Macmillan, 1927), endpaper.

test each other's reactions was discarded. As soon as we admit that each firm will consider its rival's reaction to its own policies, we have a whole range of cases, depending on what we assume about their behavior. Cournot was remarkable as a pioneer theorist of pure competition and departures from it, but modern theory, naturally, has gone far beyond his early efforts.

Sraffa

PIERO SRAFFA (born 1898), an Italian who migrated to England, studied under Marshall and taught at Cambridge University. When France fell under the German blitzkrieg in 1940, he was interned by the British as an "enemy alien." Keynes denounced the "fatheads" who were mistreating distinguished refugee scholars. He wrote, "If there are any Nazi sympathizers still at large in this country, we should look in the War Office and our Secret Service, not in the internment camps."

Sraffa was the editor of the definitive edition of Ricardo's collected works and correspondence.

In the December 1926 issue of the *Economic Journal*, he published an article that turned out to be seminal in stirring up a critique of the theory of pure competition. Sraffa pointed out that unit costs of production may very well fall as a firm increases its scale of production. This can occur because of internal economies as the firm expands output, or because overhead charges are distributed over a larger number of units produced. Such falling unit costs are incompatible with pure competition. It is necessary, therefore, to abandon the path of free competition and turn toward monopoly. Here we have a well-defined theory. These two are, however, extreme cases. In industries where competitive conditions appear to prevail, two forces are frequently found that break up the unity of markets. First, a single producer can affect market prices by varying the quantity of goods he throws on the market; second, each producer may produce normally in circumstances of individual decreasing costs. Both of these conditions are more akin to monopoly situations than to pure competition. Both derive from the fact that the producer faces a demand curve that slopes downward instead of being horizontal. Under pure competition, if a producer can sell all he produces at the going market price, he will continue to expand production as long as his cost per unit of output is below his selling price. If, however, he must lower his price in order to sell a greater quantity, he may curtail output even though a greater volume of production would lower the average cost per unit.

Everyday experience shows that a very large number of undertakings—and the majority of those which produce manufactured consumers' goods—work under conditions of individual diminishing costs. Almost any producer of such goods, if he could rely upon the market in which he sells his products being prepared to take any quantity of them from him at the current price, without any trouble on his part except that of producing them, would extend his business enormously. It is not easy, in times of normal activity, to find an undertaking which systematically restricts its own production to an amount less than that which it could sell at the current price, and which is at the same time prevented by competition from exceeding that price. Business men, who regard themselves as being subject to competitive conditions, would consider absurd the assertion that the limit to their production is to be found in the internal conditions of production in their firm, which do not permit of the production of a greater quantity without an increase in cost. The chief obstacle against which they have to contend when they want gradually to increase their production does not lie in the cost of production—which, indeed, generally favours them in that direction—but in the difficulty of selling the larger quantity of goods without reducing the price, or without having to face increased marketing expenses. This necessity of reducing prices in order to sell a larger quantity of one's own product is only an aspect of the usual descending demand curve, with the difference that instead of concerning the whole of a commodity, whatever its origin, it relates only to the goods produced by a particular firm; and the marketing expenses necessary for the extension of its market are merely costly efforts (in the form of advertising, commercial travellers, facilities to customers, etc.) to increase the willingness of the market to buy from it—that is, to raise that demand curve artificially.*

Generally each producer enjoys special advantages in his own protected segment of the total market. He would not lose all his business if he raised his price, and he would not take away all his rivals' business if he lowered his price. Therefore he enjoys certain monopoly elements even in a market that appears competitive, and the demand curve he faces slopes down to the right.

We are led to ascribe the correct measure of importance to the chief obstacle which hinders the free play of competition, even where this appears to predominate, and which at the same time renders a stable equilibrium possible even when the supply curve for the products of each individual firm is descending —that is, the absence of indifference on the part of the buyers of goods as between the different producers. The causes of the preference shown by any group of buyers for a particular firm are of the most diverse nature, and may range from long custom, personal acquaintance, confidence in the quality of the product, proximity, knowledge of particular requirements and the possibility of obtaining credit, to the reputation of a trade-mark, or sign, or a name with high traditions, or to such special features of modelling or design in the product as—without constituting it a distinct commodity intended for the satisfaction of particular needs—have for their principal purpose that of distinguishing it from the products of other firms. What these and the many other possible reasons for preference have in common is that they are expressed in a willingness (which may frequently be dictated by necessity) on the part of the group of buyers who constitute a firm's clientele to pay, if necessary, some-

* Piero Sraffa, "The Laws of Returns Under Competitive Conditions," *Economic Journal*, Vol. XXXVI, No. 144 (December 1926), p. 543. By permission of the Royal Economic Society.

thing extra in order to obtain the goods from a particular firm rather than from any other.

When each of the firms producing a commodity is in such a position the general market for the commodity is subdivided into a series of distinct markets. Any firm which endeavours to extend beyond its own market by invading those of its competitors must incur heavy marketing expenses in order to surmount the barriers by which they are surrounded; but, on the other hand, within its own market and under the protection of its own barrier each enjoys a privileged position whereby it obtains advantages which—if not in extent, at least in their nature—are equal to those enjoyed by the ordinary monopolist.*

In a stable industry, said Sraffa, a firm can lower its price and thereby increase sales and profits. If this is undertaken, it is done to the detriment of competing firms. If, however, a firm raises prices, profits are increased without injuring competition; instead, rival firms gain from the rise in prices. The second method of raising profits is therefore more acceptable to businessmen than the first, because the profits are regarded as more durably acquired, without arousing retaliation by competitors.

Sraffa's widely read and discussed article touched off an outburst of thinking and writing about the shortcomings of then-current economic theory.

Chamberlin

EDWARD HASTINGS CHAMBERLIN (born 1899), Harvard professor, published *The Theory of Monopolistic Competition* in 1933. Before that he had submitted an earlier version as his doctor's thesis at Harvard, in 1927. His book fused the previously separate theories of monopoly and competition, and it sought to explain the wide range of market situations that are neither purely competitive nor totally monopolized. Most markets contain both monopolistic and competitive elements that determine prices.

One of the key concepts of the theory of monopolistic competition is that the firm's demand curve slopes downward, and therefore the marginal revenue curve must lie below the demand or average revenue curve. Chamberlin was among the first of a considerable number of theorists in the late 1920's and early 1930's who discovered and applied the idea of marginal revenue. It may be defined as the addition to total gross revenue as a result of selling an additional unit of output. Under pure competition, with each firm able to sell all it produces at the going market price, the marginal revenue is equal to price, and both the marginal revenue curve and the demand curve are horizontal lines. Thus, if a farmer can sell all his wheat at $2 a bushel, every additional bushel he sells adds $2 to his gross revenue.

* *Ibid.*, pp. 544–45.

The situation is quite different in markets where pure competition does not prevail. With a downward-sloping demand curve, the marginal revenue curve will slope downward more steeply. For example, if an entrepreneur can sell one pair of shoes per day if he prices it at $20, two pairs if the price is $18, and three pairs at $16, in each case except the first the marginal revenue is less than the price. It is $20 for the first pair. For the second pair, however, it is only $16. This can be calculated in two ways. First, total revenue goes from $20 to $36, an increase of $16. Second, the additional pair of shoes sells for $18, but the price of the first pair had to be reduced $2 in order to sell a second pair. The marginal revenue derived from selling the third pair of shoes comes to $12.

Marginal cost is defined as the addition to total cost as a result of producing one more unit of output. As the firm expands its output toward the most efficient level, average unit costs fall and marginal costs lie below average costs. As the firm expands output beyond the most efficient level, average costs rise and marginal costs lie above average costs. Therefore the marginal cost curve crosses the average cost curve at its lowest point.

The equilibrium output for each firm is determined by the intersection of the marginal cost and the marginal revenue curves. As long as the addition to total revenue exceeds the addition to total costs as the result of producing one more unit, it pays to expand production. If, on the other hand, marginal cost is rising and it exceeds marginal revenue, it pays to reduce output. Only at the output where marginal cost and marginal revenue are equal will profits be maximized or losses minimized. This single law applies to pure competition, monopoly, and the range of situations in between.

Only where a firm enjoys significant monopoly powers will its price exceed average unit costs even in the long run; it will receive monopoly profits. But where there are many firms under conditions of monopolistic competition, free entry into the industry will cause monopoly profits to disappear in the long run. As more firms offer to sell goods that are close (although imperfect) substitutes for each other, each producer can sell less at each price than formerly. Long-run equilibrium will occur when each seller's demand curve is tangent to the average cost curve. Similarly, if too many firms enter the industry, losses will occur until some firms leave, and the demand curve for each remaining firm rises to a position of tangency with the average cost curve. These ideas are illustrated graphically in Figure 9, which is based on Chamberlin's presentation. The firm's average cost curve includes the average rate of profit that is required to keep the business operating in the long run. Goods can therefore be sold at average cost and still show a profit in the accounting sense. Marginal cost is derived from average cost. The firm's demand curve D slopes downward because the firm can increase its sales by lowering its price; if it raises its price, sales will decline. Even customers who are devoted to a particular seller or to his product's brand name will not reject close substitutes if his price becomes too high.

The marginal revenue curve *MR* intersects the marginal cost curve at the point that determines that, for maximum profit, output will be *OB* units, the price will be *BN* per unit, and the extra profit per unit will be *SN*. Total extra profit will be the extra profit per unit times the number of units produced, which can be represented by the area *LSNM*.

If the enterprise enjoys long-run monopoly power, as for example an ability to exclude new firms from entering the industry, this situation will represent the long-run equilibrium for the kind of costs and demand depicted in Figure 9. The extra profit is monopoly profit. If, however, other firms are free to enter the industry, they will do so in order to participate

FIGURE 9. Equilibrium Under Monopolistic Competition

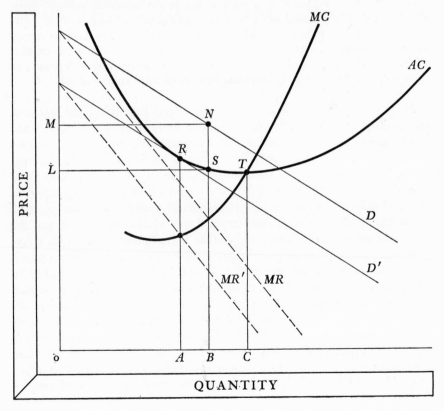

in the extra rate of return. The demand curve will fall to D' in the long run, OA units will be produced, they will sell for AR per unit, and all extra profits will disappear.

If this were a firm producing in a market of pure competition, the demand curve and the marginal revenue curve would be horizontal and identical. In the long run OC units would be produced, and the price per unit would be CT. Hence Chamberlin's significant conclusion:

The price is inevitably higher and the scale of production inevitably smaller under monopolistic competition than under pure competition. . . .

The common result of this assemblage of factors is excess productive capacity, for which there is no automatic corrective. Such excess capacity may develop, of course, under pure competition, owing to miscalculation on the part of producers, or to sudden fluctuations in demand or cost conditions. But it is the peculiarity of monopolistic competition that it may develop over long periods *with impunity*, prices always covering costs, and may, in fact, become permanent and normal through a failure of price competition to function. The surplus capacity is never cast off, and the result is high prices and waste. The theory affords an explanation of such wastes in the economic system—wastes which are usually referred to as "wastes of competition." In fact, they could never occur under pure competition, and it is for this reason that the theory of pure competition is and must be silent about them, introducing them, if at all, as "qualifications," rather than as parts of the theory. They are wastes of monopoly—of the monopoly elements in monopolistic competition.*

Many economists, following Chamberlin's lead, have reiterated that pure competition would result in a larger output, more efficient production, and lower selling prices than occur under monopolistic competition or monopoly. In saying this, they usually fail to state the implicit assumption that cost curves are the same in each situation. This, however, is an unrealistic assumption for many industries. If we were to have pure competition in the steel industry, we might have thousands of small firms producing steel. Each "steel mill" might be little larger than a blacksmith's forge, and the price of steel would be much higher than it is at present even with a few producers enjoying considerable monopolistic power. All we can say is that under pure competition each producer in the long run will tend to produce at the minimum point of his own average cost curve. If we depart from pure competition, the tendency is to restrict output and raise prices because of the downward sloping demand curve. Therefore a firm's output will generally be less and its price higher than if the same size firm were operating in pure competition. There is no doubt, however, that a modern

* Edward H. Chamberlin, *The Theory of Monopolistic Competition*, 5th ed. (Cambridge, Harvard University Press, 1946), pp. 88, 109. By permission of Harvard University Press,

steel mill is more efficient than a blacksmith's forge. The cost curves of a small firm in pure competition lie far above those of giant firms. Therefore pure competition would not necessarily give us the greatest volume of output and the lowest prices. The nostalgia for the bygone world of small business seems both futile and erroneous.

Robinson

MRS. JOAN ROBINSON (born 1903), professor of economics at Cambridge University, was a student of Alfred Marshall. Her book, *The Economics of Imperfect Competition,* published a few months after Chamberlin's book appeared, covers substantially the same ground. Since its appearance in 1933, Mrs. Robinson has expanded her activities and made important contributions in Keynesian economics, in economic development, in international trade, and in a critique of Marxist economics. Her attitude toward Marxism has been that of a friendly critic.

Mrs. Robinson added to monopoly the concept of monopsony, the position in the market of a single buyer. She first assumed a large number of buyers of a commodity. Their aggregate demand curve slopes down and to the right, for it is based on marginal utility. The more units of a good a person acquires, the lower its marginal utility falls, and the less he offers for an additional unit.

If all the buyers then form an agreement to act together, we can assume that their combined demand curve remains unaltered. We can also assume that the supply curve remains unchanged, for it indicates how much all the sellers together will offer at each price; it is based on the cost of producing each quantity, which does not change after a monopsony is organized.

Under pure competition, the buyer will purchase successive units of goods at any one time up to the point where the *price* is equal to marginal utility. Under monopsony, the buyer will regulate his purchases in such a way that *marginal cost* is equal to marginal utility. To illustrate these propositions, consider first pure competition. Suppose the going price for shoes is $10 a pair. A single buyer, of course, cannot influence the price no matter what his purchases are. Let us assume that for a particular consumer, ownership of the first pair of shoes at any one time is worth $100. A second pair is worth, say, $12 to him, a third pair is worth $10, and a fourth pair is worth $5. In this situation our consumer would buy three pairs of shoes. That is, he buys shoes up to the point where price is equal to marginal utility, and both are equal to $10.

Now suppose the same consumer is contemplating buying shoes in a monopsony market. Acquiring shoes from the first through the fourth pair still has a marginal utility for him that can be represented, as above by $100, $12, $10, and $5. Assuming that the production of shoes can be increased only under conditions of increasing cost, the more shoes our consumer wishes to buy, the higher the price will be. In effect he bids up the price against himself when he increases his purchases. Suppose he can buy one pair of shoes for $6, but two pairs would cost him $9 each. The marginal cost of the second pair is $12, which is equal to the marginal utility, and it pays him to buy it. If three pairs would cost $10 each, the marginal cost of the third pair would be $12. It would not pay the consumer to buy the third pair, because adding $12 to cost is not justified when the increased utility is represented by $10. Thus Mrs. Robinson concluded that under pure competition the buyer will purchase successive units of goods up to the point where the price is equal to marginal utility. Under monopsony the buyer will increase his purchases up to the point where marginal cost is equal to marginal utility.

It follows that with a constant supply price, when average and marginal costs are equal, the quantity purchased under monopsony will be the same as under competition. If, however, an industry is working under increasing or diminishing supply price, marginal cost to the monopsonist will not be equal to the price of the commodity; he will buy less or more than under competition.

We can illustrate the difference between average and marginal costs with rising supply price by means of a numerical example. Suppose a buyer wishes to buy 100 pairs of shoes in a certain market, and can get them at $10 each. If he wishes to expand his purchases to 101 pairs, he may have to pay $10.05, because the prices of raw materials and labor are being bid up, and plants are pushed beyond their lowest-cost output in order to fill the extra demand. While the average cost of 101 pairs of shoes is $10.05, the marginal cost is $15.05. This can be calculated in two ways. First, the total cost of 100 pairs of shoes is $1,000.00, and of 101 pairs it is $1,015.05; therefore the marginal cost, the addition to total cost, in producing the 101st pair is $15.05. Second, the cost of the 101st pair is $10.05 plus the extra 5¢ a pair on the 100 pairs in order to produce the extra one. Therefore the marginal cost curve lies above the average cost curve (which is the supply curve for the industry) when the latter is rising.

The case of increasing supply price is illustrated in Figure 10, which is based on Mrs. Robinson's presentation. AC is the average cost curve of the industry, or the supply curve. MC is the marginal cost curve to the industry, and this is the marginal cost curve from the point of view of the monopsonist. In the absence of monopsony, OB units would be bought at price BS per unit. With monopsony, OA units would be bought at price AR per unit. Monopsony profit would be RN per unit, or a total of LRNM.

FIGURE 10. Monopsony with Increasing Supply Price

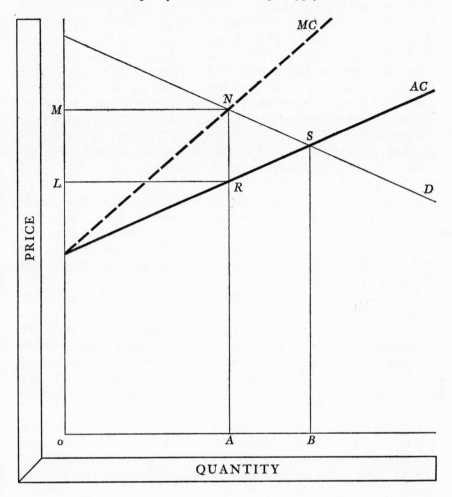

In another part of her work, Mrs. Robinson analyzed the productivity theory of distribution based on her theory of imperfect competition. In examining the demand curve for a factor of production, she used labor as an illustration. The *marginal physical productivity* of labor is the increment of output derived from employing an additional unit of labor with a fixed expenditure on other factors. It will tend to fall as more workers are employed because of the law of diminishing returns. The *marginal revenue productivity* (Mrs. Robinson called it marginal productivity) is the increment of value of the total output caused by employing an additional man. Under pure competition the firm can sell all it produces at the going market price; therefore marginal revenue productivity is equal to the value of the marginal physical product, or marginal physical product times price. When the demand is not perfectly elastic, however, the firm has to lower the price of its goods if it wishes to increase sales; then marginal revenue productivity is less than the value of the marginal physical product.

An arithmetic example may clarify this relationship. Suppose 10 workers together produce 50 pairs of shoes per day, and an 11th worker would add 3 pairs to total output. Under pure competition the price is, say, $10 per pair regardless of whether 50 or 53 pairs are sold. The marginal physical productivity of the 11th worker is 3 pairs. The value of the marginal physical product is 3 × $10 = $30. The marginal revenue productivity also is $30, which is the gross revenue added to the firm's receipts when an 11th man is employed.

Suppose that under monopolistic competition 50 pairs of shoes can be sold at $10, but to sell 53 pairs the price has to be dropped to $9.90. The marginal physical productivity remains at 3 pairs. The value of the marginal physical product is 3 × $9.90 = $29.70. The marginal revenue productivity is $24.70, the difference in total revenue between selling 50 pairs at $10 and 53 at $9.90.

Mrs. Robinson then introduced the concept of gross and net productivity. Suppose that for every extra pair of shoes produced, an extra $3 must be spent on variable inputs other than labor, such as leather, electricity, containers, etc. Under pure competition in the example given above, the marginal gross revenue productivity is $30, while the marginal net revenue productivity is $21. With monopolistic competition, the marginal gross revenue productivity is $24.70, and the marginal net revenue productivity is $15.70.

If wages were lower than $21 per day under pure competition, it would pay to hire the 11th worker. Under monopolistic competition, however, he would not be hired unless wages were below $15.70 per day, even though the net value of his marginal physical product is $20.70 ($29.70 minus $9.00).

Mrs. Robinson thus became involved in the touchy question of the exploitation of labor. She cited one definition of exploitation of a factor of production: being employed at a price that is less than its marginal net revenue productivity. If the market for labor is perfect, so that each employer can hire all the labor he wants at the going price, the marginal cost of labor to the individual employer is equal to its price. The self-interest of the employer will impel him to hire workers up to the point where the marginal net revenue productivity is reduced to equality with the wage. Exploitation under this definition normally does not occur.

She cited a second definition offered by A. C. Pigou, her colleague at

Cambridge. Exploitation occurs when the wage is less than the marginal physical product of labor valued at its selling price. Accepting this definition, she concluded that exploitation of labor occurs both under monopsony in buying labor and under monopoly or imperfect competition in selling the products turned out by labor. The remedy for exploitation under monopsony would be for a trade union or a trade board to impose a minimum wage on the industry. Then the supply of labor to the industry becomes perfectly elastic at the imposed wage, and the marginal cost of labor is identical with the average cost. Referring to Figure 10 above, if a wage of *BS* were imposed, the monopsonist would no longer be bidding up the price of labor as he increased employment. The new supply curve would be a horizontal line going through the point *S*, and employment would increase from *OA* units to *OB*. The wage would equal the net value of the marginal physical product, and exploitation would disappear.

To eliminate exploitation under monopoly, the selling price would have to be controlled in such a way that it would equal average cost. To eliminate exploitation under imperfect competition, the most common type, markets would have to become perfect or purely competitive.

When the market becomes perfect the firms will expand, and in the new position of equilibrium, when profits are once more normal, the firms will be of optimum size, costs will be lower, and the price of the commodity will have fallen.

The removal of the imperfection of the market must therefore lower the price of the commodity. It is likely also to alter the marginal physical productivity of the number of men formerly employed in the industry, since the workers are now organised in optimum firms instead of sub-optimum firms. In the old position they were receiving less than what was then the value of their marginal physical product, and in the new position they will receive the value of their marginal physical product, but it does not follow that they will be better off in the new position than in the old, since the value of the marginal physical product may have diminished: the marginal physical product may have diminished, and the price of the commodity must have fallen.*

Chamberlin did not cover distribution theory in the first edition of his book, but he did in subsequent editions. His retort to Mrs. Robinson's exploitation theory was that *all* factors, not merely labor, receive less than the value of their marginal products. The Pigou-Robinson definition of exploitation applies only to pure competition, for it is impossible under other market conditions for all factors to get the value of their marginal physical products. In their sense, all factors are necessarily exploited, and it would

* Joan Robinson, *The Economics of Imperfect Competition* (London, 1933), pp. 284–85.

be impossible for employers to avoid the charge of "exploitation" without going into bankruptcy.

Chamberlin raised another objection to the productivity theory of distribution as developed by Mrs. Robinson:

It has been tacitly assumed up to this point that the product added by another laborer in any firm is a net addition to social product, not offset by a lessened product elsewhere in the system. This may well be true. But let us examine briefly at least one case where it is not. . . . The productivity to society of any factor or of any group of factors composing an enterprise must be considered as the total product it creates less that which its presence prevents others from creating. Let us suppose that three gasoline filling stations are adequately supplying the demands for gasoline at a particular corner at going prices when a fourth company sets itself up in business. What product does the new station add? If the outcome is simply the sharing of the available business by the four at the old prices, as it is very apt to be, it is difficult to see where there has been any appreciable addition at all. The value of the services provided by the newcomer less those no longer provided by the three others is approximately zero. To be sure, there may be some additional convenience to those for whom the new station is more advantageously located. The product then will not be zero, but it will be far less than that indicated by regarding the new firm alone. There is a further complication. Since each firm is suffering a reduced volume of sales, average unit costs are higher. It is quite possible that the profits of the first three firms were sufficient before the fourth entered so that all four can now cover their costs including minimum profits without a price adjustment. It is also possible that, faced with higher costs, they will all find it necessary to raise prices, and possible to do so with little fear of undercutting, since each has a strong interest in avoiding a price so low that he cannot cover costs when enjoying his normal share of the available business. Under these circumstances the appearance of the fourth seller has actually diminished (through higher prices) the output of the group. The physical product of the resources he employs being negative, their value at current prices would likewise be negative. Wherever price competition fails to function effectively, complications such as these arise and must be taken into account in defining the net product added by a new firm or by the marginal unit of any factor which it employs. In such cases it appears that the value of the net social marginal product of a factor may even be negative, and, in any event, that it will be far less than its marginal product to an individual firm. Clearly, the value of its net social marginal product bears no relation whatever to its marginal revenue product to the firm, and hence to its income.*

Two decades after her book appeared, Mrs. Robinson criticized the type of economic theorizing she had helped to pioneer:

* Chamberlin, *op. cit.*, pp. 184–85.

The Economics of Imperfect Competition was a scholastic book. It was directed to analysing the slogans of the text-books of twenty years ago: "price tends to equal marginal cost" and "wages equal the marginal product of labour"; and it treated of text-book questions, such as a comparison of the price and output of a commodity under conditions of monopoly and of competition, demand and costs being given. The assumptions which were adequate (or which I hoped were adequate) for dealing with such questions are by no means a suitable basis for an analysis of the problems of prices, production and distribution which present themselves in reality. . . .

In principle, it is possible to set out a system of simultaneous equations showing what combination of price, outlay on production costs and outlay on selling costs would yield the best profit for a particular commodity in a particular market, taking into account the reaction upon costs and sales of other commodities produced by the same firm. Even if he had the data, the business executive would need an electric, not a human, brain to work out from the equations the correct policy in time to put it into effect. And the data are necessarily extremely vague, since the consequences of a given policy cannot be isolated in ever-changing markets. The recent development of advertising of advertisement is a witness to the difficulty which manufacturers have in knowing the consequences of advertisement, for if they knew its effects there would be no scope for persuading them that it is greater than they think. In reality, evidently, an individual demand curve (for a particular product produced by a particular firm) is a mere smudge, to which it is vain to attribute elegant geometrical properties. . . .

In my opinion, the greater weakness of *The Economics of Imperfect Competition* is one which it shares with the class of economic theory to which it belongs—the failure to deal with time. It is only in a metaphorical sense that price, rate of output, wage-rate or what not can move in the plane depicted in a price-quantity diagram. Any movement must take place through time, and the position at any moment of time depends upon what it has been in the past. The point is not merely that any adjustment takes a certain time to complete and that (as has always been admitted) events may occur meanwhile which alter the position, so that the equilibrium towards which the system is said to be *tending* itself moves before it can be reached. The point is that the very process of moving has an effect upon the destination of the movement, so that there is no such thing as a position of long-run equilibrium which exists independently of the course which the economy is following at a particular date.*

Alfred Marshall had anticipated this last objection of his illustrious pupil, although he relegated it to a minor interference with the movement toward an equilibrium price in a market for a single good. If sellers, he said, were able to get more than the equilibrium price for part of their goods, they

* Joan Robinson, "Imperfect Competition Revisited," *Economic Journal*, Vol. LXIII, No. 251 (September 1953), pp. 579, 585, 590. By permission of the Royal Economic Society.

might no longer be so hard pressed for cash, and they would continue to hold out for a higher price than they otherwise would have asked; the advantage in bargaining they obtained at the beginning of the market would persist to the end, and the price would remain higher than the true equilibrium. Conversely, if the market had opened much to the disadvantage of the sellers, their great want for ready money might compel them to continue selling below the true equilibrium price.

In turning away from the type of theory shown above and exploring other fields, Mrs. Robinson has attempted to develop a more dynamic as well as a more realistic analysis of the economic world.

CHAPTER 21

Welfare Economics and Social Control

WELFARE economics is not a distinct and unified system of ideas, and therefore cannot be properly called a school. It is, instead, a stream of thought that interests economists of different schools and of no school. Thinkers as diverse as John A. Hobson, who leaned toward fundamental reforms, and A. C. Pigou, leading neoclassicist of his day, contributed to welfare economics. J. Maurice Clark, who was perhaps an institutionalist with roots in neoclassicism, included in his wide range of interests the problems of government intervention in the economy to promote the good of society; he too, therefore, may be called a welfare economist, or at least he was an economist concerned with the social control of enterprise.

Welfare economics raises questions about how well the economy functions, how satisfactory is the system of distribution, what can be done about improving total well-being, and to what degree society must nullify the results of laissez faire in order to promote welfare.

The liberals concerned with this stream of ideas argued that laissez faire does not produce the best results, and government intervention is required. They considered the neoclassical idea of the falling marginal utility of goods and money as more of either is acquired; their conclusion was that greater equality of wealth and income will increase total welfare. They advocated social legislation, with at least part of the burden being thrown on the employers and on the wealthy through progressive taxation. Their ideas are permeated with value judgments as to what is best for mankind.

Conservative economists disavowed any possibility of interpersonal comparisons of utility. How can we be sure that a dollar transferred from a wealthy man to a beggar will add more to the beggar's joy than it will detract from the rich man's? Perhaps the latter is a more efficient "pleasure machine" than the former. The thing to do is to add to the income and util-ity of the poor man without deducting anything from the rich man. Be-sides, too vigorous efforts toward redistribution may kill the ability to accumulate wealth through saving, and they may kill incentives to invest whatever wealth has been accumulated; therefore egalitarian sentiments, if implemented, may reduce total welfare by reducing total income. Above all, conservative economists wished to perfect a purely scientific economics from which all judgments of moral value would be excluded.

Conservatives accuse the liberals of undermining the free-enterprise sys-tem. Do-gooders try to promote the well-being of the masses by deciding for them what is best. Increasing government regulation and an ever rising burden of taxation are weakening the flexibility and adaptability of the economy. The welfare state, with the increasing security it offers the indi-vidual regardless of his own efforts or abilities, is destroying his ambition, energy, and willingness to do an honest day's work. As incentives to work, save, and invest are weakened, the faltering economy requires ever more government intervention, which would not have been necessary in the first place if we had not started down the road toward the welfare state. It is only through the quest for profit and the unequal distribution of income that maximum growth is possible; as the size of the income pie grows, everybody benefits.

Liberal welfare economists argue, whimsically, that the welfare state is a state that looks after the welfare of its people. (All contestants in this de-bate claim, of course, that their policies will maximize welfare.) Value judgments must enter into policy-making decisions. Most agree that laissez faire does not necessarily produce the best results, and some government intervention is necessary to ameliorate conditions. There is disagreement among them as to how much government activity is required, for it is at the point of change that the greatest controversies occur. They all oppose, however, the conservative economist's argument that redistribution cannot demonstrably improve total welfare because we cannot compare utilities between different people. Liberal reformers argue that by shifting a dollar of wealth or income from a rich man to a poor man, we increase total wel-fare without being able to say by exactly how much. We can speak about colder or warmer temperatures without looking at a thermometer; in the same approximate manner we can say that a dollar is more useful to a poor man than to a rich one. The reformers also deplore the basically futile de-sire to increase the well-being of the poor without reducing that of the rich. They argue that almost every measure that helps some people hurts others. Full employment affects adversely the dealers in bankrupt stocks and secondhand clothes. Offering free polio vaccines hurts the doctors and the casket manufacturers, the latter through the postponement of part of their income; and postponing income and discounting it to the present reduces its value.

We should recognize that even those economists who object to welfare economics and who claim to deal with economic principles and problems with the utmost objectivity, also make certain ethical or value assumptions. Whether they are aware of it or not, whether their ideas of good and bad are stated explicitly or lurk in the background of their minds, the most impartial economists work with value judgments. Typical value judgments are the following: price stability is good; rising national income is desirable; the allocation of resources through competition and consumer choice gives the best results; productivity is the most ethical basis for rewards; increased productivity is to be welcomed. Not all people in our society, and not all societies, would agree with these preferences that are taken for granted among most of us.

There is not, therefore, a vast difference between welfare economists and their opponents insofar as both presume certain bases for the good life. The differences between them appear first, in the degree to which value judgments are openly recognized and approved; second, in the degree of reliance placed on individualism and laissez faire as opposed to collective, social controls over the production, distribution, and consumption of wealth.

We turn now to Hobson, a pioneer in welfare economics, who offered a moderately radical approach to problems of human welfare.

Hobson

JOHN ATKINSON HOBSON (1858–1940), son of a middle-class family, studied the classics at Oxford. After graduation he taught the classics and gave university extension lectures in English literature. His interests soon shifted to economic subjects, and he began to develop heretical ideas through his association with the businessman and mountain-climber, A. F. Mummery, who was killed in the Himalayas in 1895. Because of ideas that were then considered radical, Hobson lost his position as an extension lecturer at London University. Although he was excluded from academic life, he was extremely active not only as a writer of thirty-seven books, but also as a journalist and popular lecturer. One of his major themes was the interdependence of politics, economics, and ethics. A journal article he wrote on imperialism induced the editor of the Manchester *Guardian* to send him to South Africa on a study that led to his writing three books, the most famous of which was *Imperialism*. He was a pacifist during World War I.

Hobson was one of those rare social reformers who used economic theory as a foundation for his proposals. He rejected the classical and neoclassical ideas that pure competition was the typical market situation, that a harmony of interests prevailed, and that laissez faire was the best policy. In their place he developed an analysis that led to a program of reform, largely through government intervention, which can be called welfare economics.

We shall be concerned here with three major strands of Hobson's thought. First, in the 1880's he developed the idea of underconsumption and oversaving, which lead to overinvestment; for this he received Keynes's acclaim. Second, he believed that inability to keep the economy fully employed leads to imperialism; for this he was praised by V. I. Lenin, who said that although Hobson was a bourgeois social reformer and pacifist, he gave an excellent and comprehensive description of imperialism. Third, he advocated a greater equality of income both for ethical reasons and to increase consumption spending; here the role of government looms large.

The central problem of our society, said Hobson, is the recurring unemployment of labor, capital, and land. As early as 1889 he and Mummery argued against the classical doctrine that the more thrifty a nation is, the more wealthy it becomes. On the contrary, they said, an increase of capital requires a subsequent increase in the consumption of commodities, which that capital will produce. If people wish to save more now they must consent to consume more in the near future. If they persist in saving now and in attempting to invest their saving without adequately increasing their consumption, the actual formation of new capital will be limited by the extent of future consumption.

Our purpose is to show . . . that an undue exercise of the habit of saving is possible, and that such undue exercise impoverishes the Community, throws labourers out of work, drives down wages, and spreads that gloom and prostration through the commercial world which is known as Depression in Trade; that, in short, the effective love of money is the root of all economic evil. . . .

We are thus brought to the conclusion that the basis on which all economic teaching since Adam Smith has stood, viz., that the quantity annually produced is determined by the aggregates of Natural Agents, Capital, and Labour available, is erroneous, and that, on the contrary, the quantity produced, while it can never exceed the limits imposed by these aggregates, may be, and actually is, reduced far below this maximum by the check that undue saving and the consequent accumulation of over-supply exerts on production; i.e., that in the normal state of modern industrial Communities, consumption limits production and not production consumption. . . .

Reaching our main conclusion, that the undue saving of individuals impoverishes the Community, simultaneously lowering Rent, Profit, or Interest and Wages, we contradict the generally accepted dogmas that the saving of the individual must always and necessarily enrich the Community, that the individual seeking his own advantage necessarily works for that of the Community, and that wages can only rise at the expense of profit, or profit at the expense of wages, or both at the expense of rent.*

Why is there too much saving and not enough consumption? Here Hobson developed a theory of the proper distribution of income that was quite different from that of his contemporaries. Part of the income received by labor is for maintenance or subsistence, which enables workers to renew their strength from day to day and raise families to replenish the labor supply. Additional wages provide for growth in the economy, for payments above the bare maintenance level enable more children to survive infancy, and people do more work because they are healthier, better educated, and more energetic. If wages are more than enough to cover maintenance (costs of subsistence) and the productive surplus (costs of growth), the remainder will be an unproductive surplus or an unearned increment. It will not be necessary or useful in increasing output. Too high wages are unproductive because they do not call forth a greater supply of labor.

Capital likewise has two corresponding costs. The maintenance cost replaces worn-out capital. To induce growth, both profit and interest are required to evoke saving that will be invested. If interest and profit are above the level required for the maintenance and healthy growth of capital, the surplus payments are unproductive, an unearned increment.

For land, the necessary payment covers all the costs of man's efforts and expenditures to maintain and improve its productivity. Genuine economic rent is in its entirety an unproductive surplus.

Labor typically gets its subsistence costs, but not the full costs of growth, according to Hobson. In other words, higher wages generally increase the efficiency and productivity of labor. There is too much saving and not enough consumption because of the failures of competition to work effectively toward raising wages and lowering property incomes. The rich receivers of profit, interest, and rent get an unproductive surplus; they save too large a part of their incomes. They are not motivated solely by the desire to consume now or in the future, but also by the urge to save and invest, to accumulate wealth. This is possible only if the demand for consumer goods increases. To some extent this will occur, and then saving is socially useful. There always is some appropriate rate of saving that will increase the productive power of society in step with the increased effective market demand for consumption. The result is growth associated with full employment. If, however, the rate of saving is too high, this will be re-

* A. F. Mummery and J. A. Hobson, *The Physiology of Industry* (New York, 1956), pp. iv, vi, viii. [Originally published in 1889.]

vealed in unemployment. If the rate of saving is too low, productive power will be wasted, and the future will be sacrificed to the present.

Oversaving and underconsumption cause the business cycle. During prosperity, prices are high. Capital investment is high, facilitated by the expansion of bank credit. The productive power of society grows more rapidly than consumption. The first symptom of the coming depression is a weakening of prices. Profit margins are diminished as a consequence. The repayment of loans and the meeting of bills become less certain, while the value of securities held as collateral shrinks. Pessimism spreads. Banks curtail credit. Bankruptcies spread, and financial houses may crash. Suspicion changes to panic as depositors and investors seek to withdraw their funds.

Hobson disputed the view that the financial collapse is due to the psychological aberrations of men. It is based, instead, on the imbalance that arises in industry. And what reverses the downtrend? The decline of society's saving as incomes fall eventually brings about a new balance between consumption and saving.

The whole financial system is based upon actual industry: reflects, anticipates, and frequently exaggerates its forces and tendencies. Depressions, with their accompanying unemployment, must therefore be traced through their operations in the delicate mechanism of finance to the failure of consumption to keep full pace with the increase of productive power so as to furnish a full and equable employment for this power. . . .

Take the case of an economic community of a progressive type with an income of twenty units, spending seventeen, and saving three for regular investment in new productive capital, which finds full, regular employment in meeting the growing demand for commodities. Now suppose, owing to some change in distribution of incomes, some return to simplicity of living or some increased appreciation of future as compared with present satisfactions, spending is reduced to sixteen, saving raised to four, what must happen? The increased savings cannot take shape in productive capital, for, as the increase of current and prospective consumption of commodities is reduced, a smaller amount of new productive capital can be put into operation, and any attempt to put into operation as much as before must speedily be checked by the obvious glut. Instead of three units of saving taking shape in productive capital, there is now only room for two and a half. But owing to increased saving four are available. What happens to the extra one and a half? There will be some hoarding, i.e. some lingering of loanable funds in hands of financiers, from slowness in finding any sort of investment.

Let us say that this disposes of half a unit—an excessive estimate. What becomes of the remaining one?

In order to answer this question, we must look to the effect of the diminished spending of the saving classes upon the general income from industry. Since there is a reduced demand both for commodities and for new capital goods,

there will be a shrinkage of money income and real income among all industrial classes. Those among these classes whose income is reduced very low will
be disposed to part with any property, land, houses, factories, etc., they may
possess, in order to keep living and to pay their way. This means that a large
amount of such properties will at such a time become a new field of investment
for the savings which cannot take shape in new productive capital. The surplus
unit of saving will find this form of investment, consisting in the acquisition of
productive capital already existing and belonging to classes impoverished by
the very increase of saving which has glutted the investment market. Saved
by the saving class, it will be spent by the non-saving class. From the standpoint of the community it represents no saving at all, but simply a transfer of
spending from one class to another. But the class which gets it only maintains
its former spending, while the class which parts with it has reduced its total
spending. So there remains as a net effect of the operation a reduction of total
demand for commodities and new forms of capital. This means reduced employment for capital and labour, diminished rate of production, and shrinkage
of the general real income. This is the condition known as depression. Why
does it not continue indefinitely and grow ever worse? Because from the very
beginning of the maladjustment between spending and saving a process of
readjustment gradually comes into play. Directly a shrinkage in demand for
commodities and new productive capital occurs, the lessened rate of production
begins to reduce all incomes, including those of the saving class. Aggregate
income no longer stands at twenty, but falls to eighteen, or even seventeen.
The saving class who were trying to save four out of a total twenty, leaving
sixteen for spending, are not willing to save four or even three out of an aggregate income reduced to eighteen or seventeen. Their permanent standard of
comfort stands in the way. When the shrinkage of production and of income
has gone far enough, not merely is the actual amount of saving reduced, but
the *proportion* of saving to spending is brought back towards the normal rate
which preceded the attempt to oversave, or even below that rate.*

Hobson's analysis of oversaving and underconsumption led to his theory
of imperialism. An abundance of goods that cannot be sold at home can be
unloaded in the colonies. Surplus saving, which cannot be invested at home
because of inadequate consumption, can be invested in the colonies. The industrial and financial magnates persuade their governments to acquire colonies at immense public expenditures, which in themselves add further to
the profits of the industrialists and financiers. Yet if income is distributed
properly, the home market is capable of indefinite expansion, and the drive
to exploit colonies becomes unnecessary.

Every improvement of methods of production, every concentration of ownership and control, seems to accentuate the tendency. As one nation after another
enters the machine economy and adopts advanced industrial methods, it be-

---

* J. A. Hobson, *The Industrial System,* 2nd ed. (New York, 1910), pp. 301–03.

comes more difficult for its manufacturers, merchants, and financiers to dispose profitably of their economic resources, and they are tempted more and more to use their Governments in order to secure for their particular use some distant undeveloped country by annexation and protection.

The process, we may be told, is inevitable, and so it seems upon a superficial inspection. Everywhere appear excessive powers of production, excessive capital in search of investment. It is admitted by all business men that the growth of the powers of production in their country exceeds the growth in consumption, that more goods can be produced than can be sold at a profit, and that more capital exists than can find remunerative investment.

It is this economic condition of affairs that forms the taproot of Imperialism. If the consuming public in this country raised its standard of consumption to keep pace with every rise of productive powers, there could be no excess of goods or capital clamorous to use Imperialism in order to find markets. . . .

The fallacy of the supposed inevitability of imperial expansion as a necessary outlet for progressive industry is now manifest. It is not industrial progress that demands the opening up of new markets and areas of investment, but mal-distribution of consuming power which prevents the absorption of commodities and capital within the country. The over-saving which is the economic root of Imperialism is found by analysis to consist of rents, monopoly profits, and other unearned or excessive elements of income, which, not being earned by labour of head or hand, have no legitimate *raison d'être*. . . .

Many have carried their analysis so far as to realise the absurdity of spending half our financial resources in fighting to secure foreign markets at times when hungry mouths, ill-clad backs, ill-furnished houses indicate countless unsatisfied material wants among our own population.*

In the autobiography published toward the end of his life, Hobson granted that in writing about the economic basis for imperialism, he had presented an excessive and too simple case for the economic determination of history. He had not yet acquired, he said, the proper perspective on the nature of the interaction between economics, politics, and ethics.

What is the remedy for oversaving, underconsumption, depression, and imperialism? A redistribution of income toward greater equality is required to reduce the proportion of saving to consumption spending. The bulk of the saving is done by the wealthy, because "the proportion of saving is generally in direct ratio to the sizes of incomes, the richest saving the largest percentage of their income, the poorest the smallest." Would redistribution check industrial progress by unduly restricting the quantity of saving and investment? Not at all. The increased demand resulting from the readjustment of income would stimulate industry, promote full and more stable

J. A. Hobson, *Imperialism*, 3rd ed. (London, Allen & Unwin, 1938), pp. 80–81, 85–86. [Originally published in 1902.] By permission of The Macmillan Company (New York) and George Allen & Unwin Ltd.

employment, and increase the demand for goods. As a result, the absolute quantity of saving would be as large as before, although it would be smaller in relation to income.

One way to redistribute income is through labor-union action to raise wages, pensions, and other benefits in order to provide a higher standard of life for wage earners. As workers' incomes rise within certain limits, they become more productive and efficient, and total consumption spending increases. Their incomes should not rise, however, beyond the point where their productivity no longer increases. Then the state should step in and appropriate the remaining surplus for public services. If, however, an industry does not produce a surplus return above the competitive level of profits, labor cannot and should not press for higher wages and shorter hours except within the limits of the increasing efficiency of labor. Yet surplus incomes are widely diffused in modern industrial societies, and therefore unions are necessary and useful in diverting rents, excessive interest and profit, and other "unearned" income into wages.

Historically the labor movement, Hobson said, has been at best a clumsy and an unreliable instrument for redistributing income, especially as the poorest workers get the least while the aristocracy of labor gets the most. Much more effective is reliance on the state to achieve a more equitable and more socially advantageous distribution of wealth. Such public intervention takes three main forms: government regulation of industry, government operation of industry, and taxation in order to raise revenue for public consumption.

Government regulation includes all legal powers to control private industry, thereby diverting surplus income into wages or other expenses connected with improved conditions of the workers. This includes minimum wage enactments, workmen's compensation laws, limited hours of labor, improved sanitation, etc.

Government operation of industry is suitable where monopolies develop, or where public convenience requires it. There is a growing tendency for the state to assume ownership and control of transportation, communication, mineral resources, banking, insurance, water, gas, and electricity. These are industries in which large surplus profits are typical, and their socialization would mean the socialization of these profits. This kind of socialism would still leave wide areas in the economy under private enterprise, so that individual initiative would have large opportunities to serve society. Socialism cannot maintain liberty of research and personal freedom of creative expression, because human nature is too acquisitive and self-assertive. Therefore routine, unskilled industries form the right sphere for socialism, and the skilled industries for private enterprise. No wonder Hobson, in spite of his sympathies with the Labour Party, did not feel "at home in a body governed by trade union members and their finance, and intellectually led by full-blooded Socialists."

When the private sector generates too high incomes, the state should tax away the surplus. The largest and therefore the most objectionable incomes are derived from economic rent of land, and from excessive interest and profits that occur mainly when competition gives way to monopoly. This kind of taxation would strike at the root of the maladies of depression and imperialism. The money received by the state should be used to provide such necessary social services as health and education. In bad times it could be used to pay for public works. The very fact that public works that are noncompetitive with private enterprise increase total employment shows that the government is taking up funds that otherwise would not be spent; it cures the disease of oversaving.

Hobson amplified his system of welfare economics with a criticism of the valuation of cost and utility by orthodox theorists in terms of money. He preferred a "human valuation" of industry in terms of human effort and satisfaction. The standard of human well-being should replace the monetary standard of wealth. A dollar's worth of cheap gin or hand-made lace sweated out of peasant women at the cost of their eyesight should not be given the same weight as a dollar's worth of good prose or wholesome bread. A day of labor in a factory costs much more in terms of human sacrifice than a day of pleasurable artistic creation. The human cost of saving arises only when it is done by people of small incomes; there is no sacrifice involved in the saving practiced by the rich. We should be concerned, he said, with the human interpretation or valuation of industry by asking two questions about the goods we produce: What are the net human costs involved in their production? What are the net human utilities involved in their consumption? Society should distribute the costs of production according to the ability of individuals to bear these costs, and it should distribute the produced goods among consumers according to their capacity to derive utility from them. Human costs would thereby be minimized and utilities maximized. This is an interesting contrast to Bentham and his followers, who believed that all consumption represented utility and all work disutility.

Hobson's position is secure in the history of economic thought. He was a pioneer welfare economist, and he lived to see some of his ideas on the causes and remedies for depressions embodied in a much more sophisticated way in the Keynesian system.

Pigou

ARTHUR CECIL PIGOU (1877–1959) succeeded Marshall in the chair of political economy at Cambridge University in 1908, and he held this position until his retirement in 1943. He was the leading neoclassical economist after the death of his predecessor. Like Marshall, Pigou expressed humanitarian impulses toward the poor, and he hoped that economic science would lead to social improvement. In his own cautious way, Pigou was willing to go further than Marshall in allowing a role for the government in ameliorating certain undesirable features of society.

Pigou hoped to provide the theoretical basis for statesmen to enact measures that promoted welfare. As an economist, he was concerned with *economic* welfare. This he defined as "that part of social welfare that can be brought directly or indirectly into relation with the measuring-rod of money."

Basing himself on Jevons' and Marshall's principle of the diminishing marginal utility of money as more is acquired, Pigou asserted that the greater equality of incomes under certain conditions could increase economic welfare.

Any transference of income from a relatively rich man to a relatively poor man of similar temperament, since it enables more intense wants to be satisfied at the expense of less intense wants, must increase the aggregate sum of satisfaction. The old "law of diminishing utility" thus leads securely to the proposition: Any cause which increases the absolute share of real income in the hands of the poor, provided that it does not lead to a contraction in the size of the national dividend from any point of view, will, in general, increase economic welfare.*

Pigou's most significant deviation from orthodox theory lay in his abandoning the idea that what was good for the individual was necessarily good for society, or that total welfare was simply the summation of all individuals' welfare. He distinguished between social and private marginal costs and benefits. The private marginal cost of a commodity or service is the expense the producer incurs in making one more unit; the social marginal cost is the expense or damage to society as the consequence of producing that unit of product. Private marginal benefit is measured by the selling price of the commodity; social marginal benefit is the total benefit society gets from the production of an added unit.

These distinctions are significant because costs may be thrown upon people who are not directly concerned, so that social costs may be greater than private costs; in such a situation, the private marginal net product is greater than the social marginal net product. For example, sparks from railway engines may do damage to surrounding woods without their owners being compensated for the damage. If an entrepreneur builds a factory in a residential district, he thereby destroys much of the value of other people's

* A. C. Pigou, *The Economics of Welfare*, 4th ed. (London, 1932), p. 89. [Originally published in 1920.]

property. The increased sale of intoxicating beverages is profitable to the distiller and the brewer, but increased social cost is incurred when more policemen and prisons become necessary. If the excessive work of women in factories injures the health and well-being of their children, private employers get the benefits of cheap labor while society has to bear the burden of increased welfare costs.

There are opposite cases, said Pigou, where some of the benefits of private actions will spill over to society's benefit, and the person who rendered the benefit will not be compensated for it; then the social marginal net product will exceed the private marginal net product. For example, the expansion of one firm in an industry may give rise to external economies in the industry as a whole that will reduce the costs of production of other firms. Private investment in afforestation will benefit surrounding property owners. Preventing smoke from factory chimneys will benefit the community at large much more than it will benefit the factory-owner. Scientific research is generally of greater value to society than to the researcher and inventor, although the patent laws aim at bringing private and social marginal net products more closely together.

The above examples can occur even under conditions of "simple competition." Pigou, even before Chamberlin and Robinson published their works in 1933, recognized in monopolistic competition another source of divergence between social and private net products.

Where conditions of monopolistic competition—competition, that is to say, between several sellers each producing a considerable proportion of the aggregate output—are present, the way is opened up for a new kind of investment. This consists in competitive advertisement directed to the sole purpose of transferring the demand for a given commodity from one source of supply to another. There is, indeed, little opportunity for this as regards goods of a kind whose quality is uniform and, as with salt, lumber or grain, can be easily tested; but, where quality cannot be easily tested, and especially where goods are sold in small quantities, which can readily be put into distinctive packages for the use of retail customers, there is plenty of opportunity.*

Some advertising, Pigou believed, fulfills a social purpose by being informative. Much of it, however, is strictly competitive, and its social net product is therefore zero or negative.

In general, industries whose private costs are too low become too large; industries with too low a private gain, too small. Thus we may have too much investment and employment in sweated industries and too little in schools and hospitals. Pigou showed that the success of a business or the outcome of competition is not necessarily to the advantage of society.

One of the problems of society arises, said Pigou, because of people's at-

* *Ibid.*, p. 196.

titude toward the future. We prefer present rather than future satisfactions of equal magnitude because our telescopic faculty is defective, and we therefore see future pleasures on a diminished scale. This reveals a far-reaching economic disharmony, for people distribute their resources between the present, the near future, and the remote future on the basis of a wholly irrational preference. As a consequence, efforts directed toward the remote future are starved in comparison with those directed to the near future, while these in turn are starved relative to efforts directed toward the present. The creation of new capital is checked, and people are encouraged to use up existing capital to such a degree that larger future advantages are sacrificed for smaller present ones. Natural resources are consumed more quickly and more wastefully because future satisfactions are underrated.

Pigou concluded that any government intervention that strengthens the tendency of people to devote too much of their resources to present use and too little to future use will diminish economic welfare. Any tax on saving should therefore be condemned, including property taxes, death duties, and progressive income taxes, if we wish to maximize economic welfare. Heavy taxes on consumption are preferable, except that we may wish to balance equity towards low-income people against the desirability of increased saving.

Pigou thus reached a conclusion about saving that was diametrically opposed to that of Hobson. Imbued with the orthodox idea of an economy's tendency toward full employment, Pigou wanted to increase saving in order to promote economic growth. Believing that all income is automatically spent on consumption or investment, he was not concerned with Hobson's problem of excessive saving. He did make some important contributions to the analysis of business fluctuations, but they were kept out of his discussion of the welfare implications of saving and consuming.

In general, said Pigou, industrialists are interested only in the private, not in the social, net product of their operations. If private and social net products happen to coincide, the free play of self-interest, so far as it is not hampered by ignorance, will tend to raise economic welfare to a maximum. Wherever they do not coincide, and that occurs frequently, government intervention can increase welfare. Alcoholic drinks and competitive advertising may legitimately be taxed; building and zoning laws may be enacted; public subsidies to research may be granted; and laws against false weights and measures, the adulteration of foods, and fraudulent promotions may be enforced. Government conservation measures are commendable on the same basis of increasing economic welfare. The task of government is to bring into equality private marginal net cost and social marginal net cost by subsidies, taxes, or legal regulation.

Pigou insisted that interpersonal comparisons of satisfactions *can* properly be made if we are concerned with typical people of the same race and brought up in the same country. In this sense he was more of a reformer than those "purely scientific" economists who daintily abjure value judgments and proclaim the impossibility of comparisons of satisfactions among different people.

Clark

JOHN MAURICE CLARK (born 1884), the son of John Bates Clark, was educated at Amherst College and Columbia University, and he ultimately occupied the position of professor of economics at Columbia from which his father had retired. His intellectual heritage came from many men, including his father, Veblen, Hobson, and Pigou. Clark, starting where his father left off with static theory, became a leading exponent of a realistic, dynamic economics. He worked toward a fusion of neoclassical and institutional economics, and he was an important precursor of the Keynesian system. Many significant contributions flowed from his probing mind. In 1923 he published a classic titled *Studies in the Economics of Overhead Costs*. Three years later he published the first edition of his *Social Control of Business*. The National Bureau of Economic Research issued his *Strategic Factors in Business Cycles* in 1934. At a much earlier date, however, in 1917, he had published his famous article in the *Journal of Political Economy* titled "Business Acceleration and the Law of Demand." In this paper Clark developed the quantitative relationships between changes in the demand for final goods and the magnified changes they cause in the demand for machinery and raw materials. The principle of acceleration has become an integral part of the Keynesian analysis of fluctuations. In his study of business cycles, Clark concluded that the independent action of businessmen cannot eliminate fluctuations, but collective economic action can.

Clark followed Wesley C. Mitchell as the second recipient (in 1952) of the Walker Medal, awarded at intervals of at least five years by the American Economic Association to the most distinguished living American economist.

Clark defined social control as any instance when the "individual is forced or persuaded to act in the interest of any group of which he is a member rather than in his own personal interest." The necessity for social control was woven into his "social economics." This is an economics that seeks to interpret and improve the functioning of a pluralistic economy that embraces coexistence among government enterprises, government-controlled industries, large private corporate enterprises, and small-scale businesses.

Clark held that businessmen generally are responsible, but unless they seek to serve their own interests in the narrowest sense, competition will drive them to the wall. If nineteen businessmen want good conditions, they may be coerced by a twentieth competitor who is unscrupulous. Therefore in his system of social economics, social control is required to serve the general welfare. In a journal article published as early as 1916 he wrote:

By comparison with the scope of responsibility as it has been conceived and presented here the laissez-faire economics may well be characterized as the economics of irresponsibility, and the business system of free contract is also a system of irresponsibility when judged by the same standard. Of static theory we must simply say that while it does not deny social responsibilities it does to a large extent ignore them. . . .

Meanwhile the demand for control has grown with amazing speed, and in every direction experiments are being tried. This should properly be regarded as a recognition of special kinds of responsibility which the business economics leaves out of account and which the machinery of free contract furnishes no way of bringing home to the proper persons. But instead, this regulation is looked on by too many as a phase of the old irresponsible struggle, merely translated from the field of business into the field of politics. It is under suspicion as being mere irresponsible class legislation, and unfortunately the suspicion has some justification.

Hence employers often feel either contemptuous or deeply injured when laws begin to interfere with customary business practices, and when investigating committees ask prying questions which imply a demand for a righteousness that shall exceed the righteousness of the scribes and Pharisees. Business men with this point of view oppose the growth of public control with a resistance that is now adroit and now stubborn but nearly always powerful. The economics of control is at war with the economics of irresponsibility. . . .

To the extent that each of us is a factor in economic evolution, be it only that his presence adds one member to the population, he shares in all the increasing difficulties which economic evolution brings with it. He cannot do anything so far-reaching as building a house without affecting other people's property interests for better or for worse. Unless he affects them for the better he is pretty sure to affect them for the worse. And unless he leaves society stronger in its power to master the manifold troubles of modern industry he will leave it relatively weaker by just so much as those troubles have grown in size and complexity. Modern industry gives a new meaning to the text, "He that is not with me is against me," and is constantly showing new ways in which, whether we like it or not, we are our brothers' keepers.*

Clark contrasted the social and individual points of view by showing that what is a variable cost for the firm is an overhead cost from society's stand-

---

* J. Maurice Clark, "The Changing Basis of Economic Responsibility," *Journal of Political Economy*, Vol. 24, No. 3 (March 1916), pp. 218, 219, 224.

point. Labor is the outstanding example. An employer can lay off workers and thereby save a large part of his production costs as he reduces output. Yet workers have to be fed, housed, and clothed even during bad times; their costs of maintenance cannot be avoided when they are unemployed.

For the nation as a whole, its labor power is a fixed asset and any failure to utilize it is just as definite a loss as failure to utilize a mechanical plant. It pays, socially, to utilize labor so long as it produces anything toward its own necessary upkeep, which must be met somehow in the long run. Thus social cost-accounting shows a gain from employing labor in a slack season, even if the product will not pay regular day wages to the laborers: social accounting shows a gain where private accounting would show a loss.*

If wages could be converted into an overhead cost for the employer, said Clark, production would become more regularized. A guaranteed annual wage might accomplish this.

Raw materials, like labor, are a variable cost for the purchasers but an overhead cost for their original producers and therefore for society as a whole. Producers of raw materials invest funds in their enterprises, and they themselves must be maintained through good and bad times. The cattle-raiser, for example, must pay interest on his mortgage, meet his property-tax payments, allow for maintenance and depreciation on his buildings, machinery, and livestock, and maintain himself and his family. These are all overhead costs, yet the cost of live cattle becomes a variable cost to the packing house that buys them. This shifting of costs distorts economic calculations when it comes to deciding whether it is economically worthwhile to produce goods or not. Every producer has an incentive to maintain production, but the strength of his incentive is measured by his own overhead costs, not by the total overhead costs involved in the whole process from beginning to end of the chain of operations and exchanges.

Clark felt that in seeking solutions to our economic problems, no single measure, agency, or group could be held responsible for the whole task. We require a coordinated effort by many agencies, including government, banking, insurance, industry, and labor. The individual business should plan steadier production, producing goods for inventory in slow times. This would tend to fill the depression hollow of the business-cycle curve. The peak of the curve could be lopped off by requiring that the employer bear some responsibility for the overhead cost of casual labor he might hire; this would make him reluctant to handle his peak demand in this manner until he had tried his best to provide for it with his normal labor supply.

* J. Maurice Clark, *Studies in the Economics of Overhead Costs* (Chicago, 1923), p. 350.

In addition, broad social and governmental programs, including public works, should be used to promote stability.

In recent writing Clark conceded that in spite of the many social controls that have been enacted, "the existing system is far from perfect on the score of efficiency." Yet collectivism, he said, does not offer the complete answer. A collectivist dictatorship of the Russian type can be ruthlessly efficient, though it may sacrifice the higher and more creative forms of efficiency. A democratic collectivism would also sacrifice efficiency and technical progress, perhaps as much as or more than our present system. Worst of all, even a democratic collectivism would reduce personal liberty, because a central administrative authority would have ultimate power over the livelihood of every citizen. Our present system creates difficulties for radical nonconformists; the problem would become more serious if there were in effect only one employer. This argument against collectivism, said Clark, should not be taken as a brief for preserving the existing system.

Existing systems are not preserved unchanged, no matter what we decide about them. They change of themselves, if they are not altered by outside forces; and our present system is not exempt from this law. No single form of existing business liberty is sacred. But this argument is a brief for continuing to struggle onward with a system embodying the principle of liberty, economic as well as personal, in spite of the difficulties. This does not offer a quick cure of basic evils. It offers rather a prospect of generations of effort, with patience, persistence, and tolerance, to strike a sane balance between liberty and control, and to reduce our worst evils to tolerable proportions by a process of adjustment, using voluntary means to the utmost of their capacity, the whole being subject to free discussion, not directed by arbitrary fiat and suppression of dissent.

It is conceivable that at some point in such a process we might achieve enough co-ordination to reduce unemployment to minor proportions and to maintain stability in other respects without making everyone an employee of the state. At that point it would make little difference whether we called the system "socialistic" or not. "Socialism" of such a sort, reached by such a process, could still leave room for true personal liberty: it could still be democratic. But this can only be attained by a process that does not go too fast for business to adjust itself without catastrophic breakdown or violent revolution. If such a process is to continue, we must avoid committing ourselves to the experiment that would mean the end of free experimentation.*

Clark, as a social philosopher, was willing to consider and express value judgments, provocative as this attitude may have been. Opinions about how to promote man's well-being have been expressed freely by economists from Adam Smith's time, and earlier, to the present day. Those economists who

* J. Maurice Clark, *Economic Institutions and Human Welfare* (New York, 1957), pp. 100–01.

insist on an austere and Olympian disassociation from social objectives in effect endorse the status quo. One cannot write tax laws or pass on school budgets without some concept of what is welfare and how to promote it. Nor can a man readily separate and compartmentalize his scientific economic analysis from his ideas of good and bad, better and worse. The economist who spells out his predilections and his preferences can be as rigorously scientific as the economist who eschews ideas about maximizing welfare. Clark, like Hobson and Pigou, was willing to consider social policy that aimed at maximizing welfare.

CHAPTER 22

The Keynesian School

THE KEYNESIAN system of ideas represents, up to the present, the last great school of economic thought. It arose out of the neoclassical or marginalist school, with Keynes himself being steeped in the Marshallian tradition. Although Keynes sharply criticized certain aspects of neoclassical economics, which he lumped together with Ricardian doctrines under the heading of "classical" economics, he himself used many of the postulates and methods of neoclassicism. His system was based on a subjective, psychological approach, and it was permeated with marginalist concepts, including static equilibrium economics. He disassociated himself from any attacks on the neoclassical theory of value and distribution.

John Maynard Keynes (1883–1946) was the son of eminently intellectual parents who survived him. His father was John Neville Keynes, outstanding logician and political economist. His mother, who was interested in public affairs and social work, was a justice of the peace, alderman, and mayor of Cambridge. Among Keynes's teachers at Cambridge were Marshall and Pigou, both of whom recognized his brilliance. At twenty-eight years of age, Keynes became editor of the *Economic Journal*. He also managed the investments of its publisher, the Royal Economic Society, with an unusual degree of success. The finances of King's College of Cambridge University likewise were phenomenally profitable under his guidance. His own considerable fortune of a half a million pounds was accumulated mainly through dealing in foreign currencies and commodities. He was one of the speculators about whom he wrote:

Speculators may do no harm as bubbles on a steady stream of enterprise. But the position is serious when enterprise becomes the bubble on a whirlpool of speculation. When the capital development of a country becomes a by-product of the activities of a casino, the job is likely to be ill-done. The measure of success attained by Wall Street, regarded as an institution of which the proper social purpose is to direct new investment into the most profitable channels in terms of future yield, cannot be claimed as one of the outstanding triumphs of *laissez-faire* capitalism—which is not surprising, if I am right in thinking that the best brains of Wall Street have been in fact directed towards a different object.*

Keynes was an important figure both in the world of practical affairs and in academic life. He was chairman of the board of a life insurance company, he served as director of other companies, and he was on the governing body of the Bank of England. In addition to being a financier, he was a high government official, a scholar writing many theoretical works, a journalist, a connoisseur and supporter of the arts, and a college teacher at Cambridge. At the peace conference after World War I he was the principal representative of the British Treasury, with power to speak for the chancellor of the exchequer. As the result of his experiences at the Paris negotiations and his strong opposition to the peace settlement that was forced upon Germany, he resigned his official position in 1919 and wrote his polemical *The Economic Consequences of the Peace.* In 1940 he rejoined the Treasury to guide Britain through the difficulties of war finance. He was his country's chief negotiator in organizing the International Monetary Fund and the International Bank for Reconstruction and Development, and in obtaining the United States postwar loan to Britain. He became a baron in 1942, and to those of his friends who criticized his accepting the title, his joking defense was, "I had to do it in order to get servants."

After a brief summary overview of the Keynesian school, we will examine in greater detail some of its major ideas.

Overview of the Keynesian School

The social background of the school. Keynes's ideas grew out of the fearful depression of the 1930's, the worst the Western world had ever known in modern times. Yet the roots of his ideas can be traced back earlier than 1929. The work of many economists, including that of Mitchell and his associates in the National Bureau of Economic Research, was cast in the framework of aggregative economics or macroeconomics rather than the microeconomics of the neoclassical school. This was also the approach adopted by Keynes. World War I and the economic controls that were adopted required an over-all view of the economy. The growth of large-scale industrial production and trade made the economy more susceptible to statistical measurement and control, thereby making the inductive, ag-

---

* John Maynard Keynes, *The General Theory of Employment, Interest, and Money* (New York, 1936), p. 159.

gregative approach more feasible than in the past. This approach became more necessary as the idea pervaded society that something should be done by government about unemployment.

Keynesian thinking also had its roots in the spreading anxiety about secular stagnation. Somehow the mature private-enterprise economies of the Western world did not seem to be so vigorous after World War I as they had been before. The rate of population growth was declining; most of the world had already been colonized, and there seemed to be no room for further geographic expansion; production seemed to be outrunning consumption as incomes and savings rose; there were no new inventions visible like the steam engine, the railroad, electricity, and the automobile that would call forth a burst of new and vast capital investments as in the past; whatever new ways of doing things did develop seemed as likely as not to save capital, thereby reducing investment expenditures; the decline of vigorous price competition reduced the rate of replacement of old machinery with new and better machines; as capital investment increased and depreciation allowances grew larger, the economy was dragged downward when the accumulated depreciation funds were not spent quickly enough. These were the major ideas of secular stagnation that came to the fore after World War I, and especially after 1929. They were based in part on the works of Marx, Hobson, Veblen and others, and in part on actual observations and historical studies.

The essence of the Keynesian school. The major principles of Keynesian economics will be discussed later in this chapter under three headings. First, the immediate determinants of income and employment will be explored. Keynes assumed that there is a high correlation between national income and the level of employment. This of course is not necessarily true. Large investments in labor-saving capital, for example, can cause real national output and income to rise more rapidly than employment. It is even possible for the two variables to move in opposite directions. Keynes, however, was concerned mainly with the short run; he defended this with the quip, "In the long run we are all dead." In the short run we can neglect technological change, and then we can agree that the level of income determines the level of employment, and the two can be used synonymously and interchangeably.

The immediate determinants of income and employment are consumption and investment spending. Every dollar spent on final goods and services, either for consumption or investment, becomes income. If we include government, taxation represents a deduction from the income stream and therefore a potential deduction from consumption and investment spending. Government spending constitutes an addition to total spending.

The second theme of the Keynesian system to be discussed will be the ultimate determinants of income and employment, or the determinants of consumption and investment spending. Keynes assumed that consumption is a variable determined by the size of income. That is, consumption spending is a stable proportion of income at each level of income, and the proportion falls as income rises. This is the "consumption function," based on the psychological propensity to consume. It means that at any income level, people tend to spend a certain fixed proportion of income on consumption. Is it circular reasoning to argue that income depends in part on consumption spending, and the level of consumption spending depends on income? Not at all. The propensity to consume is a schedule, a whole series of values at different levels of income, and Keynes assumed that it is independent and stable in the short run. The level of consumption varies with income; income varies because the inducement to invest changes.

Investment spending is determined by the rate of interest and the "marginal efficiency of capital," or the expected rate of return over cost on new investments. The rate of interest depends on liquidity preference and the quantity of money. The marginal efficiency of capital depends on the expectations of future profits and the supply price of capital assets. The three basic psychological influences on income and employment are, therefore, the propensity to consume, the desire for liquid assets, and the expected profits from new investments. The first of these psychological influences is most stable, thought Keynes, and therefore does not cause fluctuations; the third is the least stable and one of the greatest causes of depressions.

The third heading in our discussion will be Keynes's idea that laissez faire is obsolete, and the government should intervene actively to promote full employment. This it could do by forcing down the rate of interest, thereby stimulating investment; by increased government deficit spending; and by redistributing income in order to raise the expenditures on consumption.

As early as 1926 Keynes published a little book attacking laissez faire, his hope being that by regulating capitalism it could be preserved. He accused orthodox economics of not counting the cost of the ruthless struggle that brings the most successful profit-makers to the top by bankrupting the less efficient. The giraffes with the longest necks starve out those whose necks are shorter.

If we have the welfare of the giraffes at heart, we must not overlook the sufferings of the shorter necks who are starved out, or the sweet leaves which fall to the ground and are trampled underfoot in the struggle, or the overfeeding of the long-necked ones, or the evil look of anxiety or struggling greediness which overcasts the mild faces of the herd. . . .

The important thing for Government is not to do things which individuals are doing already, and to do them a little better or a little worse; but to do those things which at present are not done at all.*

The evils of our time, Keynes went on to say, are the fruits of risk, uncertainty, and ignorance. Big business is often a lottery because some individuals are able to take advantage of ignorance and uncertainty. The consequences are great inequalities of wealth, unemployment of labor, disappointment of reasonable business expectations, and impairment of efficiency and production.

Yet the cure lies outside the operations of individuals; it may even be to the interest of individuals to aggravate the disease. I believe that the cure for these things is partly to be sought in the deliberate control of the currency and of credit by a central institution, and partly in the collection and dissemination on a great scale of data relating to the business situation. . . . These measures would involve Society in exercising directive intelligence through some appropriate organ of action over many of the inner intricacies of private business, yet it would leave private initiative and enterprise unhindered. . . .

Devotees of Capitalism are often unduly conservative, and reject reforms in its technique, which might really strengthen and preserve it, for fear that they may prove to be first steps away from Capitalism itself. . . . For my part, I think that Capitalism, wisely managed, can probably be made more efficient for attaining economic ends than any alternative system yet in sight, but that in itself it is in many ways extremely objectionable. Our problem is to work out a social organisation which shall be as efficient as possible without offending our notions of a satisfactory way of life.†

Keynes did not depart from these views during the remaining two decades of his life.

What groups of people did the Keynesian school serve or seek to serve? The great success of Keynesian economics came partly because it offered something for almost everybody, and it rationalized what was already being done out of necessity. Society as a whole gains from full or fuller employment, and those individuals or groups who lose because of it can easily be ignored. Labor favored the liberalism of the Keynesian approach, and counterdepression measures are always very much to its liking. Businessmen benefited from government contracts and government stimuli to get the economy out of deep depression. Bankers, when they had huge excess reserves in the 1930's, found a vast and profitable area for investment in government bonds, and government controls gave the banking system

* John Maynard Keynes, *The End of Laissez-Faire* (London, 1926), pp. 33–34, 46–47.
† *Ibid.*, pp. 47–48, 52–53.

liquidity, security, and stability. Reformers and intellectuals enjoyed vastly increased employment in the government service, and they could pursue with crusading zeal the mild, safe, and sane reforms that grew out of Keynesian thinking. Farmers came to rely heavily on government subsidies and regulations; their spokesmen even had a crude theory of the multiplier long before it was incorporated into the Keynesian system. In defending government intervention in order to raise farmers' incomes, they claimed that each dollar received by the farmer generated a seven-dollar increase in national income through the re-spending of the farmer's increased receipts.

How was the Keynesian school valid, useful, or correct in its time? The Keynesian approach is immensely useful even to those who do not accept the Keynesian remedies for depression. It provided the basis for national-income accounting, and it stimulated a vast and fruitful effort at inductive studies of the real world. The methodology is applicable to inflation as well as to depression, to war and to peace, to international economics as well as to a closed national economy, to public finance and to business-cycle studies. Keynes demolished the classical and marginalist assumption that a private-enterprise system tends to be self-adjusting at full employment.

Keynes was not the first to discover that as income rises in the short run, consumption will rise more slowly. He was the first, however, to integrate this principle with other relevant ideas to formulate a general theory of income and employment. He also was one of a long line of dissident economists who denied J. B. Say's principle that supply creates its own demand. On the contrary, said Keynes, all of the costs of production (which become income to the owners of factors of production) need not necessarily be spent in the aggregate on purchasing the product. Nor will any abstention from consumption spending necessarily increase investment.

The fruitfulness of Keynes's ideas can be illustrated by the light they cast on a problem that puzzled the great authority on international trade, Harvard professor Frank W. Taussig. He developed the idea that gold movements led to equilibrium in international trade by influencing prices and money wages. Based on the quantity theory of money, an inflow of gold into a country causes prices and money wages to rise, thereby stimulating imports, reducing exports, and causing the flow of gold to be reversed. An outflow of gold will cause prices and money wages to fall, thereby reducing imports, increasing exports and reversing the outflow of gold. Yet Taussig was amazed at

the closeness and rapidity with which the varying balance of payments has found its expression in the varying balance of trade. The actual merchandise movements seem to have been adjusted to the shifting balance of payments with surprising exactness and speed. The process which our theory contemplates—the initial flow of specie when there is a burst of loans; the fall of prices in the lending country, rise in the borrowing country; the eventual increased movement of merchandise out of the one and into the other—all this can hardly be expected to take place smoothly and quickly. Yet no signs of disturbance are to be observed such as the theoretic analysis previses; and some recurring phenomena are of a kind not contemplated by theory at all. . . . It must be confessed that here we have phenomena not fully understood.*

The new theory of the balance of payments, which partly supplemented and partly superseded the old price specie-flow mechanism, was a direct outgrowth of Keynes's *General Theory of Employment, Interest, and Money*, with Mrs. Joan Robinson and others playing a leading part. If country *A* increases its imports from *B*, its income and employment fall while *B*'s rise. When a country's income rises, it imports more, and when income falls it reduces imports. Therefore falling incomes in *A* will curtail imports from *B*, and rising incomes in *B* will increase imports from *A*. The imbalance in trade will be partly or completely self-correcting, even without gold movements. Keynes stimulated the thinking that solved Taussig's uncertainties.

Keynes geared economic theory to policy-making. Apparently there is at least some truth to the stagnationists' thesis that a mature private-enterprise economy is not so buoyant and viable as in its youth—unless something is done about it. World wars, worldwide depressions, and the growing complications of modern economic life undermined laissez faire. Demands that something be done about fluctuations grew more insistent, and Keynes provided both a program and a theoretical justification for it.

The neoclassical idea that reductions in money wages would overcome a depression could be questioned from the humanitarian or welfare point of view, for there are alternative ways to seek that end. More important, it was bad economics according to Keynes. He held that a single firm could increase sales and employment through wage cuts, for the demand for its product would remain unaffected. A whole economy, however, cannot easily increase sales by cutting wages (assuming it is isolated from international trade), for wages are a source of demand for goods as well as a cost of production. If wages were to begin to fall, expectations would be generated that they will fall still further; this would cause a postponement of investment spending, thereby making the depression worse. If falling wages were to result in falling prices, this would again worsen matters, because the real burden of debts would increase, thereby transferring wealth from the entrepreneur to the *rentier;* and profit margins would become smaller, thus choking off new investments. As wage-earners be-

* F. W. Taussig, *International Trade* (New York, 1927), p. 239.

come worse off through wage cuts and employers better off, the propensity to consume would be diminished. As an outstandingly practical man, Keynes also objected to wage cuts because they would touch off labor troubles. He was quite successful in converting people to the idea that wage policy should be divorced from counterdepression policy; there are other, better ways to seek full employment.

Keynes was a leading advocate of and negotiator for international financial cooperation during and after World War II. He sacrificed his health and shortened his life in this crusade, for his strenuous activities hastened a fatal heart attack. He repudiated the old laissez faire gold standard system; in the 1930's, in the spirit of nationalism, he argued that a country, through protectionism, could insulate itself from the rest of the world in unilaterally pursuing its own full-employment policies. Yet even in 1936 he expressed the belief that if nations learned to provide themselves with full employment through their domestic policies, and if population growth were limited, an international harmony of interests might prevail. The struggle over export markets could be replaced by an unimpeded exchange of goods and international lending under conditions of mutual advantage. Keynes lived to see these aspirations realized in part through the financial organizations of the United Nations that he helped to create.

How did the Keynesian school outlive its usefulness? New schools of economic thought will undoubtedly arise in the future to deal with old and new problems in a new theoretical framework. No new system of ideas, however, has yet appeared on the horizon to challenge the dominant Keynesian school. This school has therefore not outlived its usefulness. We can nevertheless point out certain weaknesses and inadequacies embodied in its ideas.

The short-run, static thinking of Keynes and some of his followers led to an exaggeration of the trend toward secular stagnation. They assumed a stable consumption function. If it were true that the higher the income the smaller the percentage spent on consumption, historically rising incomes would enormously multiply our difficulties. The Keynesian analysis of consumption is apparently true for the short run. At any moment in time, poorer people spend a larger proportion of their incomes on consumption than wealthier people. Historically, however, as national and per capita incomes have risen, the percentage spent on consumption has remained fairly stable. We learn how to live up to our rising incomes as new products are developed and new desires evoked. We have to spend more on consumption to keep up with or exceed our neighbors if they are spending more also. Yet we should recognize that there is some possible validity to the stagnation thesis, for even though the *percentages* consumed and saved out of disposable income tend to remain stable in the long run as income rises, the *amount* of saving out of income grows and may not be invested easily.

Static thinking led to excessive pessimism about declining investment opportunities and falling rates of profit. Keynes, like many economists before him, thought that the profitability of new investment would decline as the most profitable projects were undertaken first, leaving for later exploitation those projects which were less attractive.

Ancient Egypt was doubly fortunate, and doubtless owed to this its fabled wealth, in that it possessed *two* activities, namely, pyramid-building as well as the search for the precious metals, the fruits of which, since they could not serve the needs of man by being consumed, did not stale with abundance. The Middle Ages built cathedrals and sang dirges. Two pyramids, two masses for the dead, are twice as good as one; but not so two railways from London to York.*

The stagnationists underestimated the possibilities of technological change and the new capital investments it would stimulate.

Keynes was narrowly provincial with respect to both time and space. He seemed to think that unemployment might have become a problem in ancient Egypt and in the middle ages were it not for building pyramids and cathedrals. His analysis of mercantilism strongly implied that the problems of 1636 were the same as those of 1936. "There has been a chronic tendency throughout human history," said Keynes, "for the propensity to save to be stronger than the inducement to invest." He thought that at all times the weakness of the inducement to invest had been the key to the economic problem, and this the mercantilists recognized in their day. Keynes, like Ricardo, uncritically fell into the assumption that the spirit of capitalism had dominated the subsistence, agricultural economies of the past; and that, even though they were not basically money-using economies, they calculated profit, loss, investment, etc., as we do.

So much for Keynes's provincialism in time. He and many of his followers were provincial in space in believing that their economics was applicable to all countries. The doctrines of excessive saving and inadequate consumption spending do not apply to the underdeveloped areas, where inadequate saving is one of the factors limiting the growth of investment and income. In the poor countries, not involuntary but disguised unemployment is the major symptom of economic malaise. Keynes ridiculed the Victorian virtues of abstinence and thriftiness, but this bias against saving would be harmful if transplanted to the non-industrialized countries.

Keynes, in his concern with short-run problems, denied the importance

* Keynes, *The General Theory of Employment, Interest, and Money*, p. 131.

of economic growth of industrialized countries—a subject that has risen in most people's list of significant problems. He thought that if the propensity to consume were to be raised sufficiently,

full employment can be reached with a rate of accumulation little greater than at present. In this event a scheme for the higher taxation of large incomes and inheritances might be open to the objection that it would lead to full employment with a rate of accumulation which was reduced considerably below the current level. I must not be supposed to deny the possibility, or even the probability, of this outcome. For in such matters it is rash to predict how the average man will react to a changed environment. If, however, it should prove easy to secure an approximation to full employment with a rate of accumulation not much greater than at present, an outstanding problem will at least have been solved. And it would remain for separate decision on what scale and by what means it is right and reasonable to call on the living generation to restrict their consumption, so as to establish, in course of time, a state of full investment for their successors.*

The Keynesians were too blithely willing to accept a slow, steady inflation to stimulate the economy. The idea was that certain sticky costs like property taxes, public-utility charges, and fees of lawyers and accountants would rise more slowly than general prices, thereby increasing profit margins and stimulating investment. The time lag between buying raw materials and selling finished products also would increase profits if prices were rising. Investment in durable goods would be speeded up if their higher future costs were anticipated. Keynes believed that while workers strongly resist reductions in money wages, they do not fight against cuts in real wages through rising prices. With wages also being sticky, rising prices would quicken economic activity.

The Keynesian inflationary remedy has lost its charm. Since World War II there has been a pronounced repudiation of this idea by increasing numbers of people for many reasons. Wage costs are no longer sticky when unions keep up with and anticipate rising prices in presenting their wage demands. The cry against inflation has become a cry against high government budgets, high taxes, welfare spending, and the redistribution of income through government fiscal policy. A continuing inflation that is anticipated and discounted becomes dangerous; government and corporate bonds become more difficult to sell, interest rates rise, and stock prices increase to dangerously high levels. An inflation that exceeds that of the rest of the world makes it more difficult to export goods, and imports increase. Finally, an anti-inflation stand wins much support among the millions of people whose wealth and income are impaired through rising prices.

* *Ibid.*, p. 377.

For these reasons, the Keynesian propensity toward inflation has definitely lost popularity during the last decade or two.

The Keynesian school can be criticized on the ground that it too readily accepted wasteful government deficit spending. Keynes, to be sure, preferred that the state finance useful rather than useless projects. He recognized that the business community might condemn useful public works if they were competitive with private enterprise; in such a situation wasteful spending was preferred to serviceable projects, and this, he said, was much better than doing nothing at all. It is true, of course, that if increased government deficit spending scares off private investment, the effect of government spending is weakened or nullified.

When involuntary unemployment exists, the marginal disutility of labour is necessarily less than the utility of the marginal product. Indeed it may be much less. For a man who has been long unemployed some measure of labour, instead of involving disutility, may have a positive utility. If this is accepted, the above reasoning shows how "wasteful" loan expenditure may nevertheless enrich the community on balance. Pyramid-building, earthquakes, even wars may serve to increase wealth, if the education of our statesmen on the principles of the classical economics stands in the way of anything better.

It is curious how common sense, wriggling for an escape from absurd conclusions, has been apt to reach a preference for *wholly* "wasteful" forms of loan expenditure rather than for *partly* wasteful forms, which, because they are not wholly wasteful, tend to be judged on strict "business" principles. For example, unemployment relief financed by loans is more readily accepted than the financing of improvements at a charge below the current rate of interest; whilst the form of digging holes in the ground known as gold-mining, which not only adds nothing whatever to the real wealth of the world but involves the disutility of labour, is the most acceptable of all solutions.

If the Treasury were to fill old bottles with banknotes, bury them at suitable depths in disused coal-mines which are then filled up to the surface with town rubbish, and leave it to private enterprise on well-tried principles of *laissez-faire* to dig the notes up again (the right to do so being obtained, of course, by tendering for leases of the note-bearing territory), there need be no more unemployment and, with the help of the repercussions, the real income of the community, and its capital wealth also, would probably become a good deal greater than it actually is. It would, indeed, be more sensible to build houses and the like; but if there are political and practical difficulties in the way of this, the above would be better than nothing.*

Keynes was sympathetic toward private wasteful consumption spending as well as public waste. He defended Bernard Mandeville's *The Fable of the Bees: or, Private Vices, Publick Benefits* (1705), which told of the

* *Ibid.*, pp. 128–29.

appalling plight of a prosperous community that suddenly abandoned luxurious living and amusements in the interests of saving. Professor Calvin B. Hoover of Duke University reported Keynes's whimsey on this matter in a Washington hotel:

While I was preparing to share dinner with Keynes in his hotel suite in Washington in 1934, he genially ridiculed my niceness in selecting a towel from the rack so as not to muss the others. He made a sweep with his arm and knocked two or three on the floor. "I am convinced," he said, jokingly, "that I am more useful to the economy of the U.S.A. by stimulating employment through mussing up these towels than you are by your carefulness in avoiding waste."[*]

Immediate Determinants of Income and Employment

THE immediate determinants of income and employment, ignoring the government for the moment, are consumption and investment spending. Every dollar spent on final goods and services, whether for consumption or investment, generates a dollar of income. If we designate C for consumption, I for investment, and Y for income, then

$$Y = C + I.$$

Saving is the difference between income and consumption. If we were to consider taxation, we would then have to say that saving equals disposable income minus consumption. If we let S stand for saving, then

$$S = Y - C.$$

Solving the two equations, we get

$$S = I.$$

Aggregate savings and investment are equal at all times and at every moment of time. Although they are always equal, they are not always in equilibrium. Changes in the level of income bring saving and investment into a stable balance. The concept of equality between saving and investment proved somewhat puzzling when Keynes first published it in 1936. In fact, in his *Treatise on Money* (1930), he assumed that inequalities between saving and investment are likely because they are done by different people, and they cause changes in the level of income and employment.

We might well ask how saving and investment are necessarily equal at all times. If you save fifty dollars and keep it in the form of cash in your wallet, where is the increased investment to match it? Let us assume that you normally spend your weekly income on consumption, but now you suddenly decide to withhold the fifty dollars. Retailers who stocked goods

* Calvin B. Hoover, "Keynes and the Economic System," *Journal of Political Economy*, Vol. LVI, No. 5 (October 1948), p. 397.

in anticipation of selling them to you suddenly find that their sales have declined and their investment in inventories has increased. Your increased saving of fifty dollars has simultaneously and involuntarily increased retailers' investments by the same amount. Now that their sales have declined, however, they need smaller inventories. They curtail their orders from the manufacturers, people are laid off, and aggregate income and saving fall. Your increased saving is ultimately offset by the reduced saving of other people.

Let us look at another hypothetical case of the instantaneous equality between saving and investment. Suppose an entrepreneur increases his investment through the creation of bank credit, with some unemployment existing in the economy. Where is the increased saving to match the increased investment? The employer hires a worker to produce capital goods. When he pays his employee one hundred dollars on Friday afternoon, the hundred-dollar investment is matched by the hundred dollars of saving in the worker's pocket, for income is saved as long as it is not spent on consumption. If the worker spends a dollar at a tavern on his way home, the tavern-keeper's investment in beer has declined by that amount, and the total new investment and saving now stand at ninety-nine dollars. As inventories are replaced and increased because of rising business, incomes rise and saving rises to match the increased investment originating in the expansion of bank credit.

Suppose banks expand credit when the economy already is fully employed. This will generate inflation. From society's point of view, inflation will curtail consumption by people with fixed income, and reduced consumption means increased saving, which will equal the increased investment. Who are the individuals who will increase their saving as inflation develops? They are those who gain from rising prices, such as debtors, farmers, and entrepreneurs.

We will now introduce the government, thereby disturbing the equality between saving and investment. Let G stand for government spending, and T for taxes. Income is generated by consumption, investment and government spending. Therefore

$$Y = C + I + G.$$

Saving is what is left out of income after consumption expenditures and tax payments are deducted. Therefore

$$S = Y - C - T.$$

As a consequence,

$$S + T = I + G$$
$$S = I + (G - T).$$

If government spending is larger than tax receipts, the government has a budget deficit, and $(G - T)$ is positive. Therefore

$$S = I + \text{government deficit.}$$

If government spending is smaller than tax receipts, the government has a surplus and $(G - T)$ is negative. Then

$$S = I - \text{government surplus.}$$

What is the meaning of these equations? We can illustrate their essence with two examples. Suppose people save two billion dollars. One billion is used for private investment, and the other billion goes into government bonds to finance deficit spending. Then saving (2 billion) = investment (1 billion) + government deficit (1 billion).

Suppose now that the government runs a surplus of one billion dollars, and it pays off its bondholders. This sum can now be invested. Saving (1 billion) = investment (2 billion) — government surplus (1 billion).

Keynes assumed that consumption spending depends on income, rising as income rises but not as much, and falling as income falls, but again not as much. Variations in investment spending cause variations in income, which are reinforced by the induced changes in consumption. If investment falls, income falls, saving falls, and saving equals investment at a lower level of income and employment. Rising investment results in higher income, consumption, and saving. Full employment, said Keynes, is only a special case. The general and more typical case is that of underemployment equilibrium.

When consumption and investment spending are inadequate to maintain full employment, the government should be ready to add to the income stream through spending financed by deficits. The government should be the spender of last resort.

Ultimate Determinants of Income and Employment

KEYNES borrowed the theory of the multiplier from R. F. Kahn, his Cambridge colleague, and incorporated it into his general theory. The multiplier measures the effect on income of a change in spending. If we assume with Keynes that the propensity to consume is given and fixed at each level of income, we must look to autonomous changes in investment or government spending, and the multiplier indicates the effect of these changes in spending on income. Let us assume that the marginal propensity to consume at the current level of income is 75 per cent. That is, if people receive an added dollar of income, they will spend an extra seventy-five cents on consumption. An added dollar of investment spending will immediately raise income by a dollar. When three-fourths of that is spent on consumption (with twenty-five cents being saved), income goes up another seventy-five cents. Seventy-five per cent of that addition to income will in turn be spent on consumption, and 25 per cent will be saved. Given enough time, income will be increased by four dollars, consumption will go up three dollars, and saving will rise by one dollar. When the original dollar injected into the income stream is entirely withdrawn again through saving, the effect of the injection will have been completely dissipated.

The size of the multiplier is the reciprocal of the marginal propensity to save. If the marginal propensity to consume is three-fourths, the marginal propensity to save is one-fourth, and the multiplier is four. If the marginal propensity to consume were 60 per cent or three-fifths, the marginal propensity to save would be two-fifths, resulting in a multiplier of two and a half.

One of the two major determinants of investment, Keynes said, is the marginal efficiency of capital. When a man buys an investment or capital asset, he purchases the right to a series of prospective net returns during the life of the asset. A second element to consider is the supply price or the replacement cost of the asset. Keynes defined the marginal efficiency of capital as being equal to that rate of discount which would make the present value of the series of *expected* returns just equal to the supply price of the capital asset. For example, if the present cost of a capital asset is fifty-five hundred dollars, and it is expected to yield an annual return of a thousand dollars for six years, with the assets worth nothing at the end of that time, the marginal efficiency of capital is 2½ per cent. A thousand dollars per year for six years discounted to the present would be worth fifty-five hundred dollars. Alternatively, fifty-five hundred dollars invested at 2½ per cent would yield a return of a thousand dollars each year for six years. The marginal efficiency of capital really is its marginal productivity as a percentage of the original cost of the capital goods, computed over the life of the capital investment and discounted for uncertainty as well as for futurity. Or it is the expected rate of profit of a new investment, not deducting depreciation or explicit and implicit interest costs.

Investments will be made up to the point where the marginal efficiency of capital is equal to the rate of interest. In the above example, the investment would not be undertaken if the rate of interest were 3 per cent, but it would if the rate of interest were 2 per cent.

The marginal efficiency of capital is, of course, highly variable; it fluctuates with every change in people's expectations of future profits from any present investment. If there is increased investment in any given type of capital, said Keynes, the marginal efficiency of capital will tend to fall for two reasons. First, expected profits decline as more and more investments compete with each other. Second, the supply price of capital goods will rise as more is demanded. In the long run, Keynes thought, the first cause is the more significant. The overriding problem lies in the fact that the richer a society grows, the more it saves, the more difficult it becomes to maintain full employment. A private-enterprise economy may have difficulty maintaining adequate investment unless the rate of interest is low enough. If the marginal efficiency of capital is falling more rapidly than the rate of interest because of pessimism, a decline in the rate of interest will not increase investment.

Keynes, in affirming a long-run tendency for the rate of profit to fall, had come to the same conclusion (but in some cases for different reasons) as Smith, Ricardo, Mill, Marx, the marginalists, and Veblen.

The second major determinant of the level of investment, in addition to the marginal efficiency of capital, is the rate of interest. Keynes disagreed with those economists who thought that the rate of interest produced a balance between the demand for saving to be used in new investment and the supply of saving. The rate of interest, he said, cannot be a reward for saving or waiting as such. If a man hoards his savings in cash, he earns no interest. Nor is saving influenced significantly by the rate of interest; it depends much more on the level of income. The rate of interest is a reward for parting with liquidity. It depends on liquidity preference and the quantity of money (currency plus demand deposits). It is the price which equilibrates the desire to hold wealth in the form of cash with the available quantity of cash.

Liquidity preference depends on three motives for holding money, and for being reluctant to part with it except insofar as the rate of interest acts as an effective inducement. First, there is the transactions motive, or the need for cash to pay for current purchases for consumption and business needs. Second, there is the precautionary motive, the desire to keep some cash on hand for unforseen emergencies. Third, there is the speculative motive, the desire to hold cash while waiting for interest rates to rise or stock and bond prices to fall, or the general price level to fall. Liquidity gives the advantage of being able quickly to seize investment opportunities as they come along.

The quantity of money depends on central bank policy, which can increase or decrease the money supply through changes in open-market operations, reserve requirements, and the rediscount rate. An increase in the quantity of money will lower the rate of interest, unless the public's liquidity preference is increasing more than the quantity of money. A lower rate of interest will not reduce saving, as the classical and neoclassical economists thought. Instead, it will tend to stimulate investment, thereby increasing income and saving.

The independent variables which determine saving and investment are the propensity to consume, the schedule of the marginal efficiency of capital, and the rate of interest. These determinants are independent in the sense that their values cannot be inferred from one another. Consumption and investment spending determine not the rate of interest but the aggregate volume of employment. Decreased consumption, other things being equal, will not increase investment; it will increase unemployment.

Government Policy to Promote Full Employment

THE Keynesian school relied on a large role for the government to stabilize the economy at a full-employment level. One of the things the government should do, Keynes thought, is to stimulate private investment during depression by forcing down the rate of interest. This it could do through central bank policy. But there are limits to how low interest rates can fall. He quoted the nineteenth-century English economist, Walter Bagehot, who said, "John Bull can stand many things, but he cannot stand 2 per cent." How can the rates of interest be forced down toward zero and even a negative figure? Keynes drew on the German monetary reformer, Silvio Gesell, for an answer: stamped money. Money should incur carrying costs just like other stocks of barren goods. A paper currency note would retain its legal-tender quality by having a stamp affixed to it every month. If the cost were a half-cent on the dollar per month, the carrying cost of currency would be 6 per cent per year. In that case, a person might be eager to lend it out at minus 4 per cent, and an investor would be willing to push investments to the point where the marginal efficiency of capital would be minus 4 per cent. Keynes recognized that there would be a flight from currency, and checking accounts would have to be taxed in the same manner. The public could find many substitutes for money, such as promissory notes, foreign money, jewelry, and the precious metals.

The important point is that instead of allowing laissez faire conditions to determine interest rates, the government should take action to force them downward in order to overcome inadequate investment. If the rate of interest were forced down to zero, we could make capital goods so abundant that the marginal efficiency of capital would be zero. This would mean the "euthanasia of the rentier," the coupon-clipper, the receiver of interest. The capitalist could no longer exploit the scarcity value of capital, and the most objectionable features of capitalism would be eliminated. A man could still accumulate income to spend at a later date, but his income would not grow. There would still be room for private risk-taking, for active entrepreneurship, for earning profit. Only interest would disappear. Keynes's sympathies lay with the active entrepreneurs, the industrial capitalists, not with finance capitalists, speculators, and passive receivers of interest.

Keynes was not too sanguine about the effectiveness of a lower rate of interest. Stamped money presented difficulties and was not likely to be adopted. He was skeptical of the success of a merely monetary policy directed toward influencing the rate of interest. The rate of interest would not fall so low as necessary, and the marginal efficiency of capital is too fickle and unstable to govern the rate of interest, he said.

Interest charges probably are less important than Keynes thought in determining the level of investment. Except for very large long-term projects like railroads, power plants, and apartment houses, interest represents only a small part of total costs. Bankers and businessmen generally do not believe that the level of interest rates is a significant determinant of investment. That it has some limited influence, however, cannot be doubted. The *availability* of credit, which can be influenced by open-market operations and reserve requirements, has more influence on borrowing than the *cost* of credit.

A second and more effective way to overcome depression is for the government to undertake enough deficit spending to bring about full employment. In effect, current investment spending would be socialized. To Keynes this meant that the state would decide on the aggregate amount of investment. Ownership of capital could still be private, with the government determining what the returns to the owners should be. Economic life as a whole would not be socialized because the existing system does not seriously misemploy the factors of production which are in use. The state should determine the volume, but not the direction, of employment.

A third type of government action to stimulate the economy should be to redistribute income, thereby increasing the propensity to consume. Higher taxes on the rich and lower interest rates would help, said Keynes, although he did not emphasize this method of solving the problem of inadequate demand. In 1936 he considered the stimuli to expanding investment much more important than the expansion of consumption. In later years, however, he seems to have changed his mind. Professor Calvin B. Hoover, in the article referred to above, reported that Keynes stated in a conversation with him in 1942 or 1943 that after the war the "answer will lie in consumption." It would be necessary and desirable to take action to increase the consumption of the lower-income groups rather than to depend on maintaining full employment through measures to expand investment.

Keynes's great contribution was to adapt economics to the changing institutional structure of modern society. He successfully related academic economics to the economics of government. Because of his ideas, his contemporaries and successors have been able to integrate the analytical and statistical approaches to economics. His followers found, through him, a new liberalism on which to pin their hopes for reform. The Keynesian school has provided one of the most important alternatives to Marxism.

The "Stockholm School"

THE so-called "Stockholm school," basing itself on Knut Wicksell's analysis of the cumulative process, studied aggregative economic processes in a manner similar to Keynes. The English economists were for years unaware of the developments in Sweden, even though the Swedish economists paralleled and in some important points anticipated the Keynesians. Gunnar Myrdal (who will be discussed in the following chapter) chided Keynes for his "unnecessary originality." In 1931, as a result of the worldwide depression, the Swedish government asked its leading economists to analyze different policies to combat unemployment. This raised certain theoretical problems that had to be cleared up. How can output and investment expand from a depressed state, when savings are very small? When investment expands without savers deciding to save more, in what sense does investment exceed saving? Investment ultimately requires saving; where does it come from?

Professor Gunnar Myrdal in 1933 published a contribution that now seems to sharpen the Keynesian concepts that were to appear three years later. He drew a distinction between forward-looking income, saving, and investment, which he called *ex ante*, and the backward-looking categories, or *ex post*. Thus, *ex ante* investment is planned investment for a future period based on *ex ante* or planned income. *Ex ante* saving is also based on expected future income and consumption. *Ex post* saving, investment, and income were realized in some past period; they have already occurred, and can be examined in the statistical record.

To explain fluctuations, an *ex ante* analysis is required. One must examine expectations and plans for the future. While future expectations and plans are to some extent based on present or past experiences and conditions, there is no mechanical, routine, straight-line connection between the two.

Planned saving and planned investment generally are undertaken by different people. Their equality would be accidental. Discrepancies between them represent disequilibria in the economy that force changes toward a new equilibrium. The end result is that income shifts to the level where *ex post* saving and investment are equal. Thus, if planned saving exceeds planned investment, income will fall until realized saving and investment are equal. If planned investment exceeds planned saving, perhaps through the expansion of bank credit, income will rise until realized saving and investment are equal. When *ex ante* saving and investment are equal, equilibrium is reached that normally will manifest itself as an absence of gains or losses in saving and investment *ex post*. Actually, it is possible for planned saving and investment to be equal and still set off an expansion. For this to occur, the planned saving and investment must be larger than realized saving and investment in the past. This could result from a widely held belief that income is due to expand.

Suppose, because of optimistic anticipations, investors decide to increase their investments in an economy that has some unemployment. Savers have not decided to save more than formerly. Total sales will rise, more goods will be produced, aggregate income will rise, and people will save more money. At the end of the period, realized incomes will have exceeded expected incomes, and realized savings will have exceeded planned savings. It is possible also for realized investment in this example to be less than planned investment. If people save less than the amount required to bring about equality between saving and investment, they will cause inventories of goods to be reduced, thereby reducing realized investment from the planned level.

When Keynes in his *Treatise on Money* (1930) wrote about the inequality between saving and investment causing changes in the level of income and employment, he meant it *ex ante*. When, in *The General Theory of Employment, Interest, and Money* (1936), he wrote about the equality of these two categories, he meant it *ex post*. In his discussion of expectations and the fluctuation of income, however, he did weave *ex ante* considerations into his theory.

CHAPTER 23

Modern Theories of Economic Development and Growth

No one school of economic thought has a monopoly of interest in and concern over economic development and growth. Adherents of several schools and eclectics from no particular brand of economics have occupied themselves with these matters. Especially since World War II, economic growth has inspired active scholarship, with a vast outpouring of literature on the subject.

Although the terms "economic development" and "economic growth" are used synonymously and interchangeably, perhaps they should be defined more carefully in order to distinguish between them.

Economic growth may be defined as increasing total output. This can occur with no increased efficiency or rising levels of living. Growth can result from increased population; increased capital investments; longer hours of work; and a larger proportion of the population working, as when women, young people, and old people enter the labor force instead of remaining at home, at school, or in retirement. If total hours worked in a society double while total output goes up 50 per cent, there is growth even though efficiency has declined. Growth can be associated with falling levels of living if population grows faster than output, or if capital investments grow faster than increases in output.

Economic development may be defined as rising output per man-hour of labor with no reduction in employment. The last qualification is important. It is possible to raise output per man-hour by cutting production. The least efficient factories and machines are idled, and the least efficient workers are laid off. Employed workers, fearful for their jobs, can be speeded up. Even if all units of labor and capital were of equal quality, reducing the number of workers while capital investments are kept constant would increase output per man-hour because of the law of diminishing marginal productivity. Reductions in employment that lead to increasing output per man-hour do not lead to economic development.

Economic development therefore implies improvement, increasing efficiency. It is generally but not necessarily associated with economic growth and rising levels of living. We might have growing output per man-hour with the increase going into investment; then the level of living would not rise immediately, although it might ultimately. With increasing productivity, people might prefer increased leisure instead of increased income. Thus, if productivity doubled while workers chose to cut their weekly hours of labor by half, there would be development but no growth and no rising real income unless leisure is included in income.

There are a number of significant reasons why interest in economic development and growth has burgeoned during the last several decades. First, economic growth is associated with growing military power; a country that produces ten million tons of steel is potentially stronger than one that produces two million, though perhaps less efficient and certainly not five times stronger. Second, western Europe and the United States seem to have become "mature" economies suffering from stagnation and unemployment. Third, the world is watching the race of progress between the United States and Soviet Russia to see which can grow and develop more rapidly and thereby capture world attention; the rapid rate of growth of the Communist countries, as well as private-enterprise countries like Japan, has been disturbingly impressive to the Western world. Fourth, most of the poor countries, many of them colonies before World War II, are now politically free and have decided to promote growth and development; since the war the term describing them has been changed from "backward" to "underdeveloped," "developing," or "emerging," which shows the new respect they have won and recognizes their aspirations. Fifth, we and the Communists are fighting for leadership of and alliances with the poor countries, and the latter are watching closely to learn which type of approach can best suit their needs. Sixth, the idea that something can be done under government auspices to promote growth and development has become pervasive; people are generally no longer content to wait for laissez faire principles to accomplish these objectives. Finally, promoting capital investments in underdeveloped areas is significant in that the export of capital will stimulate fuller employment in the industrialized countries.

We shall examine the theories of five men who represent different types of analysis. Some, like Schumpeter and Rostow, seek to explain economic change without prescribing remedies or urging detailed policies. Others hope to influence policy in the direction of more rational and faster progress.

Schumpeter: The Decay of Capitalism

JOSEPH ALOIS SCHUMPETER (1883–1950), the son of a cloth manufacturer, was born in the Austrian province of Moravia (now Czechoslo-
vakia). He was educated in law and economics at the University of Vienna.
During World War I he made no secret of his pacifist, pro-British, anti-
German sentiments. He served briefly as Minister of Finance of the Austrian Republic in 1919. Later he accepted a professorship at the University
of Bonn in Germany. From 1932 until his death he taught at Harvard. He
served as President of the American Economic Association, the first for-
eign-born economist to attain this distinction. His encyclopedic *History of
Economic Analysis*, edited after his death by his wife, is a monument to
his gigantic scholarly achievements.

Two major intellectual influences in Schumpeter's life came from Léon
Walras (see p. 211 above) and Karl Marx (pp. 133–44). From Walras
he derived the emphasis on the interdependence of economic quantities,
but the approach was static. Although Schumpeter had a strong aversion
to Marx and all he stood for, he admired his understanding of the process
of economic change. Schumpeter was deeply devoted to the institutions
of capitalism, and he viewed with alarm the rise of forces engendered by
the very success of capitalism that in his opinion would destroy the system.
He agreed with Marx that capitalism was doomed, although for different
reasons and with profound regret.

Schumpeter constructed a theoretical system that he used to explain both
business cycles and the theory of capitalist economic development. The
key process in economic change is the introduction of innovations, and the
central figure who does this is the entrepreneur. Innovation is defined as
changes in the methods of supplying commodities. This includes introducing new goods or new methods of production, opening new markets,
conquering new sources of supply of raw material or semimanufactured
goods, and carrying out a new organization of industry, such as creating
a monopoly position or breaking one up. Innovation is much more than
invention, although it can include, not discovering or perfecting an invention, but rather its application to industrial processes.

The entrepreneur is the person who carries out new combinations, who
introduces innovations. Not all heads of firms or managers or industrialists
are entrepreneurs, for they may be running a business in a routine manner
without having any new ideas or introducing new ways of doing things.
Nor are the entrepreneurs risk-takers. That function is left to the shareholders, who typically are capitalists but not entrepreneurs. Entrepreneurs
may have only temporary connections with individual firms in the roles
of financiers or promoters. They are always pioneers in introducing new

products, new processes, new forms of business organization, or in pene-
trating new markets. They are men with exceptional abilities who seize
opportunities where others are oblivious of them, or who create opportunities through their own daring and imagination.

In the absence of innovation, economic life would reach static equilibrium, with its circular flow running along in essentially the same channels
year after year. Profit and interest would disappear, and the accumulation of
wealth would cease. The entrepreneur, seeking profit through innovation,
upsets this static situation, transforming it into the dynamic process of economic development. He raids the circular flow and diverts labor and land
to investment. Because savings generated by the circular flow are inadequate, he relies on credit to provide the means for his enterprise. The resulting development means changes in economic life that are not forced
from without, but which arise from within the economic system.

Innovations do not occur continuously, but appear in clusters. The activities of the most enterprising and venturesome entrepreneurs create a favorable climate for others to follow. Credit expands, prices and incomes rise,
and prosperity prevails. But not forever. The boom generates conditions
unfavorable to its continued progress. Rising prices deter investment, and
the competition of new products with old ones causes business losses.
When businessmen repay their debts, the deflationary process is intensified, and depression has replaced prosperity. Business fluctuations therefore represent the process of adaptation to innovation. The system tends
toward equilibrium, except that innovations always disrupt that tendency.
The process that generates economic development also generates fluctuations, with every depression representing a struggle toward a new equilibrium.

Can capitalism survive? asked Schumpeter. No, was his reply; he did
not think it could. Capitalist society is, and for some time has been, in a
state of decay. But he disagreed with most economists about the precise
nature of that decay. He rejected the Ricardian law of diminishing returns
and the Malthusian population principle which were supposed to thwart
progress. He denied Marx's contention that economic contradictions would
produce successively more severe crises. He rejected the Keynesian stagnation thesis on several counts. Opportunities for great innovations have
not been exhausted; the tendency of innovations to become capital saving
has not been established convincingly; the opening up of new countries,
even if that process has been completed, may be replaced by other opportunities; the falling birth rate may become economically significant in the
future, but it cannot explain the events of the 1930's. His diagnosis of the
fundamental sickness of capitalism came closest to that of Sombart, discussed in Chapter 11 above.

Schumpeter wrote that if the capitalist system has another run such as it had in the sixty years preceding 1928, we can achieve the objectives of social reformers without significant interference with the capitalist process. Yet this is not likely. The economic and social foundations of capitalism are beginning to crumble for three reasons: (1) the obsolescence of the entrepreneurial function, (2) the destruction of protecting political strata, and (3) the destruction of the institutional framework of capitalist society.

The entrepreneurial function is growing obsolete. Innovation is being reduced to routine. Technological progress is increasingly becoming the business of teams of trained specialists who turn out what is required and make it work in predictable ways. Economic progress tends to become de-personalized and automatized. Bureau and committee work replaces individual action. The leading man no longer has the opportunity to fling himself into the fray. He is becoming just another office worker, one who is not always difficult to replace.

To sum up this part of our argument: if capitalist evolution—"progress"—either ceases or becomes completely automatic, the economic basis of the industrial bourgeoisie will be reduced eventually to wages such as are paid for current administrative work excepting remnants of quasi-rents and monopoloid gains that may be expected to linger on for some time. Since capitalist enterprise, by its very achievements, tends to automatize progress, we conclude that it tends to make itself superfluous—to break to pieces under the pressure of its own success. The perfectly bureaucratized giant industrial unit not only ousts the small or medium-sized firm and "expropriates" its owners, but in the end it also ousts the entrepreneur and expropriates the bourgeoisie as a class which in the process stands to lose not only its income but also what is infinitely more important, its function. The true pacemakers of socialism were not the intellectuals or agitators who preached it but the Vanderbilts, Carnegies and Rockefellers. This result may not in every respect be to the taste of Marxian socialists, still less to the taste of socialists of a more popular (Marx would have said, vulgar) description. But so far as prognosis goes, it does not differ from theirs.*

The destruction of the political strata that offered the strongest defense of capitalist society also spells the self-destruction of the system. Schumpeter agreed with Marx that big business destroys small and medium-sized firms. Under conditions of democratic politics, this process weakens the political position of the industrial bourgeoisie, for numerous small businessmen are more powerful politically than a few salaried executives and large shareholders.

* Joseph A. Schumpeter, *Capitalism, Socialism, and Democracy*, 3rd ed. (New York, Harper, 1950), p. 134. By permission of Harper & Row, Publishers.

The capitalist process, by substituting a mere parcel of shares for the walls of and the machines in a factory, takes the life out of the idea of property. It loosens the grip that once was so strong—the grip in the sense of the legal right and the actual ability to do as one pleases with one's own; the grip also in the sense that the holder of the title loses the will to fight, economically, physically, politically, for "his" factory and his control over it, to die if necessary on its steps. And this evaporation of what we may term the material substance of property—its visible and touchable reality—affects not only the attitude of holders but also that of the workmen and of the public in general. Dematerialized, defunctionalized and absentee ownership does not impress and call forth moral allegiance as the vital form of property did. Eventually there will be *nobody* left who really cares to stand for it—nobody within and nobody without the precincts of the big concerns.*

Farmers, another group that strongly defends capitalism, are declining as a percentage of the population, if not in absolute numbers.

Capitalism, said Schumpeter, must even create, educate, and subsidize an intellectual group that develops a vested interest in social unrest. Intellectuals do not have direct responsibility for practical affairs; they are outsiders looking in, yet they wield the power of the spoken and the written word. Their main chance of asserting themselves is their actual or potential nuisance value. Freedom of public discussion involves freedom to nibble at the foundations of capitalist society, and the intellectual group cannot help nibbling because it lives on criticism. College graduates who are incapable of professional work and object to manual occupations swell the ranks of the discontented, and they develop hostility toward the capitalist order in rationalizing their own inadequacies. Intellectuals have also invaded the labor movement and radicalized it in order to win favor among the very people who are naturally suspicious of them.

The third reason for the crumbling of the foundations of capitalism, according to Schumpeter, lies in the destruction of the institutional framework of capitalist society. The stagnationist argument has as its chief merit the recognition of the undeniable truth that unlike other economic systems, the capitalist system is geared to incessant economic change. Capitalism implies recurrent industrial revolutions which are the main sources of profit and interest for entrepreneurs and capitalists. The stagnationist analysis hinges on the inadequacy of profit expectations. This is the valid core of the theory that tries to explain insufficient investment and employment. This is the consequence of the anticapitalist policies adopted in most European countries since World War I and in the United States since 1933. The unemployment figures of the 1930's were increased beyond what they need have been by anticapitalist policies. The policies that are destroying

* *Ibid.*, p. 142.

capitalism are taxation that is so high and progressive that it prevents private accumulation; counterdepression public expenditure; labor legislation that shifts questions of wages, hours, and factory discipline to the political sphere; and strict regulation of the behavior of big business under the threat of prosecution.

Under these conditions, public income generation will automatically become permanent, quite irrespective of the factors stressed by the theories framed to prove its necessity from causes inherent in the saving-investment process of capitalist society. Such a system will no doubt still be called capitalism. But it is capitalism in the oxygen tent—kept alive by artificial devices and paralyzed in all those functions that produced the successes of the past. The question why it should be kept alive at all is therefore bound to be put before long.*

Non-public banking and finance will no longer have a role to play in an economic world completely dependent on government financing that is itself entirely independent of private voluntary saving. Government spending as a permanent policy will develop into government planning of investment. International trade and investment will be cut off from its old background of commercial calculation and come to be managed by political considerations. This will be "guided capitalism," which will shade off into "state capitalism" as some measures of nationalization are adopted. Schumpeter defined state capitalism as government ownership and management of selected industrial sectors, complete government control in the labor and capital market, and government initiative in domestic and foreign enterprise. It is a matter of taste whether this is called socialism or not, he said. Such a state will suffer from friction and inefficiency which could be eliminated by returning to pure capitalism or advancing resolutely to full socialism. On the other hand, Schumpeter thought that state capitalism might conserve many human values that would perish in the two alternative systems.

Baran: The Marxist Analysis

PAUL ALEXANDER BARAN (born 1909) moved with his family from Russia, his country of birth, to Germany in 1920. He studied economics, history, and sociology in Germany and France. In 1939 he came to the United States and continued his studies at Harvard and the Brookings Institution. After serving with the government during World War II, he joined the research staff of the Federal Reserve Bank of New York. Later he became professor of economics at Stanford University.

* Joseph A. Schumpeter, *Essays*, Richard V. Clemence, ed. (Cambridge, 1951), p. 180.

Baran, as an ardent advocate of Marxian socialism, felt obliged to explain the brutalities of the Stalin regime as revealed by N. K. Khrushchev in 1956. The preface of his book contained his answer to the widespread characterization of Soviet Russia's system as "totalitarian socialism" in contrast to Great Britain's or Sweden's "democratic socialism."

It is not *socialism* that can be fairly charged with the misdeeds of Stalin and his puppets—it is the *political system* that evolved from the drive to develop at breakneck speed a backward country threatened by foreign aggression and in face of internal resistance. The emergence of such a political system under the unique circumstances prevailing in Russia after Hitler's seizure of power and in the countries of Eastern and Southeastern Europe during the frightening years of the cold war does not "prove" that socialism is inherently a system of terror and repression. What it does mean—and this is a historical lesson of paramount importance—is that socialism in backward and underdeveloped countries has a powerful tendency to become a backward and underdeveloped socialism. What has happened in the Soviet Union and the socialist countries of Eastern Europe confirms the fundamental Marxian proposition that it is the degree of maturity of society's productive resources that determines "the general character of social, political and intellectual life." It casts no reflection on the fundamental rationality, desirability, and potentialities of a socialist transformation in the West. Indeed, it accentuates its desperate urgency. For a socialist society in the advanced countries would not be compelled to engage in "forced marches" towards industrialization, or bound to withdraw from popular consumption large parts of miserably low incomes, or constrained to devote to military purposes significant shares of small aggregate outputs. Such a socialist society would not only attack head-on the waste, irrationality, and cultural and moral degradation of the West, it would also throw its weight into helping to solve the entire problem of want, disease, and starvation in the underdeveloped parts of the world. Socialism in the West, once firmly established, would destroy for all time the bases and the need for any reappearance of the political and social repression that marked the early stages of socialism in the East.*

Economic development, said Baran, involves the class struggle. Society has to be transformed, and in the past as in the present certain classes and groups have opposed and obstructed change while others have advanced it. In the present world situation, we already have proof that an economy based on comprehensive economic planning can function and grow without the benefits of private enterprise. The dominant interests in the advanced capitalist countries are inimical to economic development in the poor countries. The latter represent the indispensable hinterland of capitalism, supplying it with raw materials, profits, and investment outlets.

* Paul A. Baran, *The Political Economy of Growth*, (New York, Monthly Review, 1957), p. viii. By permission of the Monthly Review Press.

Aside from the interrelated political problems of class struggle and imperialism, the underdeveloped countries must consider the problem of the economic surplus. The *actual* economic surplus is identical with current saving or accumulation; it is the difference between society's actual current output and its actual current consumption. The *potential* economic surplus is the difference between the output that could be produced in a given natural and technological environment and what might be regarded as essential consumption. The actual surplus is less than the potential because of: (1) excess consumption by the rich and middle classes, (2) output lost to society because of unproductive workers (advertisers, tax-evasion specialists, makers of armaments, etc.), (3) output lost because of the irrational and wasteful organization of the existing productive apparatus, and (4) output lost because of unemployment caused by the anarchy of capitalist production and the deficiency of effective demand.

The potential economic surplus can become the *planned* economic surplus under socialist comprehensive economic planning. A socialist community, guided by reason and science, can use its resources to expand investment and production most efficiently, at the same time pursuing a scientific policy of conservation of human and natural resources. The guiding force is not profit maximization, but a rational plan reflecting society's preference as to current versus future consumption.

According to Baran, the rate and direction of economic development in a country at a given time depend on both the size and the mode of utilization of the economic surplus. The surpluses drawn from countries such as India by the dominant powers could have gone far in promoting economic development if they had been invested in the countries that produced them. The present problems in the poor countries are that the actual economic surpluses are much smaller than the potential surpluses, and much of the surplus is wasted in lavish consumption rather than being used to promote development. This surplus, while small in *absolute* terms, is a large *share* of total output—as large as, if not larger than, in advanced capitalist countries. It must be invested under government planning if it is to achieve maximum effectiveness.

Baran offered a number of observations on problems of economic development in the underdeveloped areas. A land reform that merely breaks up large estates is inadvisable because it will simply increase the peasantry's consumption, while production will be kept down because of the inefficiency of dwarf holdings; large-scale farming is required. The increase of Western assets in the underdeveloped part of the world is only partly due to capital exports in the strict sense of the term; it is primarily the result of the reinvestment abroad of some of the economic surplus secured abroad. Businesses in poor countries set up by foreign corporations constitute alien bodies artificially injected to facilitate exploitation by foreign merchant capitalism. A group of native merchants emerges within the orbit of foreign capital, and it uses its influence to fortify and to perpetuate the status quo. Native industrialists and feudal landowners also oppose change, and thus foreign exploitation is continued while popular movements for social and national liberation are suppressed—temporarily. Ultimately the expropriation of foreign and domestic capitalists and landowners will have to be achieved. Economic development will then proceed simultaneously through industrialization and the improvement of agriculture.

Some people attribute underdevelopment at least partly to the lack of entrepreneurial talent. Baran was not impressed with this argument. Marxism cannot allow a crucial role to the entrepreneur, the symbol of capitalist exploitation.

The trouble with the theory centering on this "central figure" is, however, that it either boils down to a tautology, or that its contents are simply fallacious. If it is to be given the former, more merciful interpretation, the doctrine is reducible to the finding that in the absence of industrial capitalism there are no industrial capitalists, and vice versa—which is indubitably a correct proposition but also one that is singularly unexciting. For in all parts of the world and at all times in history there have been ambitious, ruthless, and enterprising men who had an opportunity and were willing to "innovate," to move to the fore, to seize power, and to exercise authority. Yet at some times and places this elite supplied the headmen of tribes, at others it provided knights, courtiers, and ecclesiastical dignitaries, while in a certain phase of the historical process it produced merchant-princes, adventurers, explorers, and pioneers of science. Finally, during the latest period of historical development—in the age of modern capitalism—it has given rise to the capitalist entrepreneur organizing industrial production or mastering the art of finance so as to be able to bring under his control vast concentrations of capital. It should be obvious that what the theorist of entrepreneurship has to explain is not the sudden appearance of men of genius—such men have been with us since the beginning of time!—but the fact that these men in a certain historical constellation have turned their "genius" to the accumulation of capital, and that they found the best way to accomplish this end to be investment in industrial enterprises. Failing to do this and invoking instead a *deus ex machina* is not unlike "explaining" squalor by the existence of poverty, and renders the theory of the strategic importance of the entrepreneur entirely worthless.*

Baran's dictum that "the establishment of a socialist planned economy is an . . . indispensable condition for the attainment of economic and social progress in underdeveloped countries" is believed by many in those countries. It remains to be seen whether such ideas will be challenged effectively by the ideology of the non-communist world.

* *Ibid.*, pp. 235–36.

Nurkse: Balanced Development

RAGNAR NURKSE (1907–59) was born in Estonia. In the early 1930's his family emigrated to Canada, and he studied at Edinburgh University and the University of Vienna. As an employee of the League of Nations, he published some distinguished studies in international economics. After World War II he accepted a professorship at Columbia University, where he remained until his sudden and untimely death in Geneva while on leave of absence.

Nurkse gave renewed emphasis to external economies: the more investments are made, the more viable each undertaking becomes. Therefore the underdeveloped areas require progress on a broad front, with simultaneous expansion of industries that will support each other and increase the chances of success. The great difficulty has been that the poverty of countries has limited their capital formation.

Why do countries remain poor? asked Nurkse. Because of the vicious circle of poverty, was his reply.

The "vicious circle of poverty" . . . implies, of course, a circular constellation of forces tending to act and react upon one another in such a way as to keep a poor country in a state of poverty. Particular instances of such circular constellations are not difficult to imagine. For example, a poor man may not have enough to eat; being under-nourished, his health may be weak; being physically weak, his working capacity may be low, which means that he is poor, which in turn means that he will not have enough to eat; and so on. A situation of this sort, applying to a country as a whole, can be summed up in the trite proposition: "a country is poor because it is poor."

The most important circular relationships of this kind are those that afflict the problem of capital formation in economically underdeveloped countries. The problem of economic development is largely, though by no means entirely, a problem of capital accumulation. The so-called underdeveloped areas, as compared with the advanced, are under-equipped with capital in relation to their population and natural resources.

There are two sides to the problem of real capital formation: there is a demand side and a supply side. The demand for capital is governed by the incentives to *invest;* the supply of capital is governed by the ability and willingness to *save.* In underdeveloped countries, a circular relationship exists on both sides of the problem. On the supply side, we have the small capacity to save, resulting from the low level of real income. But the low real income is a reflection of low productivity, which in its turn is due largely to the lack of capital. The lack of capital is a result of the small capacity to save, and so the circle is complete.

On the demand side, the inducement to invest may be low, because of the small buying power of the people, which is due to their small real income, which in turn is due to low productivity. The low level of productivity, however, is a result of the small amount of capital used in production, which in its turn is caused, to some extent, by the low inducement to invest. . . .

It may be surprising to hear that there can be anything wrong on the demand side of the problem of capital formation in underdeveloped countries. Can there be any deficiency in the demand for capital? Are not underdeveloped areas, almost by definition, greatly in need of capital for the efficient use of their labour and for the exploitation of their natural resources? Is not the demand for capital, in most of these areas, tremendous? It may well be; and yet, in terms of private business incentives to adopt roundabout or capitalistic methods in the productive process, there may be a difficulty, arising from the small size of the domestic market in the early stages of a country's development.

The inducement to invest is limited by the size of the market. . . . In a country, for instance, where the great majority of people are too poor to wear leather shoes, setting up a modern shoe factory may be a doubtful proposition; the market for shoes may be too small. Many articles that are in common use in the United States can be sold in an underdeveloped country in such limited quantities, that a machine, working only a few days or weeks can produce enough for a whole year's consumption, and would have to stand idle the rest of the time. In such circumstances the economic incentive to install capital equipment may be lacking. . . .

The size of the market, in the last analysis, is determined by the general level of productivity. In an all-inclusive view, capacity to buy not only depends on, but is actually defined by, capacity to produce. . . . For any individual entrepreneur, the use of capital is inhibited, to start with, by the small size of the market.*

Nurkse argued that if poor countries were to advance, they would have to rely increasingly on industrialization instead of depending as heavily as they do now on the production and export of raw materials. The non-industrial countries, he said, are almost all in the low-income class, and they trade very little among themselves. The rich industrial countries show vigorous advances in real income per capita, yet they are not transmitting their own rate of growth to the rest of the world through a proportional increase in the demand for primary products. There are six major reasons for this. (1) In the advanced economies, industrial production is shifting from "light" to "heavy" industries (such as engineering and chemicals), requiring fewer raw materials relative to finished output. (2) As services become increasingly important in the richer countries, their raw-material demand lags behind the rise in their national product. (3) The income elasticity of consumer demand for many agricultural commodities tends to be low. (4) Agricultural protectionism tends to affect adversely the imports of primary products into industrial countries. (5) Substantial economies

* Ragnar Nurkse, *Some Aspects of Capital Accumulation in Underdeveloped Countries* (Cairo, 1952), pp. 1–3.

have been achieved in the industrial uses of natural materials through such developments as electrolytic tin-plating and systematic recovery and re-processing of metals. (6) The industrial countries have increasingly tended to displace natural raw materials with synthetics. As a consequence of these forces at work from 1904–13 to 1944–50 the manufacturing production of the United States increased more than three times as fast as the American economy's consumption of raw materials. Traditional international trade theory, said Nurkse, is of questionable relevance in explaining the increasing discrepancies in income levels between the manufacturing and the raw-materials-producing countries.

If primary production for export does not offer attractive opportunities for expansion, the alternative is industrialization. There can be two types of industrialization: that which aims at producing manufactured goods for export to the industrial countries, and that which caters mainly to domestic markets in underdeveloped countries. The second type generally requires a complementary advance in domestic agriculture, while the first does not. Neither type demands the abandonment or contraction of exports of the raw materials that a country is naturally adapted to produce.

Nurkse thought that production of manufactured goods for export to the industrial countries does not offer much hope of success. Therefore underdeveloped areas should expand the home market for finished goods. The size of the market depends, however, on the volume of production. The difficulty is that the impoverished farm population cannot buy the manufactured goods offered for sale because of their own low productivity and incomes. Nor can the local economy supply the food required to sustain the new industrial workers. Therefore industrial development for domestic markets requires a simultaneous rise of agricultural productivity on the home front.

The same principle applies within the manufacturing sphere. The output of any single industry cannot create its own demand, because people working in new industries will not wish to spend all their income on their own products.

Just as it is possible for manufacturing as a whole to fail if peasants can produce no marketable surplus and are too poor to buy anything from factories, so it is possible for a single branch of manufacturing to fail for lack of support from other sectors in industry as well as agriculture; that is, for lack of markets. To be sure, an expansion of one industry will have effects on income and expenditure tending to induce other industries also to expand. But if the others are only passive receivers of the external stimulus their expansion may be slow and uncertain. And their slowness and passiveness will in turn slow down and discourage the industry that first started expanding. In short, while it is true that the active sectors will tend to pull the passive ones forward (and this is what some advocates of "unbalanced growth" have in mind), it is equally true that the passive sectors will tend to hold the active ones back. Would it not be better if every sector were in some measure "active" in the sense of advancing spontaneously, imbued with some expansive élan of its own instead of waiting for signals from others? Price incentives and restraints would then be needed merely to keep each sector's rate of advance in line with the community's pattern of demand. The principle of balanced expansion can be looked upon as a means of accelerating the overall rate of output growth.*

There are limits to the diversification of output. The minimum size of efficient plant is an important practical consideration that often limits the diversification of industry in any single country. Therefore manufacturing for home markets in the less developed countries must include also production for export to each other's markets. This is particularly important for countries with small purchasing power, which have much to gain from customs unions of underdeveloped nations.

Economic progress, said Nurkse, is not a spontaneous or automatic affair. On the contrary, there are forces within the system tending to keep it anchored to a given level. Once the vicious circle of stagnation is broken, however, the circular relationships tend to make for cumulative advance. The synchronized investment of capital in a wide range of different industries will enlarge the market for all of them, even though each industry considered separately would appear to be unattractive for investment. Most industries catering to mass consumption are complementary in the sense that they provide a market for each other. The social marginal productivity of capital, in essence, is higher than the private marginal productivity.

In underdeveloped countries, Nurkse believed, the forces that are to defeat the grip of economic stagnation have to be deliberately organized through some degree of central direction or collective enterprise. The actual investing could be undertaken by private enterprise. The state might enforce compulsory saving and then coordinate investment, while the act of investment could be left in private hands. The deficiency of demand arises only in the private sector of the economy. For the economy as a whole there is of course no deficiency in the demand for capital. Therefore most underdeveloped countries will need a combination of private and government action in the field of saving and investment. Each country must work out its own combination in accordance with its own particular needs and opportunities.

Nurkse's theme of balanced growth forms an interesting contrast to W. W. Rostow's emphasis on the role of leading sectors. Rostow, who will be

* Ragnar Nurkse, *Patterns of Trade and Development* (Stockholm, 1959), p. 43.

discussed more fully below, held that growth rates in the various sectors of an economy differ widely over any given period of time. Over-all growth is based on extremely rapid expansion in certain key sectors. Thus the cotton industry in Great Britain from 1780 to 1840 played an important role in sustaining over-all growth. The railroad boom during the 1840's and 1850's gave pig iron the key position in the British economy. In the United States the construction of western railroads launched the industrial revolution.

It is possible that in the history of the leading industrial countries, Rostow's idea of leading sectors is the more relevant concept. It may be equally true that for the impoverished, emerging countries today, balanced growth is one of the prime necessities for economic progress. The oil industry in Venezuela, for example, can remain an alien enclave on the domestic scene while it is integrated into foreign economies.

Myrdal: National Economic Planning

GUNNAR MYRDAL (born 1898) was educated in law and economics in his native Sweden. He pursued advanced studies in England, France, Germany, and the United States from 1925 to 1930. As an active leader of the Swedish Social Democratic Party, he was a senator, minister of commerce, and he served in other party and government posts. After World War II he was executive secretary of the United Nations Economic Commission for Europe.

There are three major themes in Myrdal's discussion of the problems of the poor countries. The first is that there is a widening gap between the rich and the poor countries. Second, standard economic theory is inadequate to explain or to help narrow the gap. Third, the state in the poor countries will have to play a large role to promote economic development.

There is an economic upper class of rich nations, said Myrdal, that is growing richer with a momentum that is not slackening except occasionally during short periods. The underdeveloped countries are moving forward very slowly or not at all. The gap between the two groups is widening. It can be explained by "the principle of circular and cumulative causation." Myrdal endorsed Nurkse's analysis, cited above, of the vicious circle of poverty. He added that a circular relationship among less poverty, more food, improved health, and higher working capacity would sustain a cumulative process upward instead of downward.

A widening of markets often strengthens in the first instance the rich and progressive countries whose manufacturing industries have the lead and are already fortified by the surrounding external economies, while the underdeveloped countries are in continuous danger of seeing even what they have of industry and, in particular, small-scale industry and handicrafts priced out by cheap imports from the industrial countries, if they do not protect them. . . .

The main positive effect of international trade on the underdeveloped countries was in fact to promote the production of primary products; and such production, employing mostly unskilled labor, has come to constitute the bulk of their exports. In these lines, however, they often meet inelastic demands in the export market, often also a demand trend which is not rising very rapidly, and excessive price fluctuations. When, furthermore, population is rapidly rising while the larger part of it lives at, or near, the subsistence level—which means that there is no scarcity of unskilled labor—any technological improvement in their export production tends to transfer the advantages from the cheapening of production to the importing countries. Since the demand is often inelastic, the market will not be greatly enlarged.

The advice—and assistance—which the poorer countries receive from the richer is, even nowadays, often directed toward increasing their production of primary goods for export. The advice is certainly given in good faith, and it may even be rational from the short-term point of view of one underdeveloped country seen in isolation. . . .

Nor can capital movements be relied upon to counteract international inequalities. In the circumstances described, capital will, on the whole, shun the underdeveloped countries, particularly as the advanced countries themselves are rapidly developing further and can offer to owners of capital both good profits and security.*

Myrdal, in developing his second major theme, argued that orthodox economic theory cannot explain or reverse the growing gap between rich and poor countries. The doctrine of equality provides the basis for Western thought; this is the universal idea that links the philosophies of conservatives and radicals, liberals and socialists. Orthodox economic theorists tried to avoid the equality doctrine, developing certain predilections as antidotes to this dangerous thought. From John Stuart Mill on, a leading device for evading this issue was to draw a sharp line of demarcation between the sphere of production (including exchange) and the sphere of distribution. Natural laws were supposed to reign in the sphere of production. In distribution, policy based on the equality doctrine might be invoked. Therefore economists have for more than a hundred years directed their analysis almost entirely toward production and exchange while expressing doubts about the need for reforms in the sphere of distribution of income and wealth.

There were a number of ideas developed by orthodox economists to evade the equality doctrine. One was the notion of the harmony of interests, which is "a comforting thought for those who have drawn a lucky

* Gunnar Myrdal, *Rich Lands and Poor* (New York, Harper, 1957), pp. 52-53. By permission of Harper & Row, Publishers.

number in life's lottery." A second predilection was laissez faire. A third
was the free-trade doctrine, which loses its validity because of the unrealistic nature of the assumptions on which it rests, such as free competition;
from this idea comes bad advice for underdeveloped countries, like telling
them to avoid tampering with international trade and payments. A fourth
concept of inherited economic doctrines is that the economy tends toward
stable equilibrium; this, said Myrdal, is much further from the truth than
the idea of circular causation and cumulative processes.

Much of standard theory is a rationalization of the dominant interests of
the industrial countries, said Myrdal. In general, economic theory has not
been concerned with the problems of underdeveloped countries. The poor
countries should not accept this theory uncritically, but should remold it to
fit their problems and their interests.

Myrdal's third major idea was that the state in underdeveloped countries
would have to play a large role, especially through national economic planning, in promoting progress.

Economists now generally endorse the opinion that the underdeveloped countries need much more planning and state intervention if, under very much
more difficult conditions than the now-developed countries ever faced, they
are to have any chance of engendering economic development. Statesmen and
officials from the rich and progressive Western countries have also been led
to take the same stand on those other countries' behalf when the matter has
been up for discussion and resolution-making in international organizations
—although it is very apparent that they often had their fingers crossed when
swearing on that strange bible. . . .

As economic development cannot be expected to come by itself, planning
becomes a precondition for development, not, as in the Western countries, a
later consequence of development and all the other changes which accompanied
it. The underdeveloped countries are thus compelled to undertake what in the
light of the history of the Western world appears as a shortcut.

All this follows as a consequence of the fact that planning is being applied
at an earlier stage of development, and of the further fact that their conditions
for development are so much worse that this seems rationally motivated. It is
also a part of the logic of the underdeveloped countries' situation that their
programmatic planning should be comprehensive and complete, not pragmatic
and piecemeal as in the Western countries. In principle and in theoretical
approach, planning anticipates public policies. It does not grow out of the
necessity to coordinate such policies as have already been initiated.*

Every national development plan must determine the total amount of investment and the proportions of the capital to be allocated in each direction. It must spell out instructions for the specific inducements and controls

* Gunnar Myrdal, *Beyond the Welfare State* (New Haven, 1960), pp. 14–15, 122–23.

for realizing these directives. There will have to be a forceful rise in the share of the national income that is withheld from consumption and devoted to investment. The national plan should also include a vigorous population policy aimed at controlling fertility. Planning should be undertaken in terms of common, long-term needs of the community, rather than in terms of costs and profits of individual enterprises.

If an underdeveloped country is to speed up its rate of progress, its government will find it essential to intervene in many phases of economic life. Foreign trade will have to be controlled, if only to conserve foreign exchange. The import of less necessary goods will be restricted, and exports might be subsidized. Some workers may have to be offered higher wages in order to get them to move as required by the over-all plan, thereby further straining the foreign exchange situation. Infant industries will have to be protected, preferably within regional common markets of underdeveloped countries. The government will find it necessary to own and operate those public utilities that are essential to growth but usually are not profitable enterprises, such as railroads, highways, irrigation projects, port facilities, and the like. Because of the great risks in private investments in underdeveloped countries, the returns to capital frequently must be so high as to be socially intolerable; therefore intergovernmental and World Bank loans are desirable; this represents a further measure of government intervention. The state also must act vigorously for land reform, not only to raise productivity in agriculture, but more important, to shatter "the foundations of the state class structure of a stagnating society." In many cases foreign-owned natural resources in an underdeveloped country will be nationalized. If, through widespread measures of government controls, an upward cumulative process is begun, the scope for private enterprise will be enlarged rather than restricted.

Myrdal ended by conjuring up a vision of a grander, larger harmony of interests.

As long as the peoples living in the underdeveloped world were subdued and quiet their grievances could be kept away from the attention of the peoples in the richer countries by opportunistic ignorance. A new phase of the age-old struggle for greater equality—a phase in which the struggle finally encompasses the entire globe—has now begun with the Great Awakening.

I have already observed that from one point of view the Great Awakening is nothing else than the victorious spread to the peoples in the underdeveloped countries of the richer nations' inherited ideal of equality of opportunity. Those nations have themselves been sowing the seed of world revolution. . . .

In the setting of Western civilization the poorer countries, once they succeed in breaking through the barriers of opportunistic ignorance, will have, as already in earlier time the poorer regions and the lower social classes within the now-richer countries, a support in the egalitarian ideal which has an emotional and moral basis in people's feelings for what is right and wrong. Whether this support will be forthcoming so soon, and be so strong, that—in analogy to what has actually happened within the richer countries themselves—the world revolution can be canalized into a process of gradual and peaceful change is a momentous question to which the future will give the solemn answer.

Such a process toward a "welfare world," where on a world scale the principle of equality of opportunity as between nations, racial and religious groups, and individuals increasingly became realized, would, like the earlier parallel development toward the national "welfare state" in the richer countries, regularly turn out to be a paying proposition also to those who are initially better off. As in the nations so in the world at large, this process would be a precondition for raising levels of production generally and not only for promoting social justice.*

Rostow: Stages of Economic Growth

WALT WHITMAN ROSTOW (born 1916) was educated at Yale. He became professor of economic history at the Massachusetts Institute of Technology. He was a consultant to the Eisenhower administration, and was chairman of the State Department's Policy Planning Council under President Kennedy.

Rostow's analysis of economic growth was based on the developmental stages through which each country goes. This reminds one of the stages-of-history approach of many earlier economists. Adam Smith used the sequence of hunting, pastoral, agricultural, commercial, and manufacturing stages. Friedrich List thought that each nation passes through the five phases of savagery, pastoral life, agriculture, agriculture and manufacturing, and finally the agricultural, manufacturing, and commercial state. Karl Marx saw society as evolving from primitive communism to slavery, feudalism, capitalism, socialism, and communism. Werner Sombart divided man's history into three stages, depending on the degree of social interaction: the individual economy, the transitional economy, and the social economy.

Rostow saw each country evolving through five stages of economic growth. These are the traditional society, the preconditions for take-off, the take-off, the drive to maturity, and the age of high mass consumption.

A traditional society is one of low productivity based on pre-Newtonian science and technology, and on pre-Newtonian attitudes toward the physical world. Rostow used Newton as a symbol for that watershed in history when men came to believe that the external world was subject to a few knowable laws and was capable of productive manipulation. Traditional

* Myrdal, *Rich Lands and Poor*, pp. 127–28.

society included the whole world before Newton, and also those post-Newtonian societies that for a time remained untouched by man's new capability for manipulating his environment to his economic advantage. Change, even increases in output, occur in traditional society but per capita production remains low.

The second stage of growth, the preconditions for take-off, indicates a society in transition. It takes time to transform a traditional society in ways necessary for it to exploit the fruits of modern science. Western Europe reached this stage of development during the late seventeenth and early eighteenth centuries as new scientific knowledge was applied to agriculture and industry, and as world markets and rivalries expanded. Outside western Europe, this stage of growth generally arose when traditional societies were shocked or shattered by invasions. In this epoch the idea spreads that economic progress is possible, good, and necessary. Education broadens and changes to suit the needs of modern economic activity. New types of enterprising men come forward to take risks and seek profits. Commerce expands, investment increases, and some modern manufacturing enterprises appear. Politically, a new nationalism develops, along with strong central governments.

The take-off is really an industrial revolution that arrives when the old barriers and resistances to steady growth are finally overcome. Growth at a compounded rate becomes a normal condition of society. The take-off requires much investment in social-overhead capital, a surge of technological development in industry and agriculture, and the emergence to political power of a group that gives the highest priority to modernization of the economy. The beginning of a take-off can usually be traced to a particular sharp stimulus. It might be a political revolution, like the German revolution of 1848, the Meiji restoration in Japan in 1868, the achievement of Indian independence, or the Communist victory in China. The stimulus for take-off might come from a technological innovation that sets in motion a chain of secondary expansion. It might come from a newly favorable international environment, such as a sharp rise in export prices. During the take-off, the rate of saving and investing may rise from 5 per cent of the national income to 10 per cent or more. New industries expand rapidly, and a large proportion of the profit is reinvested. Agriculture also adopts new techniques and is commercialized. The take-off occurred in Great Britain roughly from 1783 to 1802, in France from 1830 to 1860, in the United States from 1843 to 1860, in Germany from 1850 to 1873, in Japan from 1878 to 1900, in Russia from 1890 to 1914, in Canada from 1896 to 1914, and in India and China from 1952 on.

About sixty years are generally required to move a society from the beginning of the take-off to maturity. The drive to maturity shows a long interval of sustained if fluctuating progress. Modern technology spreads over all economic activity. Ten to 20 per cent of the national income is invested, permitting output to outstrip population growth. The economy widens and deepens its range of activities; for example, there may be a shift in focus from coal, iron, and heavy engineering industries of the railroad phase to machine tools, chemicals, and electrical equipment. The character of the leadership changes, from the buccaneering industrial barons to the efficient professional manager of a highly bureaucratized machine.

The age of high mass consumption shows a shift toward durable consumer goods and services. Real income per capita rises to a point where people can enjoy much more than the basic requirements of food, clothing, and shelter. There is a rise in the percentage of urban population, and a rise also in the proportion of the labor force working in offices or in skilled factory jobs. The further extension of modern technology is no longer an overriding objective, and more resources are allocated to social welfare and security as well as to private consumption. The mass production of a cheap automobile is the symbol and the decisive element of a high mass consumption society. For the United States, this stage began with Henry Ford's moving assembly line of 1913; it was pressed to its logical conclusion in the 1920's and during the decade after World War II. Western Europe and Japan entered this phase fully during the 1950's. The Soviet Union is ready for high mass consumption, but so far there is only an uneasy flirtation with it; there will be difficult political and social problems of adjustment if this stage is launched.

These stages are not merely descriptive, said Rostow. They have an inner logic and continuity. This is a dynamic theory of production. There are certain similarities, Rostow agreed, between his analysis of stages and Marx's. But he felt that the latter left no other motivation for human action than economic advantage.

In the stages-of-growth sequence man is viewed as a more complex unit. He seeks, not merely economic advantage, but also power, leisure, adventure, continuity of experience and security; he is concerned with his family, the familiar values of his regional and national culture, and a bit of fun down at the local. And beyond these diverse homely attachments, man is also capable of being moved by a sense of connexion with human beings everywhere, who, he recognizes, share his essentially paradoxical condition. In short, net human behaviour is seen not as an act of maximization, but as an act of balancing alternative and often conflicting human objectives in the face of the range of choices men perceive to be open to them.

This notion of balance among alternatives perceived to be open is, of course, more complex and difficult than a simple maximization proposition; and it does not lead to a series of rigid, inevitable stages of history. It leads to patterns of choice made within the framework permitted by the changing setting of society: a setting itself the product both of objective real conditions and of the prior choices made by men which help determine the current setting which men confront.*

Economic decisions which determine the rate of growth and productivity of the labor force and of capital are not governed by the strictly economic motives of human beings. What other important human objectives are there? Rostow listed six propensities:

The propensity to develop fundamental science (physical and social).
The propensity to apply science to economic ends.
The propensity to accept innovations.
The propensity to seek material advance.
The propensity to consume.
The propensity to have children. . . .

The formal position which emerges from the analysis might now be stated in the following terms: The propensities summarize those aspects of social and political behaviour believed to be directly relevant to the level of output and the rate of economic growth; the strength of the propensities and the course of their change are not simple functions of the level of real income or its change; the strength of the propensities and their course of change are determined by a complex inter-relationship among the economic, social, and political forces of a society, long-run and slow-moving in character.†

Rostow's exposition has received very wide attention and approval, perhaps for several reasons. First, it is evolutionary; second, it is grounded in historical studies; third, it seems to show a predestined affluence for all; finally, it presents a case for an inner logic and drive from one stage to the next that requires no conscious decision-making or deliberate efforts to promote growth; it is analytic without being programmatic.

---

* W. W. Rostow, *The Stages of Economic Growth* (Cambridge, Cambridge University Press, 1960), p. 149. By permission of Cambridge University Press.
† W. W. Rostow, *The Process of Economic Growth*, 2nd ed. (London, 1960), pp. 11, 38.

CHAPTER 24

Economic History in Perspective

A Time Scale of Economic Doctrines

FIGURE 11 below illustrates the evolution of various schools and streams of economic thought. Each rectangle represents a major school or subject-matter area. The names within each rectangle are of economists who were most important or most typical in developing that school or area. The names immediately above the rectangles represent forerunners. The names directly below show followers who further changed or developed the ideas of their group.

A solid line linking two rectangles shows that the latter group was generally sympathetic with and friendly to the predecessor group out of which it grew or that it superseded. A dashed line shows that the later group was antagonistic to or rose in opposition to the earlier group. Thus the physiocrats were completely antipathetic to the mercantilists, while Adam Smith and the classical school in their turn were friendly toward the physiocrats. Again, the neoclassical school showed a sharp break with the classical school out of which it sprang, and Keynes in turn rejected some of the major ideas of neoclassicism. Therefore the dashed lines in that sequence, although it could be argued that the similarities in both cases were greater than the differences. Certainly there were closer and friendlier relations between the mathematical economists and the neoclassical school than between the welfare economists and that school. Therefore the line is solid in the first case and dashed in the second.

The Impact of Three Scientific Revolutions on Economics

MANY revolutions in science, technology, philosophy, economics, politics, culture, and other branches of human knowledge and behavior have occurred. They began even before the discovery of how to ignite and main-

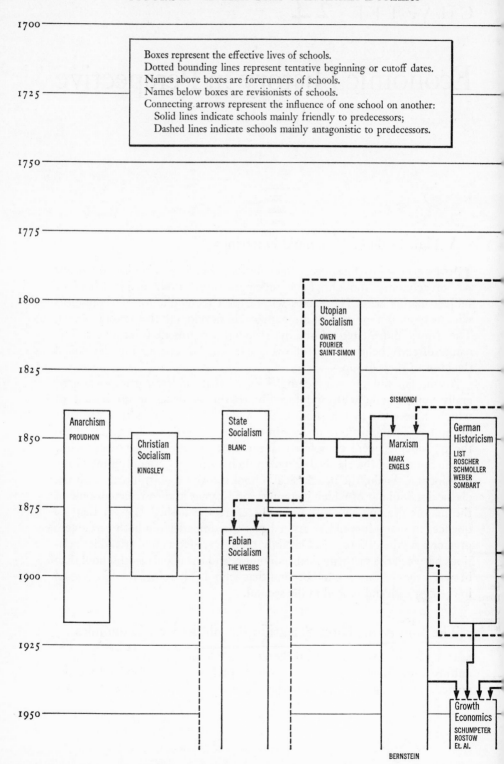

FIGURE II. A Time Scale of Economic Doctrines

Boxes represent the effective lives of schools.
Dotted bounding lines represent tentative beginning or cutoff dates.
Names above boxes are forerunners of schools.
Names below boxes are revisionists of schools.
Connecting arrows represent the influence of one school on another:
    Solid lines indicate schools mainly friendly to predecessors;
    Dashed lines indicate schools mainly antagonistic to predecessors.

1700
1725
1750
1775
1800
1825
1850
1875
1900
1925
1950

Anarchism
PROUDHON

Christian
Socialism
KINGSLEY

State
Socialism
BLANC

Fabian
Socialism
THE WEBBS

Utopian
Socialism
OWEN
FOURIER
SAINT-SIMON

SISMONDI

Marxism
MARX
ENGELS

German
Historicism
LIST
ROSCHER
SCHMOLLER
WEBER
SOMBART

Growth
Economics
SCHUMPETER
ROSTOW
Et. Al.

BERNSTEIN

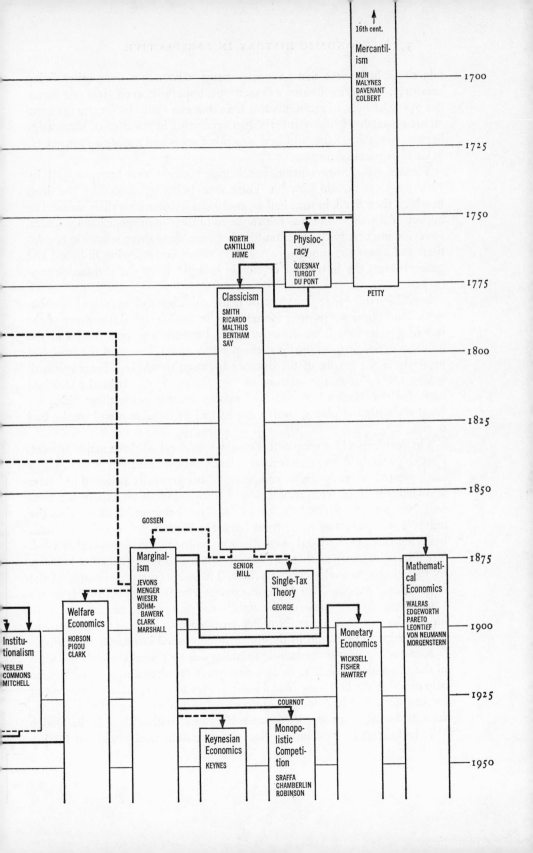

16th cent.

Mercantil-
ism

MUN
MALYNES
DAVENANT
COLBERT

1700

1725

1750

Physioc-
racy

QUESNAY
TURGOT
DU PONT

NORTH
CANTILLON
HUME

1775

PETTY

Classicism

SMITH
RICARDO
MALTHUS
BENTHAM
SAY

1800

1825

1850

GOSSEN

Marginal-
ism

JEVONS
MENGER
WIESER
BÖHM-
BAWERK
CLARK
MARSHALL

SENIOR
MILL

Single-Tax
Theory

GEORGE

1875

Mathemati-
cal
Economics

WALRAS
EDGEWORTH
PARETO
LEONTIEF
VON NEUMANN
MORGENSTERN

Welfare
Economics

HOBSON
PIGOU
CLARK

Institu-
tionalism

VEBLEN
COMMONS
MITCHELL

Monetary
Economics

WICKSELL
FISHER
HAWTREY

1900

1925

COURNOT

Keynesian
Economics

KEYNES

Monopo-
listic
Competi-
tion

SRAFFA
CHAMBERLIN
ROBINSON

1950

tain those little fires that gave man many advantages over other living creatures. These revolutions will continue, hopefully, even after our recent discovery of how to ignite nuclear fires that can easily incinerate man and all life on earth with him. Invariably a revolution in one area of knowledge became pervasive, being diffused into other areas and having an impact far beyond its point of origin.

Three significant revolutions in scientific thought were brought forth by Newton, Darwin, and Einstein. These men, being influenced by the times in which they lived, in turn had an enormous influence on their times. The impact of their thought was felt far beyond their own specialized sciences. In reviewing briefly the relationships between these three scientific revolutions and economic thought, we shall in effect be reviewing in broad and general terms the history of economic thought from the eighteenth century on.

Isaac Newton (1642–1727) made many significant discoveries in mathematics and physics. His most famous was his mathematical statement of the law of gravitation: The attractive force between any two bodies in the universe varies proportionally as the product of the masses of the two, and inversely as the square of the distance between them. This law explained, among other things, the motions of the planets. At one time the idea had prevailed that bodies had souls and tendencies that made them strive toward their natural places, so that apples had to fall down and smoke had to rise.

The revolution in seventeenth-century thinking had three major aspects. First, Newton and others relied completely on experimental evidence. His less educated contemporaries and predecessors generally believed in innate knowledge derived from reason alone without reliance on experience. Second, Newton popularized the idea (already existing in his time) that the universe was governed by natural laws. He himself was deeply religious, believing that gravitational phenomena were due to the direct will of God. Yet his critics charged that he virtually abolished God from the universe by reducing it to a self-acting machine. The role of original creator of the universe still remained for God, of course. The third aspect of Newton's system was a static view of the universe. Space, time, and matter were independent of each other. Nothing changed over time. The motion and relationships to be found in the universe continued in endless repetition.

Newton's impact on economic thinking can be traced through the ideas of the classical school. The rising businessmen required a new set of ideas to help dislodge the lingering feudal institutions and the restrictive controls of mercantilism that had become unnecessary. For them, Newtonian science furnished a nature fully as effective as the earlier will of God. If the Divine Will had created a mechanism that worked automatically without further interference, then laissez faire was the highest wisdom in social affairs. Natural laws would guide the economic system and the actions of men. These ideas were new and revolutionary in their time. No longer would men accept the ancient truths without question, such as the immorality of interest, the virtue of charity, and the requirement that men should be satisfied with their inherited station in life. Society would be served best if men were free to follow the natural law of self-interest. Newtonian thinking in classical economics provided an ideology that justified property incomes. As natural law was best if left unobstructed, and as private thrift and prudence contributed to the good of society, then rent, interest, and profit were necessary and just rewards for the ownership and productive use of wealth.

Charles Robert Darwin (1809–82) was inspired by one economist while he in turn inspired others. He told how, while reading Malthus on population one day, it suddenly occurred to him that, in the struggle for existence that he had everywhere observed, favorable variations would tend to be preserved and unfavorable ones to be destroyed. The result was the formation of new species. Darwin claimed to have applied the doctrine of Malthus to the whole animal and vegetable kingdoms.

Darwin's key ideas were the struggle for existence, natural selection based on individual differences, the survival of the fittest, and the evolution of species. These concepts influenced some, but by no means all, of the streams and schools of economic thought. Two strands of economic thought can be related to the Darwinian revolution: the evolutionary approach to economics, and social Darwinism. The evolutionary approach was incorporated in the thinking of Marxism (see Chapters 9 and 10), the German historical school (see Chapter 11), and the institutional school (see Chapter 17). Outstanding social Darwinists were the English philosopher, Herbert Spencer, and the American economist and sociologist, William Graham Sumner.

The social Darwinists applied one aspect of Darwin's ideas to human affairs. They emphasized not evolution but the struggle for existence and the survival of the fittest. They argued that the pressure of subsistence on population had a beneficent effect on the progress of the human race, for it placed a premium on skill, intelligence, self-control, and the power to adapt by technological innovation. Unrestricted competition and the struggle for existence would enable the best people to survive. The poor, the sick, the uneducated, and the hungry were inferior beings, and therefore they should not blame society or the more affluent classes for their unhappy condition. If their situation were ameliorated through social action, less fit people would survive and reproduce themselves, and the race would degenerate. In international affairs, the struggle for colonies and spheres of influence represented the more fit races surviving in competition against inferior peoples.

Social Darwinism virtually ended by World War I, although some of its ideas linger on. The world struggle was no longer between the "superior" Westerners and "inferior" indigenous people in the underdeveloped areas. Instead, the war was fought among Western societies themselves. Social Darwinism had justified militarism, and there was a revulsion against militarism after World War I. Some people pointed out that war killed the most fit, and was therefore dysgenic instead of eugenic. Finally, social Darwinism was ended as a major force by the poor, the "unfit," who found themselves fit enough to insist upon and to win certain improvements in their condition.

It is interesting to note that the social Darwinists came to the same conclusion as the classical economists who based themselves on Newton: Laissez faire is the best policy. Man must not interfere with natural processes. The social laws derived from Newton were based on the natural order as illustrated by the solar system. The social Darwinists based their social laws on the natural order as developed through biology. Both ideas accepted the environment as given, and not to be manipulated or changed; both ideas were suitable for those who had no basic grievance against the existing order.

The neoclassical school, which arose almost simultaneously with Darwinism, remained impervious to Darwinian thinking. Its basic orientation was Newtonian. It was static in its thinking, expressing universal economic laws which it believed were applicable everywhere and for all time, past, present, and future. Without interference by government, natural law would insure the best of all possible worlds.

Albert Einstein (1879–1955) developed the third great revolution in human thought that we are considering here. His theory of relativity, first presented to the world in 1905, has interesting implications for the social sciences. Yet it is doubtful if his influence in the social sciences is as great as Newton's and Darwin's influence has been in the past. There are at least three reasons for this. First, Einstein's theory may be too new to have had time to spread its influence. Second, with the explosion of knowledge, learning has become more and more specialized and compartmentalized; people are less familiar than in earlier times with what is going on in disciplines other than their own. Third, the social sciences to some extent have developed a relativity approach of their own independently of Einstein. Instead of seeking to discover Einstein's impact on the social sciences, which apparently is negligible up to the present, we should look for parallel developments in physics and in the social sciences that show certain common methodologies and patterns of thought.

In Einstein's theory of relativity one finds that what is "true" for an observer within one system may not be true for an observer in another system if the two systems are moving relative to one another. Imagine an observer in a train (a moving system), and another observer outside (a stationary system). From the exact middle of the train, two light rays are flashed at the same instant forward and back. For both observers, the light rays travel from their source at identical speeds (approximately 186,000 miles per second), because the velocity of light is constant throughout the universe and is not affected either by the motion of its source or the motion of the receiver. Will the light rays strike the front and rear walls of the train simultaneously? From the point of view of the observer within the train, the two events will be simultaneous. From the point of the observer on the ground, they will not be simultaneous. Even though both rays of light travel at the same speed, the front wall of the train is moving away from the light, and the rear wall is moving toward the light. Therefore the light ray will strike the rear wall first. What is true for the observer in one system is not true for the observer in another.

Take another example of relativity. Imagine a freely falling elevator. The passengers in the elevator are in one system. Observers on the outside are in a second and different system. Suppose we drill two holes in opposite walls of the elevator at exactly the same height. We place a flashlight in one hole and shine the light toward the other while the elevator is falling. As the passengers see it, the light from the flashlight will travel in a straight line at constant speed, and it will strike the opposite hole.

The outside observer sees the elevator falling because the gravitational field operates on it without any impediments. He sees the light ray coming from the flashlight in one wall and reaching the hole in the opposite wall. But during the infinitesimal interval of time that it takes the light ray to travel from one wall of the elevator to the other, the outside observer sees the entire elevator move down. The light appears to leave the elevator through the hole, but at a lower level than its source. The light ray, instead of traveling in a straight line, is curved in the gravitational field. The truth from the point of view of observers in one system is not true for observers of another system.

In the social sciences, the independent development of a relativistic outlook is illustrated by such useful clichés as "frame of reference," "value system," and "point of view." Anthropologists have probably led other social scientists in this respect. What would we think of a man who ate the flesh of his dead father? Would we not regard such an act as bestial and revolting? The anthropologist Bronislaw Malinowski reported that the Melanesians of New Guinea followed such practices with some of their dead. They may have felt as much aversion toward doing it as we would, for they were filled with extreme repugnance and dread and usually suffered violent fits of vomiting. Moreover, in recent times they were severely penalized by the white government when caught performing such acts. To the Melanesians of New Guinea, eating the flesh of the dead was a sacred duty, for it represented a supreme act of reverence, love, devotion, and self-sacrifice. The act is disgusting or noble, depending on one's point of view.

This relativistic point of view can be applied to ethics. Imagine a small and struggling union trying to gain a toe-hold in a company, operating in secret because its members face reprisals if their membership is discovered. Suppose that the membership secretary of the union is secretly employed by the company to turn over to it union membership lists and campaign plans. Is he a traitor, a scab, and a rat? Or is he a trustworthy employee of the company, a loyal member of one big family that is striving to exclude the disruptive influence of outside agitators?

Imagine another case in ethics. A millionaire's butler overhears plans for the grand strategy to smash a union. He rushes to the union officials to warn them, and they are able to forestall the scheme. Is the butler a traitor, a rat, and a snake? Or is he a loyal son of the working class, a hero, a paragon of virtue? Perhaps there is no absolute right and wrong; it all depends on one's frame of reference.

This relativistic approach has been applied to economics, and it should guide economic thinking more than it does. Will digging holes in the ground, which Keynes advocated, enrich or impoverish us? That depends on the alternatives. If the choice is between that and unemployment, digging holes will enrich us. If the alternatives are digging holes or doing useful work, digging holes will tend to impoverish us.

During the foreseeable future, the United States will produce more automobiles than the Soviet Union. Is this an indication that our system is superior to theirs? Only if consumers desire to own automobiles, and if we judge the success of a system by how well it satisfies individual desires. N. S. Khrushchev has already announced that Soviet Russia will never produce as many automobiles as the United States does. His people will be invited to rent cars for week-end and vacation driving. The objectives of his plan will be to prevent traffic congestion, to conserve raw materials, to reduce air pollution, and to save productive resources for other purposes. Which system is better? That depends on one's value system.

Why Study Economics and Its History?

WE HAVE examined in this book a minute segment of man's intellectual and social history over the last 450 years. Students who have struggled over this difficult terrain may well ask, "Was it worth the effort? Why study economic theory? Why study its history?"

Many answers come to mind. Omitting the private, personal advantages that might be gained, there are two major reasons justifying the study of theory. First, it elucidates how an economy works, what makes it hang together and function; we gain understanding. Second, given the economic goals that a society chooses, theory can help us reach these goals. We can make faster progress, however that is defined, through a knowledge of theory.

Why study the history of economic thought? Such a study above all gives us perspective and understanding of our past, of changing ideas and problems, of our direction of movement. Our study seems to confirm our initial idea that theory arises out of society's needs and problems. We can appreciate the fact that no group seems to have a monopoly over the truth, and many groups have contributed to the richness and diversity of our intellectual, cultural, and material inheritance. A study of the evolution of economic thought and the changing social background associated with it can illuminate changes in other areas of concern to us, such as politics, art, literature, music, philosophy, and science. There is, of course, a reciprocal relationship here, so that a better understanding of the latter areas of knowledge can help explain changing economic ideas.

The vast growth of our statistical knowledge can provide a closer check on irresponsible generalizations. Hopefully, we will make fewer errors in the future than in the past in guiding our economies. Yet there remains a vast area of *terra incognita*—of unsolved problems and unanswered questions. Much progress remains to be achieved.

Unfortunately the accumulation of knowledge and understanding does not necessarily lead to a better world; change is not necessarily progress. We cannot agree on a definitive statement of what constitutes a better world, or how progress should be defined. Even a perfect understanding of economic phenomena would leave us deeply divided. Suppose we all understand and agree that the operation of the gold standard will result in stable foreign exchange rates provided that money prices and wage rates are flexible. This means that the gold standard will not function well where unions are powerful and prevent wages and prices from falling when the exchange rate requires that they should. This analytical statement can be interpreted as an argument against unions, or as an argument against the gold standard. Even if all people were perfectly well informed on economic theory, disagreements and conflicts would remain because of different ideas about what is good and what is bad, which goals should be adopted and which rejected, and what the priority of each goal should be.

Even if we agree on goals for the economy, we will disagree on their relative importance. Suppose everybody agrees that all people should have adequate diets. We may also want people to have incentives to do good work, and the two goals may be incompatible to some extent; we would have to decide which should have the higher priority. Again, while we can all agree on the desirability of adequate diets, the vegetarian will say that avoiding the slaughter of animals should take an even higher priority. The cannibal might argue that his predilections are merely implementing what we all agree is a worthy aim—a well-fed people.

In certain combinations of circumstances, the desperately evil qualities of man rise to the surface. Hopefully, as our understanding grows, as our mastery over the forces of nature and over social problems increases, as the material well-being of the people rises, as our appreciation of the cultural, aesthetic, and intellectual facets of life enlarges, we shall become more civilized, more humane, more considerate and understanding of our fellow inhabitants on this planet. If an understanding of economic theories and problems of the past and present contributes a modicum toward these goals, it will have been worth the effort.

Bibliography

Chapter 1

BLAUG, MARK, *Economic Theory in Retrospect.* Homewood: Irwin, 1962.

FELLNER, WILLIAM, *Emergence and Content of Modern Economic Analysis.* New York: McGraw-Hill, 1960.

FERGUSON, JOHN M., *Landmarks of Economic Thought.* 2d ed. New York: Longmans, Green, 1950.

GIDE, CHARLES, and CHARLES RIST, *A History of Economic Doctrines.* 2d English ed. Boston: Heath, 1948.

HANEY, LEWIS H., *History of Economic Thought.* 4th ed. New York: Macmillan, 1949.

HEILBRONER, ROBERT L., *The Worldly Philosophers.* 2d ed. New York: Simon and Schuster, 1961.

HEIMANN, EDUARD, *History of Economic Doctrines.* New York: Oxford University Press, 1945.

LEKACHMAN, ROBERT, *A History of Economic Ideas.* New York: Harper, 1959.

MITCHELL, WESLEY C., *Lecture Notes on Types of Economic Theory.* 2 vols. New York: Kelley, 1949.

ROGIN, LEO, *The Meaning and Validity of Economic Theory.* New York: Harper, 1956.

ROLL, ERICH, *A History of Economic Thought.* 3d ed. New York: Prentice-Hall, 1956.

SCHUMPETER, JOSEPH A., *History of Economic Analysis.* New York: Oxford University Press, 1954.

SPIEGEL, HENRY WILLIAM, ed., *The Development of Economic Thought.* New York: Wiley, 1952.

TAYLOR, OVERTON H., *A History of Economic Thought.* New York: McGraw-Hill, 1960.

WHITTAKER, EDMUND, *Schools and Streams of Economic Thought.* Chicago: Rand McNally, 1960.

Chapter 2

COLE, CHARLES W., *Colbert and a Century of French Mercantilism.* 2 vols. New York: Columbia University Press, 1939.

DAVENANT, CHARLES, *Discourses on the Publick Revenues, and on the Trade of England.* 1698.

FURNISS, EDGAR S., *The Position of the Laborer in a System of Nationalism.* Boston: Houghton Mifflin, 1920.

HECKSCHER, ELI F., *Mercantilism.* 2d ed., 2 vols. London: Allen and Unwin, 1955.

JOHNSON, E. A. J., *Predecessors of Adam Smith.* New York: Prentice-Hall, 1937.

MALYNES, GERARD, *Lex Mercatoria: Or, The Ancient Law-Merchant.* 1686. [Written in 1622.]

MUN, THOMAS, *England's Treasure by Forraign Trade.* New York: Macmillan, 1895. [Written c. 1630.]

PETTY, WILLIAM, *Economic Writings,* ed. by Charles H. Hull. 2 vols. Cambridge, England: The University Press, 1899.

VINER, JACOB, *Studies in the Theory of International Trade.* New York: Harper, 1937.

Chapter 3

BEER, MAX, *An Inquiry into Physiocracy.* London: Allen and Unwin, 1939.

HIGGS, HENRY, *The Physiocrats.* New York: Langland Press, 1952. [Originally published in 1897.]

TURGOT, ANNE ROBERT JACQUES, *Reflections on the Formation and the Distribution of Riches.* New York: Macmillan, 1898. [Originally published in 1766.]

WARE, NORMAN J., "The Physiocrats: A Study in Economic Rationalization." *American Economic Review,* XXI, No. 4 (December 1931), 607–19.

Chapter 4

CANTILLON, RICHARD, *Essai sur la nature du commerce en général,* ed. by Henry Higgs and printed in French and English. London: Macmillan, 1931. [Originally published in 1755.]

NORTH, DUDLEY, *Discourses upon Trade,* ed. by Jacob H. Hollander. Baltimore: Johns Hopkins Press, 1907. [Originally published in 1691.]

POLANYI, KARL, *The Great Transformation.* New York: Rinehart, 1944.

ROTWEIN, EUGENE, *David Hume: Writings on Economics.* Madison: University of Wisconsin Press, 1955.

Chapter 5

SMITH, ADAM, *An Inquiry into the Nature and Causes of the Wealth of Nations,* ed. by Edwin Cannan. New York: Random House, Modern Library edition, 1937. [Originally published in 1776.]

Chapter 6

BLAUG, MARK, *Ricardian Economics*. New Haven: Yale University Press, 1958.

MALTHUS, THOMAS, *An Inquiry into the Nature and Progress of Rent, 1815,* ed. by Jacob H. Hollander. Baltimore: Johns Hopkins Press, 1903.

RICARDO, DAVID, *Works and Correspondence*, ed. by Piero Sraffa. 10 vols. Cambridge, England: The University Press, 1951–55.

WEST, EDWARD, *On the Application of Capital to Land, 1815,* ed. by Jacob H. Hollander. Baltimore: Johns Hopkins Press, 1903.

Chapter 7

GODWIN, WILLIAM, *An Enquiry Concerning Political Justice and Its Influence on General Virtue and Happiness.* 2 vols. New York: Knopf, 1926. [Originally published in 1793.]

MALTHUS, THOMAS, *An Essay on the Principle of Population.* London, 1798.

———, *Principles of Political Economy.* New York: Kelley, 1951. [Originally published in 1820.]

OSBORN, FAIRFIELD, *Our Plundered Planet.* Boston: Little, Brown, 1948.

OSER, JACOB, *Must Men Starve? The Malthuisan Controversy.* London: Cape, 1956; New York: Abelard-Schuman, 1957.

SCHAPIRO, J. SALWYN, *Condorcet and the Rise of Liberalism.* New York: Harcourt, Brace & World, 1934.

SMITH, KENNETH, *The Malthusian Controversy.* London: Routledge and Kegan Paul, 1951.

VOGT, WILLIAM, *Road to Survival.* New York: Sloane, 1948.

Chapter 8

BENTHAM, JEREMY, *An Introduction to the Principles of Morals and Legislation.* New York: Hafner, 1948. [Originally published in 1780.]

BOWLEY, MARIAN, *Nassau Senior and Classical Economics.* New York: Kelley, 1949.

HALÉVY, ELIE, *The Growth of Philosophic Radicalism,* tr. by Mary Morris. 2d ed. London: Faber and Faber, 1934.

MILL, JOHN STUART, *Autobiography.* London, 1873.

———, *Dissertations and Discussions.* 2 vols. London, 1859.

———, *Essays on Some Unsettled Questions of Political Economy.* London: The London School of Economics and Political Science, 1948. [Originally published in 1844.]

———, *Principles of Political Economy.* 7th ed. London, 1871. [Originally published in 1848.]

———, *Utilitarianism.* London, 1861.

SAY, JEAN BAPTISTE, *A Treatise on Political Economy*, tr. by C. R. Prinsep. 2 vols. Boston: Wells and Lilly, 1821. [Originally published in 1803.]

SENIOR, NASSAU W., *An Outline of the Science of Political Economy*. New York: Kelley, 1951. [Originally published in 1836.]

——, *Industrial Efficiency and Social Economy*, ed. by S. Leon Levy. 2 vols. New York: Holt, 1928. [Written 1847–52.]

STARK, W., *Jeremy Bentham's Economic Writings*. 3 vols. New York: Franklin, 1952–54.

Chapter 9

BEER, MAX, *A History of British Socialism*. 2d ed. London: Allen and Unwin, 1940.

BLANC, LOUIS, *Organization of Work*, tr. by Maria P. Dickoré. Cincinnati: University of Cincinnati Press, 1911. [Originally published in 1839.]

COLE, G. D. H., *The Case for Industrial Partnership*. London: Macmillan, 1957.

——, *A History of Socialist Thought*. 6 vols. New York: St. Martin's, 1953–58.

FOURIER, CHARLES, *Selections from the Works*, tr. by Julia Franklin. London: Swan Sonnenschein, 1901.

——, *Theory of Social Organization*. New York: Somerby, 1876. [Written in 1822.]

KINGSLEY, CHARLES, *Works*, ed. by Mrs. Charles Kingsley. Vol. VII, *Letters and Memories*. Philadelphia: Morris, 1899.

LOUBÈRE, LEO A., *Louis Blanc*. Evanston: Northwestern University Press, 1961.

MANUEL, FRANK E., *The New World of Henri Saint-Simon*. Cambridge: Harvard University Press, 1956.

MARRIOTT, J. A. R., *The French Revolution of 1848 in Its Economic Aspect*. Vol. I, *Louis Blanc's organisation du travail*. Oxford: Clarendon, 1913.

OWEN, ROBERT, *A New View of Society and Other Writings*. London: Dent, 1927. [Written 1813–21.]

Politics for the People. London: John W. Parker, 1848.

POPE-HENNESSEY, UNA, *Canon Charles Kingsley*. London: Chatto and Windus, 1948.

PROUDHON, PIERRE-JOSEPH, *General Idea of the Revolution in the Nineteenth Century*, tr. by John B. Robinson. London: Freedom Press, 1923. [Originally published in 1851.]

——, *Solution of the Social Problem*, ed. by Henry Cohen. New York: Vanguard, 1927.

——, *What Is Property?* tr. by Benjamin R. Tucker. London: Reeves, n.d. [Originally published in 1840.]

RAVEN, CHARLES E., *Christian Socialism, 1848–1854*. London: Macmillan, 1920.

SAINT-SIMON, COMPTE DE, *Selected Writings*, ed. by F. M. H. Markham. Oxford: Blackwell, 1952.

Sismondi, Simonde de, *Political Economy and the Philosophy of Government*. London: Chapman, 1847. [Originally published 1826–37.]

Woodcock, George, *Pierre-Joseph Proudhon*. London: Routledge and Kegan Paul, 1956.

Chapter 10

Bernstein, Edward, *Evolutionary Socialism*, tr. by Edith C. Harvey. New York: Huebsch, 1909.

Cole, G. D. H., *The Meaning of Marxism*. London: Gollancz, 1948.

Freedman, Robert, ed., *Marx on Economics*. New York: Harcourt, Brace & World, 1961.

Gay, Peter, *The Dilemma of Democratic Socialism*. New York: Columbia University Press, 1952.

Marx, Karl, *Capital*, tr. by Samuel Moore, Edward Aveling, and Ernest Untermann. 3 vols. Chicago: Kerr, 1906–09. [Originally published 1867–1895.]

————, *Theories of Surplus Value*, tr. by. G. A. Bonner and Emile Burns. London: Lawrence and Wishart, 1951. [Originally published 1905–10.]

————, *Value, Price and Profit*, ed. by Eleanor Marx Aveling. New York: International Publishers, 1935. [Originally delivered as a speech in 1865.]

————, *Wage-Labour and Capital*. New York: International Publishers, 1933. [Originally published in 1849.]

Marx, Karl, and Friedrich Engels, *Manifesto of the Communist Party*. New York: International Publishers, 1948. [Originally published in 1848.]

Pease, Edward R., *The History of the Fabian Society*. London: Fifield, 1916.

Semmel, Bernard, *Imperialism and Social Reform*. Cambridge: Harvard University Press, 1960.

Sweezy, Paul M., *The Theory of Capitalist Development*. New York: Oxford University Press, 1942.

Webb, Beatrice, *Our Partnership*. London: Longmans, Green, 1948.

Webb, Sidney and Beatrice, *The Decay of Capitalist Civilization*. New York: Harcourt, Brace & World, 1923.

Chapter 11

Hirst, Margaret E., *Life of Friedrich List and Selections from His Writings*. London: Smith, Elder, 1909.

List, Frederick, *National System of Political Economy*, tr. by G. A. Matile. Philadelphia: Lippincott, 1856. [Originally published in 1841.]

Myles, Jack C., "German Historicism and American Economics." Unpublished Princeton University doctoral thesis, 1956.

Roscher, William, *Principles of Political Economy*, tr. by John J. Lalor. 2 vols. New York: Holt, 1878. [Originally published in 1854.]

SCHMOLLER, GUSTAV, *Idea of Justice in Political Economy*. Philadelphia: American Academy of Political and Social Science, No. 113, n.d.

SOMBART, WERNER, *The Jews and Modern Capitalism*, tr. by M. Epstein. Glencoe: Free Press, 1951. [Originally published in 1911.]

——, *Der moderne Kapitalismus*. 3 vols. Munich and Leipzig: Duncker and Humbolt, 1916–27.

——, *A New Social Philosophy*, tr. by Karl F. Geiser. Princeton: Princeton University Press, 1937.

——, *Socialism and the Social Movement*, tr. by M. Epstein. New York: Dutton, 1909.

TAWNEY, R. H., *Religion and the Rise of Capitalism*. New York: Harcourt, Brace & World, 1926.

WEBER, MAX, *The Protestant Ethic and the Spirit of Capitalism*, tr. by Talcott Parsons. London: Allen and Unwin, 1930. [Originally published in 1904–05.]

——, *The Theory of Social and Economic Organization*, tr. by A. M. Henderson and Talcott Parsons. New York: Oxford University Press, 1947. [Originally published in 1921.]

Chapter 12

JEVONS, WILLIAM STANLEY, *Investigations in Currency and Finance*. 2d ed. London: Macmillan, 1909. [Originally published in 1884.]

——, *Methods of Social Reform*. London: Macmillan, 1883.

——, *The State in Relation to Labour*. London: Macmillan, 1882.

——, *The Theory of Political Economy*. 4th ed. London: Macmillan, 1911. [Originally published in 1871.]

Chapter 13

BÖHM-BAWERK, EUGEN VON, *The Positive Theory of Capital*, tr. by William Smart. London: Macmillan, 1891. [Originally published in 1888.]

CLARK, JOHN BATES, *The Distribution of Wealth*. New York: Macmillan, 1899.

——, *Essentials of Economic Theory*. New York: Macmillan, 1907.

MENGER, CARL, *Principles of Economics*, tr. and ed. by James Dingwall and Bert F. Hoselitz. Glencoe: Free Press, 1950. [Originally published in 1871.]

STIGLER, GEORGE J., *Production and Distribution Theories*. New York: Macmillan, 1941.

WIESER, FRIEDRICH VON, *Natural Value*, tr. by Christian A. Malloch. London: Macmillan, 1893. [Originally published in 1889.]

——, *Social Economics*, tr. by A. Ford Hinrichs. New York: Adelphi, 1927. [Originally published in 1914.]

Chapter 14

MARSHALL, ALFRED, *Money, Credit and Commerce*. London: Macmillan, 1923.

Marshall, Alfred, *Principles of Economics*. 8th ed. London: Macmillan, 1920. [Originally published in 1890.]

——, *Memorials*, ed. by A. C. Pigou. London: Macmillan, 1925.

Chapter 15

Cassel, Gustav, *The Theory of Social Economy*, rev. ed. tr. by S. L. Barron. New York: Harcourt, Brace & World, 1932.

Charnes, A., W. W. Cooper, and A. Henderson, *An Introduction to Linear Programming*. New York: Wiley, 1953.

Dorfman, Robert, Paul A. Samuelson, and Robert M. Solow, *Linear Programming and Economic Analysis*. New York: McGraw-Hill, 1958.

Edgeworth, F. Y., *Mathematical Psychics*. London: Kegan Paul, 1881.

Hicks, J. R., *Value and Capital*. 2d ed. Oxford: Oxford University Press, 1946.

Leontief, W. W., *The Structure of American Economy, 1919–1939*. 2d ed. New York: Oxford University Press, 1951.

National Bureau of Economic Research, *Input-Output Analysis: An Appraisal* (Studies in Income and Wealth, Vol. XVIII). Princeton: Princeton University Press, 1955.

Neumann, John Von, and Oskar Morgenstern, *Theory of Games and Economic Behavior*. 3d ed. Princeton: Princeton University Press, 1953. [Originally published in 1944.]

Patinkin, Don, *Money, Interest and Prices*. Evanston: Row, Peterson, 1956.

Walras, Léon, *Elements of Pure Economics*, tr. by William Jaffé. Homewood: Irwin, 1954. [Originally published in 1874 and 1877.]

Chapter 16

Carey, H. C., *Principles of Social Science*. 3 vols. Philadelphia: Lippincott, 1888. [Originally published in 1858.]

De Mille, Anna George, *Henry George: Citizen of the World*. Chapel Hill: University of North Carolina Press, 1950.

Dorfman, Joseph, *The Economic Mind in American Civilization*. 5 vols. New York: Viking, 1946–59.

Franklin, Benjamin, *The Papers of Benjamin Franklin*, ed. by Leonard W. Labaree. Vols. I–III. New Haven: Yale University Press, 1959–61.

——, *Writings*, ed. by Albert Henry Smyth. 10 vols. New York: Macmillan, 1907.

George, Henry, *Progress and Poverty*. New York: Robert Schalkenbach Foundation, 1942. [Originally published in 1879.]

Hamilton, Alexander, *Papers on Public Credit, Commerce and Finance*, ed. by Samuel McKee, Jr. New York: Columbia University Press, 1934.

Kaplan, A. D. H., *Henry Charles Carey: A Study in American Economic Thought* (Johns Hopkins University Studies in Historical and Political Science, Series XLIX, No. 4). Baltimore: Johns Hopkins Press, 1931.

PAINE, THOMAS, *Complete Writings*. 2 vols. New York: Citadel, 1945.
WALKER, FRANCIS A., *Political Economy*. 3d ed. New York: Holt, 1888.

Chapter 17

DORFMAN, JOSEPH, *Thorstein Veblen and His America*. New York: Viking, 1934.
GAMBS, JOHN S., *Beyond Supply and Demand*. New York: Columbia University Press, 1946.
GRUCHY, ALLAN G., *Modern Economic Thought: The American Contribution*. New York: Prentice-Hall, 1947.
VEBLEN, THORSTEIN, *Absentee Ownership and Business Enterprise in Recent Times*. New York: Viking, 1954. [Originally published in 1923.]
———, *The Engineers and the Price System*. New York: Viking, 1947. [Originally published in 1921.]
———, *Essays in Our Changing Order*. New York: Viking, 1934.
———, *Imperial Germany and the Industrial Revolution*. New York: Macmillan, 1915.
———, *The Instinct of Workmanship*. New York: Huebsch, 1918. [Originally published in 1914.]
———, *The Place of Science in Modern Civilization and Other Essays*. New York: Huebsch, 1919.
———, *The Theory of Business Enterprise*. New York: Scribner's, 1904.
———, *The Theory of the Leisure Class*. New York: Random House, Modern Library edition, 1934. [Originally published in 1899.]
———, *What Veblen Taught*, ed. by Wesley C. Mitchell. New York: Viking, 1936.

Chapter 18

BURNS, ARTHUR F., ed., *Wesley Clair Mitchell: The Economic Scientist*. New York: National Bureau of Economic Research, 1952.
COMMONS, JOHN R., *The Economics of Collective Action*. New York: Macmillan, 1950.
———, *Institutional Economics*. New York: Macmillan, 1934.
———, *Legal Foundations of Capitalism*. New York: Macmillan, 1924.
———, *Myself*. New York: Macmillan, 1934.
MITCHELL, LUCY SPRAGUE, *Two Lives*. New York: Simon and Schuster, 1953.
MITCHELL, WESLEY C., *The Backward Art of Spending Money and Other Essays*. New York: Kelley, 1950. [Originally published 1912–36.]
———, *Business Cycles: The Problem and Its Setting*. New York: National Bureau of Economic Research, 1927.
———, *Business Cycles and Their Causes*. Berkeley: University of California Press, 1941. [Originally published in 1913.]

MITCHELL, WESLEY C., "Economic Resources in Economic Theory," *Studies in Economics and Industrial Relations*. Philadelphia: University of Pennsylvania Press, 1941.

———, *What Happens During Business Cycles*. New York: National Bureau of Economic Research, 1951.

Chapter 19

FISHER, IRVING, *The Money Illusion*. New York: Adelphi, 1928.

———, *The Nature of Capital and Income*. New York: Macmillan, 1906.

———, *100% Money*, 2d ed. New York: Adelphi, 1936.

———, *The Purchasing Power of Money*. New York: Macmillan, 1911.

———, *Stabilizing the Dollar*. New York: Macmillan, 1920.

FISHER, IRVING NORTON, *My Father: Irving Fisher*. New York: Comet, 1956.

GORDLUND, TORSTEN, *The Life of Knut Wicksell*, tr. by Nancy Adler. Stockholm: Almqvist and Wiksell, 1958.

HAWTREY, RALPH GEORGE, *The Art of Central Banking*. London: Longmans, Green, 1932.

———, *Capital and Employment*. 2d ed. London: Longmans, Green, 1952.

———, *Currency and Credit*. London: Longmans, Green, 1919.

SAULNIER, RAYMOND J., *Contemporary Monetary Theory*. New York: Columbia University Press, 1938.

UHR, CARL G., *Economic Doctrines of Knut Wicksell*. Berkeley: University of California Press, 1960.

WICKSELL, KNUT, *Interest and Prices*, tr. by R. F. Kahn. London: Macmillan, 1936. [Originally published in 1898.]

———, *Lectures on Political Economy*, tr. by E. Classen. 2 vols. London: Routledge, 1934–35. [Originally published in 1901 and 1906.]

Chapter 20

CHAMBERLIN, EDWARD H., *The Theory of Monopolistic Competition*. 5th ed. Cambridge: Harvard University Press, 1946. [Originally published in 1933.]

COURNOT, AUGUSTIN, *Researches into the Mathematical Principles of the Theory of Wealth*, tr. by Nathaniel T. Bacon. New York: Macmillan, 1927. [Originally published in 1838.]

ROBINSON, JOAN, *The Economics of Imperfect Competition*. London: Macmillan, 1933.

———, "Imperfect Competition Revisited." *Economic Journal*, LXIII, No. 251 (September 1953), 579–93.

SRAFFA, PIERO, "The Laws of Returns Under Competitive Conditions." *Economic Journal*, XXXVI, No. 144 (December 1926), 535–50.

Chapter 21

CLARK, J. MAURICE, *Alternative to Serfdom*. New York: Knopf, 1948.
———, *Economic Institutions and Human Welfare*. New York: Knopf, 1957.
———, *Preface to Social Economics*. New York: Farrar and Rinehart, 1936.
———, *Social Control of Business*. 2d ed. New York: McGraw-Hill, 1939. [Originally published in 1926.]
———, *Studies in the Economics of Overhead Costs*. Chicago: University of Chicago Press, 1923.
HOBSON, J. A., *Confessions of an Economic Heretic*. London: Allen and Unwin, 1938.
———, *The Economics of Unemployment*. 2d ed. New York: Macmillan, 1931.
———, *Imperialism*. 3d ed. London: Allen and Unwin, 1938. [Originally published in 1902.]
———, *The Industrial System*. 2d ed. New York: Scribner's, 1910.
———, *The Problem of the Unemployed*. London: Methuen, 1896.
———, *Wealth and Life*. London: Macmillan, 1930.
———, *Work and Wealth*. New York: Macmillan, 1914.
HOMAN, PAUL T., *Contemporary Economic Thought*. New York: Harper, 1928.
KAPP, W. WILLIAM, *The Social Costs of Private Enterprise*. Cambridge: Harvard University Press, 1950.
LITTLE, I. M. D., *A Critique of Welfare Economics*. 2d ed. London: Oxford University Press, 1957.
MUMMERY, A. F., and J. A. HOBSON, *The Physiology of Industry*. New York: Kelley and Millman, 1956. [Originally published in 1889.]
PIGOU, A. C., *The Economics of Welfare*. 4th ed. London: Macmillan, 1932. [Originally published in 1920.]

Chapter 22

DILLARD, DUDLEY, *The Economics of John Maynard Keynes*. New York: Prentice-Hall, 1948.
HANSEN, ALVIN H., *A Guide to Keynes*. New York: McGraw-Hill, 1953.
HARRIS, SEYMOUR E., ed., *The New Economics*. New York: Knopf, 1948.
HARROD, R. F., *The Life of John Maynard Keynes*. New York: Harcourt, Brace & World, 1951.
KEYNES, JOHN MAYNARD, *The End of Laissez-Faire*. London: Hogarth, 1926.
———, *Essays in Persuasion*. London: Macmillan, 1933.
———, *The General Theory of Employment, Interest and Money*. New York: Harcourt, Brace & World, 1936.
———, *How to Pay for the War*. New York: Harcourt, Brace & World, 1940.
———, *A Treatise on Money*. 2 vols. London: Macmillan, 1930.

TERBORGH, GEORGE, *The Bogey of Economic Maturity*. Chicago: Machinery and Allied Products Institute, 1945.

Chapter 23

BARAN, PAUL A., *The Political Economy of Growth*. New York: Monthly Review Press, 1957.

HOSELITZ, BERT F., ed. *Theories of Economic Growth*. Glencoe: Free Press, 1960.

MYRDAL, GUNNAR, *Beyond the Welfare State*. New Haven: Yale University Press, 1960.

———, *An International Economy*. New York: Harper, 1956.

———, *Rich Lands and Poor*. New York: Harper, 1957.

NURKSE, RAGNAR, *Patterns of Trade and Development*. Stockholm: Almqvist and Wiksell, 1959.

———, *Problems of Capital Formation in Underdeveloped Countries*. New York: Oxford University Press, 1953.

———, *Some Aspects of Capital Accumulation in Underdeveloped Countries*. Cairo: National Bank of Egypt, 1952.

ROSTOW, W. W., *The Process of Economic Growth*. 2d ed. London: Oxford University Press, 1960.

———, *The Stages of Economic Growth*. Cambridge, England: The University Press, 1960.

SCHUMPETER, JOSEPH A., *Capitalism, Socialism, and Democracy*. 3d ed. New York: Harper, 1950.

———, *Essays*, ed. by Richard V. Clemence. Cambridge: Addison-Wesley, 1951.

———, *The Theory of Economic Development*, tr. by Redvers Opie. New York: Oxford University Press, 1961. [Originally published in 1911.]

Chapter 24

BECKER, CARL L., *The Heavenly City of the Eighteenth-Century Philosophers*. New Haven: Yale University Press, 1932.

DARWIN, CHARLES, *On the Origin of Species by Means of Natural Selection*. 1859.

HOFSTADTER, RICHARD, *Social Darwinism in American Thought, 1860–1915*. Philadelphia: University of Pennsylvania Press, 1944.

INFELD, LEOPOLD, *Albert Einstein*. New York: Scribner's, 1950.

MALINOWSKI, BRONISLAW, *Magic, Science and Religion and Other Essays*. Glencoe: Free Press, 1948.

SULLIVAN, J. W. N., *Isaac Newton, 1642–1727*. New York: Macmillan, 1938.

Index

J

K

L

M

DATE DUE
